The Westford Knight
and Henry Sinclair

ALSO BY DAVID GOUDSWARD

*Ancient Stone Sites of New England and the Debate Over
Early European Exploration* (McFarland, 2006)

With Niven's compliments + my best wishes

The Westford Knight and Henry Sinclair

Evidence of a 14th Century Scottish Voyage to North America

DAVID GOUDSWARD

Foreword by Robert E. Stone

McFarland & Company, Inc., Publishers
Jefferson, North Carolina, and London

LIBRARY OF CONGRESS CATALOGUING-IN-PUBLICATION DATA

Goudsward, David.
    The Westford Knight and Henry Sinclair : evidence of a
14th century Scottish voyage to North America / David
Goudsward ; foreword by Robert E. Stone.
      p.   cm.
    Includes bibliographical references and index.

    ISBN 978-0-7864-4649-0
    softcover : 50# alkaline paper ∞

    1. Westford Knight Site (Westford, Mass.) 2. America —
Discovery and exploration — Historiography. 3. America —
Discovery and exploration — Pre-Columbian. 4. Sinclair,
Henry, Sir, 1345–ca. 1400. 5. Templars — Scotland —
History. 6. Massachusetts — Antiquities. I. Title.
F74.W58G68   2010
974.4'01 — dc22   2010035541

British Library cataloguing data are available

Front cover: *clockwise from top* the coat of arms of Henry, Earl
of Orkney; map,background, and ship ©2010 Shutterstock;
Frank Glynn's original 1954 chalking of the full Westford Knight
(photo courtesy of Cindy Glynn)

Manufactured in the United States of America

McFarland & Company, Inc., Publishers
  Box 611, Jefferson, North Carolina 28640
  www.mcfarlandpub.com

To Elizabeth Lane, Keeper of the Knight,
and Niven Sinclair, Keeper of the Flame

Acknowledgments

Cindy Glynn
Robert E. Stone, America's Stonehenge
Dennis Stone, America's Stonehenge
Malcolm Pearson
Diane Kachmar, Florida Atlantic University
Virginia Moore, J. V. Fletcher Library, Westford, MA
Greg Laing, Haverhill Public Library Special Collections
Drew Laughland, Haverhill Public Library Special Collections
Lori Nyce, Dauphin County Library System
Richard Lynch
Inger Johansson
Kate Johnson
Carol Simmons
Vance Tiede
Cindy Lillibridge
Father Tim Goldrick
Kate Johnson
Ellery Frahm, University of Minnesota
Richard P. Howe, Jr., Middlesex County North Register of
Deeds
Mark Oxbrow
David S. Brody
Terry Welbourn
Gerald Sinclair
Rondo B B Me
Kathleen Kavet
Anne Wirkkala, NHTI Concord

And a special thanks to Heather Bernard, Terry Deveau
and Jeff Nisbet, who may or may not have realized how vital
their role as sounding boards has been to this book.

Table of Contents

Foreword
by Robert E. Stone*

The key word when discussing New England ancient stone sites seems to be "serendipity." If Frank Glynn hadn't been carpooling with Malcolm Pearson, he would have driven past Westford, oblivious to the Knight's location. If Frank hadn't brought his daughter Cindy along on his subsequent explorations, she would not have convinced her father to see "the Old Indian" carving that led to the Knight carving's re-discovery. My association with the Westford Knight came about because of a similar serendipitous event — my wife decided I needed a haircut.

In 1955, I was sitting in a barbershop, waiting my turn, thumbing through a 1952 issue of *New Hampshire Profiles* when I came across an article on "Pattee's Caves" in North Salem. I lived in nearby Derry all my life and had never heard of the location. I decided I needed to visit the site and, to make a long story short, ended up leasing and then buying it from Malcolm Pearson, who had recently inherited the property from William Goodwin. The site opened to the public in 1958 and I quickly discovered that the expense of operating it did not allow enough money to underwrite research. And since Mystery Hill Corporation was technically a profit-making entity, it did not qualify for research grants. I founded the New England Antiquities Research Association (NEARA) in 1964, ostensibly to research sites throughout the region but also to serve as the non-profit research arm of Mystery Hill.

NEARA struck a resonance and quickly became a clearing house for sites across New England. And one of those sites was the Westford Knight. Frank Glynn was already a fixture at Mystery Hill by the time I leased the site in 1956. Frank was on a quest to prove a European Bronze Age culture had colonized New England, and his work remains the standard for fieldwork both

---

*Bob Stone died December 15, 2009, as the manuscript of this book was in a final stage of preparation. I will miss his frequent calls on a variety of topics and his encyclopedic knowledge of ancient stone sites. I am honored and grateful to have known and worked with him for more than 30 years.—D.G.

at possible pre–Columbian sites and among the Native sites he excavated in Connecticut. Mystery Hill benefited from a number of Frank Glynn projects, but the Westford Knight was *his* site. I have not seen a shred of legitimate new material on the Knight since his untimely passing in 1968.

Knowing Frank and his painstaking eye for detail, I can say he would be mortified at the current claims of Knights Templar and hidden treasures associated with his Knight. I wish Frank and David Goudsward had been given the opportunity to work together. Both men consider getting the correct answer more important than getting the expected answer, and I see more than a little of Frank in Dave's relentless pursuit of original source material. I've worked with both researchers and I am proud to consider both friends.

Frank Glynn's effigy in Westford could not ask for a better advocate than Dave and this book should more than adequately illustrate why.

At the time he wrote this, the late Mr. Stone was president, America's Stonehenge, North Salem, New Hampshire, and founder, past president and research director emeritus, New England Antiquities Research Association.

Preface

This is a book about a carving on an exposed ledge in Westford, Massachusetts. And while New England has no shortage of carved stones, the Westford carving is significantly different in that it is offered as evidence that Scottish nobleman Henry Sinclair set out on a voyage of exploration a century before Christopher Columbus. The Sinclair expedition, according to the theory's proponents, landed in Nova Scotia and explored the coastline to the mouth of the Merrimack River. Sinclair then proceeded up the Merrimack until the explorers came to the hilltop in Westford, where they would leave a full-size effigy of a knight in armor carved on the ledge, a memorial to a fallen comrade from the Gunn Clan. This carving was embraced by the Clans Sinclair and Gunn as proof that their ancestors were in North America long before Columbus, Cabot or Verrazano.

Locally, published references to a carving on a ledge in Westford date back to 1874 in its earliest identification as a Native American petroglyph. It was not until the 1950s that Connecticut archaeologist Frank Glynn identified the carving as a 14th-century Scottish military person. The premature death of Glynn in 1968 meant that the Westford Knight carving never generated the great interest that other alleged pre–Columbian sites enjoy. Awareness of the Westford Knight remained limited to locals, and it was rarely mentioned except in amateur archaeology circles.

In 2003, that changed. In the wake of Dan Brown's *Da Vinci Code*, a surge in interest in neomedievalism entangled Scotland's Rosslyn Chapel and the Knights Templar with the Westford Knight. Any scholarly research on the Westford site was swept away as the fantastic claims and wildly inaccurate statements became a deluge of hastily compiled books looking to ride on the *Da Vinci Code*'s coattails. This is a pity, because the carving, whatever interpretation one subscribes to, continued to erode at an alarming rate. Where Glynn found a full-sized figure, now only a sword is clearly discernible.

This book is an attempt to sweep through the claims and counterclaims and present a brief survey of the Westford carving's history and how it went from being a local curiosity to controversial evidence of Scottish explorers and how the carving was twisted into "proof" of secret societies and sacred relics hiding in North America. Because of that, chapters have been devoted to the history of the Knights Templar and Rosslyn Chapel. Neither chapter should be considered an endorsement of the connections to Westford and they are included specifically to demonstrate the myth-building process that eventually included Westford.

My own involvement with the Westford Knight is an outgrowth of my research at the Mystery Hill site in North Salem, New Hampshire, now open to the public as "America's Stonehenge." I was researching the colonial owners of that site in 1987 when the New Age movement reached a zenith with the astrological alignment of planets that was widely acclaimed as the "Harmonic Convergence." Hundreds of sincere believers in José Argüelles' interpretation of Mayan cosmology came to Mystery Hill to sit on a damp New Hampshire hillside and watch the sun rise over the standing stone that marks the summer solstice sunrise on that site's vast astronomical calendar. The sunrise was to usher in the start of an unprecedented New Age of Peace, which doesn't appear to have worked out nearly as well as they hoped.

The memorial plaque adjacent to the Westford Knight carving was dedicated in 1976. The arms are a stylized representation of the contemporary arms of the Earl of Caithness, chief of the Clan Sinclair (photograph by author).

This impressed me, not because of any New Age epiphany but because although the astronomical calendar on Mystery Hill had been documented, researched and publicized for decades, astronomy and archaeology were irrelevant that morning. Science had been eclipsed by a modern myth. As I would subsequently find happening at Westford and other sites, Mystery Hill's peripheral involvement in contemporary folklore generates more publicity than decades of archaeological, astronomical and historical research. Worse, these new interpretations are repeated so often as to give the appearance of "facts," albeit in a constant state of flux, being manipulated and mutated as needed to give credence to the latest flavor of esoterica.

The Westford Knight is deserving of additional research, if only to cull and purge the recent accumulation of published detritus. The Westford town history of 1883 mentions the carving without any elaboration — the carving needed no explanation because it was already a local landmark, as known and familiar to a Westfordian as a church steeple or the cannon in the town square. It is part of the tapestry of history and culture that unites the Westford community. Yet there is no attempt to protect the carving from the ravages of time and New England weather. By comparison, the Dighton Rock was lifted out of the Taunton River in 1963 by the Commonwealth of Massachusetts. A cofferdam was built beneath the rock to prevent further erosion and the area became a state park. A decade later, a building was constructed around the carved boulder, and 5 years later, an interpretive museum was added to the building. More recently, climate control measures were added. Compare this to Westford, where protection consists of a plywood frame placed over the carving for the winter, when someone remembers.

It is my hope to begin removing the conflicting, nonsensical and erroneous data that have accumulated around the carving, particularly in the last decades. It may still be possible to reinvigorate both research and attempts to protect the carving. Be it Native American, Medieval or even a Gestalt reification, the carved rock ledge off Depot Road has contributed to the historical identity of Westford. And for that reason alone it should be preserved and cherished as a local landmark.

1

The Indian on the Ledge

With the rich and long period of contact with the Native Americans that Westford experienced, it was logical that the townsfolk assumed the local Indians were responsible when someone first noticed the carving on an exposed ledge off Depot Road.

The area that would come to be known as Westford, Massachusetts, was originally on the far edges of neighboring Chelmsford. The Plantation of Chelmsford was granted in 1653, incorporating as a town in 1655. By 1660, the local Natives had moved further away from the new arrivals, opening up the land to the north and west of Chelmsford for colonization, including the land that would become Westford. Westford was a separate entity by 1729 with the town line being marked by Tadmuck Swamp. The actual Native word is somewhat debatable — Tatnoc, Tadnick, Tadnuck or Tadmuck all appear in town records, depending on which colonial record keeper was phonetically transcribing the word. The origin of the word is associated with wetlands or swamp, with proposed translations ranging from "wading place" to "meadow of moving grass."[1]

Geographic historian Arthur Krim observes Tadmuck is the only wetlands in eastern Massachusetts to keep the original Algonquian root in its name and the Reverend Edwin Hodgman, in his 1883 history of the town, notes the word was used extensively by the settlers in old land descriptions: Tadmuck Swamp, Farther Tadmuck, Little Tadmuck, Great Tadmuck, Hither Tadmuck, and Tadmuck Hill, now known as Westford Hill.[2]

Native habitations of Westford were located in the wetlands near what is today called Stony Brook. Projectile points have been recovered across the town, suggesting hunting activity throughout the region. In neighboring Groton, an Indian fish weir on Stony Brook lasted until 1680, when it was dismantled to make way for a mill.[3]

In his 1874 *Gazetteer of the State of Massachusetts*, the Reverend Elias Nason discusses the geology of Westford, mentioning a ledge of andalusite "which crops out near the Centre has upon its surface ridges furrowed in former times by glacial forces. There is upon its face a rude figure, supposed to have been cut by some Indian artist."[4] In a paper read before the Eastern States Archaeological Federation in 1957,[5] archaeologist Frank Glynn repeated the interpretation of that Indian figure as it was pointed out to him by Westford residents: out-splayed feet, pipe stem legs, with a melon shaped body.

Hodgman's 1883 history also notes the andalusite ledge, adding that it was near the house of William Kittredge and that "rude outlines of the human face have been traced upon it, and the figure is said to be the work of Indians."[6] Hodgman's reference specifically to a face, as opposed to an entire figure on the ledge, raises the question of how familiar Hodgman actually was with the carving. It appears that Hodgman liberally borrowed geology notes from the 1874 Nason book but misread the reference to the carving being upon the "face of the ledge" as being a "face on the ledge."

The Kittredge house mentioned in Hodgman's town history is located at 21 Depot Street. Built in 1846, William Kittredge, Sr. lived here, as did his

The 10-room, 3-story Victorian home formerly owned by Fisher Buckshorn. It was built in the early 1890s and deeded to Fisher's widowed mother, Adaline Fisher Kittredge, by her father-in-law, William Kittredge (photograph courtesy of Allie Brody).

son William. A third generation of the patronymically inclined Kittredges, William L. Kittredge married Adaline Fisher of the locally prominent Fisher family. When William L. Kittredge died in 1892, William Jr. provided for his widowed daughter-in-law by selling an adjacent two-acre parcel with house to the widow for $1.[7] This property at 17 Depot Street had been purchased from Kittredge recently, only to have the owner default on the mortgage after building a house. Fortunately, the new driveway narrowly avoided the ledge with "the Old Indian" carving.

The carving outside her door would be familiar to Addie Kittredge. Her childhood home was the neighboring house at 21 Depot, less than ¼ mile from the carving, and she passed it daily along the route to the Westford Academy that she and her siblings attended.

In 1901, Addie remarried, to Unitarian minister Louis W. Buckshorn. He had been the minister of the First Congregation parish in Westford since 1896 and had recently been reassigned. The Buckshorns soon moved to Concord, New Hampshire, where their son Fisher Buckshorn was born in 1905. In 1916, after several additional relocations, the Buckshorns returned to Westford and the house that Addie still owned. Louis Buckshorn died in 1919 and Addie continued to live in the house. Her son, Fisher, assumed ownership after Addie's death in 1950.

The carving known as "the Old Indian" remained an obscure local curiosity off the road by the Buckshorn house and would continue as such, right up until the fateful day that an antiquarian from Hartford, Connecticut, decided he could do what so many others before him had failed to do: identify the location of Vinland.

William Brownell Goodwin (1866–1950) was a retired insurance executive, an expert in colonial furniture, a collector of early maps and an amateur archaeologist. Goodwin attempted to identify the location of Leif Ericsson's Vinland after having been intrigued by the mystery of the location by the publication of Babcock's *Early Norse Visits to North America*.[8] Babcock attempted to identify Vinland by cartographic references, an approach also employed by Goodwin. Goodwin, in his book, admits his original hope was to prove C. C. Rafn correct in his declaration that Thorwald Ericsson had explored Connecticut.[9] Goodwin had been working intermittently on a history of Connecticut, and although the Connecticut history would never be completed, much of his early work originally collected for that history was utilized in his pre–Columbian researches.

While Goodwin was formulating his placement of Vinland, machinist Charles Pearson was moving his family to their new home in Upton, Massachusetts. The property included a large domed stone hut buried in the hillside.

Entrance to the Pearson Chamber in Upton, Massachusetts. *Malcolm Pearson's determination to discover the origins of the underground beehive would be the catalyst of the series of events that would lead to the discovery of the carving in Westford (photograph courtesy of Malcolm Pearson).*

Entering the structure through a 14-foot passage barely 4½ high, the chamber itself had a ceiling over 10 feet high and it was circular with a diameter between 10 and 12 feet. The exterior was covered with glacial gravel on which topsoil had formed, effectively camouflaging the structure. Charles Pearson's 17-year-old son Malcolm was fascinated by the structure. He began an investigation of the chamber that continues to this day, 80 years after he first saw it.[10] As the teenaged Malcolm questioned Upton's oldest citizen and checked town records, the suggestion was made that he contact Harry A. Cheney of neighboring Hopkinton, who was investigating a small stone structure he had found in a Hopkinton neighbor's field. Known locally as "the Old Indian Tannery," the 5-foot stone structure perplexed Cheney, a farmer and local historian, highly regarded for an encyclopedic knowledge of the local area's history, as well as for his interests in botany, mineralogy and archaeology. Cheney's collections were as diverse as his interests and included an array of town histories, Indian artifacts and newspaper clippings on reported Viking sites. Among Cheney's clippings, Pearson spotted an article in an 1893 issue of the *Milford Journal*[11] that concluded the Upton chamber was a refuge against attacks of warriors that pre-dated the Indians' presence, which Cheney apparently took as meaning the Vikings. Pearson was not as readily convinced that the Norse were responsible; in the town's 1935 bicentennial history,[12] Pearson wrote a small article on the chamber, carefully avoiding any possible origins, but noting its antiquity and comparative size to a recently discovered beehive hut in Ireland.

As Cheney and Pearson continued to research the stone structures in Hopkinton and Upton, two separate articles ran in the *Boston Globe*, putting the final pieces in place that would affect the future direction of research at Westford's Indian carving. An inquiry appeared in the *Boston Globe* from Olaf Strandwold, superintendent of schools in Prosser, Washington, asking if anyone knew the current whereabouts of a Norse inscription in Hampton, New Hampshire. Strandwold had found a reference to the rock with runes in Babcock's *Early Norse Visits to North America*, which Babcock considered (sight unseen) to be more likely a legitimate runic site than other, better-known sites of the time, such as Newport Tower and Dighton Rock.[13] It was exactly the sort of thing Strandwold was looking for. Strandwold was compiling a book of his translation of runic inscriptions on the Atlantic Seaboard[14] as a way to prove a Viking presence in North America.

Cheney immediately wrote to Strandwold offering to help find the Hampton rune stone and asking for his opinion about the Upton and Hopkinton chambers. Strandwold was unable to offer any suggestions. He was a runologist, not an archaeologist; the structures had no inscriptions to translate, so Strandwold was at a loss. Cheney also included a drawing of a small stone he had found in river silt near Hopkinton, which Strandwold identified as runes and translated as a fragment of a longer inscription from which Cheney's stone had broken off.[15] Cheney, already an ardent supporter of Norse visitation theories in general, became a lifelong supporter of Strandwold's runic interpretations.

In 1936, as Cheney and Pearson were locating the Hampton Rune Stone, abandoned and forgotten in a local field of trash,[16] Olaf Strandwold was receiving a visitor, William B. Goodwin. Goodwin had met and married his wife Mary while a resident of Seattle from 1889 to 1899 and the two had returned for a visit. While in Washington, Goodwin specifically sought out Strandwold to discuss Strandwold's self-published booklet[17] translating the Fletcher Stone in Yarmouth, Nova Scotia, as Norse runes as well as to get Strandworld's opinion on aspects of the Norse sagas for use in *The Truth About Leif Ericsson*. Strandwold asked Goodwin if he was aware of the unmortared stone beehive house in Upton. When Goodwin admitted he had not heard of the structure, Strandwold made arrangements for Goodwin to be introduced to Harry

Cheney. Goodwin's subsequent meeting with Cheney included a tour of the Upton chamber and a visit with Malcolm Pearson.[18]

As Cheney and Pearson showed Goodwin the structures, they mentioned another stone site the two had recently visited after reading about it in a *Boston Globe* article, up on the Salem/Derry town line in New Hampshire.[19] In July 1936, Pearson, Cheney and Goodwin visited the site in North Salem, New Hampshire. Goodwin was suitably impressed.[20]

Following several additional visits by different members of the original trio, Harry Cheney began negotiating with property owner Fred Duston to purchase the site with the assumption that Goodwin would assume the majority of the cost. He was correct, but at a cost. Goodwin purchased the site by himself in April 1937. Goodwin, already distancing himself from Cheney and his Viking "stone city" theory,[21] instead saw an Irish influence on the North Salem hilltop, proposing it was the remains of *Hvitramannaland* or "White Man's Land" of the Icelandic sagas, which Pearson, already suspecting an Irish origin to his Upton chamber, enthusiastically agreed with. Cheney continued

The entrance to the "Oracle Chamber," the largest of the stone-constructed structures at Mystery Hill. Goodwin felt this structure was the nerve center of the Culdee monastery he now owned (photograph by author).

to look for Vikings, but he was relegated back to his historical research in Hopkinton.

Locating *Hvitramannaland* or "Great Ireland" in New Hampshire was a radical departure from the usual region in which it was placed. Rafn had placed Great Ireland in the area south of Chesapeake Bay to eastern Florida,[22] and most subsequent authors followed his lead, placing the lost Irish settlement in the deep South. Goodwin's identification of North Salem with Great Ireland became the key he needed to place Vinland on the coast. The "Irish village" was featured in a 1939 book, *Underground New England*, by spelunker Clay Perry, which was the first of two books on New England caves in which Perry would devote a chapter to Great Ireland and Goodwin's "artificial caves."[23]

Perry's book caught the attention of E. E. Davis, a civil engineer in Northampton, Massachusetts, who wrote to Goodwin and asked to visit the site. In the course of conversation, Davis offered his opinion that the coastline that best matched the descriptions in the sagas was around Portsmouth Harbor in New Hampshire. Goodwin reviewed the cartographic maps of the area and concurred.[24] Because both *Íslendingabók* and *Landnámabók* state Great Ireland was near Vinland, Goodwin declared his newfound Irish monastery was the center of Great Ireland, proving his theory that Leif Ericsson's landfall was near Portsmouth, New Hampshire, in a shallow channel of the Piscataqua River.[25]

Goodwin's search for definitive proof that Great Ireland and Vinland were in New England resulted in a collection of reports of stone structures scattered across New England, found both by scouring town histories and by a network of correspondents who passed the data to Goodwin.

Another site mentioned by Perry was an Irish cross carved on a ledge in Westford, Massachusetts.[26] Perry, whose writing essentially repeated what Goodwin told him, was dutifully reporting Goodwin's opinion that a carving in Westford, like any other possible pre–Columbian site (inland, away from the coast and the Norse), was a relic of Irish missionaries.

Westford residents still knew it as Indian in origin; some of Goodwin's circle of correspondents considered the carving something very different — the hilt and broken blade of a Viking sword.

2

The Sword and the Cross

Harry Cheney's uncompromising belief that the ruins at Hopkinton, Upton and North Salem were Viking relics had alienated him from Goodwin and Pearson who were now of the belief that Irish monks[1] were the builders of both Upton and North Salem. So when Cheney reported to Goodwin that he had identified a carving of a broken Viking sword in Westford, his claim was essentially ignored. Goodwin's Irish monastery included a proviso that the monks stayed inland to utilize the Indian trails and avoid the Norse presence on the coast. A Viking carving as far inland as Westford, according to Goodwin's theory, would have driven the Irish out of the area.

Goodwin's Irish theory had begun to gain in popularity and was receiving national media coverage, in no small part due to the efforts of Clay Perry. A published novelist, the cave enthusiast Perry had decided to branch out into nonfiction by writing a book on New England caves and their lore. Perry had been running a query in regional newspapers asking about local caves, preferably with local legends attached to them. Goodwin, as owner of a "manmade cave" at North Salem, dropped him a note. Perry then published Goodwin's monastery theory in magazines and newspapers across the country. Perry's book on caves, *Underground New England*,[2] devoted an entire chapter to Goodwin's theories. Because of Perry's comparative speed in publication, his articles and book offer a more contemporary view of Goodwin's theories as they evolved, with more clarity and cohesion than Goodwin's later book would provide.

As a result of Perry's advocacy, reports of additional sites, usually smaller stone chambers, were brought to Goodwin's attention. Some were never located and some were immediately dismissed as colonial outbuildings, but Goodwin and Pearson found more inexplicable stone structures scattered across New England than originally anticipated. Goodwin began to hypothesize that the range of the Irish missionaries was greater than he originally envisioned and that the attempt to convert the American Natives to Catholicism was widespread and systematic. His evidence was the stone ruins across

William Goodwin examines the Quitsa Dolmen on Cape Cod in a photograph from *The Ruins of Great Ireland in New England* (1946).

the region near Indian trails, outposts of the monks who sought out converts by traveling along the trails.

In 1936, Harral B. Ayres joined the Connecticut Historical Society to research the major Indian routes in southern New England.[3] Goodwin, a staple of the historical society, was also researching Indian trails as his theory of Great Ireland using the trails for missionary work began to evolve. The two would eventually meet in the society's research library while reviewing material on Saybrook, Connecticut.

Ayres had already invested time into the issue, so Goodwin, rather than duplicate the effort, became an impromptu patron for Ayres, offering advice based on his own research as well as access to his personal collection of rare colonial maps. Goodwin had also suggested Ayres, living in northern New Jersey, make contact with Harry Cheney. Ostensibly the suggestion to Ayres was because of Cheney's background in Indians and colonial history in the Upton area, but Goodwin probably also considered it a method of keeping Cheney distracted from the work at North Salem.

Clay Perry's book, reflecting Goodwin's opinions of the time (1939), somewhat dismissively refers to Cheney's Hopkinton stone structure: "The beehive at Hopkinton is but five feet high over all, and may have been merely an outdoor fireplace or smokehouse."[4] Goodwin would include the Hopkinton site in his 1946 book as proof of the Irish settlement because it was identical to Irish sweathouses, but he never mentioned that it had been found by Cheney.

With a little behind-the-scenes maneuvering by Goodwin, Ayres' book was published in 1940, several years after Ayres had completed the text. *The Great Trail of New England*, with a chapter on early exploration of the Connecticut written by Goodwin, was well received, particularly in Hartford, where it arrived in the wake of the 300th anniversary of the city's founding by Thomas Hooker, who followed Indian trails from Massachusetts.[5] Before *Great Trail* had been published, Goodwin was already looking ahead with plans to have Ayres write a supplementary volume on the Mohawk Trail. The two books would give Goodwin a documented source for all the major trails to and from the Upton and North Salem sites and would allow him to illustrate the proximity of his growing collection of stone structures to those trails.[6] Cheney had been able to help Ayres locate the original path in the Upton/Hopkinton area, but Goodwin surely must have felt a tinge of chagrin when Ayres' book mentioned the Upton chamber as "Norse or earlier" and that Cheney had "a Norse Rune stone that he found near Upton."[7]

The original scope of Ayres' book was to include the Mohawk Trail as well as trails out of Boston and northward (material Goodwin later anticipated in the second book), but time and size constraints limited him to the Connecticut trails and those leading up to Boston. Some of the material north of Boston did make it in to the final book; Chapter VI includes Indian sites on the Merrimack River, particularly around Lowell. Ayres and Cheney had reviewed printed material for references to Indian trails on and off the Mohawk Trail, so it was inevitable that either Ayres or Cheney (who owned a large collection of local history books[8]) would have encountered Hodgman's *History of the Town of Westford* while searching for trails from the Merrimack River at Lowell that led back to the main Mohawk Trail. Among the discussions of Indians in the Westford history is, of course, the reference to the Indian carving on the ledge.

With or without direction from Ayres, who had returned to New Jersey, Cheney was lured, by his interest in Indian artifacts, to Westford to investigate the Indian petroglyph. With his unwavering belief in a Viking origin of North Salem, Upton and the other sites being found, the Westford carving acted like a lithic Rorschach test. The local residents saw an Indian caricature; Cheney saw the broken half of a Viking sword. He sent the report to Goodwin, who asked Malcolm Pearson to visit the site during one of his visits to the southern New Hampshire sites. In the spring of 1937, Pearson found the location, took a few photographs, and continued on his way.

Goodwin, in a July 1937 letter to William Sumner Appleton, Jr.,[9] notes that if a branch trail could be found that went from the Mohawk Trail to Lowell as expected, it would include the "sword rock at Westford." This letter, which also mentions his efforts to get Ayres' book published, is the earliest found reference to the Norse association with the Westford carving. It indicates Goodwin had already been made aware of the Westford site. Other than the suggested tie-in to the Mohawk Trail, Goodwin doesn't elaborate on the reference to the rock, indicating that both men had discussed the site previously and that this follow-up correspondence needed no elaboration.[10]

Sharing a possible Norse site with Appleton was a logical choice for Goodwin; Appleton had a pedigree in Norse visitations to America. His aunt Frances "Fanny" Elizabeth Appleton married Henry Wadsworth Longfellow and his uncle was writer and art patron Thomas Gold Appleton, who also served as chairman of the Scandinavian Memorial Association of Boston, the society that erected a statue of Leif Ericsson in Boston.[11] The association became a veritable who's who in Bostonian society as Norse became the new haute couture among the Boston Brahmins, and any possible Norse ruin or carving in the greater Boston area was of interest to the Appleton clan.[12]

There are problems with identifying the carving as a broken Norse sword, not the least of which is that Viking burials did not use a broken sword as a grave symbol. Although there have been burials excavated that were found with damaged weapons near the body, these weapons had been ceremonially rendered unusable.[13]

The symbol of the broken sword is more prevalent in Arthurian literature when Percival visits the Fisher King at the Grail castle. There he encounters a number of symbolic items, including a broken sword that the hero must restore to fulfill his destiny. Ironically for Cheney, the broken sword myth is derived from an earlier Irish myth where the Irish hero kills the Norwegian king.[14]

In some ways, it is surprising that neither Nason nor Hodgman had previously attempted to interpret the Westford carving as evidence of Vikings in their histories of the area. At the time they were writing their books, an obsession with Norse exploration was sweeping New England, triggered by Carl Christian Rafn's 1837 publication of *Antiquitates Americanae*[15] in Copenhagen. This monumental tome gathered all the Icelandic sagas in one source, with the text in Old Icelandic, Modern Danish and Latin. A subsequent supplement[16] included a section on the North American monuments that were "proof of the veracity of the sagas." Suddenly every odd carving, misplaced boulder and unrecognized stone structure in New England was a Norse relic. References to Norse visitations began to creep into the New England consciousness. New England icons Longfellow and Whittier popularized the Norse visits even further, publishing works about the intrepid Northmen.[17] Even the 1861 history of nearby Haverhill[18] does not start with the city's settlement in 1640, opting instead to open with Bjarni Herjolfsson and Leif Ericsson in the New World.

As Goodwin further examined the photographs of the Westford carving, he didn't see an Indian or a Norse sword; he saw an Irish face-cross similar to one found on Skellig Michael. Goodwin reinterpreted the carvings by extending the parallel lines that were the Indian's legs (or sword blade) down to create the body of a cross similar to the anthropomorphic "face-cross" on the Irish island. In a series of letters sent to European experts on Vinland and the Norse in 1938, Goodwin mentioned he had located a number of previously unknown sites as well as a "so-called carving of a Norse Sword which I think is not Norse but is an Irish cross."[19]

Goodwin was familiar with the island monastery of Skellig Michael — his 1946 book on Great Ireland would specifically note beehive huts on Skellig Michael as being similar to his own structures on Mystery Hill, making an Irish gravestone a better fit with his theory of Culdee monks traveling the Indian trails while avoiding the coasts where their feared enemies, the Norse, were doing a bit of colonization of their own.[20]

Goodwin's 1941 book on his search for Vinland, *The Truth About Leif Ericsson*[25] introduces his theory of Great Ireland, but it does not mention the Westford carving, either as a Norse sword or an Irish cross. Apparently, he was having second thoughts as to whether the carving was Irish or Norse. In a December 1941 reply to a letter from a student, David Smith, looking for further information on the carving,[22] Goodwin admits he had only seen photographs of the carving and now suspected it could be a sword, as was commonly believed. The student had written to Clay Perry about a reference to the carving in *Underground New England* and Perry had directed him to Goodwin for an answer. Considering that the student lived in the Nabnasset section of Westford, it suggests that the identification of the carving as either Norse or Celtic was not commonly recognized, at least in Westford, where residents still knew the carving only as the Old Indian.

Goodwin's reversal of opinion about Westford may be symptomatic of his growing health problems. The letter to Smith specifically notes that the cross should have a face at the point where the arms intersect the upright but that the carving had a face at the top.[23] This would suggest Goodwin was now confusing a face-cross, where the figure of Christ is integrated into the crucifix design, with a Celtic cross, where a ring encompasses the arm intersection.

In November 1943, Goodwin received a letter[24] from Vincent F. Fagan, a professor of architecture at Notre Dame. Fagan had come to Mendon, Massachusetts, to visit his parents. Fagan was formulating a book on colonial New England architecture, rendering his sketches into accurate line art. He had been jotting down notes when he learned of the chamber on the Pearson farm in Upton, less than 10 miles away. Visiting the farm, he met both Malcolm and his father, and returned to Indiana with copies of *The Truth About Leif Ericsson* and *Norse Runic Inscriptions along the Atlantic Seaboard.* Fascinated, he proposed that he and Goodwin join forces to research the ruins, each working on their own individual book. Fagan did not entirely embrace the Culdee monks as the specific Irish sect that built the structures, but he was willing to let Goodwin pursue the research. Fagan added an Irish Catholic perspective to Goodwin's staunch Presbyterian views, and Fagan had access to the Notre Dame library. Goodwin's correspondence brought Fagan up to speed on Goodwin's theories and progress along with photographs from Pearson, including several of the carving in Westford, which Goodwin was currently interpreting as a broken sword, but not committing to it being specifically a Norse artifact.

This correspondence with a novice unfamiliar with his work allowed Goodwin to put down his thoughts in writing. Much of this correspondence, including excerpts of Fagan's replies, would be edited into text for Goodwin's planned book, *These Strange Stone Houses,* later renamed *The Ruins of Great Ireland in New England.*

Fagan took an academic sabbatical to visit New England and sketch the various stone structures. After his return, he continued to work with Pearson on North Salem, trying to determine elevations for an accurate architectural map. He became a neutral figure, willing to discuss the sites with people who had opposing views on the sites. He and Pearson became the center of the operation, tracking research, forwarding requests and extinguishing minor turf wars.

By 1945, research among Goodwin and his collaborators had ground to a standstill. Goodwin's health was deteriorating quickly, and he was spending more time being hospitalized or bedridden than handling correspondence and coordinating research. Without his presence overseeing work, spats began breaking out, particularly between the original researchers and later arrivals. Fagan became more interested in a site he found near his parents' house in Mendon and was pursuing contacts to get his book published of architectural renderings of the sites. This left Pearson in the middle, dealing with internecine feuds. Fagan's correspondence from this time period is on file with the archives at Notre Dame University. It contains updates from Pearson and a litany of letters from other correspondents bemoaning slights, complaints and spats ranging from irritation that Pearson's father was beginning to refuse admittance to the Upton Chamber to Strandwold's paranoia about Goodwin publishing a book first and stealing the thunder from his own book.

Pearson, working full-time, raising a family and conducting his own research, was overwhelmed. The final straw was when Strandwold "translated" a series of stones in Byfield, stones that Pearson and Goodwin had examined in 1937 and dismissed as grooves created randomly when struck by farming implements, specifically ploughs and harrows.[25] Strandwold translated them in spite of Pearson's warning, so Pearson simply became unavailable to do further photography for Strandwold's book.

Oblivious to the breakdown in his network, Goodwin announced he felt well enough to proceed with plans to publish a book about his Stone Village. *Ruins of Great Ireland in New England* was published the following year, and even Goodwin's most staunch allies were dismayed by the book. It is painfully apparent that Goodwin did not allow anyone to review or edit the material. The text jumps from topic to topic, using random notes, excerpts from previous correspondence and (uncredited) typescript copies he had made of pertinent passages written by other authors. The text is disjointed, disorganized and includes materials that should not have been included all, such as a lengthy diatribe against Goodwin's mortal enemy, Samuel Eliot Morison.[26]

Meador Publishing, not adverse to a fully or partially subsidized project on occasion, merely typeset the book as presented to them. Pearson had seen the test prints of the book pages and knew how badly the book was put together. His subtle suggestions to Goodwin about changes went unheeded. The only delay in publication was caused by war-induced paper shortages. Misgivings aside, Pearson was able to secure a supply of paper that he personally transported to the publisher.

Two of Pearson's Westford photographs[27] appear toward the back of the book, uncaptioned and unidentified in the text. These photographs were taken from the side and show the sword with minimal distortion. In the front of the book is a line drawing of the Norse sword, traced from another photo.[28] The line art is stylistically different from the other images by Fagan and was probably meant to be no more than a rough draft. Among Fagan's archived files at Notre Dame is a print of the photograph that was the source of the line art. It is apparent that the line art was created from the photo — both have the same incorrect proportions and a line in the upper left corner corresponds with the encroaching plant life in the photo. The photograph was taken at an acute angle to capture shadows in the carving, but because there is no scale or landmark, it is not obvious that the angle has affected the image. Because Fagan drew it from the photo, having not seen the original site, the rendering is inaccurate: the pommel is round instead of prolate, the handle shortened and the cross-guard is a fraction of the actual thickness.

More telling is that the caption simply notes the carving was a "line carving on a vertical stone surface in Massachusetts." It does not specify that it is a Norse sword nor does it list a location; Fagan did not know where the "sword rock" was located; in 1944, Fagan was still asking Goodwin the location of the carving, and Goodwin was still mistakenly telling Fagan the carving was on a cliff in Weston, Massachusetts near Route 2.[29] The previous year, Goodwin had further complicated the matter by mixing up the carvings found in Hampton, New Hampshire, and in Westford.[30] This is reflected in the map in *Ruins of Great Ireland* as well.[31] This was also drawn by Fagan, revised in March 1944, and because he still did not know where the carving was located, both Weston and Westford are marked as places of interest, although neither appears in the text of the book.[32]

Various early interpretations of carving in Westford. From left to right: (1) Broken Norse sword, after Fagan's original skewed perspective drawing. (2) Irish face cross, per Goodwin, based on Fagan's incorrect drawing. (3) Composite of corrected Fagan rendering and Glynn's original chalking. (4) Westford "Old Indian" with Edward Fisher's peace pipe addition. Headdress is actually part of the Knight's chainmail aventail. (5) Fowler's French & Indian War era tomahawk.

Ruins of Great Ireland in New England was published with little fanfare and was as poorly received as Pearson feared. Because there is no text on the Westford site, there is no indication of whether Goodwin had finally decided the carving was indeed a sword or if the Fagan rough sketch was accidentally included in the rush to print. Four years later, Goodwin died in Virginia.[33]

As *Ruins of Great Ireland in New England* was being published, so was another book by Clay Perry. *New England's Buried Treasures* was an updated version of his 1939 book, being marketed by the publisher as the first in a short-lived "American Cave Series."[34] Perry devoted a chapter of the book to Goodwin's "artificial caves," virtually verbatim from the original book. In both books, Perry refers to the Westford site as depicting a "cross with a human face atop of it, typical of Irish carvings of sacred significance in the old country."[35] Perry also notes that the carving is on the main old Mohawk Indian trail from Albany to Boston Bay, an error in geography dating back to Goodwin's inability to recall the carving's location.[36] Perry's books may be the most accurate (and only) published record of Goodwin's "Westford Irish Cross" identification.[37]

Whether the carving was Indian, sword or cruciform, neither Goodwin nor Perry saw significant sales or distribution of their 1946 books.[38] Other post-publication effects of *The Ruins of Great Ireland* were less quantifiable but more significant. As far as Westford was concerned, the carving remained an Indian. Harry Cheney, having seen his role diminished and his work ignored, returned to his farm and his local research. Vincent Fagan abandoned efforts at publishing his own book. There is no indication in the correspondence between Fagan and Goodwin that suggest Fagan was aware that Goodwin had intended to use his illustrations for *Ruins of Great Ireland*—Fagan had been submitting them as samples in proposals for his own book. Whether he dropped the project voluntarily or because he was academically tainted by Goodwin's book is undetermined. In 1948, Fagan was horrified by rumors that Irish-American poet Shaemas O'Sheel was writing a book on the Irish stone ruins of New England with Goodwin's book as a primary source, prompting Pearson to write to O'Sheel to warn him away from the book and distance himself and Fagan from the book, if not all of Goodwin's theories.[39] Fagan died in July 1951, less than a year after Goodwin.

Olaf Strandwold's concern that Goodwin was trying to steal his thunder was not entirely incorrect, but, because of unanswered questions about his translations and feuds over translations with such high-profile figures as the Kensington Rune Stone's Hjalmar Holand, Strandwold became a pariah among publishers of Scandinavian topics.

The recalcitrant Strandwold's insistence on "translating" conspicuously non–Norse markings such as the plough strikes in Byfield made him an easy target for discrediting, just as Pearson had predicted. When Johannes Brøndsted, Director of the National Museum of Denmark, toured alleged Norse sites in North America in the autumn of 1948, his report[40] mentions Strandwold's 1939 book, which Brønsted had received in Denmark while deciding which sites he would visit. Brøndsted passed the book along to Denmark's foremost runologist, Erik Moltke, also of the National Museum. Moltke was succinct in his opinion, excerpts of which Brønsted included in the report: "Olaf Strandwold's book 'Norse Runic Inscriptions along the Atlantic Seaboard,' 1939, shows that this author lacks the most elementary knowledge of the Scandinavian languages; he is able to find runes in any crevice of groove and decipher them. He is lacking in all scientific qualifications for occupying himself with runological subjects...."[41] As far as Moltke was concerned, the only inscriptions he reviewed that were even remotely runic in nature were the Kensington Rune Stone in Minnesota and Noman's Land Island in Massachusetts and neither was ancient nor Scandinavian in origin.[42] An edited version of the 1951 English summary was published by the Smithsonian in 1954.[43] This version doesn't mention Strandwold at all; his work doesn't even appear in a bibliography at the end.

Strandwold's vaunted expanded edition of his 1939 107-page booklet was published posthumously in June 1949 as *Norse Inscriptions on American Stones*, a 69-page pamphlet with 32 pages on American translations, over half of which were the collection of field stones with plough strikes in Byfield.[44] Strandwold died December 1948 at his home in Washington State, three months after traveling to the East Coast to meet Johannes Brøndsted during the autumn tour of Norse sites. There is no record of how well the meeting went.

Both William Goodwin and Clay Perry, regardless of how poorly their respective 1946 books sold, did make a significant contribution to continuing interest in the Westford carving. In 1958, archaeologist Frank Glynn corresponded with Clay Perry,[45] noting that the chapter on "Pattee's Caves" in *Underground New England* was the start of his interest in that site. Glynn's subsequent work at Mystery Hill would lead to his shipping a copy of *Ruins of Great Ireland in New England* to a heretical British archaeologist named T. C. Lethbridge. That international parcel would result in the transformation of the Westford Indian into the Westford Knight.

3

A Knight Is Found

In 1948, British archaeologist T. C. Lethbridge published a collection of essays on Britain in the Dark Ages entitled *Merlin's Island.*[1] One of the essays included Lethbridge's opinion that prior to Leif Ericsson and the Norse journeys to Vinland, there were frequent transatlantic voyages from the British Islands to North America, primarily by Irish missionaries.[2] Eleven years prior to the publication of *Merlin's Island,* Lethbridge had privately published *Umiak,* a brief study of the similarities between the umiak (a skin-covered boat used by Eskimos) and the skin-covered currach used in Britain.[3]

Such opinions in 1940s Britain by an established and respected academic bordered on heresy. Lethbridge, the Director of Excavations for the Cambridge Antiquarian Society and the University Museum of Archaeology and Ethnology, freely (and gleefully) admitted his heretical stance in his introductory notes. As a response to his peers, Lethbridge elaborated on his theory in 1950's *Herdsmen and Hermits,* going so far as to suggest that the Kensington Rune Stone could be a legitimate artifact, which would offer the alternative that Vinland might not be located on the East Coast but in Minnesota, by way of Hudson Bay.[4] Lethbridge was never one to bow to convention, and his later books wandered seamlessly from archaeology into the supernatural, prompting a 1968 editorial in *Antiquity* that referred to Lethbridge as "[standing] firmly on that narrow line which delimits the lunatic fringe of archaeology from established orthodoxy and he has often written to the benefit of both sides."[5]

Merlin's Island was reviewed by Eric Forbes-Boyd in the *Christian Science Monitor.*[6] Forbes-Boyd, an author, historian and regular contributor to the newspaper, recommended the book for its approach to the material and lack of technical jargon. The review specifically mentioned Lethbridge's theory of Celtic pre–Columbian crossings.

This review brought Lethbridge to the attention of Frank Glynn, a well-respected avocational archaeologist in Connecticut. A member of the board of directors of the Archaeological Society of America, and past president of the Connecticut Archaeological Society, Glynn had developed a theory that there was a connection between the New England sites and European Bronze Age cultures. After Malcolm Pearson inherited the Mystery Hill site from William Goodwin, Frank Glynn was among the researchers who Pearson encouraged to reexamine the site.

Lethbridge's book fascinated Glynn, so much so that he wrote to Lethbridge praising the book and asking about parallels between New England stone structures and the sites Lethbridge had mentioned. This was the start of a vibrant correspondence between the two that continued until Glynn's death.[7]

In a January 1951 letter, Lethbridge told Glynn he was unaware of a dry masonry village in North Salem, New Hampshire, and wondered if data on the site had ever been published.[8] In response, Glynn shipped him a copy of Goodwin's *Ruins of Great Ireland in New England.*

Formal portrait of Frank Glynn, taken in December 1963 (photograph courtesy of Cindy Glynn).

Lethbridge had little use for Goodwin's Culdee monastery theory but, ironically, the one thing that he immediately focused on was the photographs of the sword that arguably should not have been in the publication. In a 1954 letter to Arctic explorer Vilhjálmur Stefansson, Lethbridge wrote, "There is one very important photograph in Goodwin's book — p.362–3. This sword carved on a rock can hardly be anything but a mediaeval sword."[9] He initially considered the sword Norse, dating it to 1200–1300 A.D. if not earlier, ending his note with the opinion that "this sword is one of *the* most important things found in America."

Lethbridge needed a better view of the sword to study the hilt and hopefully identify the origin of the sword. He urged Glynn to investigate Goodwin's sword site immediately and get a clearer image of the sword. Unfortunately, although Goodwin did include a map of southern New England in the book[10] (with Westford marked as a community of note), there is no key to the map, nor is there any mention of the sword's location other than "in Massachusetts." Glynn had met with Goodwin briefly in 1949 but

T. C. Lethbridge sorting pottery shards, circa 1966 (photograph courtesy of A. E. U. David — T. C. Lethbridge copyright).

the discussion was limited to a site in Connecticut that Glynn had found.[11] Glynn asked Pearson if he recalled the broken sword.

Malcolm Pearson was preoccupied with trying to reinvigorate research at Mystery Hill, working full time and raising a family. Pearson, assuming he remembered the site at all out of the dozens he had examined for Goodwin, would be familiar with the Westford carving as Goodwin's Irish Cross, not as Cheney's Viking sword. Thus, when Glynn asked about the sword, Pearson incorrectly recalled the carving as being one of the spurious ones in Byfield, Massachusetts, that Strandwold had "translated." These stones had been subsequently destroyed during road construction. The Byfield "runic inscriptions" were not photographed by Pearson and he had not visited them after the initial 1937 visit with Goodwin.[12] Glynn queried the local historians in Byfield, who did confirm the destruction of several alleged runic inscriptions during road widening but did not specifically recall a carving of a sword being among the casualties.

Glynn, not convinced that the destroyed carvings included the Norse sword, worried that the location had died with Goodwin, assuming the sword still existed. So Glynn began a systematic search of Massachusetts. Using Goodwin's notes, Olaf Strandwold's books and lists of known sites compiled by Pearson's newly founded research group, Early Sites Foundation, he began to visit locations as weather and time permitted. For two years, Frank Glynn searched for the elusive sword.

Lethbridge continued to examine the images in Goodwin's book more closely. As Glynn searched for the sword's location, Lethbridge began to suspect that the carving might not be Norse in origin but might depict a hand-and-half broadsword, used in Britain between 1300 and 1400 A.D. Lethbridge had already published his suspicion that Irish and Scottish explorers made it to North America earlier than suspected and this looked like the evidence he needed.

Lethbridge was hoping that Glynn would find a sword that had been rendered more accurately than the book's photographs suggested, with a carving distinct enough to determine the style and age of the sword so he could use that to date the carving. He cited examples from Iona and the Hebrides for Glynn to look up for comparison, not necessarily expecting either location would be the source. Photocopier technology was not yet common, so Lethbridge chose images of weapons widely discussed among antiquarians and authors, turning to such works as Graham's *Antiquities of Iona* and Drummond's *Archaeologia Scotica* for images to compare against the sword in Westford.[13] Both titles were considered standards for such studies, with subsequent inventories often referring back to them to avoid repeating the same material over again.[14] More importantly, such titles would be available on both sides of the Atlantic, allowing Glynn to review the same images as Lethbridge by visiting libraries at locations such as Harvard and Yale.

It is interesting to note that Lethbridge, who in *Herdsmen and Hermits* had already suggested that Henry Sinclair could have made the voyage to North America, did not use the floriated cross and sword adorning a grave slab believed to be Henry Sinclair's grandfather, Sir William Sinclair of Rosslyn (1297–1330).[15] This marker, although not widely known until becoming the pivot point of Andrew Sinclair's 1992 book, had been mentioned in British antiquarian journals at least as early as 1876.[16] The stone was one of several with floriated crosses and sword found by 19th-century gravediggers in the ruins of St. Matthew's Church, the Rosslyn village chapel used as a burial ground after the construction of the Sinclair family's proposed collegiate church in 1446, now known as Rosslyn Chapel.

In the spring of 1954, Frank Glynn and Malcolm Pearson were returning from a research trip to the North Salem site. As they drove along State Route

110, Pearson, in a sudden flash of recognition, suddenly pointed to Boston Road, a turn-off leading into Westford and casually remarked that the sword carving was about two miles beyond Westford on that road.

On May 30, 1954, Glynn headed back to Westford with his daughter Cindy. Passing through Westford, they found themselves in Graniteville. Asking around, he was directed to a local historian, who had never heard of any local carvings of a sword. The historian made a number of phone calls to no avail — none of the locals knew of a sword. Several did suggest that since he was in the area, perhaps Glynn should stop and see an old Indian carving on Prospect Hill. The sporadic rain that had plagued him all day had turned into a steady downpour and Glynn had no interest in looking at "the Old Indian," especially in a cold May rain. His daughter uncharacteristically insisted that they should investigate. When he continued to balk, Cindy, in her own words, "threw a tantrum."[17] So, begrudgingly, he got directions and drove to the site.[18]

In a later interview, Frank Glynn recalled how the sword "jumped right out at us"[19] on the wet rock face. Goodwin's broken sword and Westford's Old Indian were one and the same. It was raining too hard to take photographs, so an elated Glynn came back the next day. By then, word had gotten out that an archaeologist was looking at the Indian carving, and locals began stopping by to chat.

In a paper read before the Eastern States Archaeological Federation in 1957, Glynn repeated the interpretation of the Indian as it was pointed out to him by Westford residents: the out-splayed feet, pipe-stem legs, with a melon-shaped body of a 20-inch-long stick-figure caricature of an Indian, "gazing to the west toward his happy hunting ground."

Glynn cleared the sword, chalked in the pecked holes and then connected them. He then sent a copy to Lethbridge. Reviewing the image, Lethbridge felt the sword was not merely a carved sword grave marker as he had originally suspected. Finding the image more reminiscent of swords on full effigies common in the British Isles, Lethbridge suggested to Glynn that there almost certainly had to be more to the carving.

Lethbridge was now certain that this was carved by explorers from the British Isles and his prime suspect was Henry Sinclair. Extrapolating from the Glynn image, Lethbridge proposed that the sword was part of a larger funerary monument, similar to an English memorial brass etching or a recumbent grave slab such as those found in the Hebrides and Ireland.[20] To illustrate what Lethbridge expected Glynn to uncover, he drew a rough sketch of an effigy found on the Isle of Lewis. The effigy Lethbridge chose was of a Macleod, found on the south side of the ruins of St Columba's Church in

Aignish on the east coast of Lewis.[21] A high relief of a figure carrying a spear and a sword, it is typical of the effigies that Lethbridge expected, with quilted armor and pointed bascinet helmet.

With the assistance of his daughter Cindy, Malcolm Pearson and land owner Fisher Buckshorn, Glynn spent several weekends clearing away the moss, lichen and soil that had built up on the rock. When they were done, Glynn began chalking in any marks that he didn't think were natural. The first version of the Knight was crude when compared to later versions, but Glynn only chalked in the most pronounced punch marks.[22] The result was a knight in armor with a shield. It was at best a rough representation, but it was sufficient to convince Glynn that he and Lethbridge were on the right track. If Glynn had merely been randomly connecting marks to subconsciously recreate the image suggested by Lethbridge, it would have resulted in an entirely different image. Lethbridge had predicted there was an effigy, but his Macleod effigy example bore little resemblance to the Westford counterpart in pose or weaponry.

Glynn now decided to chalk in the smaller punch marks, painstakingly examining each depression on the ledge to determine man-made marks from natural markings. This would turn out to be a more arduous task than expected. The ledge of mica schist was glacially striated and laced with the andalusite as noted by Elias Nason back in his 1874 gazette. Unfortunately, as geology texts of the same time noted,[23] andalusite decomposes readily into a soft talc or clay-like form, meaning Glynn was faced with differentiating between small pockmarks of eroded andalusite and the man-made punch holes. The Westford variety of andalusite is a sub variety known as chiastolite. In chiastolite, carbon impurities arrange along the axis of the crystal and alter the appearance of the crystals, causing black and white variations in regular symmetrical shapes. When cut in cross sections, the crystal appears as a white cross or an X. So, the ledge where the Westford Knight was memorialized may have been chosen because the ledge was near an omen-like outcropping of crystals bearing a white X or cross on a black background, evocative of the black engrailed cross upon a white background that was an armorial bearing of the Sinclairs.[24]

Although the andalusite may have slowed Glynn down, it would also add to the authenticity of his work. When he was finished, what lay before him was a life-sized image of a knight in full regalia, which bore a striking resemblance to effigy grave slabs still extant in Western Scotland, particularly on the Isle of Iona.

One of those stopping by to supervise was 84-year-old Lila Fisher. When Glynn sought permission from Fisher Buckshorn to examine the ledge on his property, he also met Buckshorn's aunt Lila, who had recently moved back to Westford to be near relatives.[25] Miss Fisher recalled that the carving had been there when she was a child and that it was always known as "the Old Indian." Miss Fisher thought there was evidence of erosion — she recalled the carving being deeper in her childhood than it was in 1954.[26]

She also recalled the time her brother Edward decided to "improve" the Indian by taking a hatchet and adding a carving of a peace pipe.[27] Glynn admitted to Lethbridge that he still couldn't see the head of the Indian in the carving, but the placement of the peace pipe carving indicated that the Fisher children easily saw it 70 years before.[28] Glynn actually was pleased with the attempt — the crude V-shaped cuts into the rock were easily identifiable and, in at least one case, superimposed over existing lines. This showed that the carving was not done by local children, a popular explanation of the carving at the time.

As the summer turned to fall, Lethbridge reviewed the progress and offered interpretations as to what Glynn was finding. Glynn expanded his search with Fisher Buckshorn's assistance. Buckshorn was able to confirm that the carving was on his property, not the town's berm, meaning a proposed sidewalk would not affect the Knight. And when Buckshorn was preparing to turn over his post-harvest garden, he bulldozed away the top layers of soil so Glynn could look for disturbances in the soil stratigraphy that would indicate any additional features. Glynn spotted several promising burnt piles of stones that turned out to be post-colonial. The Knight was alone on the hill.

Although Lethbridge was convinced Glynn was looking at an effigy by a carver from somewhere in the British Isles, Glynn still continued to lean toward a Norse carving. That changed when Glynn sent images of the shield to Lethbridge in late May. There was no doubt in Lethbridge's mind that a circular image on the shield was a heraldic buckle and probably Orcadian. To Lethbridge, there was no question that Glynn had found a life-sized military of a knight in armor that was somehow connected to Henry Sinclair's voyage to North America.

The process was not entirely seamless. Lethbridge's attempts to have a professional herald review the heraldic symbols on the shield were rebuffed first in England and then in Scotland. Meanwhile, the Lowell, Massachusetts, newspaper recorded an ill-fated attempt to make a plaster casting of the ledge[29] that resulted in a massive block of plaster attached to the rock face so firmly that even a local tow truck winch couldn't budge it. Glynn later elaborated on the story to a bemused Lethbridge, noting that a local policeman was called in to handle the crowds and rubbernecking drivers. When the plaster mass wouldn't move, the only local truck with a heavy-duty hoist was owned by a man with a long-standing feud against Fisher Buckshorn who had to be wooed into using his truck so close to the enemy camp. The truck hooked up the embedded wire grips, tightened the slack and pulled. Immediately, the back of the truck began sinking into the soil and as the tension increased, the wires pulled out of the plaster, leaving a mortified Glynn, amused crowds and a newspaper reporter without a story. The plaster cast did eventually come off, in small pieces after a rainstorm.[30]

The plaster fiasco aside, Glynn's discovery was beginning to generate widespread press coverage, including articles in the *Christian Science Monitor*[31] and *Yankee* magazine. Suddenly, there was a great deal of interest in the Westford Knight, both pro and con. Among the proponents were Frederick J. Pohl, a historian who had previously suggested that Henry Sinclair had crossed the Atlantic to Nova Scotia in a small book on the topic in 1950[32] and several of the curators of the John Woodman Higgins Armory in Worcester, Massachusetts. The curators came to Westford at the behest of Glynn and immediately focused on the helmet, narrowing down the date of the design to circa 1376 to 1400.[33]

But not everyone was prepared to cede the Westford carving to the Sinclair expedition. Archaeologist William Fowler visited the site and published his own theory[34] that the only actual carving was in the area of the sword's hilt and that the rest of the markings were natural striations and pockmarks on the ledge. Instead of a sword, Fowler saw the image of an iron tomahawk, circa 1700–1750, carved by an unknown settler as a memorial to a battle against the Indians. Fowler specifically thought the carving looked like a tomahawk wielded by William Denison of Stonington, Connecticut, during the French and Indian War (1754–1763).[35] Fowler doesn't elaborate on why his unknown settler would choose to carve his memorial with the handle pointing away from the road, making it appear upside-down to passersby, or why it was carved on a stretch of road that led away from the center of town and had no houses on it except the local parsonage.[36]

Fowler's suggestion of Westford as a tomahawk, in spite of his familiarity with the type of weapon,[37] did not convince the Knight advocates and did not impress the skeptics. It was, however, sufficient impetus for a meeting at the Westford Knight between Frank Glynn, historian Frederick J. Pohl, and author Charles Michael Boland. Pohl was finishing *Atlantic Crossings Before Columbus*, his latest book on transatlantic crossings and Boland was in the process of writing a similarly themed book, *They All Discovered America*, in which he would claim nineteen separate discoverers of North America before Columbus.[38] The two books came out within a week of each other, with Pohl's more scholarly text faltering in sales against Boland's hyperbolic prose. Both authors glowingly record Glynn/Lethbridge's work at Westford. Pohl ignored Fowler's report while Boland excoriated Fowler for trying to make a 6-foot knight into a 15-inch tomahawk.[39]

In spite of all this press, after a brief spike in interest, the Knight returned to the status of a local curiosity. Frank Glynn was appointed Postmaster for Clinton, Connecticut. The position brought additional civic responsibilities as well — moderating town meetings, Little League, the boards of the Library and Chamber of Commerce; all in addition to editing the *Bulletin of the Archaeological Society of Connecticut* and countless speaking engagements around the state.

By the time he oversaw the remodeling of the Clinton Post Office in 1965, he was rarely able to find time to continue his Westford or Mystery Hill research. His correspondence with Lethbridge became less frequent and his health began to falter.

In 1967, Glynn returned to Westford with his teenaged daughters and chalked in the image again. Compared to the earlier versions, the Knight demonstrated the clarity with which Glynn now saw the effigy. Glynn died the next year in August 1968.

Also in 1967, Lethbridge published *A Step in the Dark*,[40] a book on the vibration rates of life and death, supernatural and parapsychology, topics he had increasingly become interested in. In the final chapter, Lethbridge recalls the Westford Knight and his correspondence with Glynn; although Lethbridge refers to it in the present tense, the careful phrasing suggests that the great transatlantic research collaboration had already ended by attrition.

In 1974, Frederick J. Pohl published a greatly revised and expanded study of the Sinclair expedition[41] that included a chapter on the Westford Knight with very few changes from Frank Glynn's interpretation.

Lila Fisher's reminiscence of her brother Edward "improving" the carving with a peace pipe had evolved locally into his having carved the entire image, in spite of the fact that he was born in 1874, the same year that Nason published his *Gazetteer of the State of Massachusetts* with the earliest reference to the carving. This was typical of the schism — either you believed Frank Glynn's theory or you believed it was a local hoax.

When Andrew Sinclair visited Westford in the early 1990s while researching his book on his ancestor's voyage, he found Westford still divided into two camps — those who believed that the Knight was a pre–Columbian effigy as proposed by Glynn and those who believed Edward Fisher and his brothers had too much time on their hands as children.[42] The division over the carving's origins remains unabated 60 years after Frank Glynn first began stripping away the lichen around Goodwin's broken sword.

4

A Knight in Armor

When Frank Glynn finished chalking in the marks on the newly exposed ledge, he found himself face to face with a life-sized image cut into the ledge. Wielding a 39-inch sword and a great shield, the Westford Knight in quilted armor and helm was outlined on the ledge using a combination of the striations in the rock and man-made punch holes. The holes vary in size and depth but appear to have been punched into the stone by a sharp tool such as a metal punch or awl, standard tools in an armorer's repair kit.[1]

Frank Glynn corresponded with Frederick J. Pohl, who had published a booklet in 1950 chronicling the voyage of Henry Sinclair to Nova Scotia.[2] The Westford Knight was evidence that the Sinclair expedition went further south than originally theorized, well into New England. If this was the case, the effigy marked the spot where one of Sinclair's companions died.

Pohl immediately visited the site and embraced the carving as unquestionably authentic. Pohl began to study his previous research to see if there were data to support or disprove a continuation of Sinclair's voyage. That research would result in a section of a new book, *Atlantic Crossings Before Columbus* and a book in 1974 on the Sinclair voyage that included Glynn and his work in Westford, expanded biographical material on Henry Sinclair and new material on the Native American folk hero Glooscap.[3]

Pohl found the method of creating the Knight effigy to be a confirmation of his theory that Henry Sinclair had crossed the Atlantic to Nova Scotia. The varying depth and size of the punch holes was an indication of the legitimacy of the image. Pohl explained that as the punch tool was struck repeatedly into the resisting New England ledge, it dulled and the tip flattened; a prankster would have had the time and means to sharpen the tool as needed.[4] The prankster would also need to be familiar with the weapons and armor found in Scotland in the late Middle Ages. Pohl also notes that the same punch-hole technique was used to inscribe Århus Rune Stone 6 (No.68), found in Denmark in 1905.[5]

The Scottish clans were some of the earliest to use the longer swords as

Frank Glynn's original 1954 chalking of the full Westford Knight. His daughter Cindy adds scale (photograph courtesy of Cindy Glynn).

they became available, while the style of the sword hilts, as found on the effigies and in art, were often already out of fashion in Britain and Europe. This combination of up-to-date blades on obsolete hilts, often with Norse influences, makes identification difficult under normal circumstances. Combined with the theory that the Knight was carved by an armorer, not an artist, trying to render an image on a rough ledge with simple tools, it must be assumed that the armorer created a technically, not aesthetically, correct image.

Steer and Bannerman, in their 1977 study of monumental sculpture, note that the weaponry and armor displayed in such a sculpture represent an image both derived from the wardrobe actually worn in life and as a symbol of status.[6] Determining the Westford carving's armor could therefore identify the time period and possibly even the identity of the person memorialized.

Frederick Pohl never altered his interpretation of the image as he first saw it, using it in all of his subsequent books on Sinclair. Glynn, on the other hand, was constantly modifying the image as he discussed the matter with Lethbridge and reexamined the markings on the Westford ledge. His initial image in 1954 featured a short quilted tunic with a jagged hem and a disproportionately thin right arm that crosses the chest with the hand resting above the sword's pommel. Pohl saw other details, such as a falcon with jesses and bells alighting on the pommel of the sword instead of an arm across the body. Pohl also saw a rampant lion on the pommel and a break in the blade of the sword. Glynn concurred with these points and added them to a subsequent chalking of the ledge. Details were beginning to clutter the image; the revised image showed a knight in a full-length tunic with a rampant lion and a St. Andrew's Cross within the sword's pommel, a falcon with jesses alighting on the pommel and a fleurette on the right breast which Glynn suggested represented a lance rest.

The St. Andrew's Cross is appropriate; in 1385, the Scottish Parliament decreed that as a preparation for a joint attack by French and Scot forces on England that "all men, French and Scots, have a sign in the front and at the back, namely, a white cross of St. Andrew,"[7] confirming the use of the cross as a military insignia. The lion rampant was the heraldic symbol of the Scottish crown, but Pohl noted that the lion's torso is merely a discolored patch on the ledge with punches that he felt were deliberately added to the lighter color to add legs and tails to the image.[8]

The Westford effigy wears a quilted tunic, known as an *acton* or *aketon*. Two pieces of material were sewn together to create long, vertical pockets which were then stuffed with any material that would cushion a blow — cotton, wool, even grass. The aketon thus took on a quilted appearance.[9] The aketon was designed to be worn beneath metal armor as a buffer between armor and body during attacks with blunt objects. However, as armor historian Ewart Oakeshott notes, there is ample literary and effigy evidence to suggest that the aketon was also worn by itself as protective gear, particularly when fighting on foot.[10]

The Westford Knight also wears a bascinet, a tall, pointed helmet with a hinged visor. As was common with bascinets of the 14th century, the Knight also wears an aventail or camail, a flexible curtain of chainmail that attached to the helmet to cover the neck and shoulders.

Because of the style of the visor, tapered outward to deflect blows away from the face, the helmet acquired the nickname "pig-face bascinet." Frank Glynn's first attempts fluctuated between showing the image with this visor open and closed. Subsequent reexaminations by Glynn with Pohl reinterpreted the markings showing the visor raised or missing.[11] Medieval literature professor Derek Brewer notes that bascinets without visors were common in the late 14th century; limitations to visual range and claustrophobia prompted some knights to forego the added protection of the visor.[12] Brewer further notes that the majority of English effigies and funerary monuments which include bascinets do not depict them with visors.[13]

Although the drawing of the sword in *The Ruins of Great Ireland* shows a short grip and round pommel, subsequent examinations indicate that Fagan's illustration was inaccurate and that the grip should be significantly longer. Reexamined and chalked in, the carving became the hilt of long-sword with a shaped grip, straight cross-guards and a longer handle, which allowed use by one hand or both hands, giving it the name "hand-and-half" or "bastard" sword. Glynn's image showed an elongated pommel[14] on a tapered grip and a simple cross-guard (aka a cruciform hilt). Pohl essentially saw the same sword as Glynn, but with a straight grip.

Most telling was the heater shield[15] with images of a crescent, a star, a buckle and a ship. While Glynn continued to examine and reinterpret the lines that made up the image, Lethbridge was finally able to attract the interest of a member of the Court of the Lord Lyon, the official heraldry office for Scotland. The Unicorn Pursuivant of Arms, Sir Iain Moncreiffe, found the Westford site "absolutely fascinating,"[16] and immediately corrected several errors in the Lethbridge and Glynn interpretation of the symbols. The most significant revision was Moncreiffe's statement that the shield could not be of Sinclair or his immediate kin since there was no indication of the family's distinctive engrailed cross. Sir Iain's initial opinion was that the shield indicated that the image fit within the context of the Sinclair expedition as a memorial to one of Sinclair's companions on the voyage, possibly of Norse blood.

Moncreiffe, in a later letter,[17] felt that the Westford shield solved a puzzle he had been pondering — the composition of the medieval coat of arms of the chiefs of the Gunn clan. It was difficult to distinguish friend from foe in the heat of battle when all that was visible was armor. So, to identify allies, the practice was introduced of painting an insignia or "arms" on the shields to differentiate combatants. When embroidered on the surcoat worn over the armor, the "coat of arms" was born. A shield on a grave effigy represented the battle shield of a knight and would display his arms. As such, the shield could also be referred to by the heraldic term of "escutcheon." Sir Iain identified emblems on the shield as the arms of the chief of the Clan Gunn, who Moncreiffe considered second only to the Sinclairs in 14th-century Caithness.

Moncreiffe, discounting modern Gunn coats of arms as mistaken, declared the Westford image was the original Gunn arms, making the image so early that Sir Iain felt there were no more than four or five heralds in the world who would have known of the arms and also have sufficient knowledge of the armor to accurately carve the rock. None of these heralds were in North America, let alone carving an image into a ledge in Massachusetts. Sir Iain was so certain of the legitimacy of this shield that in his book, *The Highland Clans*, he referred to the Westford Knight's shield as "the earliest surviving example of the Gunn chief's coat-of-arms...."[18]

As Moncreiffe interpreted the shield, the crescent was actually a badly eroded second buckle, meeting a heraldic tenet that the chief's star would be placed between two identical objects. The lines crossing above the ship were more problematic. Moncreiffe's initial opinion was that they represented oars crossed to form a saltire or St. Andrew's cross, a design found on Scottish coats of arms. Thinking that punches in the correct place were furled sails, Moncreiffe also assumed there had been a mast as well that was lost through erosion. Sir Iains's final report suggested that the blazon, in heraldry terminology, was *Gules a lymphad, sails furled, oars in saltire, and in chief a mullet Gold between two large buckles Silver.*[19]

The colors, Moncreiffe explained, were based on the earliest surviving Scottish armorial role (1332) which showed the shield of the Earl of Caithness as a golden galley on red. Since there is some indication that some of the original effigies were painted to make them noticeable,[20] this raises the question of whether the Westford Knight effigy was originally painted in the tradition of incised effigies. A bright red shield on a knight would certainly be distinctive, serving the purpose of the marker to be seen and Gunn remembered but then the question arises of what coloring agents would be available. If the Westford Knight was painted, the palette would be limited to dyes from local plants and powdered rock. Geologist James Dana and gemologist George Kunz both note that the chiastolite crystals in Westford are sometimes pink or rose-colored.[21] Imperfect crystals, such as those found on the Knight's ledge, powdered easily.

A memorial to a fallen warrior on a hilltop in 1399 Westford requires an opponent, and by inference, that indicates Indians. Hodgman notes a local tradition of a pre-settlement battle between the Nashoba and Wamesit tribes on Frances Hill, about 3 miles northeast of the Knight effigy,[22] so it is possible that the Sinclair expedition stumbled into long-disputed territory and was attacked by one side or the other.

It seems unlikely that the Sinclair party would take the time to grind stone or gather flowers on the edges of a battlefield to render color for the effigy, but the assumption that the Gunn chieftain fell in battle dates back to the original broken sword image in *Ruins of Great Ireland*. As early as 1961, Frederick Pohl offered less heroic options for the death of the Gunn chieftain. In his earliest work on the Westford Knight, *Atlantic Crossings Before Columbus*, Pohl offers the possibility that Gunn, climbing up the 465-foot hill in full armor, suffered a fatal heart attack. By his 1974 book, Pohl had noted that proximity of Rattlesnake Hill and added snakebite as the possible cause of death.[23] If time constraints associated with a battle are factored out, there is no reason that the effigy could not have had some rudimentary tint added.

Glynn's design changed as he reviewed his material, reexamining the punch holes under different lighting conditions. He experimented, connecting pock marks that might be eroded punch holes. Glynn took the design to such an extreme at one point that Lethbridge gently chastised Glynn's "stage magician" coat.[24] By Glynn's final visit to the site in 1967, he had dropped a number of the original components — the cross and lion were gone from the pommel, as were the falcon and the lance rest. Glynn's most drastic revision was removing the oars saltire from the shield, falling back on Moncrieffe's alternative suggestion of the diagonal lines being support ropes for the missing mast. However, his basic design remained the same — a full-sized effigy of a knight with a shield on his left arm and his right arm at his side, the hand resting on the misericorde dagger on his belt.

Subsequent researchers would build from Glynn's prototype with varying degrees of success. Tim Wallace Murphy's 2004 book[25] features an image of the Knight carving with both hands clasped together on the sword hilt. The shield has been removed from the image, in spite of the shield being the key component in identifying the Knight, and the author quotes extensively from Moncrieffe about the heraldic features of the shield.[26] James Whittall based his rendering of the Knight on a composite of Glynn chalkings, later exchanging the misericorde for a rosary.[27]

As Lethbridge had noted, the effigy on Prospect Hill is similar in design

Frank Glynn's final chalking of the Westford Knight in 1967, showing a significantly cleaner image. Again, Cindy Glynn adds scale (photograph courtesy of Cindy Glynn).

to incised grave slab effigies from Henry Sinclair's time. Although Scottish grave markers had evolved from incised images into low-relief carvings and then high-relief carvings which were the fashion in 13th-century Scotland, art historian Robert Brydall notes the inscribed style did not entirely disappear on the introduction of the figure in full relief.[28]

Because there was no sculptor along with Sinclair on his expedition to create a relief carving, the armorer would have been called into service, creating an incised image reminiscent of the slab that would be placed over the fallen Gunn knight had his body been interred back in Scotland.

Various interpretations of the full-sized Knight carving in Westford redrawn to scale and simplified. From left to right: (1) Glynn's original sketch, using only the punch marks that were the most obviously artificial (1954). (2) Glynn's subsequent sketch (1954). It would also be the one he would return to. His final sketch in 1967 is virtually identical except for the removal of the falcon. (3) Frederick J. Pohl's partial Knight image, which he believed was combined with natural striations already on the ledge to give the effect of a full body. (4) Glynn's short-lived "stage magician" coat. Lethbridge's mild chiding was sufficient to reassess the decorated armor.

Brydall noted in 1895 the alarming rate at which the grave slabs were disappearing, citing surviving examples scattered across Scotland and her islands. He also notes that although there were no extant markers, "[d]oubtless the great St. Clairs of Orkney were at one time represented in the far North, being connected with the Douglas and more southern Scottish families, as we find some of the great island chiefs in the north-west attempting to perpetuate the memory of their ancestors after the manner of the descendants of the Norman knights."[29]

It is to those northwest islands Lethbridge turned his attention. He mentioned funerary art generally found in the Hebrides and Ireland, but his letters to Glynn focused particularly on the Hebrides markers, noting that Glynn's sketch seemed to show quilted armor, a trait found on the Hebridean carvings. Lethbridge was not showing preference by focusing on Irish and Hebridean grave markers; it was simply that he had limited examples to draw from. A recent study notes there are only about 150 Irish medieval effigies remaining from the time period circa 1200 A.D. to 1600 A.D. and of these, just over 50 are figures in armor. Of those, less than half are from the 1200 to 1350 time period.[30]

Even with these limited choices, Irish effigies do exist that have design similarities to the Westford carving, most notably in the town of Hospital, County Limerick. Among the effigies in the ruins of a church founded in 1215 is a 14th-century slab carved in very low relief of a knight wearing mail and a surcoat.[31] The left hand grasps a sword with a straight short cross guard and a large round pommel. The primary difference is the lack of a shield.[32]

The Hebrides hold a number of low-relief effigies that evoke the design of Westford's Knight, but perhaps the most striking examples are at one of the oldest and most revered religious centers in western Europe — Iona, the island considered the point of origin for the spread of Christianity throughout Scotland.[33]

A wide range of monuments were erected through the ages in the burial ground, *Reilig Odhrán* — "St. Oran's Burial Ground." In a nearby museum in the restored abbey infirmary, a wide collection of grave slabs, carved stones and architectural fragments are displayed, rescued from the area surrounding the abbey and removed from *Reilig Odhrán* to protect them from the elements.

Among the abbots, prioresses and knights are several carvings that share design elements with the Westford Knight figure in full armor with sword and shield, originally recumbent. Some carry spears as well, but between the bascinet and quilted armor, it is quite evident why Lethbridge specifically mentions the Hebridean effigies for comparison.

The Royal Commission on the Ancient and Historical Monuments and Constructions of Scotland survey of ancient monuments on the isle of Iona[34] includes a late 14th-century grave slab for Bricius MacKinnon showing him wearing an aketon and bascinet, bearing a shield with a galley, and wearing his sword. Steer and Bannerman note that the MacKinnon grave slab is the best surviving example of a group of twenty-two surviving armored effigies that are clearly from the same sculpture workshop, generally known as the Iona School. There are actually only five of these effigies on Iona, and the rest scattered around the western Highlands, with specific examples in Kintyre and Knapdale, Skye and a number of the other Inner Hebrides.[35]

The MacKinnon effigy carries a spear, which Steer and Banner note as an exception to the majority of the monuments, with most of the carvings showing the left hand holding the scabbard while the right hand usually grasps the free end of the sword belt.[36] Glynn's initial chalking has the right hand grasping a dagger. Erosion has taken a toll on that arm, and subsequent examinations position the arm in a variety of locations. Of note is the fact that even with the arm's questionable positioning, the sword belt itself on the Knight is clearly defined.

Spear aside, the similarities between Westford and MacKinnon and the other Iona School slabs are striking. The Westford Knight is more crudely rendered and does not show the distinctive foliaceous decorations that surround the main sculpture, but considering the work was done under less than optimal conditions by a non-artist, the Westford Knight is a fair rendering of a contemporary style of grave marker.

Based on the inscriptions that surround the figure, the MacKinnon monument also marks the resting place of five MacKinnons.[37] So, it is possible that more than one Gunn perished on Prospect Hill, all of whom were collectively represented by the same effigy. Any inscriptions in Westford near the Knight are long eroded away and Gunn records are extremely limited prior to the mid–15th century. As such, the question of single or multiple casualties must remain strictly conjecture.

Funereal monuments dressed in armor first appear in Scotland in the early 13th century, a century after they gained popularity in England.[38] The practice of depicting deceased warriors in their armor began in mainland Europe and was brought to Britain by the Normans. The Westford Knight may suggest that the Sinclair expedition may have brought the practice to North America.

5

Jarl Henry and the Sinclairs

The Orkney Islands lie in the North Sea off the northernmost point of the tip of Scotland. Archaeological data indicate the Picts came to the Orkney Islands during the Bronze Age and remained until the arrival of the Vikings in the latter part of the 8th century.[1] The details of the earliest Norse contact with Pictish Orkney are vague, with various theories of genocide, integration or subjugation being offered. The circumstances surrounding the founding of the Orkney earldom is chronicled in the *Orkneyinga Saga*,[2] telling of the conquest of the Orkneys by Haraldr Hárfagri (Harold Fairhair) as part of his consolidation of power in Norway, during which he also laid claim to Shetland, Hebrides, and Man.

In 1379, Norway's Håkon VI granted the jarldom of Orkney to Henry Sinclair. *Burke's Peerage* includes Henry Sinclair, "who on 2 August 1379, was formally invested by Haakon, King of Norway, as Jarl of the Orkneys."[3] Henry was given his title from the King of Norway, but he was also entitled by the Scottish throne as the Baron of Rosslyn, making Henry obligated to both monarchs.

Descended from Scottish nobles through his father and Norse Jarls on his mother's side, Henry was the first of three Sinclair generations to be Jarl (or Earl in English) of Orkney. Already controlling the ancestral Sinclair Barony of Rosslyn, the addition of the Orkney jarldom gave Henry oversight of 200 islands and control of 5,000 square miles of major sea lanes between Norway and Scotland. With his income for collection of the *skat* (the land tax paid by the owners of Udal land) for the Crown, Henry Sinclair was able to afford the navy and troops to keep his earldom safe. Earl Henry was a military and political presence to be reckoned with.

Henry Sinclair was born in 1345 at Rosslyn Castle near Edinburgh, the son of Sir William St. Clair of Rosslyn and Isabel, daughter of Malise, the 8th Earl of Strathearn and Jarl of Orkney. The death of Henry's maternal grandfather Malise without male heirs triggered a succession dispute that was not resolved for decades. Crawford's listing of the family in the *Oxford Dic-*

tionary of National Biography explains the problem succinctly: "Earl Malise had had five daughters altogether, from two marriages. The process of dividing his lands among them was a lengthy one, complicated by the differences in inheritance customs in force in Caithness and Orkney."[4]

Henry was embroiled in a long-term struggle for the possession of the jarldom, losing his first attempt at the title at age 8 when his aunt Agneta, the older sister of Henry's mother, married Erngisl Sunesson in 1353. Sunesson was named Jarl of Orkney that same year by the Norwegian throne. Jarl Erngisl supported the losing side in an attempt to replace Norway's Magnus VI in 1375 and was deprived of the title as a result.[5] With Erngil's forfeiture, Henry found himself in contention for the Earldom of Orkney with two cousins, Alexander de l'Arde and Malise Sperra.[6]

When Henry Sinclair was eventually granted the jarldom by Håkon in 1379, his title was granted with conditions, such as to defend of Orkney and Shetland and to provide Norway with military support as needed. Eldbjørg Haug of the University of Bergen suggests Sinclair did fight, at least on one occasion, at the battle of Falköping in 1389, but, not atypically, records are scarce from the time period and the data are not conclusive.[7] Roland Saint-Clair, in his book on the family,[8] also places Henry in Scandinavia in 1389 at the subsequent ascension of Erik to the throne. Saint-Clair's declaration aside, Sinclair did sign a 1389 letter, along with the Archbishop of Nidaros, several bishops and a number of other nobles supporting Erik's right to the Norwegian crown under Margaret's regency.[9]

The early coat of the Sinclair family: *Argent, a cross engrailed sable.* The coat later appears in the Rosslyn Chapel and is used in subsequent shields. The earliest known use was as the armorial seal of Sir William Sinclair in 1292, when Rosslyn was acquired from Henry de Roskelyn.

Scottish historian Stephen Boardman[10] suggests that Henry would have also been active in military action in Scotland as well. Boardman believes Henry almost certainly would have fought alongside his wife's family at the 1388 Battle of Otterburn, although Roland Saint-Clair disagrees.[11]

Sinclair would be forced to settle his family disagreement with Malise Sperra in 1391. Although Earl Henry, in 1379, had to promise an apparently prescient Håkon that he would not alienate or sell any properties of the earldom away from the king, Barbara Crawford notes Earl Henry considered Shetland part of his earldom, even if the crown didn't.[12] Crawford hypothesizes that Malise Sperra was most likely a royal foud or administrator in Shetland,[13] possibly given the position as assuagement for the loss of the earldom. When Sperra seized the properties owned by Herdis Thorvaldsdatter, it was the excuse Sinclair was looking for. Crawford's research into the estate[14] suggests the land had originally belonged to the Orkney earls before Shetland was placed under royal control in 1195, and Sinclair came to Shetland to reclaim what he could have considered his holdings and settle the matter with Sperra.

Sinclair was forced to confront Sperra in Tingwall at the law-thing, the assembly of free men of Shetland. The disagreement turned violent, and Sperra and a number of his followers were slain. A Neolithic menhir in the vicinity has become associated with the internecine fight, becoming an impromptu monument marking the site.[15] Crawford notes although the Herdis Thorvaldsdatter land was restored to her closest relatives, Sigurd and Jon Hafthorsson, the heirless Malise Sperra's Shetland estates reverted to Earl Henry.[16]

In 1391, Henry Sinclair also appears in documents recorded in *Registrum Magni Sigilli Regum Scotorum* and *Diplomatarium Norvegicum*.[17] Of note is one document that records

The coat of arms of Henry, Earl of Orkney, as illustrated by the *Wapenboek Gelre*, a 14th-century heraldic manuscript now preserved in the *Bibliothèque Royale de Belgique*. The Sinclair coat of arms is topped by a crest of a camel's head couped, proper, langued of gules, gorged by a coronet argent, the base of which forms a chapeau on the heume Gold. The crest appears only in *Wapenboek Gelre* and was soon replaced by the new coat of arms with the Orkney coat quartered with the engrailed cross.

Henry conceding the lands of Newburgh and Auchdale in Aberdeenshire to his brother David in return for David's claims to the Orkney.[18]

Frederick J. Pohl, one of the Westford Knight's staunchest advocates, perpetuates an error by referring to David Sinclair as a "half-brother" of Henry. The term does not appear in the 1912 Latin version of *Registrum* nor in the Clouston translation in *Records of the Earldom of Orkney*.[19] Although it would be a minor point of confusion when the Sinclairs launched a project to trace specific branches through DNA, it is also an indication of some of Pohl's source material. The only other researcher who specifically refers to David Sinclair as Henry's half-brother is Caithness antiquary and questionably accurate genealogist, Thomas Sinclair.[20]

Several Sinclair family members have subsequently suggested that this property transfer was also an opportunity for Henry to make contingency plans for his holdings as a preparation for his expedition, a supposition presuming the 1390 date of the Zeno Narrative is correct. Crawford suggests that the appearance of Shetland witnesses among the Scots is an indication of Sinclair's growing control of Shetland, the beginning of a "Scotticisation" that would eventually bring Shetland under the Scottish flag.[21]

Boardman also notes that an Earl of Orkney was involved in sporadic skirmishes between George Douglas and Douglas of Dalkeith over Douglas lordship issues, circa 1398.[22] Somewhere in the midst of all these conflicts would be the period when Sinclair made his voyage of discovery that would result in the creation of the Westford Knight. The date of the voyage still fluctuates among researchers, ranging from 1380 to 1398.

Henry Sinclair's death came soon after any involvement in a 1398 Douglas internecine spat, according to the "Sinclair Diploma,"[23] a document written by Thomas, Bishop of Orkney to Eric of Norway in 1443, affirming the right of succession for Henry's grandson William to the Jarl title. The document was required because of a rather contentious situation. After Henry's death, the earldom passed to his son, Henry, who apparently was more interested in affairs in Scotland than the Orkney Earldom.

Sir David Menzies of Weem had been appointed Foud of Orkney and Shetland under the King of Norway to run the government for his brother-in-law, the absentee Earl of Orkney, Henry Sinclair II.[24] Sir David was apparently such a tyrant that a formal "Complaint of the People of Orkney" was sent to the Norwegian crown in 1424.[25] Clouston suspects the petition was effective in forcing Menzies out — he doesn't appear in Orcadian records after March of 1425.[26]

Whether Menzies removed pertinent records or his mismanagement merely raised questions about the Sinclair rights to the Earl title, the Bishop of Orkney sent the diploma to reaffirm William's right of ascension to the Jarldom. The document also notes that first Earl Henry had returned to the Orkneys in the later part of his life where, in behalf of the defense of his land, he was savagely killed by enemies.[27]

Pohl believes the aforementioned defense was in 1400, citing in a 1636 history of England by John Trussell which refers to an attack "whereof the English invaded, burnt and spoyled certaine Ilands of Orckney" in retaliation for an October 1399 attack by Scottish forces on England's Castle Wark.[28]

In 1446, Jarl Henry's grandson William would begin construction on a collegiate church dedicated to Saint Matthew now known famously as the Rosslyn Chapel. This new church was built above an earlier structure, possibly a mausoleum housing the remains of the family, interring the family in the new church without having to actually exhume and re-inter the remains.[29] This previous structure, mausoleum or other, was associated with the church that Rosslyn Chapel was built to replace. *Theatrum Scotiæ*,[30] John Slezar's 1693 book of engravings of Scottish architecture, contains the earliest known description and image of Rosslyn Chapel. Among his notes is the fact that all three Earls of Orkney are buried there.[31] Although details of the first Earl Henry's death may be sketchy, his final resting place appears to be among his kin beneath Rosslyn Chapel.

Although the Sinclair genealogical descendancy is well documented, the origin of the Sinclair dynasty is a source of debate in genealogical circles, neither surprising nor uncommon for

The coat of arms of Henry, Earl of Orkney, Quarterly first and fourth Azure a lymphad within a double tressure flory counterflory Gold, second and third Argent a cross engrailed Sable. The images represent both the Sinclair and the Earl of Orkney coats joined together to create a new coat of arms appropriate for the first Sinclair Earl of Orkney. It first appears in the 13th-century *Armorial du Hérault Vermandois*, compiled circa 1285–1300, an armorial that still exists in a 15th-century copy in the *Bibliothèque Nationale de France*.

family trees dating back as far as the Sinclair's. The origins of the family are clouded by family traditions, lost records and overreaching genealogists. The confusion is not necessarily deliberate, but centuries later, the family roots remain a point of debate.

Father Richard Augustine Hay (1661–1736), a Canon-Regular of Sainte-Geneviève and Prior of St. Piermont in France, was an antiquarian with a passion for old records. In his search for records in the area around Edinburgh, he was able to use family connections to gain access to archives that no one else could. One such familial connection was to the Sinclairs of Rosslyn[32] and he began compiling Sinclair family records and oral traditions. In 1700, Hay completed a manuscript that was equal parts Sinclair family history, a record of Rosslyn Chapel and a chronological compilation of deeds, charters and documents. His manuscript, now in the National Library in Scotland, was edited down and published by James Maidment in 1835 as *A Geneologie of the Sainteclaires of Rosslyn*.[33] Maidment's publication barely extended the accessibility to Hay's work — only 120 copies were printed.[34] Hay's work is considered by default to be, prima facie, the primary authority on the history of Rosslyn Chapel, but this expertise is suspect — much of what Hay recorded were centuries-old family traditions and the questionable work of a previous genealogist. Maidment, in his introductory notice to the 1835 publication, remarks on Hay's use of "curious, but sometimes inaccurate" works archived in the library, and Hay himself cautions that more work is needed on the early genealogy because a major source was Frederick van Bassan, "a Dane, who understood not our printed historys [*sic*], and had not knowledge enough of our manuscripts and charters."[35]

Nonetheless, Maidment notes, the work is invaluable because the original materials used by Hay had been destroyed or lost in the intervening years. Some of these missing records which cloud the early history of the Sinclairs may also have been stolen. Father Thomas Innes, in his 1729 *Critical Essay*, notes that England's Edward I carried off ancient histories to search for validation of his claims to the crown of Scotland, which medievalist E. L. G. Stones confirms, citing records that documents were carried off from 1296 to 1323.[36] The record loss continued when Stirling Castle surrendered to Monck in 1651; records that had been moved to Stirling from Edinburgh Castle when Edinburgh surrendered eight months before were then shipped off to the Tower of London. After the Restoration, the records were going to be returned to Scotland, but the majority of them never arrived. In 1660, 85 hogsheads packed with records were lost at sea in a storm,[37] including most of the Charters of Robert I (1306–1329) and David II (1329–1371), a time period that covered the early years of Henry as Baron of Rosslyn.

According to van Bassan by way of Father Hay, the Sinclair dynasty started with the arrival in Scotland of William "the Seemly" Saintclair, a Norman in the service of Princess Margaret,[38] the Hungarian-born sister of Edgar Ætheling, Saxon heir to the English throne. Margaret, her sister and mother were fleeing back to Hungary after William the Conqueror usurped her brother's throne, but a storm forced their ship to seek refuge in Scotland. Malcolm of Scotland was immediately taken with Margaret (or saw opportunity to extend his power base). The next year Malcolm married Margaret and William St. Clair was made her steward.

The van Bassan/Hay version then has Malcolm granting Rosslyn as life-rent. This status changed to "in free heritage" after William's death in service to the King defending the Scottish borders against William the Conqueror. The fact that the Normandy-born William the Seemly was fighting against fellow Norman William the Conqueror and his own kin in defense of the sister of the Saxon heir to the English throne is explained away by subsequent researchers as evidence of a family squabble. Thomas Sinclair, who uses Hay's work extensively in his own 1887 book, has William at the Battle of Hastings, fighting alongside his father Walderne and his brothers Richard and Britel and having a falling out with William I after the battle and then heading to Scotland.[39]

With such unreliable sources, Father Hay's version of Sinclair matters cannot be accepted as accurate. When Trinity College professor H. J. Lawlor examined the surviving manuscripts from the Sinclair library,[40] he also examined Father Hay's notes. Lawlor carefully worded a polite dismissal of Hay: "...it is probably universally admitted that Father Hay is not a writer whose unsupported testimony can be explicitly accepted."[41] Even Father Hay was not convinced that the material he used was correct: "All what is above recorded by the Genealogists doth not agree with the Evidences, Historys [sic], Registers, and other privat Memiors [sic] I have found in Gentlemen's hands."[42]

It is almost certain that some Sinclairs were involved with the Battle of Hastings. Sir Edmund Lodge, the Clarenceux King of Arms, in his major work on heraldry, *The Genealogy of the Existing British Peerage,* lends his support to St. Clairs arriving with William the Conqueror.[43] The Sinclairs first appear in English history courtesy of the Domesday Book, a land survey from 1086, commissioned by William I to assess his new kingdom and potential tax base. William gave out vast parcels of land to his allies after the Battle of Hastings and both Richard de St. Clair and his brother Britel appear in the Domesday Book.

Back in Scotland, King Malcolm Canmore had married Margaret, whose influence, political sociologist Colin Pilkington[44] observed, resulted in the children of Margaret and Malcolm being more English than Scottish. Their son, David I, extended an invitation to the Normans to migrate to Scotland. Many did, eyeing the opportunity to become major landholders in Scotland, creating a new class of Scottish nobility made up of Norman families with such familiar names as Bruce, Balliol and Sinclair.[45] The first record of Sinclairs was the grant of the lands and the barony of Rosslyn to Sir William Sinclair on September 14, 1280.[46]

At some point in the evolution of the Sinclair family lore, Jarl Henry was promoted to "Prince Henry Sinclair." This is not a title ever used in contemporary sources and it seems to have originated several centuries later. It may simply be a subsequent misunderstanding of the word's usage — the use of the term "prince" during the Renaissance was that of a catchall term of respect, used regardless of actual title or rank.

Father Hay lists Henry as marrying Florentina, the daughter of the King of Denmark,[47] which subsequent authors took to mean that Henry, in marriage to a princess, had become a prince. There is no surviving record of such a marriage taking place, so assuming Hay did run across some record, he may have come across a record of negotiations for a betrothal that never took place. The title "Prince" appears to first have been used for a title for Henry's son, also named Henry (the second Sinclair Earl of Orkney), in David Hume's 1633 massive two-volume verse hagiography[48] of the Douglas family. Hume's interest is not the Sinclair family, merely in establishing the credentials of Earl Henry as sufficient to warrant his marriage to Egidia Douglas.[49] Hume, a leading Presbyterian intellectual, may have influenced future writers — the 1693 publication of *A Description of the Isles of Orkney*[50] by the Rev. James Wallace also makes the second Earl Henry a prince. However, Wallace misidentifies his father as being named William, making the second Earl Henry the first in line with the forename. This could also be the beginning of the prince title being associated with the first Earl Henry.[51]

The 1468 marriage of James III of Scotland to Margaret, daughter of Christian I, King of Denmark and Norway, forced Christian to mortgage the Orkneys to Scotland as security for his daughter's dowry. In 1469 Shetland was added to the impignoration (held in pledge) until redeemed by payment of the outstanding amount. Orcadian historian John Mooney[52] notes that this pledge only covered suzerainty and demesne. Suzerainty gave James legal control of the islands as a dominion of Scotland but not the domestic sovereignty. He could collect income but not replace the existing government, then in the hands of the third Jarl of Orkney, William Sinclair. Demesne lands were the properties kept by the king and did not include control of those previously granted.

In 1470, James, seeing an opportunity to keep the islands, swapped Ravenscraig in Fife for the Sinclair Earldom and their stronghold in the Orkneys, Kirkwall Castle, by excambion. This gave James the title of Earl of Orkney, Kirkwall Castle and his own royal demesne.[53] William Sinclair was in the middle of constructing Rosslyn Chapel and probably felt he was getting more than a fair trade; in return for properties he rarely visited, he received Ravenscraig, a practically new castle built in 1460 by James II just across the Firth of Forth from Rosslyn. The annexation of the Earldom of Orkney to the Crown was set on February 17, 1471, and confirmed by Act of Parliament on May 16, 1471.[54]

Although this was the end of the Sinclairs as Jarls of Orkney, the Sinclair family would continue to be a force in Scottish history. By the sixteenth century, the Sinclairs, in addition to significant holdings of land, held power as justicars, chamberlains and sheriffs for the bishopric of Caithness, everything north of the Dornoch Firth. "The Lords of Roslyn made Scotland ring with the renown of their deeds."[55]

6

A Knight Gunn

The original cadre of researchers responsible for identifying the Knight as a member of the Clan Gunn (Lethbridge, Glynn, Moncreiffe and Pohl) never specified which member of the clan they thought the effigy represented. This is because of a lack of Gunn records from their arrival in Caithness until the middle of the 15th century. The loss of these records can be attributed to numerous causes — fire, war, Reformations — but Dr. Kathleen Hughes of the University of Cambridge suggests a more prosaic culprit.[1]

Dr. Hughes notes that record keeping commences in the wake of conversion.[2] Northern Scotland was converted by Irish missionaries, meaning the earliest manuscripts would be written in Irish. By the middle of the 12th century, thanks to Malcolm III and Margaret, the Scottish episcopate had shifted from Celtic to Anglo-French influences, including moving to Latin for record keeping. Hughes believes early manuscripts could have survived into the 12th century only to languish in the cathedral libraries, neglected until discarded as irrelevant because they were written in a common language instead of Latin.[3] The same fate would await any records in Norwegian, which James Graham-Campbell notes rapidly became the dominant language in the Northern Isles and Caithness before being replaced by Scottish.[4] As a result, there are no documentary sources from Scandinavian Scotland until the late 12th or early 13th century. Barbara Crawford further notes that in the Hebrides, there are no records until well after the islands were in Scottish possession (1266) and that no document survived in the Western Islands from the Norse era.[5]

The earliest verifiable records of the Gunns do not appear until Sir George Gunn, who was killed in 1464 by Keiths at the Chapel of St. Tears in a battle of folkloric proportions.[6] And even then, the records remain somewhat nebulous. Mark Rugg Gunn, in his history of the clan, observes that even George's name is suspect, noting that several previous genealogists don't agree on the name.[7]

George Gunn was known as "Crowner of Caithness," a hereditary office with functions and duties that have become vague over the centuries. According to Jamieson's *Dictionary of the Scottish Language*, a crowner is a judiciary in cases involving the crown. R. H. Wellington, a 19th-century crowner, or coroner, in London, goes into more specifics, observing that the coroner's primary function was to monitor the king's interests within his region, including revenues from shipwrecks, found treasure troves, and sudden deaths.[8] Felony, murder and suicide were cause for forfeiture of land and goods to the Crown, so the crowner was always on the lookout for sudden or unexplained deaths, a function the crowner or coroner continues to do, albeit for different reasons.

Antiquarian Hugh Cowan notes the crowner was a hereditary office that shows up in records at least back to the reign of David I (1124–1153) and appears to have initially been based on territorial possessions.[9] This echoes the work of Charles Gross, who places the creation of the English coroner as being during the reign (1100–1135) of Henry I.[10] Gross feels that by the reign (1154–1189) of Henry II, the English coroner's

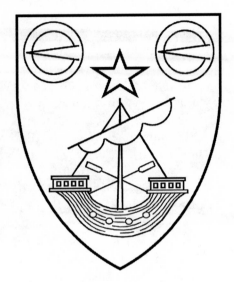

The shield of the Westford Knight, representing the chieftain of the Gunn Clan, as interpreted by the Unicorn Pursuivant of Arms, Sir Iain Moncreiffe. Moncreiffe suggested that the blazon, in heraldry terminology, was *Gules a lymphad, sails furled, oars in saltire, and in chief a mullet Gold between two large buckles Silver.*

position was firmly established, not only to protect the king's interests, but to reduce the authority of the sheriff with some of the sheriff's duties being reassigned to the coroners as a system of checks and balance.[11]

The main qualifications for the coroner office in England by the 13th century were knighthood and residence in the same county, with tenure for life.[12] Scotland made the office one that could be passed down to a son. Both Innes and Maitland believe that the officer of coroner was equal to that of the sheriff in both Scotland and England, and that by James V's reign (1513–1542), German, French, English and Scottish law were very similar, with each borrowing from each other, suggesting that the Gunns had been entitled at some time in Scotland's past.[13]

However, unlike the English coroner who continued to evolve, the Scottish coroner "went early out of use."[14] This opinion echoes that of John Rastell, who published in 1579, noting the same thing: "But at this day, either ye aucthoritie of the Coroner is not so great, as in fore tyme it was, whereby the office is not had in like estimation."[15]

Regardless of the duties, the actual term "coroner" is derived from the Latin *coronae*, "of the crown."[16] Scottish references interchangeably use crowner and cruner. Cruner may be a vernacularized version of *coronae* but it is more likely a pronunciation that betrays the Norse roots of the area and is derived from the Norse *krūna,* also a reference to the Crown. George held the ancestral office with pride and was noted for wearing the badge of his office, a large silver buckle which earned him the nickname *Am Braisdeach Mor* or "the great broached one."

The buckle carried on the shield of the Westford Knight indicated to Moncreiffe that he was looking for a Gunn. As he continued to scour heraldic and genealogical records for clues, his research arrived at the same source that genealogist Thomas Sinclair relied on before him — the manuscripts of the Reverend Alexander Gunn (1773–1836).[17] A biographic sketch of the Reverend Gunn[18] does not mention his genealogical research, but it does mention that prior to his installation as a Free Church of Scotland minister in the northeastern Caithness village of Watten in 1805, Gunn spent two years as assistant to the minister at Orphir, Orkney. Orphir is the site of the ruins of an ancient round church that had been partially dismantled in 1757 to build the church where the Reverend Gunn served. The ruins of the Orphir Round Church have outlasted its successor; 300 years later, those ruins would become associated with Henry Sinclair's voyage to North America as a proposed prototype for the Newport Tower in Rhode Island.

The Reverend Gunn's unpublished research does not cite sources but is nonetheless still considered a viable genealogy of the Gunn chiefs. Although the origins of the Norse line are still debated, the line appears to arrive in Caithness with Harald Eriksson, known as Harald ungi (or Harald the younger), whom Scotland's William the Lion made earl of South Caithness in 1184. An 1198 battle between Harald ungi and his rival Harald Maddadarson, Earl of Orkney and North Caithness, resulted in the death of Harald ungi. Harald's sister Ragnhild, married to Gunni Andersson, inherited the estates in Caithness. It is from Gunni that the clan name is derived and Moncreiffe considers him the first Gunn chieftain.[19]

Gunni was succeeded by his son Snaekol Gunnisson. Snaekol forfeited the jarldom titles that had descended through both his paternal grandparents after a land dispute with the Jarl of Orkney resulted in the death of Jarl John, severing any ties to Norway and the Orkneys. Snaekol, bereft of title in Norway, managed to keep the Caithness estate, going to Scotland and effectively creating a clan that was predominantly a Caithness presence. Snaekol was

The apse and a small section of the eastern wall of the nave are all that remain of the round Romanesque-style St Nicholas Church (dated 1090–1060 A.D.) at Orphir in the Orkney Islands. The structure was partially dismantled in 1757 to build the church where Reverend Alexander Gunn served while working on his Gunn genealogy. Philip Means would subsequently find the double-splayed window to be similar to the windows in the Newport Tower (photograph courtesy of Elizabeth Lane).

eventually executed after an abortive attempt to overthrow Norway's Håkon IV in a battle at Oslo in April 1240.

Snaekol's son Ottar Gunn has an unsubstantiated tale associated with him in which he had made several trips to the Norwegian Royal Court, presumably to mend the bridges burned by his father. On one of these trips, Ottar married a daughter of the king. However, Ottar neglected to mention beforehand that he already had a wife in Caithness. When arrangements were made for the Norwegian princess to arrive with her dowry, Ottar had the beacon moved to wreck the ship, planning to eliminate the spare wife but maintain the dowry. It did not take the Norwegian king long to learn what happened and retaliate by slaying Ottar and his retainers, then destroying Castle Gunn at Bruan. In fairness to Ottar, this may be a later elaboration — early records of the runic stone associated with the drowned princess, such as Calder's *Sketch of the Civil and Traditional History of Caithness* and *An Account of the Danes and Norwegians in England, Scotland, and Ireland,* recount the story attached to the stone without mentioning which Gunn married the princess and that the wreck was an accident.[20] Thomas Sinclair's version makes the shipwreck deliberate but doesn't specify which Gunn.[21]

Ottar's son Ingraham or Ingram was of interest to Moncreiffe[22] because the name was not usually seen that far north. It was, however, a favorite in the family of Sir Gilbert de Ummfraville, the Norman husband of Maud, daughter of Malcolm, the Earl of Caithness. Moncreiffe hypothesized that Ingram was born and named at a time when Maude's descendants still had some influence in Caithness. The attempt to pander to the Earl of Caithness seems to have helped the Gunn standing since Ingram was witness to a charter of King David II. This indicates that Ingram was alive until after David's ascension to the throne in 1329, a rare specific date in the sparse early Gunn timeline.

Ingram's son Donald and Donald's son James are complete mysteries. Even the traditional burial ground of the Gunn chiefs, the chapel of St. Magnus in Spittal is of little help in this case. Still in occasional use as late as 1911, the Royal Commission on the Ancient and Historical Monuments of Scotland notes that the ruins of the chapel and graveyard are filled primarily with uninscribed gravestones.[23]

James Gunn is usually identified as the Gunn memorialized as the Westford Knight effigy, but this is a recent identification. As late as 1973, Sir Iain Moncreiffe, the Scottish heraldic expert who had originally identified the shield for Lethbridge, remained convinced that the shield was that of an early Gunn chieftain but could not name the chief who fell in Westford.[24]

The earliest identification of Sir James Gunn of Clyth, Crowner of Caithness, as the Westford Knight appears to have been in the first issue of a Gunn family newsletter.[25] The author of the piece was Michael Gunn of Wick, Caithness, past president of the Clan Gunn Society. He based his identification on a 1438 legal document known as a "retour of inquest"—a report of the jury finding whether an heir is duly entitled to properties. This 1438 document dealt with lands claimed by Alexander Sutherland as third Lord of Duffus at an inquest held at Wick. This document, according to Gunn,[26] listed a Caithness crowner Magnus Gunn. That would make Magnus the father of Crowner George and make James a logical choice in such a chronology.

However, in reviewing the material, it appears Michael Gunn made a slight error. The 1438 retour, abstracted in 1900,[27] typically lists the jury of local landowners who were assembled to hear evidence and to determine the rightful heir. This jury lists a "Mawnis[28] Crownar of Cathness" as well as a Thomas Crownar, confirming that this is Crownar as a surname, not a title of office. There is no reference to the surname Gunn, nor do the few other documents from the time period list a crowner as an office. This, according to Wellington's history of the coroner office, is because the inquest was held before the coroner was involved[29] which would remove any need for his name to be listed in such a document.

The appearance of the surname Crownar in 1438 is by itself interesting. The name has recently begun appearing in lists as a possible sept of the Clan Gunn.[30] Major compilations of historical clan names do not include Crowner or a derivative as a sept and neither do the Clan Gunn histories.[31] Genealogist Melville Henry Massue, the Marquis de Ruvigny et Raineval, in his 1906 genealogy of the Moodie family, does come across an Agnes Crownar, wife of Gilbert Mudie of Caldwell (Ayrshire) in a 1469 charter, which he attempts to associate with the Gunns without further clarification.[32] Considering most current septs of the Gunn clan are derived from the sons of George, if the appearance of the Crownar surname in the 1438 and 1469 documents is indicative of anything, it is only that the surname existed. It could have been a Gunn sept derived from an early Gunn crowner that died out until more recent times, or it could just as easily be a corruption of the Gaelic word for roundness, *cruinne*, a surname derived from a nickname for a fat man.

Michael Gunn further speculates that James Gunn, as crowner of Caithness, was responsible for the security of the Orcadian harbors.[33] Why the crowner, an appointment of the Scottish Crown, would be overseeing harbors in Norwegian territory is not explained. Mr. Gunn cites several documents in the *Registrum Magni Sigilli Regum Scotorum* as his source.[34] These sources do not support the claim.[35] Removing this fallacious Magnus Gunn, the crowner line of succession returns to that as listed by the Reverend Alexander Gunn several centuries earlier.

So, to determine who the Gunn clan chief was at the time of the Sinclair expedition, we need to superimpose the historical record over the scant Gunn records. We know Ingram was Gunn clan chief when David II took the throne in 1329. Since he was of sufficient standing to witness a charter by the king, it is probably safe to assume he held the Crowner title that would subsequently be passed down in sequence to Donald, James and George. Thomas Sinclair's history of the Gunns supports the timetable for Ingram as Crowner, noting that as of 1331, the termination of the Norwegian line of earls of Orkney and Caithness created a power vacuum as claims and counterclaims by Scottish earldoms of Straithness and Caithness made the area ripe for a Scottish Crown representative in the form of a coronership.[36]

A 1764 history of clan battles notes a battle in 1426 at Blar-Tannie (Tannach Moor) between the Caithness natives and invading Keith clansmen.[37] Two Caithness chieftains were slain, which, considering the region and the

Gunn history, could easily include a Gunn chief among the casualties. The date of 1426 would be within the correct time period for George to assume the coroner title from his father James. If Crowner James Gunn is a casualty at Blar-Tannie, he could not have died in Westford. Because of the timeframe, James almost certainly had to be alive beyond the Sinclair expedition date since no reference to George the Crowner mentions extreme age in his final battle at the Chapel of St. Tears in 1464.

Continuing the chain of logic, if James was Crowner until his demise in 1426, he could have easily assumed the title after learning of the death of his father Donald with the return of the Sinclair expedition from North America. Working with circumstantial evidence and minimal records, it appears that Donald Gunn of Clyth is the most likely candidate as the Gunn represented by Westford's effigy.

An act was passed by the Scottish Parliament in July 1587 "for the quieting and keeping in obedience of the ... inhabitants of the Borders, Highlands and Isles" and included an attachment with "the roll of the clans that have captains, chiefs, and chieftains upon whom they depend, often against the wills of their landlords, as well on the Borders as Highlands, and of some special persons of the said clans." There is no listing for Clan Gunn. This, according to Thomas Sinclair, indicates that by 1587, the Gunns were considered, at best, a local clan. This fact is reinforced by the lack of mention of Gunns in the *Acta Parlimentorum* until 1647.[38]

Thomas Sinclair, one of the principal chroniclers of Gunn history, blames this on the Gunns' Norse roots, giving them an inclination to avenge slights and defend lands by sword instead of with diplomacy. The blood-feud with the Keiths starting in 1426, countered the Gunn expansion (and wiped out half the George the Crowner's male lines), followed by a feud with the MacKays and by 1520, the Gunns had begun feuding with their former allies, the Sinclairs.

Thomas Sinclair is correct to a degree, but the loss of Gunn territory was as significant as loss of life. While neighboring clans increased their landholdings through marriage, alliance and grants, the Gunn-controlled lands were gradually absorbed into those other holdings, primarily through grants of the Scottish kings to new arrivals, such as the Sinclairs and Keiths.

Thomas Sinclair notes Henry's appointment as Jarl of Orkney in 1379[39] gave Henry an edge in dealing with the Gunns — with a Caithness father and an Orcadian mother, he had an understanding of the unique Gunn perspective *aut pax aut bellum*, the Gunn motto. "Either peace or war" seems to suggest their unyielding nature but it may also have spelled doom in an age where political maneuvering was far deadlier and efficient than a Gunn sword.

7

The Zeno Narrative

The story of how a Scottish nobleman ended up in Westford, Massachusetts, is a complicated tale of translation and interpretation, based on a small book and map now known as the Zeno Narrative. The Narrative tells of the travels of the Zeno brothers, Nicolò and Antonio, as compiled from letters from Antonio Zeno at the end of the 14th century to his brother, the Venetian military hero Carlo Zeno.[1] In spite of its longevity, it is a text fraught with controversy and debate, or as Barbara Crawford, formerly of University of St. Andrews School of History, referred to it, "an exceedingly difficult and corrupt text."[2]

The chronicle commonly called the Zeno Narrative was published in Venice in 1558 as *De i Commentarii del Viaggio in Persia di M. Caterino Zeno il K. & delle guerre fatte nell' Imperio Persiano, dal tempo di Vssuncassano in quà*, a title no less cumbersome in English.[3] It was not the featured text in the book; that was Caterino Zeno's observations in Persia. The commentaries were published anonymously, but the compiler is generally recognized as Nicolò Zeno, the great-grandson of Caterino and 3rd great-grandson of Antonio Zeno, the author of the letters that were the body of the Zeno Narrative. The younger Nicolò was a member of the Venetian ruling Council of Ten and was related to the reigning families of Persia and Cyprus through his great-grandmother Violante Crespo.[4]

This latter Nicolò related how, as a child, he discovered a stack of papers in the attic of the family home. Being a child, the younger Nicolò then admits he tore up the documents in youthful abandon. He later returned to the attic as an adult and viewing the tattered papers, realized they were important historical letters and attempted to reassemble the surviving pieces. Finding a map in the family library too badly decayed to utilize, the younger Nicolò made a copy and included it in the book. The map, as published, is dated 1380 and shows the coastlines of Norway, Iceland, Greenland in varying degrees of accuracy within less accurate lines of latitude and longitude, as well as other islands named Frisland, Estland, Icaria, Estotiland, and Drogio, all located in the North Atlantic or Arctic seas.

DE I COMMENTARII DEL

Viaggio in Persia di M. Caterino Zeno il K.
& delle guerre fatte nell'Imperio Persiano,
dal tempo di Vssuncassano in quà.

LIBRI DVE.

ET DELLO SCOPRIMENTO

dell'Isole Frislanda, Eslanda, Engrouelanda, Esto
tilanda, & Icaria, fatto sotto il Polo Artico, da
due fratelli zeni, M. Nicolò il K. e M. Antonio.

LIBRO VNO.

CON VN DISEGNO PARTICOLARE DI
tutte le dette parte di TRAMONTANA *da lor scoperte.*

CON GRATIA, ET PRIVILEGIO.

VERI   TAS.

IN VENETIA
Per Francesco Marcolini.   M D LVIII.

The original 1558 publication of the Zeno Narrative in *De i Commentarii del Viaggio in Persia di M. Caterino Zeno il K. & delle guerre fatte nell' Imperio Persiano, dal tempo di Vssuncassano in quà. Libri due. Et dello Scoprimento dell' Isole Frislanda, Eslanda, Engrouelanda, Estotilanda & Icaria, fatto sotto il Polo Artico, da due fratelli Zeni, M. Nicolò il K. et M. Antonio.*

The book was released at the height of the Age of Exploration when travelogues and maps were eagerly sought and accepted at face value. The Zeno brothers were immediately added to the roster of intrepid explorers of the North Atlantic regions. In addition to recording visits to Iceland and Greenland, the other islands mentioned as being visited by the Zeni were incorporated into subsequent maps.

Within 50 years after the narrative was first published, even Richard Hakluyt, the great chronicler of English exploration, listed the Zeno brothers side by side with Ribaut, Verrazano and Laudonnière as notable foreign explorers in his compilations of first-hand narratives of exploration such *Principal Navigations, Voyages, and Discoveries of the English Nation.*[5] Hakluyt notes that there were questions about the Zeno map, but he would defer to the judgment of cartography's foremost mapmaker, Abraham Ortelius, who had incorporated map details into his *Theatrum Orbis Terrarum.*[6]

Ortelius had followed the lead of fellow cartographer Gerardus Mercator who had placed the Zeno islands on his 1569 map,[7] establishing the Zeno map's authority and legitimacy. Because Estotiland actually runs off the edge of the Zeno map, it is not possible to determine if it represents an island or an outcropping of a larger land mass to the east. Mercator modified the Zeno map, dividing Greenland with a strait and placing the name of Estotiland off the coast of the New World between 61° and 63°, roughly where Baffin Island is located. This would lead to Cornelis Wytfliet's 1597 atlas *Descriptionis Ptolemaicae Augmentum,*[8] the first atlas devoted exclusively to the New World. Wytfliet included a map of *Estotilandia et Laboratoris Terra,* putting in print what Mercator and Ortelius had identified cartographically — Estotiland was on the North American mainland, adjacent to Labrador. Suddenly, the Zeno Narrative was "proof" that the Venetians had reached North America before their rivals in Genoa, or more specifically, Columbus.

The Zeno Narrative, as evidence that exploration and settlement of the North Atlantic was accomplished much earlier than Columbus's voyage, became embroiled in a larger argument with greater implications — the prolonged biblical exegesis on the origins of the American Indians.

Hugo Grotius's 1642 *De Origine Gentium Americanarum Dissertatio* (*Dissertation of the Origin of the American Peoples*) suggested that the names of the lands of the Zeno voyage such as Frisland and Estotiland were toponymic evidence of the Norse first settling the new world, spreading south to Panama, as evidenced by similar name patterns in such locations as Quaxutatlan, Icatlan and Tunoxcaltitlan, the last letter being dropped by the Spanish pronunciation.[9] This was utter nonsense, according to historian Johannes de Laet, who immediately published a pamphlet[10] disputing Grotius's analysis, advocating a Scythian origin and warning that the Zeno narrative should be treated with caution. The two would issue pamphlets back and forth until the death of Grotius in 1645.

The position of de Laet, as a prominent historian, raised the prominence of doubts about the narrative, or at least the map, but the focus of debate on the Zeno Narrative had diverged into two separate debates. While cartographers argued about the accuracy and veracity of the map, another group was less concerned about whether the Zeni reached Labrador and more about whether or not Grotius was correct in his belief that the narrative indicated northern European origins of the American Indians. The leading theory of the time was a literal interpretation of Noah's pronouncement upon his three sons in Genesis 9:25–27 that the Japhetites (i.e., the Indo-Europeans) dwelling in the tent of Shem (i.e., Semitic origins of Christianity) would expand across a new continent. The Indians as the degenerate descendants of Canaan like those other Canaanites, the African slaves, were to be pitied, but are doomed by Biblical decree to be subjugated and eventually vanish. Giving the Natives a European origin would negate the perception of the natives as degenerate descendants of the Canaanites, a perception that absolved the colonists of any guilt associated with fraud, cruelty or genocide of the Indians that lasted well into the 18th century. Ezra Stiles, president of Yale University, was so convinced that the carved stones on New England (most notably the Dighton Rock) were written in Phoenician and as such, were confirmation of the Canaanite origins of the Indians, that he declared so in a sermon before Connecticut Governor Jonathan Trumbull in 1783.[11]

The journey that was causing all this discussion is a fairly straightforward travelogue pieced together from the surviving letters of Antonio Zeno to his brother Carlo in Venice. According to the narrative,[12] Venetian Nicolò Zeno, after the Battle of Chioggia, wanted to see the world. He was on a voyage to England when his ship encountered "a great tempest." Driven helpless by the storm for days, the ship was driven aground on Frisland, an island larger than Ireland. Nicolò and his exhausted crew were about to be overrun by local fishermen intent on salvaging the wreck when they were rescued by Prince Zichmni, lord of the island kingdom known as Porlanda who had won a great victory against Norway the year before. Now owing Zichmni his life, Nicolò entered the service of Zichmni as a pilot. Antonio joined his brother at Nicolò's urging and the Zeno brothers embark on a series of adventures with Zichmni, engaging in battles and exploring the lands of the North Atlantic. So useful were the Zeno brothers with their superior Venetian navigation skills that Nicolò was soon made Captain of the fleet. After a battle which saw Zichmni and the Zeni take possession of the island chain named Islande from the Norwegian king, Zichmni built a fort on one of the islands and left Nicolò in command with a small fleet, a crew and provisions. With the rest of his fleet, Zichmni returned to Frislanda to repair and restock the rest of his ships.

Nicolò set out on his own voyage of discovery and set sail to the north, reaching Engroueland where he found a settlement of mendicant monks and a church dedicated to St. Thomas near a "mountain which cast out fire like Vesuvius and Etna." In spite of the geothermal properties of the area that the monks utilized to heat their monastery and supply hot water year-round, Nicolò, not being used to the freezing weather, fell ill and died soon after his return to Frisland.

Antonio begged Zichmni to allow him to return home, but Zichmni had learned of a presumed-lost fisherman who had returned after 26 years from lands to the west and he needed the Venetian maritime skills to find the land in the fisherman's tale, laden with timber, fish and game, and other riches. Zichmni mounted an expedition to find these unknown lands known as Estotilanda and Drogio.

The fisherman's tale told of four vessels caught in a storm which drove them so far off course that when the skies cleared, the vessels were completely lost. The fishing vessels found the island called Estotilanda where one of the boats wrecked upon the shore. The six men aboard were seized by natives and taken to a large city. The king could find no one who spoke the language of the fisherman, but finally found another shipwrecked visitor who spoke Latin. The king decided they could stay and for five years, the fishermen dwelt among the natives, learning the language. As the men explored the island, they found evidence of prior contact in the form of Latin books in the king's library, which none of the natives could read. Estotilanda had a distinct language with a written component and traded with Engroueland.

The Estotilandan king sent the fishermen, as part of a trade fleet, south to the country of Drogio, but because a storm arose they were driven to a country of cannibals where most of the survivors were devoured. The fishermen who avoided this fate showed the natives how to catch fish with nets. By fishing every day, they provided sufficient fish and became famous and honored by the tribe. The fame prompted a neighboring chief to wage war for the knowledge of fishing nets. Overwhelmed by superior forces, the fishermen were handed over. For the next thirteen years, the men were continuously passed from one tribe to another as spoils of war.

The one fisherman that subsequently returned claimed he had been sent to more than twenty-five chiefs. He finally decided to make an escape and made his way to Drogio, where after three years, a vessel from Estotilanda arrived. He joined the ship as an interpreter and gained enough wealth to build his own ship which he used to return to Frislanda where Zichmni learned his amazing tale of survival.

Antonio Zeno noted the trip started under bad omens. The fisherman died three days before the start of the voyage and Antonio was informed he would not be the captain of the fleet because Zichmni himself would lead the expedition. The guide, instead of the recently deceased fisherman, would be some of the sailors who had sailed with him from Estotilanda.

Prevailing winds forced Zichmni and his fleet to the island of Ilofe and from there out into the deep oceans. Soon after, the fleet was caught in a storm "so fierce that, for eight days at a stretch, it kept us at work, and cast us about so that we knew not where we might be." The fleet regrouped after the storm and made for land. After terse encounters with armed natives at an island called Icaria, the fleet proceeded west and discovered "a very good country and a still better harbor." Entering the harbor, they saw a mountain sending smoke into the air. While anchored, the month of June arrived and the explorers had still not discovered signs of any inhabitants. They named the harbor Trin and waited for the return of an expeditionary force Zichmni had sent to investigate the plume of smoke coming from the mountain. Their report was that there was a "great fire" near the base and there was a spring that had a pitch-like material flowing down to the sea and that there was a local population of natives who fled to their caves when the soldiers approached.

Zichmni was enamored of the climate and prospects and began to discuss plans of establishing a city on Cape Trin. The crew, already having endured storms, hostile natives and near starvation, began to rebel at the thought of winter in this new land. Zichmni asked for volunteers to stay with him and the rest sailed back to Frislanda under the leadership of Antonio Zeno.

The younger Nicolò then interjects into the dialogue by noting that Zichmni explored the land and islands extensively, based on the details on the map, but the description of the exploration was apparently among the destroyed parts of the letters.

Subsequent maps became progressively more accurate from additional explorations and the ability to determine longitude by development of marine chronometers which came into widespread use toward the end of the 18th century. As the maps of the North Atlantic became standardized, locations found in the earlier explorations became more difficult to reconcile with the modern maps. Islands were being removed from maps because of navigational errors, duplicate discoveries under different names and the misidentification of icebergs, fog banks and sand bars viewed from a distance as islands.

By this point, the debate over the Zeno Narrative's accuracy had been raging for centuries — Rasmus B. Anderson, a staunch proponent of the Norse discovery of North America, lists published records of the debate in an appendix to his *America Not Discovered by Columbus.*[13] Dating from Hakluyt in 1589 through to the publication of the list in 1877, the debate was primarily among the scholars and antiquarians.

The collection of misplaced islands would normally assign an early travelogue to obscurity. Instead, the Zeno Narrative became a verification of claims of national pride. English explorer Martin Frobisher, in search of the fabled Northwest Passage, sailed from Iceland to Greenland, into the Labrador Sea, reaching what is now called Frobisher Bay in Baffin Island in 1576. Unfortunately, Frobisher, using a map based on Mercator's 1569 map with the Zeno map islands, had erroneously calculated his landfall in Greenland as a landing in Frisland, which the Zeno map places southeast of Greenland. So when Frobisher arrived on Baffin Island, he assumed that he was now in Greenland. The resulting cartographic confusion resulted in new maps with a strait on the southern end of Greenland that was actually a bay in Baffin Island (later named after Frobisher). As the extent of the mistake was realized, cartographers made corrections to the maps and added to the confusion. As one example, Michael Lok's 1582 map *llustri viro, domino Philippo*[14] adjusted Greenland's position southward nearly 4° and moved Frisland nearly 10° west of its position in the Zeno map.

This Frobisher confusion becomes important because, if Zeno and Zichmni are excluded, England-born Frobisher becomes the first European with a documented visit to Greenland after the Norse settlements. Britain's naval power was gaining in prestige and power, reaching an apex during skirmishes in 1792–1815 that demonstrated her superiority with decisive wins over French, Dutch, Danish and Spanish navies. Having Frobisher visit Greenland first gave the British navy a legacy of exploration to supplement the current military pride.

The German writer Johann Reinhold Forster, a naturalist who accompanied James Cook on his second expedition, published *Geschichte der Entdeckungen und Schiffahrten im Norden.*[15] In this book, and *History of the Voyages and Discoveries Made in the North,*[16] an English edition that followed two years later, Forster discusses the voyage of the Zeni. In a lengthy footnote, Forster suggests that Latin books found in Estotiland were evidence that the Norse had reached Newfoundland.[17] As a casual aside in the same footnote, he also makes the suggestion that Prince Zichmni was actually Henry Sinclair. The reason for the confusion of the location of Frisland, Forster concludes, is that the island simply no longer existed, having been destroyed by seismic activity triggered by volcanic activity sometime after the Zeni voyages. This destruction was supported by other scholars and cartographers with Frisland's destruction becoming associated with the Island of Buss just south of Iceland.[18]

Although Forster's theory of Frisland's watery doom garnered support, his proposal that Zichmni was Henry Sinclair wasn't popular, even among some of the staunchest advocates of the veracity of the Zeno voyages. Placido Zurla, Cardinal Vicar of Rome and an expert on medieval geography, was a high profile supporter of the Zeno voyage. He had no issues with the destruction of Frisland to explain its disappearance, noting other navigators had visited the island, including Christopher Columbus, who, according to his son's 1571 biography, visited Frisland in 1477.[19] Zurla, however, was not impressed by the Zichmni-Sinclair connection. Zurla published his own book on the subject,[20] studying the genealogy of the Zeno family. He felt the chronology of the voyage did not coincide well with Henry Sinclair's history. Zurla believed that if Zichmni had indeed won a decisive naval battle against Norway, it had to be after the Black Death had decimated Scandinavia and weakened the Norwegian navy, circa 1348, a date too early for Zichmni to be Henry Sinclair.[21] Additionally, Zurla noted that Nicolò and Antonio were still in Venice in 1380, the date listed on the map. He advocated treating the map and the narrative as two separate items that had been arbitrarily combined by their descendant with an erroneous date added during preparations for publication. Zurla's evidence to support this approach was his discovery of fellow Venetian Marco Barbaro's manuscript genealogy of the Venetian patricians, *Discendenze Patrizie,* with a section on the Zeno family that mentions the time spent in Frisland by the Zeno brothers.[22] More important, notes Zurla, Barbaro started the genealogy of the Zeni no later than 1536, predating the younger Nicolò's publication of the narrative in 1558 minimally by 22 years.

French geographer and cartographer Phillipe Buarche was less concerned with Zichmni's identity as he was with Forster's claim of the catastrophic disappearance of Frisland. In a paper read before the French Academy of Sciences on July 9, 1785,[23] Buarche declared that the destruction of an island of that size was completely unfeasible due to the complete lack of records on neighboring islands of effects from such a disaster, particularly in light of how many other similar events are recorded. His suggestion is that Forster's supposition is untenable but that a reasonable supposition is that the map was simply incorrect. His alternative: Frisland was actually the Faeroe Islands.[24]

In 1794, H. P. Eggers advanced the theory that Österbygde, the missing Norse settlement on Greenland, was actually on the southwest coast and not on the east as was generally presumed. One of his pieces of evidence was the Zeno map, which he felt showed the east and west Greenland colonies were on the coast along the Davis Straits.[25] He also agreed with Buarche that Frisland was actually the Faeroe Islands.

This prompted a response from Captain Christian Christopher Zahrtmann, a hydrographer in the Danish Navy.[26] Zahrtmann's work, translated into English in 1835,[27] was ostensibly a confirmation of Eggers's work, concurring with the location of Österbygde. His primary assertion in the article was that the narrative, particularly the parts relating to Nicolò, was predominantly fiction. The map was a collection of pieces and hearsay taken from other sources, not a chart compiled by anyone who had actually sailed the region and that both the history and the chart were most probably compiled by the later Nicolò Zeno in the middle of the 16th century as accounts arrived in Venice about Greenland and the search for the lost colony. Zahrtmann also made note of a map by Donnus Nicolaus Germanus that he had seen in the University Library at Copenhagen. This "Donis Map," he stated, was undoubtedly the original chart from which the Zeno map had been derived.

Zahrtmann's article was in support of Eggers's placement of Österbygde on the southwest coast by removing the use of the Zeno Narrative; Zahrtmann considered "the whole object being a tissue of fiction"[28] and suggests that it might not be a coincidence that Nicolò Zeno headed into the North Atlantic at the same time that the Dukes of Mecklenburg were recruiting privateers to wage war against Denmark. Known as the "Vitalian Brotherhood," the Vitalians subsequently turned to piracy, which, Zahrtmann notes, made them one of the suspected causes of the failure of the Greenland colony. Zahrtmann's repudiation of the Zeno Narrative made him one of the most prominent opponents of the Zeno voyage, still quoted by critics today.

The research of Eggers and Zahrtmann was part of a growing movement which Dr. Oscar Falnes would later call a renaissance in Scandinavian studies.[29] This renaissance left academic circles with the publication of Carl Christian Rafn's *Antiquitates Americanae*[30] in 1837, which collected the sagas in one volume, translated them and used them as evidence of transatlantic explorations.

Longfellow, America's most popular poet, had been in Europe studying Scandinavian languages and literature, including the Norse sagas. He returned from this trip in 1835 during which he took lessons in Icelandic from Rafn and was made a member of Denmark's Royal Society of Northern Antiquaries.[31] By the time Rafn's book came out in 1837, Longfellow was already considering a series of ballads about the Norse explorations of New England.

Longfellow's Norse ballads stoked the enthusiasm for the Norse and the momentum did not diminish. As the United States celebrated its centennial, interest in the country's history spiked, and riding that wave was Leif Ericsson and the Norse colonization of America. A flood of books identifying the location Vineland appeared, Leif Ericsson was given a statue in Boston, and architectural features on new buildings and bridges included Norse ship motifs.[32]

J. M. Mancini of University College Cork suggests that such wide mainstream acceptance of the theoretical Norse discovery of New England was a reaction by the "Anglo-Saxon elite" to the increased presence and growing political power of recent immigrants such as the Irish, Italians and Jews.[33] By having colonized New England 500 years before the Italian Columbus, the Vinland Saga reaffirmed the social superiority of the blue-blooded, Protestant families. Janet Headley of Loyola College and Robin Fleming of Boston College concur, noting that through Leif Ericsson, the proper Bostonians were able to "take back the discovery of America from a Catholic Mediterranean people and appropriate it for their imagined ancestors."[34] Some of the writers of the time were less subtle in their endorsement, such as Marie Shipley, who triumphantly published an "exposé of the plot" to keep the Icelandic discovery of America under wraps by a pro-Columbus (i.e., Catholic) conspiracy.[35]

Although Zahrtmann's opinion cooled interest on the Zeno Narrative in Europe,[36] his suggestion that the Zeni were pirates responsible for the destruction of the Greenland colonies instead of being part of the rediscovery did not sit well in North America and public interest in the United States provided ample volunteers to leap to the defense of the Zeno brothers.

Among those leading the charge was George Folsom, a prominent antiquarian in both New England and New York historical circles.[37] Folsom reviewed Zahrtmann's notes and disputed all of the arguments except for the map, which he also feels post-dates the voyage. Folsom focuses on two major points of disagreement: the first is Zahrtmann's aspersions on the character of the younger Nicolò, whom Folsom notes was a highly regarded geographer in his own rights, and as such, would certainly have access to current data on the North Atlantic coastlines which he added to the map when he copied it, making parts of the map more accurate than others. He also takes Zahrtmann to task for the Dane's disbelief in the Zeno account of St. Thomas's monastery and their use of hydrothermal power, noting that use of hot springs is common in literature.

The Reverend B. F. DeCosta, a high-profile author supporting the Norse discovery of America, repeatedly questioned Zahrtmann's cartographic evidence.[38] Zahrtmann refers to a map in the University Library in Copenhagen where Greenland is rendered as if copied from the 1528 *Isolario* by Benedetto Bordone as well as having sufficient style and name similarities as the Zeno map to suggest it was a source of the Zeno map.[39] DeCosta notes that Zahrtmann could not determine the age of the Copenhagen map yet assumes that

Zeno borrowed from it, when it could just as easily be the Danish map borrowing from Zeno.[40] DeCosta identifies Columbus's Frisland as Iceland, giving him ample opportunity to learn of the Norse lands to the west, assuming he hadn't already gathered that information from maps he was able to locate in Genoa, most notably provided by Toscanelli.[41] DeCosta notes that Columbus not only sailed to Iceland, he went beyond the island, coming within a few sailing hours of discovering Greenland. DeCosta believed Columbus was testing a specific chart's accuracy in preparation of the 1492 trip — the Zeno map.[42]

Although the debate had continued in Europe, it did not generate the widespread ardor that it did in North America. That changed in 1873 when R. H. Major entered the discussions, triggering the debate again. Richard Henry Major (1818–1891) was curator of the British Museum's map collection from 1844 to 1880. During his tenure, he published a number of books related to maps of historical significance. In addition to his work on the Zeno map, he published works on such diverse topics as the early exploration of Australia, the colonization of Virginia and early voyages to India. He also edited material for the Hakluyt Society, including a collection of the letters of Columbus.

When Major introduced his Zeno theory in a paper read at a June 1873 Royal Geographical Society meeting,[43] it reinvigorated interest in the Zeno Narrative and the credibility of the Zeno tale was again widely accepted. Major believed that the narrative was the last recorded reference of a visit to the lost Greenland colony of Österbygde. His theory and the translation of the original document was published soon after by the Hakluyt Society.[44] His original paper on the Zeni in Greenland, originally positioned as a response to Zahrtmann, is reprinted as a 100+ page introduction to the translation.

Major's version of the Zeno Narrative reflects his belief that although Estotiland was in North America, it was of minor significance compared to the evidence of the longevity of Österbygde. The discovery of the North American continent, Major believed, should probably still be credited to John Cabot, based on his review of the Cabot map.

Using the map collection under his custodianship, Major decided to approach the Zeno problem by following the route as written in the narrative, placing it on ancient maps and transferring the results to a modern map. He started by eliminating the Zeno map, which the younger Nicolò freely admitted to having copied due to the poor condition of the original. Major suspected it had been modified based on the younger Nicolò's reading of the narrative, changing what he thought was incorrect based on the maps of his time. Major then questions the results of both opponents and proponents, noting that Zurla's theory of Frisland's submersion and Forster's theories are just as conjectural and incorrect as Zahrtmann's dissection of the narrative. Only with cartography and a literal interpretation of the names of Northern locales as misheard and phonetically remembered by the Zeni, could the Zeno Narrative's route and validity be unquestionably demonstrated. Starting with Frisland, which Major demonstrated was the Faeroe Islands, Major then identifies Zichmni's kingdom of Porlanda as Pentland, which was part of the holdings of Henry Sinclair.

Major continues to demonstrate the lands in the narrative, generally noting that the narrative itself is consistent with modern geography; it is the younger Nicolò's corrections to the map and his misreading of the handwriting of his ancestor that have caused all the confusion. The great battle against the king of Norway, which Zahrtmann and other opponents of the narrative had justifiably noted as impossible to reconcile with Henry Sinclair's fealty to Norway as part of the jarldom, was the senior Nicolò's limited grasp of the language and the dynamics of the politics. The battle against Norway, Major explains, was Sinclair's 1391 battle against his usurping cousin Malise Sperra.

Major returns to the map, with a prominent 1380 date written across the top in the title, a direct contradiction to the document's internal evidence of the 1391 Sinclair battle. Major turned to the data of Marco Barbaro that Cardinal Zurla uncovered, noting that Barbaro used 1390 as the date, not 1380. Barbaro also refers to the northern mariner as "Zicno," not Zichmni, suggesting another possible misreading of the tattered letters by the younger Nicolò.

Andrew Sinclair would later suggest that the original Latin form of his family's name, Sancto Claro, if abbreviated to San Clo and combined with the Norse spelling Zinkler, would result a pronunciation phonetically close to Zicno.[45] Aside from the inherent difficulty in deriving a phonetic pronunciation from an abbreviation used exclusively in written documents, the family name in Latin in that time period in question, de Sancto Claro, is written out in legal documents and diplomas. Scandinavian records do record his name as Hinrik Zinkler,[46] which also precludes a Latin abbreviation. The most logical abbreviation of the name in Latin, $S^t Cl^o$, does suggest that that damaged, handwritten letters could be misread as Zicno, but Zurla only mentions the name once in recounting Barbaro, while the younger Nicolò repeats the name Zichmni repeatedly, making it more likely that either Zurla or Barbaro misread the name, not Zeno.[47]

Major continues his article by picking away at Zahrtmann's arguments until he arrives at Eggers's proposed location of the lost Norse settlement Österbygde, which Major also believed was actually on Greenland's southwest coast but took it one step further, stating it was a confirmation of the Zeno reference to the monastery near hot springs in Engroueland. He proposes that

St. Thomas was a mistranslation of St. Olaus, the dedicatee of a monastery mentioned by an early Norse geographer, Ivar Bardsen in *Descriptio Grœnlandiœ (1364)*.[48] Based on Bardssen's description, Major places the monastery on the Tasermiut fjord, noting a nearby mountain named Suikärssuak that could easily be a dormant volcano. Major notes there are no hot springs on the Tasermiut fjord, but points out that there are hot springs less then 25 miles away on the island of Uunartoq, where there are traces of a Norse settlement.

Major concludes with the fisherman's tale, noting that the data he provided to Zichmni while in Estotilanda and Drogio were fair approximations of the eastern seacoast of North America, with the fisherman reporting tales he had heard from other traders from areas he had not personally visited, possibly as far south as Mexico. Major concludes that this was a combination of data gleaned from the earlier Norse explorations and the contemporary traders who still frequented the coasts. His final conclusions were that the younger Nicolò added details where pieces of the original letters were missing, and Nicolò modified the map when he copied it. Major announced that the original document, with the later "excrescence" removed, was the last record of the lost Greenland East Colony, evidence of European settlement in North America and that these settlements had survived until at least a century before Columbus.

Major's work reinvigorated interest in the Zeno Narrative on both sides of the Atlantic. It was reprinted as a book by the Hakluyt Society and Major was featured as a guest contributor to the Massachusetts Historical Society, an ironic twist considering it was the same organization that had suggested that the country be renamed Columbia in honor of Columbus and would, in the immediate future, lead the fight against erection of the Leif Ericsson statue in Boston.[49]

The narrative was essentially accepted as a legitimate, albeit flawed, record of explorations of the North Atlantic with evidence that the Norse settlements extended to the North American mainland, depending on where you placed Estotilanda.

The biggest argument was no longer the validity of the narrative but whether Major was correct in his identification of the various lands. Danish Admiral Irminger, a noted explorer of the North Atlantic, took both Major and Zahrtmann to task for their identifications.[50] Using his personal familiarity with the area, Irminger declared that Frisland had to have been Iceland, noting that in 1394, there was a major skirmish at Budarhófdi, a commercial fish operation in Hvalfiord. Waged between the inhabitants and foreign sailors who had been continually looting the Icelanders, Irminger noted that this battle was about the date of the expedition of Zichmni to Frisland.[51] Irminger contacted Johannes Japetus Smith Steenstrup at the University of Copenhagen who had been on expeditions in southern Greenland and was able to confirm that Major's placement of the monastery near Suikärssuak was incorrect because Suikärssuak was not a volcano, nor were there any reports of volcanoes in southern Greenland.[52] Steenstrup also published on the topic,[53] confirming Irminger's opinion that Frisland was actually Iceland.

The polar explorer and cartographic historian Baron Nils Adolf Erik Nordenskjöld was researching a history of exploration when he became interested in the Zeno Narrative. He subsequently published his analysis in 1883 in *Studier Och Forskningar*, a companion book to his earlier book *Vegas Färd Kring Asien och Europa*, a popular accounting of his Arctic explorations and transversal of the Arctic by boat from Pacific to Atlantic, the fabled "Northwest Passage."[54]

The Nordenskjöld article in *Studier Och Forskningar* approached the topic by comparing the Zeno map with all the printed and manuscript maps known at the time of its publication in 1558. His conclusion was that the general accuracy of the descriptions compared to the lack of materials available at the time proved that the Zeno brothers must have been personally acquainted with the islands described in the narrative as well as the eastern shore of Greenland, regardless of the origin or accuracy of their names. He further stated that the details on American Indians predate European information on the Natives, which does not appear until the colonization of North America in the 17th and 18th centuries. The only source could be people who had visited the New World. Therefore Nordenskjöld concluded this was evidence of Norse colonies surviving into the 14th century.

Nordenskjöld, who would later publish several books on early maps and charts, noted that, in addition to the Zeno map, there were basically three maps available at the time of the publication of the Zeno Narrative, all of which were based on Northern sources, all of which predated Columbus. The most significant of these was a manuscript map dated 1427 with accurate renderings of Scandinavia and parts of America. Nordenskjöld had learned of this map, based on a Claudius Clavus chart under the direction of Cardinal Guillaume Fillestre. Attached to a manuscript copy of Ptolemy's *Cosmographia*, the map is now identified as the "Nancy codex," named after the town in France where it was found.

Nordenskjöld found the Nancy codex was very similar to the Zeno map and hypothesized that the Zeno map was either a copy of, or derived from, the Clavus map. Since the Clavus map was far more accurate than the 1482 Donis Map which Zahrtmann claimed the Zeno map was based on, Nordenskjöld was certain that the Clavus charts came from an independent source, meaning that the Zeno map predated the Donis Map.[55] This, as far as Nordenskjöld was concerned, negated Zahrtmann's strongest argument that Nicolò Zeno the younger had fabricated the map and narrative.

The Norse fascination in America was being supplanted by the 400th anniversary of the Columbus voyage, but Major's work brought a counterpoint to the festivities. The World's Columbian Exposition, now usually referred to as the Chicago World's Fair, was planned for 1893 to celebrate the 400th anniversary of the Columbus voyage, and the decades leading up to the event were filled with newspaper reports of the bickering, international intrigue and technological marvels being assembled at the fairgrounds. By the time the exposition opened, it was only nominally a celebration of the Columbus quadricentennial, instead becoming a cultural showcase of the modern world.

Material continued to appear as the Columbian Exposition captured the public's imagination. Fiske, in his *The Discovery of America,* takes great umbrage at Zahrtmann's inference that the younger Nicolò was setting up a Venetian claim for the discovery of America, considering that Zeno never claimed discovery of America.[56] He concludes that although certain parts of the narrative could describe North America, like the Norse visits before Zichmni, the visits were irrelevant because they were ephemeral. It was not until Columbus that contact was established and maintained with North America. Essentially, the most valuable part of the narrative is that it is a late record of the lost Greenland colony of Österbygde.[57]

The Norse discovery of America was well represented at the Exposition — *The Viking,* a replica of the Gogstad ship[58] crossed the Atlantic from Bergen, Norway, to be exhibited at the Exposition. The original plaster of Anne Whitney's Leif Ericsson statue that stands in Boston was bronzed and sent to the fair. Thomas Sinclair, the author of genealogical histories of the Gunns and the Sinclair lines of England, was invited to travel from Caithness to Chicago for a gathering of the Society de Sancto Claro. His remarks, subsequently reprinted in Scotland, reflect the evolution of the Sinclair-Zeno theory and the widespread popularity. Thomas Sinclair inexplicably assigns Sinclair's son, Henry, the second Jarl of Orkney, as Prince Zichmni the explorer, using references for father and son interchangeably as he weaves his version of Earl Henry's biography.[59]

This hybrid version of Henry Sinclair offers one new item, one that would reappear decades later — Sinclair suggests that the Scots and Norse would never neglect land, so there must have been multiple trips to the new area. Thomas Sinclair also highlights the work of May Whitney Emerson, who, in addition to being an officer of the Society de Sancto Claro and the

DAR, published a variety of articles about the Norse origins of the Sinclairs, culminating in a piece in which she notes that America was discovered by seven different explorers: five 9th century "Norse Rovers," Sinclair and finally Columbus. She notes all but the Italian were related back to Rollo, the Norse Duke of Normandy and presumed progenitor of the Saint Clair line.[60]

This widespread acceptance of the Sinclairs and the Zeno Narrative as predecessors of Columbus to America would be short lived. The charge would be led not by a Columbus proponent but by an irate English solicitor who felt John Cabot had been given short shrift. Fred W. Lucas entered into the fray and the Zeno Narrative has never been the same.

8

A Knight Under Siege

The acceptance of the Zeno Narrative, primarily on the strength of Major's work, reached a zenith in 1898. The Society de Sancto Claro was opening chapters across the country and Roland William Saint-Clair, an Orcadian-born member of the family that had moved to New Zealand as a child, published his magnum opus *The Saint-Clairs of the Isles*.[1] Equal parts a family genealogy and a hagiography of Henry, the author refers to the Zeno voyage as "Orcadian Argonauts" in a summation of Major's translation.[2]

Unfortunately for the euphoria, 1898 also saw publication of *The Annals of the Voyages of the Brothers Nicolò and Antonio Zeno, in the North Atlantic About the End of the Fourteenth Century, and the Claim Founded Thereon to a Venetian Discovery of America; A Criticism and an Indictment* by Fred W. Lucas.[3]

Frederic William Lucas (1842–1932) was a British solicitor with an interest in early explorations of America. His first book on the early colonization of America[4] casually dismissed various pre–Columbian explorers including the Zeno brothers, placing emphasis on Columbus, an early indication of his opinion of the Zeno Narrative.

Lucas had several advantages as his book came to print, not the least of which was the support of the group of ardent Anglophile antiquarians who accepted that although Columbus was the discoverer of the New World, it was John Cabot, another Venetian navigator, who was the first European to actually set foot on the North American continent. Supposedly landing in Newfoundland in 1497, Cabot did so under the flag of England. This was the beginning of British claims in North America and arguably the nascence of British maritime supremacy. Equally important to Anglophiles was that his son Sebastian, who accompanied Cabot on his first voyage, was widely believed to have been born in Bristol, making him a Brit by birth, even if his father was merely a Venetian in the employ of Henry VII under the British flag. However, research was casting doubts on Sebastian Cabot's nationality and it was becoming evident that Sebastian had also been born in Venice, not Bristol.

The Annals of the Voyages of the Brothers Nicolò and Antonio Zeno
in the North Atlantic about the end of the Fourteenth Century
and
the Claim founded thereon to a Venetian Discovery of America

A Criticism and an Indictment
By Fred. W. Lucas
Author of "Appendiculae Historicae" and part
Editor of "The New Laws of
the Indies"

Illustrated by Facsimiles

LONDON
HENRY STEVENS SON AND STILES 39 GREAT RUSSELL STREET
OVER AGAINST THE BRITISH MUSEUM
MD CCC LXXXX VIII

Cover of the Fred W. Lucas translation and dismissal of the Zeno Narrative. Three hundred and fifty copies were available on hand-made paper (£2.2s) and 50 copies on Japanese Vellum (£4.4s), both on uncut folded sheets. Half-leather, gilt-top binding was available for the discerning bibliophile who did not wish to have the book bound himself.

Needless to say, this transformation of Sebastian from British to Italian did not sit well. Anglophiles were being assailed on all sides as the 19th century drew to a close. The newfound legitimacy of the Zeno Narrative was discrediting the claims of Yorkshire-born seaman Frobisher as the first post–Norse European to visit Greenland, with the Zeno map causing Frobisher's confusion as to where he was. Now, Bristol-born Sebastian Cabot's nationality was being questioned.

Charles Henry Coote, a map librarian at the British Museum and heir to R. H. Major's title of Britain's map expert, was particularly chagrined by Sebastian Cabot's sudden change in birthplace. His 41/2-page entry on Sebastian Cabot in the *Dictionary of National Biography* warns of recent books that "injudiciously rejected" Sebastian's Bristol roots in favor of the "comparatively new but suspicious" claims of a Venetian birth.[5]

Coote, to whom Lucas dedicated his book, gave Lucas access to the same vast British Museum collection of early maps that Major had used. Coote's obituary[6] notes that he assisted Major on a number of projects, and it appears that Coote provided Lucas with specific points to cast aspersions on Major's use of the maps as supporting evidence. Whether Coote was merely doing his job or had his own reasons, it is interesting to note that Major's scholarship eclipsed Coote even in death — Coote's obituary regretfully observed that he had produced no major research of his own, unlike his colleague's biography of Henry the Navigator.

In addition to Coote, this coterie of Cabot supporters included Lucas's publisher, Henry Stevens. A Vermont expatriate and prominent bookseller in London, Lucas was noted for his eccentricities[7] as much as for his expertise in locating, verifying and selling early texts on Columbus. Stevens also published the work of Henry Harrisse, the foremost Columbus bibliographer of the time and a highly respected researcher on the Cabots.

Indicative how volatile the situation about Cabot was in England at the time, when Harrisse published a biography of the Cabots that included his reasons for agreeing with Sebastian's birth in Venice,[8] he went to another publisher — Henry Stevens's brother, Benjamin Franklin Stevens. Another Anglophile, Miller Christy, wrote a 1900 book on Francis Drake[9] that also was published by Henry Stevens. This book, with a foreword by Coote, included an appendix critical of Zeno and highly supportive of Lucas's work, barely mentioning that Christy's book had been proofread and edited by Lucas himself.

Fred W. Lucas's *Annals of the Voyages of the Brothers Nicolò and Antonio Zeno* was presold by subscription. Henry Stevens, knowing the target audience, included 18 plates of early maps at the end of the book, most provided by

Coote from the British Museum collection. Excluding these plates, the indices and the appendices that include facsimiles of the original 1558 edition of the narrative and Hakluyt's 1582 translation, the book is 157 pages long, which includes maps in the text and elaborate chapter headings. The book starts with Lucas's revised translation, his notes on the illustriousness of both the younger Nicolò and the original publisher, Francesco Marcolini. Lucas then discusses the map's impact on early navigation, including the Frobisher confusion using a map that included the Zeno islands followed by a chapter on the growing doubts of the narrative's authenticity, stressing the opponents and minimizing the proponents. Having done with the niceties, solicitor Lucas ends his overview with a 3-page chapter on the "present status" of the Zeno Narrative, ending the first section of the book with Oscar Brenner's 1886 discovery in Munich of a 1539 Olaus Magnus map which Brenner believed demonstrated the original from which the Zeno map was copied.[10] Comparing the Olaus Magnus map, Brenner found that the islands of Tile, Hebrides, Orcades, and Hetland corresponded to the Zeno map's placement of Icaria, Estotiland, Drogio, Frisland and Estonia.

Lucas concludes by again discrediting the map, not the text. He mentions a number of other authors who had addressed the material in recent years and then sums up his case with a surprising show of largesse, noting that the matter has not been conclusively proved one way or the other.

Lucas's legal approach did not go unnoticed; the American Geographical Society of New York's review was non-committal, dryly noting that the "the counsel for the defendant, if there were one, could make an equally good showing."[11] The Reverend B. F. DeCosta, a high-profile advocate of the Norse discovery of America who had already questioned Zahrtmann's research, reviewed the book for *The American Historical Review*.[12] DeCosta criticizes the tone of the text, noting that, although Lucas claimed "the final word on the topic," Lucas's position was far from impregnable. He notes that Lucas objected to apocryphal anecdotes in the text, a position that DeCosta observed as overly broad, allowing the dismissal of significant early American texts such as Cotton Mather's *Marginalia*. He further complained that although Lucas claimed the younger Nicolò forged the map from existing maps, he doesn't actually offer any proof. DeCosta concludes by calling Lucas out — if Lucas wants to discredit the Zeno Narrative, he'll need to start from scratch, declaring he could personally make a stronger argument against Zeno than Lucas and still not prove Nicolò Zeno the younger had perpetuated a fraud.

Even Lucas's circle of Cabot devotees weren't able to ignore Lucas's tendency toward arrogance and rigidity and tried to temper Lucas with moderation in their reviews and essays on the topic.

In a book on the Drake Voyage, Miller Christy wrote that he didn't believe there is anything necessarily fraudulent in the data, merely the main problem is the Zeno map itself. Christy suggests that the younger Nicolò did use an old map in his family library to create the Zeno chart, one dating back to the time of the voyage, but unrelated to the narrative. He suggests that the accuracy of Greenland indicates a lost map from ancient Scandinavian explorations of the North Atlantic.[13]

C. Raymond Beazley, another Cabot proponent, reviewed the book in such a way as to appear favorable in the first paragraph but raises doubts about Lucas's prose with such admissions as Lucas having a "certain ruthlessness of temper ... [creating] a more absolute denial than is necessary or advisable" and "somewhat too severe a pen."[14]

Brian Smith, Shetland Archivist and noted critic of the Zeno Narrative, published an article in 2002 that repeated the Lucas criticisms of the narrative as part of his dismissal of Henry Sinclair's expedition.[15] In a footnote, Smith mentions that Lucas's book was very rare and that most people discussing the material had probably not read it.[16] This is a valid observation — the prospectus for the book notes that the entire press run was 400 copies and geared toward bibliophiles, not scholars. Subsequently, as time passed, most researchers' familiarity with the book was from the reviews by Lucas's associates in mainstream antiquarian publications, not the book itself.

Ultimately, Lucas's dismissal of the narrative became the final word on the topic, not because of his scholarship, but because of his timing. R. H. Major had died in 1891, and was unable to defend his work as he had vigorously done against earlier critics. Then, in November 1898, Minnesotan farmer Olof Öhman uncovered what was immediately dubbed "the Kensington Rune Stone" and by February 1899, the debate on the stone's authenticity had eclipsed Lucas and made the debate over the Zeno Narrative passé— why debate whether Trin Harbor was in Greenland or North America when "new" physical evidence was in Minnesota?

In 1907, Hjalmar R. Holand purchased the stone from Öhman and began a lifelong quest to prove it was a record of Paul Knutson's expedition to America. Other than a few minor attempts at revitalizing the Zeno Narrative, Lucas became the final word on the topic, at least for 50 years, because those who would argue against the book simply were pre-occupied with what they considered more substantial pieces of evidence of early exploration. The comparatively esoteric hair-splitting over the narrative was far less interesting to the public than the substantive proof of Vikings in the form of the Kensington Rune Stone, Dighton Rock and Newport Tower; all revived interest in Vineland.

Unveiled in 1887, the Leif Ericsson statue by Anne Whitney still stands along Commonwealth Avenue in Boston, more a symbol of the Norse mania of New England than of the actual voyage it represents (photograph courtesy of Terry Deveau).

With Fred W. Lucas's book difficult to locate from the start,[17] later authors couldn't review Lucas's conclusions other than through reviews. To a casual observer, it appeared that Lucas's book had indeed destroyed the Zeno Narrative's credibility.

The Nancy codex that Nordenskjöld discovered would be addressed again in 1956 by Ib Kejlbo of the Royal Library in Copenhagen. In his article for the Royal Library's annual *Fund og Forskning*,[18] Kejlbo notes there was a map by Clavus that dated no later than 1425. Although this subsequent map is lost, the notes and geographical tables survived and were discovered in Vienna at the start of the 20th century.[19]

Kejlbo suggests Clavus had an ego that would not allow him to name locations after other people as was the norm. Clavus's process for selecting place-names for this map was unique. Clavus wrote a parody of a verse of a Danish ballad and then took each word, in succession, and assigned it to a place-name.[20] Starting at the northern headland on the east coast and reading clockwise along the coast, the names recombine to create the verse. Fridtjof Nansen explains the translations, noting Karl Aubert's identification of the verse was the same prototype as that of the opening stanza of a Swedish ballad "Kung Speleman."[21]

Kejlbo notes that these same nonsensical toponyms appear on the Zeno map but not in a discernible order, suggesting that the place-names on the map were jumbled when derived from a subsequent copy by an intermediate cartographer who copied Claudius Clavus's work without being aware of the hidden stanza.[22] So, there is more than sufficient toponymic evidence to suggest that the Zeno map was not created until more than a century after the 1380 date in the Zeno Narrative as the map's distinctive nomenclature postdates the Zeno map to after the 1425 Clavus map.

The discovery of the Clavus geography tables by Björnbo and Petersen, coupled with Kejlbo's research proved the Zeno map was less than 150 years old when the younger Nicolò published it in 1558. However, the compiler had admitted in the opening text of the narrative that the map was not originally associated with the letters that became the narrative.[23] Treating the map and narrative as two distinct items instead of one had been suggested by Cardinal Zurla back in 1808 and reiterated by Major in 1873.[24] Zurla and Major held that the map and the narrative are two entirely unrelated items, combined by the younger Nicolò, with an erroneous date added during preparations for publication. The Clavus tables discredited the map but left the narrative itself unscathed.

Although the Zeno Narrative ends with Zichmni ordering Antonio Zeno back to Europe while the Prince remained behind with a handful of men to establish a base of operation for further explorations, Zichmni's ultimate fate is not disclosed. The end of the narrative has Antonio writing to Carlo one last time, telling him he has another book with the customs of the lands he had visited. The list of place includes Estotiland. The narrative has Zichmni building his city at Trin, but the reference to additional, lost text on Estotiland was enough to convince some Zeno proponents that Zichmni had continued westward in his explorations and had returned home at a later date.

The major issue remained the date of the voyage. The map had 1380 written across the top, which was supported by the reference to the Battle of Chioggia. Major believed it was a transcription error and should have been 1390, a date repeated by Barbaro. Extant materials on the Sinclairs restrict the window of opportunity further — if Jarl Henry is already in a record, he cannot have been sailing west at the same time. Since the younger Nicolò destroyed many of the letters from Antonio to his brother Carlos, it may be safe to assume that in addition to any omissions, the sequence of the letters may also have been jumbled when Nicolò attempted to recompile the narrative, confusing the order of events as he attempted to translate centuries-old handwriting on damaged and decomposing paper. So in addition to transcription and translation errors, the entire chronology is suspect.

Forster was the first to make the suggestion Sinclair was Zichmni, noting that the Sinclair name could easily be transliterated into Zichmni by an Italian who was trying to write down unfamiliar words phonetically. Pohl concurs with Forster's identification of Sinclair with Zichmni and, in his three books on the topic, presents two different scenarios in which the name Sinclair could have evolved into Zichmni. His first book on the expedition explains how "Sinclair" in 14th-century script could be misread as "Zichmni."[25] He returns to the topic in *Atlantic Crossings Before Columbus* by including graphics of how similar "Sinclair" and "Rosslyn" in 14th-century handwriting were to "Zichmni" and "Soran" in 16th-century handwriting.[26] A trip to Italy gave him a new perspective on the topic.[27] He compared the medieval Italian letter forms, as given by Cappelli's *Lexicon Abbreviaturarum*[28] to examples of a capital letter "Z" found in the collections of Venice's Biblioteca Nazionale Marciana, and developed a new stance on the mistranslation. His final book on the expedition repeats the discovery; a small crossbar and a flourish are all that separate the cursive "Z" of the younger Nicolò's time from the medieval "d'O" of his ancestors, turning "Principe d'Orkeney" into "Principe Zichmni."[29] Crawford's review of the book[30] felt that Pohl's interpretation of the name "Principe Zichmni'" as a misreading of "Principe d'Orkeney" was nothing short of ingenious, although she questions Pohl's "uncritical acceptance of what was known to be a text fraught with difficulties."

Pohl's loyalty to the text is evident when he addresses the date of the voyage, the one major point upon which he disagreed with Forster. Since most researchers assumed that the Zeno map and text were contemporary to each other, the 1380 date on the Zeno map was causing chronology problems. Major first suggested that the 1380 date was a transcription error and the younger Nicolò actually meant 1390. However, the narrative notes that after the Battle of Chioggia ended the Genoese war in 1380, Nicolò wanted to see the world. Da Mosto agrees that there is evidence Nicolò visited England and Flanders but that he returned to Venice by 1385.[31] But if Sinclair is indeed Zichmni, it would be inappropriate for the Earl to consider an extended voyage in 1380, barely a year after being awarded the Orkney jarldom.

Pohl stuck with the 1390 date and used it as a basis to identify the specific date that Sinclair dropped anchor in Nova Scotia's Guysborough Harbor as June 1, 1398.[32] His rationale was the naming of the harbor by Zichmni as "Trin Harbor" and a note in the text that while they were harbored there, June arrived. Lucas questions the date, noting that early in the narrative, the expedition stayed seven days at Ledovo, and arrived at Ilofe on the 1st of July. Lucas therefore calculates the start date as on or before the 23rd of June.

Pohl does not address this conflict, which could be explained away by letter sequence, transcription mistakes or translation errors. Instead, he concentrated on the naming of Trin Harbor. He felt that Sinclair would have continued a tradition of naming discoveries after the day in the church calendar upon which they were founded. Using this as a base, Pohl found that Trinity Sunday was June 2, 1398, the only year that matched Pohl's criteria within his time frame.

Stephen Boardman's subsequent research into the Stewart Dynasty[33] suggests Henry Sinclair was involved in the English border wars in 1398, making Pohl's date untenable as well. Pohl's time frame was the nine-year period between 1395, which he calculated as the date of death of Nicolò Zeno and 1404, when Antonio Zeno returned to Venice, a possible indication that Antonio's obligation ended with Henry's death. Since neither date is confirmed by primary source material, Pohl's time frame is somewhat arbitrary.

Using similar logic but modifying the parameters of the search, alternative dates can be suggested. Keeping Pohl's basic assumption that Trin Harbor was named because of Trinity Sunday, but expanding the time period to include the decade between Sinclair being awarded the Orcadian Jarldom in 1379 and his reported involvement in the battle of Falköping in 1389, Pohl's criterion that Trinity Sunday had to be in early June expands to include June 1, 1382, June 5, 1384, and June 2, 1387.

The 1387 date would give Sinclair time to bring the Orkneys under his control and allow Nicolò Zeno to depart for England after the treaty signing in 1381 that ended the Chioggia war with Genoa and Venice. Zeno could return from England in 1385 per da Mosto and still have time to set sail again, be wrecked, rescued and recruited for the Sinclair crew. It also gives Sinclair time to return to Scotland from Trin for the 1391 battle against his cousin Malise Sperra.

Andrea da Mosto's 1933 paper on the genealogy of the Zeno family was highly critical of the voyage, with da Mosto suggesting that Venetian records of the time indicated that Nicolò Zeno was a political prisoner in Venice at the time he would have been with Prince Zichmni. However, da Mosto concedes in the same article that Nicolò Zeno was a common name in Venice in that time period.[34] Assuming he has the correct Nicolò, da Mosto finds sufficient documentary evidence of his career to track Nicolò from 1389 until his death around 1402.[35]

Da Mosto and Zurla both note Nicolò was a respected navigator and functionary and appears in the records earlier, but since both genealogists were focusing on the dates listed in the narrative and on the map, the earlier records were not examined as closely and Nicolò is not as readily referenced in the earlier dates, suggesting a 1387 date for the trip is still feasible.

There remain two additional stumbling blocks to the Zeno Narrative: Zichmni's battle against the Norwegian king, and Nicolò Zeno being alive and well in Italy after the date the narrative claimed he died in the frozen North Atlantic. Other writers had suggested either that Nicolò Zeno misunderstood (or the younger Nicolò mistranslated) the battle between Sinclair and Sperra as being an international, not an internecine war. But Crawford, who is generally noncommittal about the narrative, acknowledged in 1999 that if Malise Sperra was the Shetland foud as she suspected, Sinclair's assault would technically be against an appointee of the Norwegian crown and would explain the passage, an interpretation that Major had also suggested in 1873.[36]

The younger Nicolò's transcription errors and mistranslations might offer an explanation for the death/non-death of his earlier namesake. In modern Italian, as one example, the different between stating Nicolò died on his return to Frisland and stating he *almost* died on his return to Frisland is one word — *quasi*. If the younger Nicolò missed the word or it was too damaged to read, "*Nicolò quasi morto al suo ritorno a Frisland*" (Nicolò almost died on his return to Frisland) becomes "*Nicolò morto al suo ritorno a Frisland*" (Nicolò died on his return to Frisland). If Nicolò was too ill to serve Zichmni, he could have been allowed to return to Venice, leaving Antonio in his stead. With the 1387 date of the voyage, this would allow Nicolò to return to Venice to convalesce and place him back in the records where da Mosto tracks him from 1389 forward.

Although proponents continued research, Lucas and da Mosto had repositioned the Zeno Narrative as a "proven forgery." The demise of the Zeni voyage would again prove premature.

9

The Sinclair Expedition

In 1949, Arctic explorer and glacial geologist William Herbert Hobbs published an article in *Imago Mundi—The International Journal for the History of Cartography*.[1] He had been asked by the editors of *Imago Mundi* to use his extensive background on Greenland to write an article on the country's early maps. By sheer luck, one of the few libraries that held a copy of the Fred W. Lucas book was University of Michigan, where Hobbs had been the head of the Geology department until his retirement in 1934. Using the Zeno map as reproduced in Lucas's book, Hobbs found a revelation. He declared that his study of the medieval maps of the world indicated that the first map to show any resemblance to the actual outline of Greenland was the Zeno map.

Hobbs believed that the map's inaccuracies were caused by the younger Nicolò attempting to superimpose a contemporary longitude and latitude grid on his ancestor's map, which would already have had inaccuracies from the map's use of magnetic north for true north. Allowing for the confusion between magnetic and true north, Hobbs found the estimated distances on the map became surprisingly accurate. Hobbs places Estotiland in Newfoundland in his illustrations but does not address it in the text.

Alternatively, former U.S. Navy cartographer, engineer and ancient-map enthusiast Arlington Mallery[2] argued that the Zeno map version of the Greenland coast, although inaccurate at first glance, was actually an accurate outline of the coastline beneath the massive ice cover. This, according to Mallery, is because the Zeno map was compiled from an ancient map that predated the glaciation of the landmass. Mallery hypothesized that Nicolò may have rescued a map from the monastery he visited and sent it back to Venice.[3] Mallery's origin of the map is essentially the same as his identification of Piri Re'is map — an unknown civilization mapped the world centuries prior to the ice cover obscured the coast line.

Mallery announced his Piri Re'is map findings in 1956 on a radio forum on Antarctica.[4] Among the listeners was Charles H. Hapgood, a professor at Keene State College in New Hampshire. Hapgood had gained notoriety for his theory that the off-center accumulation of polar ice sporadically caused changes in the axis of the earth that forced rapid pole shifts with catastrophic results and had done so in recorded history.[5] Other parts of his work would be the foundation of the now widely accepted plate tectonic theory, but Hapgood used ancient maps to document his theory of pole drift. The Piri Re'is map was the sort of cartographic data Hapgood collected. His subsequent study of the Zeno and Piri Re'is maps became *Maps of the Ancient Sea Kings*.[6] Hapgood noted that these maps were unexpectedly accurate for being drawn in the centuries prior to the development of marine chronometers in Europe. His conclusions were similar to Mallery's; the early European cartographers were using copies of ancient maps charted before the Ice Age by an ancient civilization and handed down piecemeal through the centuries until the original significance had been lost.[7]

Hapgood's work was received coolly in academic circles, but since his 1958 book was graced with a foreword by Albert Einstein, it was at least acknowledged. It did not sell well until 1970, when it was briefly cited by Erich von Däniken in his bestselling *Chariots of the Gods?*[8] as evidence of extraterrestrial visits. Hapgood's material was similarly hijacked by subsequent von Däniken knock-off titles. It sold additional copies of Hapgood's book but destroyed the theory's credibility among mainstream scholars.

There was a solitary benefit to the tangent that Mallery/Hapgood led the Zeno Narrative off upon — it focused attention back on Hobbs and his studies of the topic. Hobbs began lecturing and publishing on the subject again.[9] In 1950, Frederick J. Pohl attended a lecture by Hobbs in New York where the geologist announced he had located the site of the Zeno landfall.[10] Hobbs based his claim on a description in the narrative that stated that the boats entered "an excellent harbor" where they saw a great mountain in the distance that poured out smoke. Zichmni sent out a reconnaissance party that discovered the smoke was coming from a fire at the bottom of the hill and that there was a spring spewing forth pitch which ran into the sea.

Hobbs believed this to be a reference to the area near Stellarton, Nova Scotia, with a well-documented history of exposed coal seams prone to fire, frequent releases of methane and most importantly, a stream of asphalt seeping to the surface that worked its way into Coal Brook and then the East River between Stellarton and New Glasgow.[11] Goodwin's old nemesis Samuel Eliot Morison, who had won a Pulitzer Prize for his biography of Columbus, would summarily dismiss Hobbs's conclusion in a two-volume study of the early European explorations (and take a few additional shots at Goodwin, who had died 22 years earlier).[12] Morison's rationale was that Hobbs was incorrect because there are no volcanoes in Nova Scotia. Apparently Morison was too busy being clever writing doggerel mocking pre–Columbian theorists to actually read the material he was lambasting, since one of Hobbs's points was that the reference wasn't to a volcano.[13]

Pohl however, was intrigued by Hobbs's work and began his own investigation. Pohl's 1950 book *The Sinclair Expedition to Nova Scotia in 1398* addressed the question as to exactly where the Zichmni/Zeno expedition might have landed on the North American mainland,[14] using Hobbs's identification of Stellarton as a starting point. Pohl matched descriptions in the Zeno Narrative to geographic features and calculated that Sinclair's fleet sailed into Nova Scotia's Chedabucto Bay and made landfall at Guysborough Harbor. Pohl notes this was not only "an excellent harbor" from a navigational perspective, but also from a business perspective — the fishing in the area was nothing short of spectacular, citing the writings of Nicolas Denys.[15] Denys, Cape Breton Island's first permanent French settler and a major figure in Acadia for over half of the 17th century, established a trading post to profit from the abundance of cod which he dried and shipped to France.

One of Jarl Henry's descendants, author Andrew Sinclair,[16] also researched his ancestor's voyage, using the Pohl identification of Guysborough Harbor as a fixed point in the journey. Andrew Sinclair mentions a breech loading cannon found in the collection of the Fortress of Louisbourg National Historic Site in Canada.[17] It was snagged on an anchor and pulled out of Louisbourg Harbor in the 1880s.[18] Sinclair identifies it as a peterero, a type of cannon similar to the type developed for naval warfare by Carlo Zeno. Although an 1891 article in the *Proceedings and Transactions of the Royal Society of Canada* tries to establish an evidence trail for locating a lost Portuguese colony in the vicinity, naval historian Jean Boudriot finds the light artillery piece to those similar to others found in a French context at other locations.[19]

Andrew Sinclair's inference was that Sinclair lost or scuttled one of his ships at a stop at Louisbourg, en route between Stellarton and Guysborough. The Zeno Narrative does not specify how many ships were in the expedition, but Johann Forster's inventory of Sinclair's military strength in the Orkneys[20] suggests that several vessels could make the trip and still leave a strong navy to guard the Orkneys.

The Zeno Narrative ends with Zichmni ordering Antonio Zeno back to Europe with most of the ships and men to avoid winter in the new land, while the Prince remained behind with a handful of men to establish a base of operation for further explorations. Pohl has Sinclair wintering with the Mi'kmaq and then, as the Glooscap tale states, departing to the west.

In light of Glynn's discovery of the Westford Knight, Pohl, Lethbridge and subsequent researchers believed that Sinclair did not immediately return to Europe, instead continuing his explorations following the coast of Nova Scotia. Crossing the Bay of Fundy to the Maine coast, the Sinclair expedition would pass by Machias Bay, noted for Native petroglyphs including three carvings of European sailing ships found at three different locations among the nine identified petroglyph sites. Here Native Americans pecked the image of a European ship into the rock, part of a 3,000-year-old tradition of imagery on these ledges. Archaeologist Mark Hedden of the Maine State Historic Preservation Commission identifies all three as early 17th-century sailing vessels.[21]

Two of the ship petroglyphs are recent discoveries, first published by Hedden in 2002. The remaining ship first appeared in an illustration attached to ethnologist Garrck Mallery's 1893 study[22] and subsequently lost again until 1977.

The earliest of the ship petroglyphs is smaller and significantly different from the later discoveries. It is adjacent to a Christian cross, which Hedden suggests limits the country of origin to one of the Catholic kingdoms such as France, Spain or Portugal.[23] Although Hedden finds records to document early English colonial visits at times that correspond to dates suggested by the latter two ships, he has difficulty finding a visitor in a small single-masted ship with square sails that was associated with a large cross.[24] There are two parallel lines trailing off the aft end of the ship which Hedden identifies as a symbol in a pictographic sign language denoting transitioning from the earth to a spiritual plane even though a century before, Garrick Mallery of the Smithsonian, the first to document the petroglyph, had warned future researchers of associating concepts with simple symbols.[25]

Archaeologist James Whittall identifies these same lines as wake or steering oars.[26] Whittall was noncommittal on the identity of the ship's master in 1984 but does include the Sinclair expedition as a possibility. Within a decade, Whittall would be a leading figure in research on the Sinclair expe-

Composite of Machias Bay petroglyph showing a single-masted ship with a square sail, based on images by Garrick Mallery in *Picture-writing of the American Indians* (1893) and James Whittall in *Early Sites Research Bulletin*, volume 11, number 1 (December 1984).

dition, but he does not actively connect the Sinclair trip with the Machias Bay carving.

Following the Maine coast, the Sinclair expedition would proceed past Machias Bay and continue down the coast past the mouth of the Morse River, home of the Popham Beach Stone and the notorious Spirit Pond Rune Stones.[27]

In spite of the opinions of experts in the field, these stones continue to attract new amateur researchers with a variety of explanations. These discussions continue, in spite of what Erik Wahlgren points out as a "staggering [...] disproportion between demographic factors and the runological production," noting that several thousand Norse Icelanders lived on Greenland for several centuries, but only 40 runic inscriptions exist. Iceland has 53 inscriptions all dated after 1200, but North America has hundreds of alleged inscriptions with no verified long-term habitation.[28]

So, although Sinclair had Norse familial associations, it is safe to assume that his voyage had no connection to any of the rune stones on the route. Even assuming there are legitimate runic inscriptions along the Atlantic coast, there is little reason to associate them with the Sinclair expedition. The crew of sailors would have been illiterate, speaking the Orcadian variant of Old Norse known as Norrœna or Norn.[29] Among the officers, Henry Sinclair was probably fluent in several languages, Donald Gunn spoke either Caithness Norrœna or Gaelic, and Zeno spoke Italian. Any communication among the three would be in Latin, the universal tongue of Catholic areas.

Almost due east of Popham Beach is Monhegan Island. Ida Proper in *Monhegan, the Cradle of New England*[30] lists all the documented, probable and possible explorers who visited the area, such as Verrazano in 1524 and Champlain in 1604. But she also lists pre–Columbian explorers that may have visited Monhegan Island such as the Norse, the Phoenicians, St. Brendan, Culdee Monks and Nicolò Zeno. More important to Proper were the annual visits by Basque, Spanish, Portuguese and Breton fishermen heading to the Grand Banks.

This history of the island's involvement in the dried fish trade has been eclipsed by an "inscription tablet" on adjacent Manana Island, subsequently identified as an erosion pattern as a softer intrusion vein weathered out of the neighboring rock.[31] The controversy about the runes aside, there is on the ledge above the marks, a series of drilled holes, "made to fit rounded ends of poles or timbers, used to hold upright some structure."[32] Although Proper suggests a signal tower of some sort, another possibility is a fish flake, the platform of poles used for drying split, washed and salted cod.

By the 16th century, French, Portuguese and Basque fishing vessels were regular visitors to the waters of the Maritime provinces and Maine. By the early 17th century, the Dutch and English were also fishing on the Grand Banks. Some of these fishing vessels established settlements near the fishing banks to dry and salt the cod.[33] Even Captain John Smith was dabbling in the dried fish trade with stages and fish-flakes on Monhegan in 1614 while exploring the coast, according to Samuel Eliot Morison.[34] The Sinclair expedition found territories for the Earldom, but the immediate profit center was the fishing grounds (the Grand Banks) as described by the Zeno Narrative's sailor, so the fish flake on Manana could just easily be evidence of the expedition drying cod to replenish their provisions or underwriting the expedition by filling the cargo holds on the return voyage.

Jarl Henry would have continued down the New England coast, exploring navigable rivers, including the Merrimack River, which empties into the Atlantic at Newburyport, Massachusetts. The Merrimack was a popular location; a history of the river notes that as early as 1603, Pierre Dugua, Sieur de Mons, learned of the Merrimack from Indians along the St. Lawrence River.[35] More important to Sinclair, one of the reasons for the river's renown was the fishing. The history of Lowell, Massachusetts, notes that the fishing and meadowlands of the areas along the Merrimack and Concord Rivers attracted colonists within 30 years of the Sieur de Mons initial discovery.[36] The falls at Pawtucket on the Merrimack and the Wamesit Falls on the Concord were both sites of large seasonal Native settlements which gradually died out after smallpox decimated the tribes in 1617. As Dr. Donald R. Hopkins, a former director of the Centers for Disease Control and Prevention, notes in his book on smallpox epidemics through history, this outbreak may have wiped out nine-tenths of the coastal Indian population.[37] The abandoned village of Patuxet was discovered by English colonists and the cleared fields and lack of Natives made the site optimal to found a new colony, now remembered as Plymouth. The decimated population could easily lose enough of their traditions and stories, including an encounter along the Merrimack with a Scottish ship sailing up the river four centuries before. Paula Underwood's book of the oral traditions of her Native American ancestors includes the Walking People arrival in the East and their encounters with a Stone Hill People who built stone structures.[38]

The Merrimack would have been an ideal route for exploration; the river's channel was more than adequate to allow the ships' progress inland. Haverhill, fifteen miles upriver, was among several river communities building ships in the colonial era.[39] In an 1861 history of Haverhill, the author mentions that ships were regularly built that sailed down the river and out to the British ports.[40] Sinclair's ships, most likely a variation of the cog used throughout

Northern Europe, would weigh in fully laden at 50 to 150 tons.[41] Compared to the 340-ton *Ulysses* built in a Haverhill shipyard in 1798,[42] Sinclair would have had no difficulty sailing up the Merrimack.

Heading upriver, their first obstacle would have been Bodwell Falls in Lawrence, now the site of the Great Stone Dam. With a 9-foot drop blocking the route, it would have been possible to anchor in the vicinity and portage shallow draft boats around it and continue another 10 miles or so until they reached the 32-foot Pawtucket Falls in modern day Lowell. To the west, they might have seen a hilltop 10 miles away, which local tradition claims was where Indians frequently sent smoke signals. The explorers could have made the trip overland or portaged their vessels around the falls and continued to Stony Brook and followed that to within a few miles of the hill.

Alternately, Pawtucket Falls may have been sufficient enough of an obstacle that Sinclair reversed direction and sailed down to the Concord River, which empties into the Merrimack River less than 5 miles downstream from the falls. The area south of Westford is low with numerous swamps, the remnants of glacial ponds that dotted the area after the last ice age. It is possible that some of these glacial ponds were still extant and of adequate depth for Sinclair to approach Westford from the south.

Regardless of his approach, the story relates how Sinclair and his crew proceeded to the summit of what is now called Prospect Hill in Westford, Massachusetts. Its 465-foot height afforded a good view in all directions. It was there that tragedy struck. Whether it was from battle, a heart attack, a snake bite or some sort of accident, a member of Sinclair's party died. Based on the shield's heraldic symbols, the fallen knight was Donald of Clyth, chieftain of Clan Gunn.

A battle on a hilltop in 1399 Westford requires an opponent, and by inference, that indicates Indians. Hodgman notes a local tradition of a pre-settlement battle between the Nashoba and Wamesit tribes on Frances Hill, about 3 miles northeast of the Knight effigy,[43] so it is possible that the Sinclair expedition stumbled into long-disputed territory and was attacked by one side or the other. Frederick Pohl suggests a less heroic alternate in his earliest published work on the Westford Knight, *Atlantic Crossings Before Columbus*.[44] In this version, Gunn, climbing up the 465-foot hill in full armor, suffered a fatal heart attack.[45]

New England soil's inherent acidity decomposes bone in a short time,[46] so even if the carving on the ledge in Westford marked a nearby burial, the body would be long gone by the arrival of Westford's early colonists. Alternately, the Knight carving could be a cenotaph placed atop Prospect Hill to mark Gunn's burial elsewhere. It may have been chosen because it was a better landmark than the actual burial location. Since Sinclair anticipated returning to Scotland, it would seem logical that the Gunn clan would wish to visit the site of their fallen leader after Sinclair returned and notified the Gunns. It may also offer a "directional sign" to the possible interpretations of the "Boat Stone," also uncovered in Westford.

In spite of the return of Sinclair, Zeno and the expedition, the journey apparently did not receive any notice at the time. Numerous reasons for this obscurity have been offered, ranging from the ongoing debate over the nonexistence of the voyage versus Sinclair being slain in battle soon after his return to Scotland to such absurdities as Sinclair returning to North America to live out his life.[47]

The lack of voyage documentation may not be deliberate. It could be a casualty of the Scottish Reformation, specifically the particularly enthusiastic destruction of churches in 1559–1560. The intensity of the mob was so notable that nearly two centuries later, Innes still noted the "promiscuous burning of religious houses, with registers and libraries of churches."[48]

Archbishop John Spottiswood's 1655 *History of the Church and State of Scotland* noted the mob iconoclasm was in a comparatively small area radiating out from Edinburgh,[49] but the area that bore the brunt of the damage around the ecclesiastic seat would also house documents of the voyage. Rosslyn Castle was partly burnt by an accidental fire in 1447. It was also burnt by the English in 1554; and in 1650 it was besieged and all but demolished by General Monk. Assuming records were in the castle, they did not survive the periodic onslaughts.

Aside from questions as to when or if Sinclair visited North America, the question also arises as to why. The motivation for the trip can be summed up in two words—fish and territory. The conflict between Sinclair and his cousin Sperre demonstrates how aggressively Sinclair defended his territories, granted or presumed.[50] Between his family in Caithness and his jarldom of Orkney, Henry Sinclair would have known that deep sea fishing and the export of dried fish from Orkney, Caithness and Shetland had been a tradition from the earliest of times and was an increasingly lucrative growth industry.[51] Zooarchaeologist James H. Barrett points out that the trade of dried fish was already an economic feature of northern Scotland when written records begin to provide detail in the post–Medieval period, and his fish-bone studies suggest that it was an influx of Vikings that triggered an increase in fish in the diet of Orkney and Shetland by a greater investment in deep-sea fishing.[52] Based on his examination of over 40 sites in Scotland, Orkney and Shetland, Barrett believes fishing intensified in the Middle Ages as a result of a developing export trade in dried fish, particularly cod.

Barrett notes Przemysław Urbańczyk's book *Medieval Arctic Norway*,[53] which proposed fish trade as a key role in the transformation of Arctic Norway into a Norwegian Christian state. Barrett muses on the possibility that the arrival of the Norse and the dried fish trade may have similarly transformed northern Scotland.

All this profitable fishing lends itself to an alternative theory as to why the Sinclair expedition went unheralded — simple economics. If Sinclair had discovered the Grand Banks southeast of Newfoundland, he would not advertise the location of one of the world's richest fishing grounds when a monopoly would be more profitable.

Portuguese and Basque fishermen are known to have fished these waters in the 15th century with some texts of the period referring to a land called *Bacalao*, the land of the codfish.[54] However, it was not until Cabot reached the area in 1497 that the existence of these fishing grounds became widely known in Europe.

However, the final answer may rest with one man — Johannes Gensfleisch zur Laden zum Gutenberg. Johannes Gutenberg would not develop movable type until 1447. This technology advance would allow faster dissemination of information across Renaissance Europe, a definite advantage for later explorers.

10

Glooscap

The Zeno Narrative ends with Zichmni wintering over in the new land he had discovered. Frederick J. Pohl subsequently identified Guysborough Harbor at the head of Chedabucto Bay as the initial landfall and Pictou Harbor as the point of first contact with the local Mi'kmaqs. He ends his research on Sinclair with the assumption that Sinclair explored Nova Scotia with small boats while some of his men constructed a new ship to return to Europe and that they returned to Scotland in the spring.

In the wake of the discovery of the Westford Knight, Pohl began to review his original 1950 self-published book on the Sinclair expedition for possible expansion and inclusion in his latest book, *Atlantic Crossings Before Columbus*.[1] As with his subsequent book,[2] revisions reflect the changes and discoveries since he had first published.

Pohl had been searching for the specific location for the winter quarters of Sinclair in Nova Scotia[3] when he discovered additional material he had not considered before. He had been studying the placement of Mi'kmaq camps in hopes of finding an anomaly that might indicate the Sinclair camp.[4] What he discovered, while reviewing literature on the Mi'kmaq Indians, was that there appeared to be certain parallels between Sinclair's visit and the Mi'kmaq folk figure Glooscap.[5]

Most of the printed material about Glooscap is derived from a number of sources in a variety of styles, but Pohl went to whom he considered the earliest Mi'kmaq. Rand, more successful as an anthropologist than a cleric, compiled dictionaries, translated scripture and recorded the folklore of the Mi'kmaq.[6]

It was in Rand's collected stories that Pohl claimed seventeen parallels between Sinclair and Glooscap,[7] ranging from both of them being royalty who came from the east across the great sea to their weapon of choice being a sharp sword. Most notable to Pohl was that Glooscap was not considered a deity; "He looked and lived like other men; he ate, drank, smoked, slept, and danced along with them."[8]

In one of Glooscap's adventures, he examines a *wĭchkwĕdlakŭncheejŭl* (little

Erected in 2005, a 40-foot statue of Glooscap towers over the Glooscap Heritage Centre in Truro, Nova Scotia (photograph courtesy of Terry Deveau).

bark dish), which gives him an advantage while pursuing enemies.[9] Compare this to the description of the early mariner's compass as a magnetized needle floating in a wooden bowl of water, which Barbara Kreutz notes, was already in use in the Mediterranean by the time of the Sinclair expedition.[10]

Pohl completes his association of Glooscap with Sinclair by showing how the two names could be linguistically derived from each, based on Rand's dictionary of the Mi'kmaq tongue.[11] Rand uses the transformation of the words "Jesus Christ" into "Sāsoo Goole" to demonstrate how words become unrecognizable when unfamiliar consonants meet phonetics[12] and Pohl feels the transformation of "Jarl Sinclair" to "Kuloskap" is "phonetically reasonable."

Pohl was not alone in his identification of Glooscap as an overseas visitor. Rand himself, according to one biographer, felt that a number of the tales were Biblical narratives, all but unrecognizable after years of oral transmission.[13] This fit with Rand's theory that the Indians were the Lost Tribes of Israel.[14]

Rand's work was first published by Wellesley College under the auspices of Eben Norton Horsford, the college's benefactor. Horsford, better known for his claims of the lost Viking city Norumbega being along the Charles River in Cambridge, Massachusetts, was also active in Indian philology both as an amateur scholar and as the benefactor of the Wellesley College Department of Comparative Philology.[15] Horsford felt that several of the Glooscap stories showed a definite Icelandic influence, a stance also taken by folklorist Charles Godfrey Leland.[16] Leland refers to Glooscap as "by far the grandest and most Aryan-like character ever evolved from the savage mind,"[17] believing the Glooscap legends were heavily influenced by tales derived from the Icelandic Edda. Leland felt the Edda could have been introduced to North America by the Norse or via the Eskimos who traveled between Labrador and Iceland.[18]

In 1691, Father Chrestien le Clercq,[19] recounted a 1677 encounter with a Mi'kmaq tribe on the Gaspé Peninsula, a mountainous peninsula in eastern Québec jutting out into the Gulf of St. Lawrence just north of New Brunswick. In January 1677, Father le Clercq was traveling to Miramichi near present-day Chatham[20] when he became lost. Nearly dead, he was rescued by a passing Native. To his delight, the Mi'kmaqs of the area already considered the cross a sacred symbol although they had not been exposed to Catholicism. Giving them the name of *Porte-Croix* (Cross-Bearers), le Clercq tried to discover the origins of their veneration of the cross. Father le Clercq interviewed a 120-year-old member of the tribe who claimed to remember the first arrival of the French and that the veneration of the cross came from their ancestors, long before the missionaries arrived.[21] Acadian historian William Ganong, in the foreword to his 1910 translation of le Clercq, tends to dismiss the matter by suggesting it is either an artifact from a previous missionary visit or a stylized bird in flight as a tribal totem.[22]

Father le Clercq's report of the Porte Croix was affirmation of French scholar Eugene Beauvois' stance that the Norse, Celts and Zeni had been in

Canada — how else could the Christian icon have predated the French missionaries?[23] Beauvois located Great Iceland at the mouth of the St. Lawrence River, extending it inland along the river on an accompanying map to include the area of the Great Lakes.[24] Two years later, he added the Zeno Narrative into the mix[25] theorizing "Estotilanda" of the narrative was a transcription error that should read "Escocilanda." This would make Zeno's western land "the land of the Scots," using the word Scot as in "Scoti," the generic term of the Romans to describe the Irish raiders. In other words, Zeno had found the fabled Great Ireland.[26] Beauvois would repeatedly publish articles supporting the accuracy of the Zeno narrative until his death in 1912. In the wake of the Lucas book and Beauvois' indiscriminant acceptance of any evidence of Irish in North America, including his proposal that the Mesoamerican serpent god Quetzalcoatl was proof of the Irish colonies,[27] his work was essentially disregarded.

Pohl was aware of Beauvois, noting his theory of Estotilanda being a misspelling of Escocilanda and adopting Beauvois' placement of Great Ireland in Canada when discussing St. Brendan's voyage.[28] By his next book, Pohl had begun to modify his stance, suggesting Beauvois' "Estotiland as a transcription error" could still be Escociland, but since Newfoundland was too far away to affect Pohl's placement of Sinclair's Trin colony in Nova Scotia, it was less relevant.[29]

Pohl would return to the Sinclair expedition again in 1974 with *Prince Henry Sinclair — His Voyage to the New World in 1398*, and Beavois was now relegated to a brief, tepid mention.[30] The 1974 book included an expansion of Pohl's theories of the Nova Scotian landfall, with the addition of the Westford Knight material and more background material on the Sinclairs and the Zeno Narrative. His basic theory of Glooscap being Sinclair remained unchanged. Pohl has Sinclair wintering with the Mi'kmaq and then, as the Glooscap tale states, departing to the west.[31] Only now, Pohl had Sinclair continuing his journey by paralleling the coast of Nova Scotia.

Pohl noted that it was Glooscap who introduced fishing nets, a logical gift from a Scotsman from an area that had been commercially drying and exporting fish since at least the 9th century,[32] although it is erroneous — it is Zichmni's informant, the unnamed shipwrecked fisherman, who first introduced European fishing techniques to the Mi'kmaq, not Sinclair. Quoting Leland and Prince's book of Glooscap legends, Pohl notes that before Glooscap came, the Mi'kmaq didn't know how to make nets.[33] Rand does not address nets, only weirs[34] but in this case, the Zeno Narrative actually seems to support Leland, using the argument that the Zeno text only mentions the shipwrecked man using a net to provide fish to his captors in exchange for his life, not that he taught the Natives how to use a net themselves.

James Whittall's study of the Machias Bay ship petroglyph does admit that the two lines off the vessel's aft could also illustrate dragging ropes,[35] which would support Pohl's interpretation with the parallel lines representing the expedition replenishing their provisions using the long line method of fishing. Long line fishing, as the name suggests, is one or more long lines with dozens of hooks attached to the main line by short branch lines. The technique doesn't appear in Scottish records until the 16th century, but in an appendix to an Orkney excavation report, British Museum archaeo-ichthyologist Alwyne Wheeler suggests that distribution and types of fish bones found at Buckquoy indicate that the long lining was in use on Orkney as early as the Viking Age.[36] Alternatively, the lines on the Machias Bay petroglyph could indicate a ship dragging a trawl net, a method usually associated with two ships, but also feasible for one ship.[37]

Ultimately, the possibility of the Machias Bay carving being of Sinclair's ship depends on when the petroglyph was created. Hedden dates this ship by its proximity to moose petroglyphs, which do not appear in Maine petroglyphs until the Contact Period (c.1500–1650 A.D.). This timetable is based on post-glacial flora conditions evolving into coastal spruce fir forests, conducive to moose grazing.

Paleoecology is not an exact science and other studies based on pollen stratigraphies suggest that the spruce forests began to proliferate closer to 1000 years ago.[38] This allows enough flexibility in the date that the moose petroglyph could be created to leave open the possibility of the ship petroglyph chronicling the arrival of Henry Sinclair or the departure of Glooscap.

Over a century has passed since the Glooscap legends were first published and they remain popular with the public. They are not as popular with scholars such as Thomas Parkhill, who feels that they have been altered by the transcribers, particularly Leland, to be more palatable to American readers.[39] Leland, an advocate of the German Romanticist movement, was trying to introduce the concept of folklore as an affirmation of what geographer Yi-Fu Tuan identifies as geopiety, an emotional bond between man and his sense of place.[40] Leland's alterations to the texts and the emphasis of certain stories over others, Parkhill continues, has affected the study of Native American religions both within and outside of the Native American community.

As a result, Pohl's identifying European aspects to the Glooscap stories must be looked at cautiously. The parallels he finds may not be due to Glooscap being Sinclair as much as Leland's manipulating the stories. Fortunately, Pohl focused on Rand as his primary source, as had Leland and later authors, including Ruth Holmes Whitehead of the Nova Scotia Museum, who considers Rand's body of tales "still the best source of Micmac stories."[41]

Kenneth M. Morrison's work on the Eastern Algonkian religions indicates their world view demonstrated a degree of rationality that was completely misunderstood by missionaries and anthropologists.[42] He concludes that the Eastern Algonkians didn't convert to Catholicism, instead using their traditional values to develop a sense of Christianity and meld it into their pre-contact way of life.[43] Mark Finnan, in his book on Henry Sinclair, took the opportunity to ask a Cape Breton Mi'kmaq his opinion on the Glooscap legend. His answer was that there were a number of figures spread out over time that were of notable skills and adventures, all combining into the concept of the folk hero Glooscap.[44]

If Glooscap is a composite figure of different individuals from Native legends and Catholicism, it is certainly possible that Henry Sinclair is one of the facets of Glooscap, similar to how Glooscap could be a facet of Henry Sinclair's voyage.

11

The Knight Tower

James Whittall offered an alternative to Sinclair's expedition sailing back to Scotland after the Westford sojourn. Whittall suggested that Sinclair continued to explore, sailing down the coast before finally deciding to return to Europe. His evidence as to how far along the coast may still stand, overlooking the Narragansett Bay in Newport, Rhode Island.

The Newport Tower stands in Newport, Rhode Island's Touro Park. A cylindrical tower of local stone rising approximately 26 feet on eight columns, the tower is located on one of the highest points on Aquidneck Island. It is roughly a half-mile from the ocean both to the east (Narragansett Bay) and to the west (Atlantic Ocean at the Sakonnet River). Without trees or other buildings blocking the horizon, the tower would also offer a view of the Rhode Island Sound to the south.

The mortared stonework shows sufficient remnants of mortar remaining in spots to suggest that at one time the entire surface of the structure was covered, giving the tower a finished surface. Arches connect the eight columns, with the height of the columns ranging from 7 feet 2 inches to 7 feet 10 inches. The arches are made of flat stones set on edge, and the top of each pillar extends outward slightly from the body of the tower above it, suggesting a possible use as support for an additional structure extending outward.

Sockets on the inside wall above each of the columns are theorized to have once supported beams that held up the floor on the first of two stories. There are three windows in the tower and seven niches on the inner wall that do not go all the way through to the exterior. A fireplace built over a pillar has two flues to the outside running within the wall. Both flues curve up and outward away from the firebox and come out on the exterior.

The controversy with the Newport Tower or Old Stone Mill initially was a minor debate between proponents of Carl Christian Rafn's work on Norse antiquities in America and local historians who felt it was the exterior shell from an early colonial windmill of Governor Benedict Arnold.[1] After the tower began appearing in the works of well-known writers such as Henry

The Newport Tower in Touro Park, Newport, Rhode Island (photograph courtesy of Malcolm Pearson).

Wadsworth Longfellow and James Fenimore Cooper, the debate battle between the Norse and Colonial schools took national stage where it remains a topic of great passion and debate.[2]

Archaeologist Philip Ainsworth Means was intrigued by the controversy after reading an article comparing the Newport structure to the Church of the Holy Sepulchre in Cambridge, England.[3] He studied the tower for a number of years and published his research in 1942.[4] Means's primary finding was that the tower predated the colonial settlement of Newport and that Arnold merely modified it for use as a windmill.

Means honed in on the key point of Governor Arnold having ordered the structure built between 1675 and 1677 as a replacement windmill for Newport. This theory was first proposed in 1851 by Newport clergyman Charles Brooks,[5] apparently in response to the growing popularity of Longfellow's Norse origins of the tower.

Means casts doubts about the Arnold theory but does not present a strong case for the Norse. Initially, Means believed Rafn was correct in identifying the tower as a 12th-century Norse baptistery, but before he could go to press, Hjalmar Holand swayed his opinion. Means had favorably reviewed Holand's

1940 book, *Westward from Vinland* for the *New York Times* and was contacted by Holand.[6]

Holand was working on a subsequent book of new evidence in his lifelong mission of authenticating the Kensington Rune Stone. Half of this new book would be devoted to the Newport Tower as the headquarters of a Viking expedition in 1355 that headed inland, resulting in the 1362 massacre documented on the Kensington Stone.[7]

Means adopted Holand's position that the only way to determine the age and origin of the Newport structure was to compare its features to similar features on stone structures in Europe. Means focused on three features that he felt distinguished the tower from any other building in the western hemisphere — the columns, the windows and the fireplace.

Although it does not have a chimney like the Newport Tower, an octagonal church in Store Hedinge in Zealand, Denmark, is the structure that Means found most closely resembled the Newport Tower. This church has windows splayed in both directions and eight columns surrounded by an ambulatory with the columns supporting a clerestory — exactly what Means envisioned as the original form of the Newport Tower.

Means was also intrigued by the window in the apse of the remains of the Orphir Church in the Orkney Islands. The Orphir Church, the remains of a round Romanesque Church, was dedicated to St. Nicholas and disassembled in the middle of the 18th century in order to use the stone to construct a since-demolished parish church. Today, all that remains is the apse, along with a small section of the eastern wall of the nave.

The Royal Commission on the Ancient and Historical Monuments of Scotland considers the ruins unique in Scotland, having been "built after the model of the Church of the Holy Sepulchre in Jerusalem through Scandinavian prototypes and it can be dated between A.D. 1090 and 1160."[8] The building is also mentioned in the *Orkneyinga Saga* as being next to the Earl's Bu or drinking hall in 1135.[9]

Means found the window at Orphir to be double-splayed, similar to the windows in the Newport Tower.[10] This, he noted, was as opposed to windows that splay inward as is typical in 12th- and 13th-century structures. The similarity between Orphir and Newport, Means concluded, must indicate both structures were constructed around the same time.[11]

The other problem with the Newport Tower as Arnold's windmill is the placement of the flue and chimney, as noted by civil engineer Edward Adams Richardson in his 1960 study.[12] Sparks and gases would escape from the chimney flue due to it venting out of the wall only seven feet above the fireplace. In order for the tower to function as a windmill, the cap containing the sails must overhang the tower and freely turn. The overhanging roof, as well as the sails and turning arm, would be vulnerable to any of the sparks and flames emitted from the flue. Richardson's conclusion was that the tower's builder constructed an ordinary fireplace if built prior to 1400 A.D., but a 1675 A.D. or later date indicated a "very inferior design and concept."[13]

Richardson concurred with Means's suggestion that an ambulatory or some sort of round structure surrounded the lower level and calculated the size of the enclosure as potentially extending out 24 feet, based on the weight-bearing capacity of the structure.[14]

Based strictly on its design, Richardson contends there are absolutely no possible ways that the tower was built for a milling operation — the floors are not the correct strength, the fireplace would explosively ignite dust from the milling operation, there was no way to get the equipment into the structure and the surrounding ambulatory would interfere with the turning sails. Richardson does believe that the tower could have been converted to a windmill later at slightly less cost than constructing a new windmill from scratch,[15] but that the Newport Tower was originally built for one purpose — as a signal tower.

Richardson analyzed the window placement and concluded that the upper-story windows were for observation, with the upper floor designed so that a sentry could scan the horizon at night without the light from the lower floor affecting vision. The lower floor would be bright with light from the fireplace reflecting off the plastered walls and out the larger windows into the night sky. The varying sizes of the larger windows would affect intensity and distance of the light projection. Depending on the window, Richardson calculated the candlepower emanating to be visible at sea upwards of 6 to 8 nautical miles offshore.[16] Calculating the azimuths from the windows, Richardson explained how using the lights from the windows could easily be used as course correction beacons to navigate the route from Vineland Sound into Rhode Island Sound and finally into Narragansett Bay.

Richardson's belief that the windows were specifically oriented as navigation aids was echoed by William Penhallow, an astronomer at the University of Rhode Island, who published findings on possible archaeoastronomical significance of the windows.[17]

Andrew Sinclair sees a similarity between Richardson's beacon theory and a church at Corstorphine, near Edinburgh, where Henry St. Clair's daughter Jean is buried. Sinclair claims it is "a similar beacon tower, where the firelight was reflected on the second story to guide the way for travelers by land or sea."[18] The comparison is a stretch. The Corstorphine Old Parish Church did historically function as a guide for travelers prior to the Scottish Reformation, but on a very different scale from a beacon for ships at sea. The church has a niche in the external wall of the east gable of the chancel where an oil lamp was raised each night to guide travelers along the path through the marshes between the stream and the village.[19]

The age of the Newport Tower came to the forefront again in 1991 with the arrival of the Committee for Research on Norse Activities in North America A.D. 1000–1500, a multi-national consortium studying the Vikings in North America as a whole. The Newport Tower was to be one of the sites examined. After a thorough photogrammetric survey, an attempt to date the tower was made using carbon-14 to test the lime mortar. The use of C-14 dating on inorganic material, a new testing tool, was successfully used to date medieval churches in Scandinavia.[20]

Norse Committee founder and chairman Jørgen Siemonson held a press conference announcing that the C-24 test results showed that the tower was probably built in the mid–17th century and possibly as early as the 16th century.[21] Siemonson closed the press conference by jokingly suggesting that if anyone could disprove the dating of the tower, it would be James Whittall and his Early Sites Research Society. Siemonson was aware of Whittall's interest in the tower, which Whittall believed was constructed by Henry Sinclair and his Knights in the style of Norman Romanisk architecture, inspired from the Holy Sepulchre in Jerusalem, as were many churches in Europe.[22] Whittall honed in on the photogrammetric results of the unit of measurement to build the tower. The Norse Committee's report was detailed enough to determine the standard unit, something numerous previous attempts had tried with great variation in results.

Johannes Hertz, a medieval archaeologist and head of the Danish State Antiquary's Archaeological Secretariat, considered museum curator Helge Nielsen to be one of the best in the field for determining units of measure.[23] Nielsen fed the data into a computer, resulting in a calculated unit of 23.3 centimeters. When compared to the English foot at 30.48 cm and the Danish-Norwegian foot at 31.5 cm, it posed a problem for both pre–Columbian and colonial construction advocates. Nielsen had no explanation, suggesting that the standard of 23.3 cm was similar to half of an "alen" or "ell," used in Norway and Iceland in the transitional period between the Viking Age and Middle Age.[24] This measurement matched up with Whittall's theory that Henry Sinclair built the tower as a church toward the end of his voyage. Suddenly Philip Means's notes on the Orphir Church apse in the Orkneys[25] were looking prophetic.

At the same time that the Newport Historical Society was publishing the results of the Norse Committee in their journal, a panel of experts on

Henry Sinclair and his 1398 expedition convened the Sinclair Symposium in Kirkwall, Orkney.[26] Among the speakers was James Whittall. He presented his conclusions on the Newport Tower, based on his comparative studies of key features such as the arches, windows and key stones. His conclusion was that the tower had far more in common architecturally with medieval Orkadian and Norse structures than it had to colonial New England buildings.[27] His conclusion was that the Sinclair expedition was the most likely candidate and that Sinclair built the tower specifically to employ the same sacred geometry of round towers built by Knights Templar. Suddenly the Westford Knight went from memorial to a fallen explorer to a Knight Templar outpost.

Whittall was building on research first published in 1948 by Herbert Claiborne Pell, Jr., U.S. Minister to Portugal from 1937 to 1941. Pell returned from his diplomatic duties with the thought that the Newport Tower was similar to the charola located in the Templar Castle and the Convent of the Knights of Christ in Tomar, Portugal.[28] *Castelo Templário and Convento da Ordem de Cristo* is a combination castle and convent, built by the Knights Templar in 1160.

The charola, an octagonal altar painted and carved in the Byzantine style, still stands, as do many other round and octagonal altars throughout Portugal.[29] After the Templar Order dissolved in 1314, Portugal's King Dinis founded a new order, the Knights of the Order of Christ, which assumed the functions, properties and members of the banned Templars, including the castle at Tomar. This new order would achieve results more long lasting than military battles under the aegis of Grand Master Infante Dom Henrique, Duke of Viseu, better known as Prince Henry the Navigator. Portuguese ships and soldiers went forth, charting new maps and transforming Portugal into a world power with colonies in Africa, India, and South America.

Pell theorizes that the Newport Tower was built in the style of the Portuguese charola by shipwrecked Portuguese explorer Miguel Corte Real, the same Portuguese explorer credited with the Dighton Rock inscription.[30]

According to Pell's theory, the Corte Real crew built the Newport Tower as both a chapel and a watchtower, fully expecting that Miguel's oldest brother, Vasco Añes Corte Real, would come searching for him, as Miguel had gone looking for his missing brother Gaspar.[31] Corte Real chose to build a stone tower instead of a wooden one, Pell continues, because fewer tools were required for a stone tower.[32] If Corte Real had the tools to build a wooden tower, he could have simply built a replacement boat instead. Since Pohl has Sinclair building a new ship to return to Scotland, he had the tools to work in wood, raising doubts as to the Sinclair association with the Newport Tower.

Manuel Luciano da Silva, the most ardent of the contemporary scholars of the Dighton Rock, agrees with Pell.[33] Dr. da Silva goes further, stating that the actual use of the Newport Tower could be a watchtower, a Catholic chapel or even a windmill — any one of those origins would still suggest a Portuguese builder, since contrary to American perceptions of the Netherlands, Portugal had many more windmills than even the Dutch.[34]

Although the charola in Tomar is unquestionably Templar, as architectural historian Sir Howard Montagu Colvin notes, a circular church building is not exclusively a Templar design nor did the Templars exclusively build circular churches.[35]

Even if research could identify the function of the Newport Tower, it still would not pinpoint the builders as colonial, Portuguese, Norse or English without a specific age for the tower. Pell's Portuguese theory did, however, produce an extremely tenuous association between the Newport Tower and the Knights Templar that Whittall would use to connect the tower to the Westford Knight.

12

The Boat Stone

In 1967, Frank Glynn published a report on a second carved stone found nearby in Westford depicting a single-mast ship, an arrow and the number 184.[1] Local resident Howard Smart recalled the rock from his youth and dutifully reported it to Glynn in 1956. Glynn encouraged Smart to track down the rock, which had been moved to safety in a neighborhood barn when the roads were widened in 1932.

Originally located about 2 miles from the Knight at Wyman's Corner, the intersection of North Street and Groton Road (State Road 40), the stone was also considered an Indian carving by local residents. In 1963, the stone was finally tracked down by Smart, who obtained it from the barn of William Wyman and convinced Wyman to donate the carving to the Westford Historical Society.

Glynn's letter to Lethbridge[2] announcing the Boat Stone specifically notes the stone being donated to the Historical Society, which did not have storage or display facilities (the society's museum did not open until 1980) with arrangements made to display the rock in the lobby of Westford's Fletcher Library. The president of the Historical Society added signage identifying the rock as an 1840 marker on the Indian trail to let the Natives know there was a trading ship in Boston accepting furs. Glynn was scornful of the identification, there was no fourth digit to suggest a 17th-century date and the ship was not typical of the time period.

Glynn's more detailed talk at the Eastern States Archaeological Federation conference in 1966, later excerpted in the newsletter of the New England Antiquities Research Association,[3] indicated that by the ESAF conference Wyman had deeded the rock to the Fletcher Library. The rock remains at the Fletcher, now prominently displayed on the lower level near the meeting rooms and parking lot entrance.

Glynn interviewed Wyman and Edwin Gould, a direct descendant of one of Westford's original settlers. Both recalled the rock being located in the gore formed where the road intersected at least as far back as when they were teenagers, some 60–70 years prior.

The oblate spheroid stone is a glacial erratic, roughly 250 pounds in weight, roughly 26" × 18" × 7½" thick. It is inscribed with the image of a ship, an arrow and three characters that appear to be the number 184. The 8 numeral appears to have an unusual open upper loop, which could be indicative of the style of the lettering when the rock was carved or an attempt to avoid carving in a preexisting fracture on the rock surface that would intersect the numeral at the top of the upper loop. There is an early photograph of the Boat Stone that was taken by Glynn soon after the rock arrived at the Fletcher Library that could be evidence that the top of the 8 was actually a closed

Also found in Westford, the "boat stone" is now on display at Westford's J. V. Fletcher Library (photograph courtesy of Cindy Glynn).

loop. If the fracture in the face of that rock was actually a vein of a softer mineral or the top of the loop was a more shallow cut than the rest of the numeral, the appearance of an open top loop may be from decades of curious fingers tracing the numbers and gradually wearing down the surface to appear flush with the surface. The photo is inconclusive and Glynn's subsequent chalking of the stone seems to indicate Glynn felt the loop was not closed.

If the open loop on the number 8 is deliberate, it offers a possible age. The open top 8 was used in some medieval texts, most notably by Johannes de Sacrobosco,[4] the 13th-century Augustinian scholar who wrote some of the most widely read and influential books on mathematics and astronomy of his era. Sacrobosco's *Tractatus de Sphaera*[5] was one of the most popular astronomical books at the time. Before the development of the printing press, it was widely used in manuscript form and in 1472, became one of the first science texts to be published. Sacrobosco's book reintroduced Greek astronomy to Europe and provided the basis for teaching astronomy including celestial navigation. In manuscript form, it would certainly have been of interest to a literate nobleman with a vested interest in navigation such as Henry Sinclair.

The image of the ship on the stone is consistent with that of a cog: flat-bottomed with a single-mast with a square sail, all trademarks of a style of ship used into the 14th century. The ship shows a single row of eight circles which have been identified variously as oarports, portholes or cannon ports. The ship image also depicts a short bowsprit extending out with rigging correctly placed from the bowsprit to the top of the mast. The surface of the stone makes it difficult to tell, but there may be a faint line etched along the stern indicating a sternpost rudder. There is one possible discrepancy in the ship's sail. There is a second yard, either acting as a crossbeam on the sail, or alternately, suggesting the addition of a topsail. The few images of cogs that exist from the period appear to have a single square–rigged sail,[6] but design modifications were made as conditions dictated. If Pohl is correct and Sinclair built a new ship after the departure of Zeno, there is no way to determine what changes Sinclair would have added based on local conditions and available resources.

Most images of cogs typically portray them with forecastles and aftcastles;[7] the image on the Boat Stone shows neither. This lack of castles may actually be evidence of the accuracy of the image. N. A. M. Rodger of the National Maritime Museum in Greenwich, England, points out that the castles, light staging erected on the ship, were originally temporary constructs added when the vessel was used for military purposes.[8] Jaap Morel, Director of the Nederlands Instituut voor Scheep en Onderwaterarcheologie, concurs, pointing out that of the 35 cogs recovered and examined by archaeologists, none showed evidence of a castle.[9]

Cogs were shell built, the exterior hull being built first with a skeleton of support framing added into the completed hull. The eight small divots carved into the hull of the ship carved on the Boat Stone may represent cross-beams, used in cogs for lateral support of the hull. These beams were part of the framework added to the completed hull and protruded through the hull.

By comparison, the Bremen Cog, capsized in a 1380 shipwreck and salvaged in 1962, has five such crossbeams. Now on display in the Deutsches Schiffahrtsmuseum in Bremerhaven, the Bremen Cog's keel is 15.6 meters long with a carrying capacity of little more than 50 tons.[10] The cog also bears more than a passing resemblance to the oldest of three ship petroglyphs found in Machias Bay, Maine.[11]

T. C. Lethbridge was less concerned with the ship image on the Boat Stone than with the number 184. He felt that the ship and arrow were a heraldic symbol and pointer respectively, representing directions to a location 184 paces away where the blazon of Sinclair hung on his winter quarters, a custom of medieval times to indicate the lodging of a Knight at the local inn for the illiterate.[12]

Glynn divided the area into quadrants and began a systematic search in a radius 184 paces around the original location of the stone, the junction of two Indian trails. In 1966, Glynn found a 32' × 40' stone enclosure, about three feet high, with a fresh water spring nearby, now dried up. The low walls and proximity to water suggest a colonial structure, an animal pen or oversized spring house, not a 12th-century campsite.[13]

Frank Glynn's locating a stone structure 184 paces away is tentative proof at best. Between stonewalls, cellar holes and glacial debris, you're liable to find something that could be interpreted as significant in any search of the New England countryside. Additionally, Glynn appears to have used U.S. units of distance. In the United States, a pace is 30 inches. 184 paces would be a search radius of 460 feet. In England, however, since at least the 12th century, one pace is 60 inches, creating a search radius of 920 feet.

Using either radius, the search would be on property that had been actively farmed almost back to the 17th century. The house nearest the stone enclosure was the Wyman house, better known in local history circles as the Jacob Wright house. The house was erected before the 1729 incorporation of Westford and it has a stone in the walls of the cellar bearing the chiseled date of 1717.[14]

The house was demolished in 2000 and the property has had several new houses built on subdivided lots. Using James Whittall's maps, it is possible to plot comparative locations, and it is apparent that a diagonal line starting at Wyman's Corner near where the Boat Stone was recovered and ending at Glynn's stone enclosure would also intersect the Jacob Wright House, placing the alleged Sinclair relict about 150 feet into a farm yard that had been in use for 300 years. Occam's razor suggests that any structure in the immediate vicinity of a farm is going to have an ancillary function to that farm.

Wyman's Corner is at the junction of Indian trails that became colonial paths that evolved into municipal streets. Hodgman's town history indicates that roads past the Jacob Wright house were among the first laid out by the new town in 1730.[15]

As an alternative, instead of pointing to a Sinclair base, the stone could just as easily be a marker pointing a traveler to the Knight carving at the crossroad. The distance from the Boat Stone to the Knight is roughly 184 chains or 2.3 miles (3.7 kilometers).[16] Since Sinclair anticipated returning to Scotland, it would seem logical that the Gunn clan would wish to visit the site of their fallen leader in the future, so with a theoretical marker along the Merrimack indicating where to moor and head up the trail, there would need to be directional aid at the path's fork, such as the Boat Stone. This use of the galley would be appropriate — the galley occurs frequently as a design element in grave art. Antiquarian Lord Archibald Campbell's study of Argyllshire grave art finds galleys common on grave slabs, effigies and crosses, even noting a font in a churchyard with a simple galley as the only decoration.[17] Not only is the ship a component of the Gunn coat of arms and the use of a galley prevalent on gravestones, but it is used as a component in heraldic art with appropriate symbolism — an 1898 treatise on heraldic symbolism notes that the lymphad or galley symbolizes a notable sea expedition.[18]

Steer and Bannerman[19] note that although the terms galleys, birlinn and lymphad are used interchangeably today, the records of the time indicate they were distinctively different vessels. In 2004, Wallace-Murphy identifies the image on the Boat Stone as an Orkney Galley, also known as a Hebridean Birlinn.[20] A direct descendent of the Viking longships with steeply pitched stem and stern, the most significant difference was the replacement of the steering-board by a stern rudder.[21] The eight oarports on the Boat Stone would indicate some vessel smaller than a birlinn, based on a 1615 Scottish Privy Council document differentiating birlins from galleys by the number of oarports.[22] There are discrepancies in this identification: the Boat Stone shows a topsail, a bowsprit and a less pronounced pitch to the stem and stern. The image of a ship carved on the Knight's shield with a high stem and stern could more readily be interpreted as a birlinn, but Wallace-Murphy could not compare the ship on the Knight's shield with a Hebridean birlinn; the image of the Knight used in his book is a variant interpretation of the Knight, drawn without the shield with the image that might bolster his case.

In 2007, the Boat Stone was sent to Minnesota for petrographic analysis to see if the age of the carvings could be determined using microscopic examinations.[23] The tests were conducted under the supervision of Scott F. Wolter, a Minnesota geologist who had previously published a book on the Kensington Rune Stone[24] declaring that geology proved the carving was too old to be a hoax by Olof Öhman (1855–1935), based on mica degradation within the inscribed runes. Although anthropologist Alice Beck Kehoe, author of her own book on the Kensington Rune Stone[25] and a longtime advocate of pre–Columbian transpacific contact, wrote the foreword to Wolter's 2005 book on the Kensington Rune Stone, most archaeologists remained unimpressed. Dr. Larry J. Zimmerman, professor of anthropology and museum studies at Purdue University,[26] is among the critics, noting that although Wolter and his co–author Richard Nielsen both are trained scientists, their technique of dating inscriptions via mica weathering and surface alteration has never been published in a peer-reviewed journal, so it has not been evaluated by independent sources.[27]

Wolter's results in Westford were less than impressive, restating the obvious — the rock was a glacial erratic and the carvings were man-made, created by a dull pointed tool used to peck out the lines. He also noted the carved area "has a dark gray to black colored, organic-like material" of unknown origin, apparently unaware that 40 years of contact with hands that touch and trace the carvings on the rock will leave oils and grime. The Boat Stone was returned safely to its home in Westford's Fletcher Library, no worse for wear other than a 1¾" by 2½" long hole that was drilled in the stone where a core sample was taken.

In his subsequent book, Wolter gives his opinion on the two Westford carvings. He feels the only man-made portion of the Knight carving is the sword itself, which was still significant in that a sword represented the burial of a Templar.[28]

Wolter also suggests that the open-end 8 might actually be ♉, the zodiac symbol of Taurus and the numeral 4 might actually be ♃, the astrological symbol for the planet Jupiter, making the Boat Stone a directional map for astronomical navigation.[29]

James Bennett, Director of the Museum of the History of Science at Oxford University, notes that common navigation instruments in use at the time of the Sinclair expedition were the quadrant, the cross staff and the astrolabe.[30] These instruments all work by lining up the horizon and a celestial object through the navigation device, which allowed the viewer to compute

Westford's J. V. Fletcher Library overlooks the town common. A half-mile from the Knight, it has become a key location for research, both because it has a "Westford Knight Collection" and because it is guardian of the Boat Stone (photograph courtesy of Terry Deveau).

a simple altitude angle that can be used to determine latitude. James Morrison's study of the astrolabe notes that astrolabes were firmly established in Europe by the end of the 13th century, but Bennett adds that they were "practically impossible to use at sea, and the navigator had to go ashore to make any worthwhile observations."[31]

The need of the navigator to leave the ship to take readings on the shore could also be a factor in determining the viability of the Machias Bay petroglyph, the drilled holes on Manana Island and even the Newport Tower as landing points for the Sinclair expedition.[32] 1४4 would not be standard citation, but it is within the realm of possibility, assuming it could be interpreted.

The lack of frame of reference is the crux of the problem with the carving on the Boat Stone; without the key, the 184 is at best permutable in the various theories. The distance from Bodwell's Falls on the Merrimack River to Prospect Hill via Stony Brook and the Merrimack River is roughly 184 furlongs or 23 miles. Bodwell's Falls would be impassable for Sinclair's ship. Anchored there, now the site of the Great Stone Dam in Lawrence, Massachusetts, by foot or by portage of smaller boats, 184 furlongs would bring Sinclair to Westford. Unfortunately, there is no evidence to support this or any other interpretation of the numbers.

Without knowing the unit of measure or purpose of the images, there is ample room for interpretation of the message on the Boat Stone. An arrow and 184 rods (.575 mile) would suggest a colonial-era boundary marker but doesn't explain the ship. Without context, the stone could just as easily be a secret road marker from the 1860s as a medieval carving. The Samuel Fitch house on Westford's Powers Road, now a bed & breakfast, is locally known as a local Underground Railroad stop. It is roughly six miles from Wyman's Corner. Historian Wilbur Siebert spent decades tracing fugitive slave routes but did not note a Westford stop, but he does refer a route heading from Concord, Massachusetts, via Concord, New Hampshire to Canterbury, New Hampshire, which would run right up Route 3.[33] A route from Powers Road away from the center town would lead up Concord Road toward Forge Pond and would connect to North Main Street, becoming North Street and leading straight to Wyman's Corner and Groton Road, the most direct way to Route 3.[34]

Also, 184 miles is the approximate distance to the Canadian border up Route 3 before I-93 was constructed.[35] With the stone positioned so that the arrow designates which road to take at the fork at Wyman's Corner to reach Route 3 (3.7 miles) further along Groton Road (or 5 miles to the Merrimack River), the ship becomes a symbol of freedom as in the slave spiritual "Old Ship of Zion."

Alternately, if the path followed the river, it would lead past Old Tyng Road and the "Tyngsboro Map Stone." Within sight of the Merrimack River on an outcropping of bedrock, the carving was first discovered circa 1920 and assumed to be an Indian petroglyph. Named "The Wannalancet Map Rock" accordingly, after Wannalancet, a Pennacook Indian chief believed to be buried nearby, the image carved into the rock appears to show the path of the river from its source at the confluence of the Pemigewasset and Winnipesaukee Rivers in New Hampshire, the southward flow into Massachusetts and then the sudden turn northeast to the mouth at Newburyport, Massachusetts. The carving shows heavy patina and at least one researcher[36] has suggested it is old enough to be pre–Columbian in origin. When the New England Antiquities Research Association rediscovered the carving in 1970, it was noted as atypical of Indian petroglyphs and potentially affiliated with the Westford Boat Stone.[37]

Whether it's an Underground Railroad relic or somehow associated with the Sinclair party's further explorations up the river, it is interesting to note that the Tyngsborough stone map is affiliated with a river navigation hazards by proximity; it is located near Wicassic Falls, roughly halfway between Pawtucket Falls, Massachusetts, in Lowell and Taylor's Falls in Nashua, New Hampshire.

The use of lithic directional aids, like the interpretation of southern slave spiritual lyrics as secret directional aids, is fraught with controversy, as demonstrated by use of the spiritual "Follow the Drinking Gourd" as specific directions rather than the "poetic articulation of black desires for freedom expressed through the syncretism of early African American religion" and Christian belief systems.[38] James Kelly, a historian, notes that the "propagation of the claim of a coded message in the lyrics of 'Follow the Drinking Gourd' reflects a propensity of all peoples, not just enslaved African Americans, to organize their past and present through shared, popular stories rather than researched histories."

Similar sentiment could be offered for both the Boat Stone and the Westford Knight. In pursuit of popular story, the carvings veered from carefully considered, well-researched but controversial historical artifacts into the realm of speculative non-fiction, the home of Knights Templar, lost ancient wisdom and alternative science.

13

The Knights Templar

Although James Whittall had been considering the Sinclair voyage for some time,[1] his theories never reached the mainstream press. However, his work suggesting a connection between the Westford Knight and the Newport Tower reached the Internet just as the technology was hitting its stride.

The various Sinclair clan associations were creating websites to discuss their common ancestors and the subsequent proliferation on the Internet brought Henry's trip and speculative Knights Templar affiliations of the Westford and Newport sites to the attention of untold thousands. The new social connectivity allowed the Sinclairs and Gunns to plan and launch a 600th-anniversary celebration of Henry's trip to North America in 1998. By this time, both *Holy Blood, Holy Grail* and *The Temple and the Lodge* had been published, laying the groundwork for Andrew Sinclair's *The Sword and the Grail*.[2] Suddenly, the Sinclairs were part of the bloodline of Jesus and Mary Magdalene's secret offspring and Rosslyn Chapel was a hotbed of Knight Templar–inspired Freemason ancient relicts/wisdom.

The original Knights Templar, a monastic military order, was formed during the 12th-century Crusades. It was originally a small order of nine warrior monks pledged to protect pilgrims on the dangerous route to the Holy Land. The order was granted quarters atop the Temple Mount within the Al-Aqsa Mosque, which the Knights believed to be have been built atop the Temple of Solomon—hence the name *"pauvres chevaliers du temple,"* Poor Knights of the Temple or the Knights Templar.

The leader of the fledgling Knights, Hugues de Payens, was at the Council of Troyes in 1128 where St. Bernard de Clairvaux was a major figure. The Knights Templar adopted the Rule of St. Benedict as embraced by the Cistercians, taking vows of poverty, chastity and obedience as they waged religious war in the Holy Land.

The Order grew rapidly with the support of such a major church figure as Bernard, gaining Papal privileges that effectively placed the Order under Papal control, bypassing bishopric and sovereign influence.

Stylized figure of Knight Templar Jean de Dreux, based on his grave marker in St.Yved de Braine, created by Abbé Bernard de Montfaucon for the second volume of his *Les Monumens de la Monarchie Françoise* (1730). The garb is consistent with the few other extant Knight Templar graves.

The Order was supported by a growing infrastructure primarily focused on funding the military campaigns. They developed a system of letters of credit for pilgrims who were journeying to the Holy Land where the pilgrim deposited funds with the Order in Europe before beginning their journey in return for a document to be used for reimbursement at their destination.

Through the 12th and 13th centuries, the Order received large donations of land in Europe and the Middle East. Their operation expanded beyond building churches and raising castles into farms, manufacturing and shipping, geared toward underwriting crusades. Although things were going well in Europe, the Crusaders were losing ground in the Middle East.

After the Crusader forces were driven entirely from the Holy Land, orders such as the Templars and the Hospitallers (Knights of St. John) began to lose their luster. Blame for the humiliating loss of Jerusalem and the Middle Eastern lands began to shift to them. The Knights Templar was now a wealthy order with property holdings across Europe, but the loss of the Holy Land essentially eliminated its purpose and therefore made it an easy target, vulnerable to political machinations.

That vulnerability was exploited on October 13, 1307, when the Knights Templar properties in France were simultaneously raided by agents of King Philip the Fair. British historian Peter Partner suggests that Philip's attack on the Templars was based not only on a way to default on the considerable amount of money he had borrowed from them but also his belief that the Templars were undermining his plans for a new Military Crusading Order to be formed by the merger of the Templars and Hospitallers (and led by a son of Philip).[3] Arrested knights were later tortured into admitting a variety of charges ranging from generic heresy and apostasy to specific acts such as defiling the cross and worshipping Baphomet.[4] Philip began pressuring other monarchs to arrest Templars and seize their holdings.

Within a month, with the French Templars beginning, under torture, to admit their guilt, Pope Clement V ordered that Templars should be detained throughout Christendom. Malcolm Barber[5] notes that on the Iberian Peninsula, the situation was different; the Templars had been on the front lines of a crusade against the Muslims in Portugal and were still an active military presence in Alemtejo, along with the Hospitallers and the Knights of Calatrava. Other historians suggest that the Military Orders were the sole military force keeping the province out of Muslim control.[6] When the Papal decree to detain the Knights was issued, the Military Orders had been maintaining control of Alemtejo and the Algarve for over 50 years, driving out Muslims and finally occupying the area between 1225 and 1250. Having roughly doubled the size of Portugal from 55,000 to 90,000 square kilometers,[7] Portugal's

Dinis I was not inclined to lose his control over Algarve. The trials of the Portuguese Templars were torture-free and expedient and the Knights were soon found innocent by the ecclesiastical court of the Bishop of Lisbon. When the Order was subsequently dissolved, Dinis created a new order in 1317 — *Christi Militia*, The Knights of Christ. By 1319, Dinis had Papal permission for the Knights of Christ to assume the Templar estates,[8] with a headquarters in the Algarve as a base against the Muslims. Between the former Templars who became Knights of Christ and the Templar holdings that the new Order controlled, for all intents and purposes, the military presence continued uninterrupted.

Meanwhile, the interrogations conducted across Christendom produced varying results, depending on how strongly the local monarch disliked the French king compared to the Templars. Alan Forey notes that while the Knights in Cyprus and the Iberian peninsula maintained their innocence, seriously incriminating confessions were gained primarily in France and parts of Italy, usually after deprivation, torture and threats.[9]

In England, Edward II had been monarch for only four months when the arrests in France started. He refused to heed Philip's request for immediate arrest and waited until he was required to do so by Pope Clement.[10] Helen J. Nicholson's study of the trials in the British Isles[11] emphasizes the variation in scale between the Templar presence in France versus the British Isles. At the time of the British apprehensions in 1308, there were only a total of 144 Knights[12] in England, Scotland and Ireland combined and none in Wales.

Forey notes that the three men in England who made significant admissions of guilt — Stephen of Stapelbrigg, Thomas Totty and John of Stoke — did so at a late stage in the interrogation, when torture was finally demanded by Papal authorities after English authorities stalled.[13] Although only these three confessed serious charges, most of the other Templars held in custody in 1311 admitted that they were so defamed that they could not clear themselves. They abjured their errors, and eighty-one Templars received absolution in two group ceremonies in London and York.

In 1813, literary scholar François Raynouard published a fairly well-balanced study on the Templar trials based on newly uncovered Papal documents shipped to Paris.[14] He noted Templar holdings in Scotland and Ireland were so comparatively sparse that they remained part of English jurisdiction until the Order's dissolution.[15] So, in spite of limited Scottish documentation, it is possible to postulate what was happening. The Templar arrests started in England in January 1308. Robert Aitken[16] notes that by the time trials began in Edinburgh in 1309, only two Templars, Walter de Clifton and William de Middleton, were left to be arrested. When the Knights Clifton and Middleton appeared before the inquisitors at Holyrood, they vowed that they were the only two of the Order left in Scotland and that the rest "fled beyond the sea."[17] This comment has fueled claims of the Templars escaping to North America, but Aitken later expands on the comment reporting the only specific example he could find of a Knight fleeing over the sea was not heading west; John de Hufflete fled over the sea to Norway or Denmark.[18]

The trials of the Templars between 1307 and 1312 rapidly escalated into a battle of political will between King Philip IV of France and Pope Clement V. Clement was well aware he had limited options without provoking a military intervention and/or another schism within the church. Barber points out that these actions by a secular monarch actually represented a "frontal assault" on the authority of Clement V and the Church in general. Clement V knew it was not simply the Templars, but the Papacy itself which was at stake.[19]

Clement knew he could not control the deteriorating situation unless he had papal representatives interview the Templar leaders, whom Philip held incommunicado at the castle of Chinon in Tours, rather than allowing them to appear before a Papal Curia. Eventually his representative did interrogate the leaders, but the evidence for this was lost and the proof was contained in a letter preserved in the French Chancery, making the incident appear apocryphal. Barbara Frale's recent discovery of the Chinon Parchment[20] shows that Clement initially absolved the Templar leaders of heresy, though he did find them guilty of the considerably less serious charge of immorality, and that he planned to reform the order. However, as Frale interprets the political machinations, Clement, to preserve the unity of the church against Philip, reversed his decision and suppressed the order in 1312, sacrificing the Order to preserve the Church.[21]

The Papal Bull "Vox in Excelsis," dated March 22, 1312, decreed the dissolution but not the condemnation of the order, citing the scandal of the trial and the probable poor condition of Templar properties. The Order was technically abolished due to obsolescence, not because of any crime. Because the Templars were not guilty under Clement's legal hairsplitting, the Knights were allowed either to join a different military order or return to the secular life with a pension for life. The remaining Templar holdings were turned over to the Knights Hospitaller. The Templar leaders, still imprisoned by Philip in spite of having been granted judicial immunity by Clement, continued to declare their innocence. This sent the Bishops back to the Pope to see how to proceed. Philip used the opportunity to seize the Templar Grand Master Jacque de Molay and Geoffrey de Charny, the Preceptor of Normandy and had them burned at the stake as relapsed heretics. Frale notes poet Geoffrey de Paris witnessed the execution and reported that de Molay called upon God to judge Philip, for attacking the Templars without provocation, and Clement, for abandoning the Order. Both were dead within a year, giving rise to the first of the legends of the Templar, that of a curse placed by de Molay.[22]

Along with the various charges of heresy, defilement of the Cross and sodomy leveled against the Templars, charges of black magic were leveled. In the trial itself, the Templars were accused of worshipping Baphomet. The supernatural charges were convenient for Philip and a precursor of two centuries of witch hysteria about to sweep Europe. Trevor-Roper, in his essay "European Witch-Craze of the Sixteenth and Seventeenth Centuries," considers the Templar ordeal a "sorcery trial" similar to Joan of Arc's trial (who was also burned as a relapsed heretic); there were "political exploitations of a social fear and a social ideology whose origins were to be found at a deeper level," similar to the later advent of McCarthyism.[23] Partner concurs with this assessment, noting that the late medieval church was experiencing a shift in values that was causing a sense of alienation in the populace that evolved into a pathological fear of demonic possession.[24] In 1307, Partner continues, charges of witchcraft were a popular way of denouncing one's competition in the court of Philip. The practice then spread to England and the Papal courts.[25]

Social historian Peter Gay designates the period of 1300 to 1700 "the era of pagan Christianity" as Europe struggled to reconcile orthodox faith with a new interest in ancient paganism, particularly the Greeks and Romans of antiquity.[26] Astrology, necromancy, and alchemy worked alongside Christian spirituality—Gay notes one example of Roger Bacon explaining the rise of Christianity as "a fortunate conjunction of the planets Mercury and Jupiter."[27]

Just as the Templars appeared to be relegated to a footnote in history obscured by the roots of the Reformation and the Hundred Year's War, German magic scholar Heinrich Cornelius Agrippa von Nettesheim wrote *De Occulta Philosophia*.[28] Agrippa's 1533 book lists the Templars as an example of evil magicians, right alongside witches, heretics, pagans and Gnostics. Agrippa's book, although widely read at the time (and still in print), was not influential in opinions of the Templars at the time. Other authors, such as Guillaume Paradin in his 1561 history of Savoy, salaciously elaborated on the story even as other authors such as Jean Bodin sowed the seeds of revolution with such symbols as the Templars as victims of persecution by an unjust monarch.[29]

Even as Templars were juxtaposed by authors as needed, the medieval stone mason guilds were developing into a fraternal order. Originating in the Middle Ages as a way to preserve their professional trade secrets and to protect their wages, historian Margaret Jacob[30] notes that by the 18th century, the

English and Scottish lodges had moved beyond their origins into a social entity, evolving through the Renaissance and Reformation to become the incubator of the Enlightenment.

Robert L. D. Cooper, Curator of the Grand Lodge of Scotland Museum and Library, in his 2006 book notes the development of Freemasonry as a separate entity that appeared in 1599 and developed over nearly a century, as Scottish Masonic lodges began to admit members who had no connection to stonemasonry, evolving into three distinct types of lodges: operative (trade organizations), mixed and speculative (ceremonial fraternities).[31]

Sociologist Mary Ann Clawson theorizes that these fraternal groups developed across Europe as a means to construct social ties that transcended national, religious and social boundaries by creating rituals and ceremonies that were specific to the organization and consistent from one location to another.[32] UCLA historian Margaret Jacob concurs, suggesting that these Masonic lodges functioned as microcosms that incubated the radical concept of social equality and constitutional government.[33]

Sometime during this evolution, the Temple of Solomon begins to appear in Masonic literature. Masonic scholar Alexander Horne pinpoints the change in the origin legend in the period 1390 to 1410, as noted in the transition from Nimrod and the Tower of Babel as found in the Regius manuscript of 1390 to Solomon and the Jerusalem temple in the Cooke manuscript of 1410.[34] According to Horne, this shift arises because the Regius manuscript represents pre–Reformation Catholic attitudes about the Old Testament. Horne suggests that the Cooke manuscript represents the emergence of a Protestant influence in the Masonic traditions.[35] Among the new facets on the influence is association with Solomon's Temple and the pillars Jachin and Boaz.

There are elements in speculative masonry that had their origins in Scottish operative masonry of the 16th century, based on the lack of equivalents in English operative masonry. The most relevant to the Sinclairs and Rosslyn Chapel is the legend of the Two Pillars.

Knoop and Jones[36] noted that the two pillars referred to in the Cooke manuscript were traditionally explained as being Seth's Pillars, those on which the *artes liberals* (seven liberal arts) were carved to perpetuate the knowledge beyond the flood or fire predicted by his father Adam. In his widely popular 1499 book[37] *De Inventoribus Rerum (The Inventors of Everything)*, humanist Polydore Vergil advocated first-century historian Flavius Josephus's position that Adam received all knowledge available to man, which he then passed on to his son Seth. Josephus credits Seth's descendants with discovering astrology, the first mathematic science. To prevent their discoveries from being lost to future generations in the destruction of the universe predicted by Adam, they erected two pillars, one of brick and one of stone, and inscribed their discoveries on both, so that, whether fire or flood destroyed the world, one pillar would survive.

Knoop and Jones stress that these were not Jachin and Boaz, the two pillars set up in the porch of the Temple, as described in 1 Kings VII:21. Stevenson, in his later study agrees, noting that Seth's Pillars had a long Masonic tradition, and that the merging of the Seth Columns into Solomon's Pillars was a fairly late development.[38]

Seth's pillars, continue Knoop and Jones, evolved into the pillars of Solomon's Temple through the Scottish ceremonies associated with the "Mason Word," the term that indicated one mason to another, another Scot-specific element.[39] Robert Kirk, a Scottish clergyman, knew the decreasingly secret words by 1690, casually bringing them up in dinner conversation in London, resulting in the first published record of the secret words being Jachin and Boaz.[40] The Masonic tradition that the pillars set up by Solomon were made hollow to store the Masonic archives appears at the same time, which may represent an attempt to meld the two different legends into one set of pillars.

On May 1, 1707, the Acts of Union resulted in Scotland's political union with England. Scotland's inclusion in the growing British Empire gave rise to a period of peace and economic growth. Freed of the constant war with the English, Scottish philosophers began to emerge. With Scotland's traditional ties to France, the Enlightenment cross-pollinated philosophy in the two countries. While the French embraced humanism to such a fever pitch that it gave birth to revolution, the Scottish blend of practicality and moderation caused a philosophical rift between the two countries. Voltaire, ignoring the Seven Years' War and England's gradual eclipse of France as a world power, was finally provoked by Lord Kames and his *Elements of Criticism*. Kames had the audacity to criticize French playwrights Corneille and Racine, while praising Shakespeare. This was the final straw for Voltaire, who reviewed the book for the *Gazette Littéraire de l'Europe*.[41]

Voltaire's review was published April 4, 1764, and is laden with irony and sarcasm, noting to his amazement that humanity now looks to Scotland for its rules of taste in all the arts instead of the iconic French savoir-faire:

> "C'est un effet admirable des progrès de l'esprit humain qu'aujourd'hui il nous vienne d'Écosse des règles de goût dans tous les arts, depuis le poème épique jusqu'au jardinage. L'esprit humain s'étend tous les jours, et nous ne devons pas désespérer de recevoir bientôt des poétiques et des rhétoriques des îles Orcades."[42]

Sarcasm aside, Voltaire's observation is not entirely incorrect. The Scottish Enlightenment brought forth such significant figures as David Hume,

Adam Smith and James Hutton. This moderation also gave rise to a new philosophy that affected science, politics and the arts — Romanticism.

As the Enlightenment continued its reign in France, the last decades of the 18th century saw the rise of Romanticism in Great Britain and Germany. The Romantic Movement was a reaction to the rational approach of the Enlightenment, with emphasis now on trying to peacefully exist in harmony with nature and the universe instead of trying to control nature and reduce it to formulae.

Romanticism also stressed that culture was what created and defined a nation. The focus shifted to the preservation and development of national languages and folklore, and the spiritual value of local customs and traditions. This included the arts, where Scottish schoolmaster James Macpherson published a collection of Gaelic poems, *The Works of Ossian*.[43] The prose poems in a loose, rhythmical style were filled with supernatural imagery. The book heavily influenced the nascent Romantic Movement and launched new studies of folklore and Celtic languages and inspired such subsequent authors as Johann Wolfgang Goethe,[44] Robert Burns and Walter Scott.

The Enlightenment had viewed the Middle Ages as ignorant and dark times; Edward Gibbon's *History of the Fall of the Roman Empire* denounced the Crusades as "savage fanaticism."[45] Ergo, Romanticism's reaction was to look at the Crusades with nostalgia. Sir Walter Scott's work is typical of the time, with chivalrous knights, fresh from the Crusades, in search of heroic quests and damsels to rescue. Robert Cooper notes that Scott differentiates between Crusaders and Templars, casting the Knights Templar as completely unredeemable villains in *Ivanhoe* (1819) and both of his "Tales of the Crusaders" novels: *The Betrothed* (1825) and *The Talisman* (1825).[46]

Ironically, the use of the Templars as the antithesis of chivalry may have completed a full circle for the ill-fated knights. There are scholars[47] who believe that the entire concept of chivalry and knight-errantry may have been diffused from the Bedouin concept of *al-furusiyya* (horsemanship) and *muru'ah* (courage and honor) by the Templars and the other Military Orders who brought the concept back to the west. This also brings up the question as to whether the original accusation against the Templars of worshipping Baphomet (Mohammed) could have been a distortion of interest in this Arabic chivalry.

The idealized knights of Romantic literature and the Masonic association with the Temple of Solomon had already combined into a new Templar origin legend within Freemason circles, and the myth-building process has never slowed down. Andrew Michael Ramsay, a Scottish-born writer, became an author in France and was knighted into the Order of St. Lazarus of Jerusalem in 1723, a French military order dating back to the Crusades. Initiated into

Freemasonry in London in 1730, Chevalier Ramsay soon became associated with the fledgling Freemasonry movement in France. He was well aware that the humble beginnings of the Masons as a stone laborer guild would not appeal to the French aristocracy that patronized the organization. So, in 1737, Ramsay wrote a speech[48] now commonly known as *Ramsay's Oration*, in which he gave the Masons a pedigree by connecting Freemasonry with the military orders of the Crusades. Although he did not mention the Templars by name, subsequent writers had no problem bridging the short span between the Masonic origins at Solomon's Temple and the original Templar base atop the Temple Mount.

Joseph Freiherr von Hammer-Purgstall, an Austrian-born orientalist of dubious translation skills,[49] made the assertion that the Templars held the Holy Grail, which he surmised through symbols illustrating Gnostic ceremonies on coins, medals and markers found in old Templar churches and buildings in the Danubian Provinces. Hammer-Purgstall further identified the Cup of the Holy Grail as a relict of the Ophites, a Gnostic serpent-worshiping sect of the 2nd century, as was the idol Baphomet that the Templars were accused of worshipping. He claimed this was proof that the Templars were an Ophitic sect. Hammer-Purgstall doesn't stop at the Grail. Guilty by association, he finds evidence of Gnosticism in such classic medieval works as Wolfram of Eschenbach's *Parzifal* and Malory's *Morte D'Arthur*. Such extreme views would be of little note, particularly since they were self-published in *Fundgruben des Orients*, a research journal that Hammer-Purgstall edited, except that the claims incensed the aforementioned literary scholar François Raynouard.[50]

In 1813, Raynouard was determined to counter such nonsensical claims as Hammer-Purgstall's. Raynouard published an article that included his own French summary of the Hammer-Purgstall article as he disputed its key points.[51] In addition to the article running in *Journal des Savants*, a significantly more popular periodical, both the Hammer-Purgstall piece and the Raynouard refutation appeared in Michaud's popular *Histoire des Croisades*.[52] The Templars were now the keepers of the Grail in their growing résumé of lore.

Freemasonry historian René Le Forestier[53] suggests that 18th-century German Freemasonry saw a resurgence in interest in the medieval blend of alchemy, astrology, and necromantic magic known as Hermeticism. Partner concurs, noting that the "Age of Reason" was also "a period of runaway superstition, especially in the Germanic lands, where alchemists were as common as bakers."[54] The German Freemasons rediscovered Agrippa's text on magic which was used by unscrupulous poseurs to create new Masonic myths of secret knowledge passed down from the Templars and only available at the highest (usually fictional) grades of Masonry.[55] In addition to creating a myriad of new Masonic guilds, this "guardians of ancient secrets" lore was a vital key in the metamorphosis of the Templars into a mythical, quasi mystical semblance of their former selves. Once "secret knowledge" became part of the growing myth attached to the organization, every attempt to control or abolish the various secret societies then became obvious conspiracies to either destroy or gain access to the secret knowledge.

Partner considers the 1785 governmental suppression of the Bavarian Illuminist Freemasons as the birth of the first conspiracy plot associated with the Masons, brought to full fruition by Abbé Augustin Barruel, a Jesuit priest exiled to England during the French Revolution. Barruel published his *Mémoires pour Servir à l'Histoire du Jacobinisme* in England, a multi-volume conspiracy theory stating the Knights Templar, the Bavarian Illuminati and the French Jacobinians were not only responsible for the French Revolution, but part of a long-term plot to overthrow Christianity.[56]

Cooper notes that although Barruel specifically excludes "English" freemasons from the conspiracy, a subsequent attempt at a rebuttal by Scottish Freemason Alexander Lawrie in 1804 actually ends up associating Scottish Freemasonry with the Knights Templar.[57] In addition to bringing the Scottish Freemasons into the conspiracy, Lawrie also brought to the forefront a pair of documents that have perpetually been used to associate the Sinclair family to Freemasonry — the Sinclair Charters.

14

Rosslyn Chapel

Scottish Freemason Alexander Lawrie's 1804 attempted refutation[1] of Abbé Augustin Barruel's claims of Templar/Freemason conspiracies against Christianity brought to the forefront a pair of documents that have since perpetually been used to associate the Sinclair family to Freemasonry — the Sinclair Charters.

The Sinclair Charters, now housed in the museum of Freemasons Hall in Edinburgh, were transcribed by Father Hay in his family history.[2] In addition to recording the family history and oral traditions of the Sinclairs, Father Hay compiled deeds, charters and documents, including the two documents that, with no surviving context, are open to interpretation. Robert Cooper, Curator of the Grand Lodge of Scotland Museum and Library, dismisses the documents outright, identifying them not as charters but correspondence asking the Sinclairs to reestablish lapsed patronage of the stonemasons, essentially no more than an attempt at a fundraising/membership drive.[3]

David Stevens of St. Andrews University disagrees,[4] believing that the chapel's construction presented a challenge to stonemason's skills which, when added to the length of time involved in construction, may have endeared Sinclair to the craftsmen, making him a protector and champion of their guild, at least on the local level. His theory was that succeeding generations of masons were inspired by the work, and in trying to account for the uniqueness of the building, gave birth to the idea that Sinclairs must have had a special relationship to the craft. This re-emerged around 1600 and might have been believed by the Sinclairs themselves via the charters from Hay.[5]

The charters request the Sinclairs to resume their monarch-approved, ancestral patronage and supervision of the stonemasons, a claim that Cooper notes is only made by the stonemasons, not Freemasons, with no verifying documentation from other sources that would be expected to mention such an appointment, such as Hay's Sinclair genealogy or records of the Scottish monarchy.[6]

Father Hay doesn't date the documents, but subsequent research roughly dates them to 1601 and 1628, far too late to show a direct association between the Freemasons and the construction of Rosslyn Chapel.[7] The documents do coincide with the evolution of stonemasonry into Freemasonry. Stevenson also believes that the first charter's claim that the Sinclairs had a history as patrons of the craft was based on a genuine belief, based on the poor choice of a patron presented by William Sinclair. Even Father Hay disapproves of William Sinclair, calling him a "leud man" who "kept a miller's daughter, with whom he went to Ireland."[8] Stevenson concludes that if the masons had a choice of patrons, Sinclair would not be the noble they would approach.[9]

In 1736, several prominent speculative lodges gathered to form a Grand Lodge, a governing body over all the lodges. At the meeting, a descendant also named William St. Clair of Rosslyn renounced the hereditary rights that the Sinclair Charters claimed he was entitled to and was immediately elected First Grand Master Mason of Scotland. Historians Mark Oxbrow and Ian Robertson note that the renunciation, like the documents, was meaningless but was used to establish an ancient tradition that didn't exist.[10] Cooper further notes that as late as six months prior to his installation as Grand Master Mason, William St. Clair of Rosslyn wasn't actually a freemason, having been fast tracked through the ranks in order to attend the meeting where he renounced his hereditary rights.[11]

The connection between Freemasonry and the Sinclairs took place nearly three centuries after construction began on Rosslyn Chapel. The connection between stonemasons and the Sinclairs, conversely, dates all the way back to the construction of Rosslyn Chapel.

As recorded by Father Hay in the family history, William Sinclair (third Earl of Orkney), in recognition of his own mortality,[12] decided in 1446 to construct a Collegiate Church dedicated to Saint Matthew, now known as Rosslyn Chapel. Father Hay's belief in the mortality of William Sinclair was a tad premature; Sinclair spent the next 40 years supervising the construction of the building. After Sinclair died, he was buried in the unfinished chapel. His successor, son Oliver St. Clair, roofed the choir and stopped the project at that point with no further attempts to complete the cathedral as planned in his father's original design.[13]

The actual name for the chapel was to be the Collegiate Church of St. Matthew, one of over forty Collegiate Churches built in Scotland between the reigns of James I and James IV (1406–1513). In earlier times, Scottish nobles such as William Sinclair would have donated to the monasteries, but as the Middle Ages drew to a close, building a Collegiate Church became more popular. This, architecture historian George Hay[14] notes, was partially due to the rise of the Chantry Movement. A chantry is a mass said on behalf

Postcard by J S & S, Edinburgh, circa 1910, part of their "St Giles" series of cards, looking south toward the northern exterior of Rosslyn Chapel (reproduced with acknowledgment to Peter Stubbs, www.edinphoto.org.uk).

of the donor while alive, and on behalf of his soul after his death, in theory minimizing the time spent in purgatory. Although a chantry college's primary function was the offering of the masses, it also served some additional charitable or educational purpose. Hay notes that Sinclair was already providing for both his impoverished tenants and the poor who came asking for help.[15] Considering a fire in the castle during construction nearly cost Sinclair all of his papers,[16] he may also have planned to relocate his scriptorium into the new stone cathedral.

Several successive generations of the Sinclair family[17] created a collection of manuscripts that was so extensive that many papers survived the subsequent destruction of the castle. Lawlor,[18] as late as 1898, opens his study on the extant manuscripts by noting that Scottish antiquarians were indebted to the library at Rosslyn Castle. Chesnutt notes a number of documents attributed to Henry's descendants that were translated from Latin into Scottish.[19]

It is the unfinished church that connects the Sinclair family to the reworked Knights Templar through various carvings that are claimed to offer proof of the Sinclair expedition. As the mythification process continued, this proof evolved into evidence that Henry Sinclair was part of an attempt to reestablish the Templar Order in North America.

The church foundation broke ground on St. Matthew's Day, September 21, 1446, and the foundations alone took four years to put into place. The existing chapel is a fraction of the full-sized cathedral planned. The original building was to be cruciform in shape but was not completed. The choir was constructed, as was the Lady Chapel, before Sinclair died. Angelo Maggi's study of the chapel[20] notes that many Collegiate Churches were left unfinished west of the transepts. Because the construction was done in phases, the emphasis was in getting the choir completed first, in order to begin use of the building for services while the next phase of construction continued. Since the building, complete or not, was in use, it was considerably easier to justify abandoning the project due to dwindling resources or, as at Rosslyn, due to disinterested heirs.[21]

The cathedral, had it been completed, would resemble a typical Gothic cruciform cathedral. The foundations of the uncompleted transept and naves were laid but never built upon. Architectural historian Colin McWilliam[22] calculates that had the building been completed, the building's length would have gone from 70 feet (21 meters) to 180 feet (55 meters).

Oxbrow and Robertson note that Rosslyn is a scaled-down version of the East Quire at Glasgow Cathedral, with a "near identical floor plan of 14 pillars, the same north aisle and south aisle, and a Lady Chapel in the east behind a row of three pillars."[23] This similarity between Rosslyn and Glasgow is not a recent observation. Andrew Kerr noted in 1877 that "the entire plan of this Chapel corresponds to a large extent with the choir of Glasgow Cathedral."[24] Even earlier (1851), Daniel Wilson, in his *The Archæology and Prehistoric Annals of Scotland*, noted "that many of the most remarkable features of Rosslyn Chapel are derived from the prevailing models of the period, though carried to an exuberant excess ... [and] is nearly a repetition of that of the cathedral of St. Mungo at Glasgow."[25] This sentiment is elaborated upon by architects MacGibbon and Ross, the definitive source for Scottish architecture, who devote 30 pages to the architectural details of Rosslyn, both pointing out specific details and drawing parallels to other churches with similar features, concluding that "these comparisons are probably enough to prove that Rosslyn Church was built after the manner and style of its age and country, and only differs from other Scottish churches of the same period in possessing a superabundance of rich detail and carving in excess of what is usually found."[26] Oxbrow and Robertson further note that Sir William's first wife, Elizabeth Douglas, was the sister of Archibald, the 5th Earl of Douglas. When fire damaged Glasgow Cathedral, it was the Earl of Douglas who underwrote much of the reconstruction, giving Rosslyn a familial connection to Glasgow Cathedral. Hay suggests that Sinclair himself provided the designs on wooden planks to be rendered in stone at Rosslyn,[27] possibly suggesting his brother-in-law Archibald had provided a set of plans that Sinclair scaled down for Rosslyn, which Sinclair could then return for Glasgow's reconstruction.

The interior of Rosslyn Chapel is filled with carvings ranging from angels and musicians to green men[28] and dragons. As varied as the carvings are, so are the interpretations. Karen Ralls,[29] a medieval historian and Celtic scholar, feels there is biblical and pagan imagery, a nod to the area's Celtic roots. Historian Michael Turnbull[30] and Robert L. D. Cooper both feel they are entirely Christian in derivation. Oxbrow and Robertson suggest that among the biblical carvings are renderings of the Arthurian legends growing in popularity at the time of the church's construction.

Any or all of them could actually be correct when factoring in William Sinclair's literary background. His library almost certainly had to include at least one of the dozens of collections of exempla circulating among the clergy who used the anecdotes to augment the sermon. This would offer the interpretation of the sculptures as stone-carved images created to reinforce both biblical topics and exempla.[31] At the time of Rosslyn's construction, the lessons had become less popular than the story itself. As Cornell professor T. F. Crane[32] noted, the popularity of the anecdotal stories grew because the Crusades brought more exotic Eastern tales that could be used as exempla. Infused with new stories, the setting and performance began to overshadow the message itself and began to be told for entertainment value. The popularity reached the point where the Council of Sens in 1528 forbade use of any humorous tales as exempla under penalty of interdiction.[33] Not only could some of the various carvings reflect exempla, the most enduring story associated with the chapel could be a partially remembered exemplum warning against hubris — the tale of the "Murdered Apprentice" associated with the Apprentice Pillar.

The earliest published account of the "Murdered Apprentice" legend, in association with Rosslyn, was in a travel diary from 1677, first published in 1832 as *An Account of a Tour in Scotland* by Thomas Kirk:

> *...this story he told us, that the master builder went abroad to see good patterns, but before his return his apprentice had built one pillar which exceeded all that ever he could do, or had seen, therefore he slew him; and he showed us the head of the apprentice on the wall with a gash in the forehead, and his master's head opposite to him.*[34]

Kirk's wording indicates there were already local tour guides leading visitors around the chapel and that the column was part of the tour. The 'Prentice Pillar is a plain fluted shaft, with a floral garland twined around it that spirals upward from the base to the capital. Unique at first glance, MacGibbon notes that the ornamentation of the wreaths corresponds stylistically with the other carving in the building, and the base of the pillar, depicting eight dragons from whose mouths the vines originate, is similar to the column in the chapter house at Glasgow Cathedral.[35] The capital carvings are similar to those at Melrose, according to James Richardson, the first Inspector of Ancient Monuments of Scotland, who suggests that masons had completed enough work at Melrose by 1450 to proceed to Rosslyn and create a similar design.[36]

Above the capital of the pillar is the story of Abraham and Isaac in stone, Isaac bound upon the altar, a ram trapped in the brush, and a now-missing figure of Abraham praying. Turnbull suggests that the story of a father about to murder his son is the source of the "Murdered Apprentice" story attached to the Pillar; the statuary is so badly damaged that the original meaning has been lost.[37]

Even the name of the pillar has been debated over the centuries. Slezer mentions the pillar in his 1693 *Theatrum Scotiae* as the "the Prince's Pillar so much talk'd of," and Daniel Defoe is erroneously credited with referring to "the Princess's, or rather Prentice's Pillar" in his 1723 *A Tour Thro' the Whole Island of Great Britain*.[38] The "princess's pillar" reference was added to later editions by editors as the book was expanded to four volumes and transformed from an economy-oriented travelogue into a travel guide.

Richardson notes that the original name of the column could actually have been "Prentis' Pillar,"[39] named for one of the creators, a son or student of Thomas Prentis (or Prentys), half of a small but eminent alabaster quarry and carving workshop in Chellaston, England. Stewart Cruden, former Inspector of Ancient Monuments for Scotland, concurs, noting that the alabastermen were working in Scotland at the time.[40] Prentys, as an Englishman, would fit with Father Hay's declaration that William Sinclair "caused artificers to be brought from other regions and forraigne kingdomes."[41]

Saul's *English Church Monuments in the Middle Ages: History and Representation*[42] notes that the workshop of Prentys and Sutton probably employed no more than two or three sculptors, plus one or two assistants. The best alabaster supplies were exhausted by the 1440s, and the workshop began shutting down operations in the early to mid–1450s.[43] The sculptors, who specialized in standing angels with shields, would have the credentials to immediately be hired at a sculpture-intensive project such as Rosslyn.[44]

Richardson notes it could be a coincidence that there is a pillar named after a member of a family associated with stonework, but with at least four different masons' marks on the stone composing the Pillar's shaft,[45] it seems more likely that a Prentis worked on the pillar, not an apprentice.

The lack of reference to the apprentice legend in Slezer is more telling. Slezer mentions the legend of the chapel erupting in spectral flames before the death of a Sinclair, later immortalized by Sir Walter Scott in 1805, but there is no mention of the "Murdered Apprentice" story. Nor does Father Hay, working in the same time period, mention the pillar's alleged sanguinary origins. Considering Hay's proclivity for transcribing documents and family oral traditions, the omission is significant. It appears that locally, the "Murdered Apprentice" had begun to attach itself to Rosslyn's pillar via tour guides, but as evidenced by Kirk's bare bones rendering of the story,[46] it was not yet firmly established.

It was made a permanent part of the chapel's lore when Robert Forbes, the Bishop of Caithness, jotted down the tale in a newspaper article in 1761.[47] Forbes reprinted the text in a 1774 pamphlet that proved popular enough to require a reprint:

> ...a tradition that has prevailed on the family of Roslin from father to son, which is—That a model of this beautiful pillar having been sent from Rome, or some foreign place; the master-mason, upon viewing it, would by no means consent to work off such a pillar, till he should go to Rome, or some foreign part, to take exact inspection of the pillar from which the model had been taken; that, in his absence, whatever be the occasion of it, an apprentice finished the pillar as it now stands; and that the master, upon his return, seeing the pillar so exquisitely well finished made enquiry who had done it; and, being stung with envy, slew the apprentice.[48]

Forbes completes the story by adding that the head of the apprentice, with a head wound, was added among the other carvings, as was the image of his grieving mother. The murderous mason was also added to the carvings, forced to gaze out on the apprentice's masterpiece. Although this made the "Murdered Apprentice" a permanent and perennially favorite component of chapel lore, it was not necessarily a popular choice.

When Rosslyn Chapel chaplain John Thompson was compiling his *Illustrated Guide to Rosslyn Chapel and Castle, Hawthornden* in 1892, the 4th Earl of Rosslyn, Thompson's patron, had made the suggestion that the "hackneyed legend" be omitted from the book.[49] The booklet, hackneyed legend included, proved popular among the tourists (11 editions had been issued by 1934), and Thompson became intrigued by the pillar's history. He added an appendix to subsequent editions that included the 1677 reference by Thomas Kirk. Although skeptical about the story, he began to reconsider after coming across a reference in Robertson's *Concilia Scotiae, Ecclesiae Scoticanae Statuta*, an attempt to collect the canons and constitutions of medieval Scottish church. Robertson notes a document in the "Gray Manuscript" collection now housed in the National Library of Scotland.[50] The unpublished text notes that William Schevez, Archbishop of St Andrews, while in Rome at the Papal Court, was given a bull authorizing the privilege of reconciling churches by proxy. Schevez then used the privilege to commission certain clerks of his diocese to reconcile the Collegiate Church of Rosslyn, which had profaned by violence and bloodshed.

Although Thompson felt the reconciliation of the chapel was evidence of the "Murdered Apprentice" legend originating in Rosslyn, medieval historian Barbara Crawford disagrees,[51] noting that in 1481, William's sons were battling over shares of the estate. Crawford feels this tension and the barrage of court cases between the brothers eventually escalated to bloodshed and was probably the source of the profane act in the chapel.[52]

As noted in Synodal Statutes, sports and wrestling in churches or churchyards were also among banned activities because they often led to profaning the church, so there is also the somewhat anticlimactic possibility that the bloodshed was the aftermath of an accident during impromptu athletic competition among the workers.[53]

More telling is that the "Murdered Apprentice" story also surfaces elsewhere contemporaneously. Dom François Pommeraye's *Histoire de l'Abbaye de Saint-Ouen de Rouen*[54] recounts the identical tale of the master outdone by the apprentice, with fatal results. Instead of pillars, Dom Pommeraye's version has architect Alexandre de Berneval embarrassed when his design of the rose window in the south transept was outdone by that of the design of the rose window by his apprentice in the north transept. Nor are Rosslyn Chapel and the Abbey of St. Ouen the only two examples. Among others, Gloucester and Lincoln Cathedrals in England and Melrose Abbey in Scotland all have a variation of a story attached to the construction where an apprentice outdoes the master with fatal results.[55] The versions at Rouen, Melrose and Lincoln featured in construction of windows, which obviously would not work at Rosslyn where stained glass was not introduced until the 1860s.[56]

The proliferation of the story, notes Cambridge historian G. G. Coulter,[57] was a result of the itinerant nature of the stonemason trade. As they traveled, they left their stories behind them. Coulter notes that there are so many quarrels and rivalries in stonemason record that the story begins to appear archetypal.[58] This itinerancy was later verified by Stewart Cruden, Inspector of Ancient Monuments for Scotland, in a study of nearby Seton Collegiate Church, where Cruden notes a number of mason marks that appear in both Seton and Rosslyn.[59]

Father Hay's note about foreign craftsmen on the chapel project could also be due to Alexandre de Berneval's death in France in 1440, giving some of the St. Ouen stonemasons ample time to learn of the new project in Scotland, heading to Rosslyn, with the "Murdered Apprentice" legend following.

By coincidence, de Berneval had traveled to England in 1414 in search of alabaster for the Abbot of Fécamp, which he purchased from Thomas Prentys at the Chellaston quarries.[60]

James Richardson suggests that some masons went from Melrose to Rosslyn after work at Melrose had progressed.[61] The migration of masons from Melrose to Rosslyn might also suggest that Melrose's Apprentice Window was the predecessor of the Rosslyn version of the Apprentice Column. Richardson notes that the Master Mason at Melrose was John Morrow of Paris and that Melrose also used stylized foliage in the design.[62] Historian Louise Fradenburg[63] also believes that Rosslyn's Master Mason was French and hired specifically by Sinclair to build the church using motifs from France and Spain. This might explain the overabundance of decoration in the chapel; the excessive style of late Gothic architecture known as Flamboyant was the fashion in France and Spain in the 15th century. Fradenburg notes that Scotland in that time period was a place that was curious and fascinated by foreign designs and literature. She notes Joanne Norman's study of the William Dunbar poem "Dance of the Seven Deadly Sins"[64] which points out that Rosslyn Chapel contains the only stone-carved representation of the dance in Britain and that the seven representations of the sins are easily recognized by their counterparts in France.

The Apprentice Pillar, keeping with the exuberant style of the chapel, may simply be a stylized representation of one of the twelve spiral columns surrounding the shrine in Old St. Peter's Basilica in Rome.[65] According to tradition, Constantine took these columns from the Temple of Solomon and sent them to Rome for the Basilica, although art historian Eric Fernie has shown that such a claim was an invention of the Renaissance. Fernie's study of the spiral columns at Durham Cathedral notes that such pillars are placed to emphasize the dignity of a specific location, and the reference to St. Peter's is intentional.[66]

Assuming the Solomonic pillar at Rosslyn was similarly placed at a liturgically significant point, the location appears logical, even if the specific placement of altars has been lost. The pillar is located near an altar slightly elevated to allow headspace to the crypt, which Kerr, based on his reading of Forbes,[67] believes was the altar dedicated to Saint Peter. Forbes bases his placement of the altar on his translation of a 1523 charter transcribed by Father Hay[68] which listed the altars from left to right when standing in the chapel facing the east wall. The February 5, 1523, charter is the deed of resignation of the provost and prebendaries, whose revenues and endowments were being forcibly kept from them, courtesy of the Scottish Reformation sweeping the country.

The ensuing years were not kind to the building; On February 26, 1571,

Photograph (2002) of the "Apprentice Pillar" of Rosslyn (photograph courtesy of Jeff Nisbet).

the provost and prebendaries again resigned because their endowments were confiscated as part of the Reformation campaigns against Catholicism. The Catholic Mass accoutrements, including the altars, were demolished in 1592, and a Protestant mob sacked the building in 1688 in a fervent burst of Reformation iconoclasm. Cromwell's troops under General George Monck are reported to have used the chapel for a stable in 1650, a charge repeated at various Catholic buildings.[69] As Willsher notes in her study of Scottish graveyards, churchyards were public open spaces and as such, were used for a variety of secular activities such as meetings, weapon inspections, archery practice, fairs and markets.[70] To a Protestant militia, the use of an idolatrous Catholic church as a stable is a logical progression from using the churchyard as a corral. Willsher also notes Monck used churchyards for a variety of military purposes such as confiscating the grave slabs to build fortifications.[71] His use of ruins of the original St. Matthew's church to construct the battery that still exists to the north of the castle[72] may also include grave markers, adding to the damage and loss of graves in the area.

Although a good portion of the statuary was removed, damaged or eroded by exposure, one item remained a constant that continued to draw the attention of the visitors — the Apprentice Pillar.[73] Stewart notes that prior to 1620, the use of Solomonic columns was primarily as design elements on the title pages of books such as Arthur Golding's 1574 translation of *John Calvin's Commentaries on the Book of Job*.[74] This distinctive version of the column — entwined with a simple spiral of grape vines, became a very popular motif in Protestant texts. The similarity of the Apprentice Column to the image on Protestant title pages may have contributed a glimmer of recognition to the Reformation mobs. Compared to other parts of the chapel, the Apprentice Pillar escaped unscathed.

The chapel remained a tourist destination, but, without maintenance or repairs, it was essentially abandoned until 1736, when General James St. Clair attempted to slow the deterioration by glazing the windows for the first time, repairing the roof, and securing the building from locals. This slowed down the damage from exposure to the environment and vandalism, but Rosslyn Chapel was a battered derelict, showing its age with effusive moss and algae growing throughout the damp interior. This actually increased the building's popularity as the Romantics adopted the building as a Scottish equivalent of the Roman ruins, a monument to the past now devolving back into part of the natural landscape.

By the mid–19th century, most histories of the various churches had dismissed the local version of the "Murdered Apprentice" story. The 1865 *History and Antiquities of Lincoln* refers to the "Murdered Apprentice" story as "scarcely worth noticing" due to the realization that one of the windows was a century older than the other.[75] French historian Jules Quicherat had debunked the Abbey of St. Ouen version by noting the Rouen apprentice was the son of master Berneval, who succeeded his father as master mason.[76] Early references to the apprentice's head at Rosslyn, such as in Kirk (1677) and Forbes (1761), simply mention a mark on the head of the figure, easily explained as damage from neglect or the Reformation mobs. However, references begin to appear that refer to a painted wound on the head. Such diverse sources as antiquarian Francis Grose's 1797 book *The Antiquities of Scotland* and the 1853 *Topographical, Statistical, and Historical Gazetteer of Scotland* recount the story, noting a smear of red ochre on the forehead and specifically noting the apprentice face is that of a bearded old man.[77]

The longevity of myth at Rosslyn may have boiled down to simple economics. In 1892 Thompson noted that until 40 years before, the chapel was only accessible via arrangements at the adjacent Rosslyn Inn. The innkeeper rented the farm, castle, chapel and inn and made a living off the various components.[78] The appearance of the added color in print coincides, Thompson notes, with when David and Annie Wilson were the innkeepers at the inn.[79] Although the family left the hotel business soon after David's death, the widowed Annie continued to lead tours of the chapel up until her death in 1823, when a visitor reported her passing and that her son was leading the tour, but with considerably less fervor than his mother.[80]

Annie Wilson led tours of the chapel for nearly 50 years and had gained some notoriety, having dealings with Sir Walter Scott and Robert Burns. Angelo Maggi believes that Annie Wilson may have been the one to relay the story of the chapel erupting in spectral flames before the death of a Sinclair lord that became part of Scott's "The Lay of the Last Minstrel"[81] and in 1787, Robert Burns jotted down an epigram for her in appreciation of breakfast at the inn.

An article in the September 1817 edition of the *Gentleman's Magazine* includes a report on a recent visit to the chapel with the elderly Annie still leading the tour with her trademark, a long pointing stick, boasting that she had outlived three other guides.[82]

So, unlike other sites, Rosslyn was leased to a private party with a vested interest in keeping Rosslyn Chapel visitors entertained, including pandering to the public's love of tragic spectacle.[83]

Neither Annie Wilson nor Reformation vandalism explains the other damage inflicted on the carving — someone crudely chiseled off the "apprentice" figure's beard, in an attempt to rectify a perceived flaw in the story — since apprentices traditionally started their service as youths, the figure was

This drawing of Rosslyn Chapel tour guide Annie Wilson appeared in the September 1817 edition of the *Gentleman's Magazine*.

simply too old to be an apprentice. Professors of Economics in the University of Sheffield, Douglas Knoop and G. P. Jones, question whether the point is moot — their research into medieval stonemasonry and the connections to Freemasonry suggest that at the time of Rosslyn's construction, there were no apprentices among masons.[84] Although the other trade guilds were well established, stonemasons were an itinerant population, moving from project to project to find employment as buildings were completed or suspended for want of funds. Knoop and Jones question, under such conditions, if an apprentice could be trained or housed in a manner that would be required under an apprenticeship contract.

The beard remained intact on the carving when extensive repairs started in 1861 under architect David Bryce, commissioned to restore the chapel by James Alexander St. Clair-Erskine, 3rd Earl of Rosslyn.

The plans immediately drew the wrath of the Architectural Institute of Scotland, who already had concerns about the amount of original ornamentation Bryce had removed.[85] *The Building News* was more blunt in its opinion, suggesting the Earl had "desecrated" the building by replacing sculptures with facsimiles, modernizing the stairwell into the crypt, acid washing the stone and a litany of other changes.[86] The replacement sculptures seem to have been predominantly concentrated along the east wall, although McWilliam also warns that most of the sculptures along the south wall had also been "renewed."[87] The Earl of Rosslyn swept aside the complaints[88] and on April 22, 1862 (Easter Tuesday), the chapel was rededicated as an Episcopal church.

In 1863, English novelist and clergyman Edward Bradley, writing under his penname Cuthbert Bede, published his travels in Scotland,[89] which specifically concurs with Grosse that the head is that of a bearded old man. However, an article on the chapel in *The Book of Days* published the same year includes line art of the three heads with a clean-shaven apprentice.[90] This appears to indicate the beard that repudiated the "Murdered Apprentice" tale was removed after the restorations of David Bryce.[91]

Art historian Nigel Llewellyn suggests that the amount of damage inflicted by iconoclastic mobs is not as significant as is usually assumed. David Bryce's replacement sculptures and the 1862 vandalism to create the beardless apprentice head seem to verify Llewellyn's stance that the most damage to ecclesiastical sculpture and ornamentation was done in the Victorian Age.[92]

The most significant work was carried out by the 6th Earl of Rosslyn in the 1950s. By this time, parts of the chapel ceiling were again covered with algae and sandstone carvings were crumbling from the moisture, as feared and predicted by opponents of the restoration work a century before.[93] To bind and harden the stone, the stonework was covered with a white cementitious paint. In hindsight, it was the worst possible choice. In addition to obscuring fine lines in the carvings, making original stone indistinguishable from replacement work, destroying any remaining trace of paint and removing the stone's natural color variations, it also sealed the rock, making it impermeable. The rock became saturated with water absorbed through the exterior walls and roof.

By 1995, the chapel was deteriorating faster than ever, and a free-standing roof was erected over the entire building. This will allow the exterior stone surfaces to dry outwards, theoretically leaching the water away from the carved interior surfaces. Currently, the Rosslyn Chapel Trust is planning to remove the roof shield, experimenting with laser removal of the cementitious paint and seeking government funds to halt the damage.[94]

When Rosslyn Chapel was rededicated on Tuesday, April 22, 1862, the Bishop of Brechin preached from Psalms 26:8: "Our Lord, I have loved the habitation of thy house, and the place where thine honour dwelleth." The Bishop's words were ironic in light of the future appeal of the structure to a wide variety of eclectic studies: perhaps the chapel has been loved a little too much.

15

A Knight Mythologized

Umberto Eco, in his introduction to Barbara Frale's book on the Chinon Parchment,[1] notes that when Pope Clement V disbanded the Knights Templar in 1212, he forbade any attempts to restore the order without Papal consent and made the use of the name or Templar symbols an excommunicable offense. So the possibility of the devoutly Catholic Sinclairs incorporating Templar symbolism in the design of Rosslyn Chapel is patently absurd. Either the symbols are later additions or they are not related to the Templars. Aside from making all claims of modern-day Templar organizations invalid under pre-existing Papal decree, both explanations demonstrate the unfamiliarity of the modern world with medieval icons and symbolism.

The Scottish Reformation destroyed monasticism, eliminated the concept of purgatory and waged war on Catholic traditions and symbolism, creating what historian Norman L. Jones, in his study of the English Reformation, refers to as "an intentional introduction of religious and social amnesia."[2] The end result, Jones says, was a refocused emphasis on the family that led to the creation of secular family histories such as Hay's genealogy of the Sinclairs that confirmed the purpose, honor and status of family. This cultural amnesia would lead to ramifications for Rosslyn Chapel and eventually, the Westford Knight.

As the medieval stonemason guilds evolved into a fraternal order, the Temple of Solomon begins to appear as a symbol in Masonic literature. This system of symbolism and allegories derived from construction of the temple of Solomon became overlaid with Rosslyn Chapel.

The element of the "Murdered Apprentice" story where the Master Mason proceeds to Rome to study the original Pillar could originally have been explained as a garbled recollection of the mason creating a pillar similar to the Solomonic pillars in Rome, but as the entire "Murdered Apprentice" legend became associated with the Masonic allegories, more details arise in the chapel's version of the story. Hiram, the chief architect of the original Solomon's Temple, is murdered by three apprentices unsuccessfully forcing him to divulge the Mason Word so that they may identify themselves as Master Masons.

Although a master murdered by apprentices is the exact opposite of the Rosslyn story of a master killing an apprentice, it resonated with the Freemasons. Other Masonic references begin to appear into the chapel's iconography, most notably the sculpted head of the apprentice's widowed mother weeping at her son's fate, a later addition to the Rosslyn story, derived from the reference in 1 Kings 7:13–14 that specified that Hiram of Tyre, summoned by Solomon to build the pillars Boaz and Jachin, was a widow's son.

An 1861 letter by architect David Bryce[3] notes that the pillar later known as the "Master's Pillar" had also been more ornate than the other pillars. He noted it had been decorated with upright ornaments that had been partially removed, with new stone introduced to repair damage that was then plastered over. Bryce restored the pillar as part of his work, revealing delicate floral latticework on the inside faces that had been covered over during previous repair. The letter itself appears to be in response to questions as to whether the two pillars might have had matching designs at some point in the past, which would support Rosslyn Chapel being an early Freemason temple by having the two columns.

Architect Andrew Kerr's brief history of the chapel in 1877 refers to the "Murdered Apprentice" as a legend of the Freemasons.[4] Based in Edinburgh, Kerr was hired by Robert St. Clair-Erskine, 4th Earl of Rosslyn, to assess the chapel. Kerr was quite familiar with the building and environs (he had previously published a history of Rosslyn Castle[5]). Although Kerr believed the Prentice Pillar story to be a legend, he wasn't averse to having fun with it. As the current guide book dryly recounts,[6] Kerr repeated an anecdote to the Earl that during construction of a new baptistery with an organ loft on the west end of the building, a party of visitors had remarked that it was "wonderful that such young men should be entrusted to execute such carving," to which the estate steward replied "that it was not wonderful here, as the finest pillar in the Chapel was the work of an apprentice boy."

Ramsay's Oration in 1737 had established the ground work to position Freemasonry as the heir apparent of the Knights Templar. The 1870 elevation of Francis Robert St. Clair-Erskine to Grand Master Mason of Scotland (David Bryce was also elected Grand Architect) brought the revived Knight Templars in the guise of Scottish Freemasonry into Rosslyn Chapel. The December 1 newspaper report of the event[7] was misread at some point, creating a myth perpetuated to this day. The incorrect version states that a Grand Masonic fete was held in the chapel in 1870 with a thousand Freemasons in attendance.[8] In actuality, the event, a banquet to celebrate the Earl of Rosslyn's election to Grand Master Mason, was held in the large hall at Edinburgh's Freemason Hall with 400 Freemasons. It would not be the last or worst convoluted connection between the Sinclairs, Rosslyn Chapel, the Freemasons and the Knights Templar. In the mid–20th century, the myth process began to build momentum that shows no signs of subsiding.

The public's wholehearted embracing of the Knights Templar as an esoteric cult guarding lost ancient wisdom falls neatly within Harvard psychiatrist Eugene Taylor's identification of the 1960s counterculture as a third "Great Awakening" in the United States.[9] Like previous revivals,[10] Taylor notes this current period of religious activism was also ushered in simultaneously with a rise in social activism and the emergence of a "shadow culture," spiritual experimentation and belief systems outside of mainstream religion.

It was an eventuality that Rosslyn Chapel, already perceived as associated with the birth of Freemasonry, would also be embraced in alternative science texts as being everything from the resting place of the Holy Grail to location containing the Head of Jesus. It was similarly inevitable that someone would recall the Sinclair expedition and introduce Jarl Henry into the mythology. That introduction was made by Andrew Sinclair in his 1992 book *The Sword and the Grail.*[11] Sinclair made the claim based on information gleaned from various publications generated by the success of *Holy Blood, Holy Grail,*[12] and Sinclair's book would immediately place Henry Sinclair and the Westford Knight into the mix of fodder being used to churn out additional books that modified the "facts" in prior books as needed. The roots of *The Holy Blood and the Holy Grail,*[13] demonstrate how quickly and widespread the myth process developed.

In 1967, Gérard de Sède, no stranger to Templars or lost treasure myths (having previously penned a book claiming that lost treasure was hidden in the Templar stronghold of Gisors in Normandy[14]), published *L'Or de Rennes,* in which he describes how Abbé Bérenger Saunière discovered ancient parchments in his church in the village of Rennes-le-Château, which enabled him to locate lost treasure. *L'Or de Rennes,* with secret messages and lost treasures, was successful enough to warrant reprints, including a paperback edition as *Le Trésor Maudit de Rennes-le-Château.* It was this version that first attracted the attention of Henry Lincoln. Lincoln wrote an episode of the BBC-Two network's long-running science series *Chronicle* called "The Lost Treasure of Jerusalem?" The 1971 episode proved sufficiently popular and two additional episodes aired on the topic: "The Priest, The Painter and the Devil" in 1974 and "The Shadow of the Templars" in 1979.

Lincoln chronicled the origins of the original episode in a collection of essays from the TV series even as his primary source material was being debunked in France.[15] De Sède's work was subsequently exposed as a hoax by his disgruntled co-conspirators, Philippe de Chérisey and Pierre Plantard, who sued de Sède for a share of the royalties from *L'Or de Rennes.* Philippe de Chérisey, the self-confessed creator of the "medieval" documents that play a pivotal part in *L'Or de Rennes* and established the origins of an allegedly ancient secret society, the Priory of Sion, admitted his complicity in small pamphlets such as *L'Enigme de Renne* and in correspondence.[16]

Lincoln, oblivious to the fraud's exposure in France, joined forces with two Templar enthusiasts, novelist Richard Leigh and photojournalist-turned-screenwriter Michael Baigent, to produce the aforementioned third episode of *Chronicle* in 1979.

Even as the episode aired, French journalist Jean-Luc Chaumeil published a more widely available book debunking the Priory of Sion.[17]

If Lincoln, Baigent and Leigh were unaware of the unreliability of a significant part of their source material, they were well aware of the ratings from the broadcasts, converting their notes into a book. The result was the aforementioned *Holy Blood, Holy Grail,* with claims of lost treasures, secret messages and the secret society called the Priory of Sion that took over from the Templars, sworn to protect the bloodline of Jesus Christ. According to the book, a trail of hidden clues starting at Rennes-le-Château suggested that Jesus and Mary Magdalene married and had at least one child. Mary Magdalene traveled to France, where her descendants eventually founded the Merovingian dynasty.

The 1982 publication of *Holy Blood, Holy Grail* launched controversy and debate. Before the book was released in the States, the *New York Times* had already noted the book's impending arrival on a wave of controversy (a.k.a. free publicity).[18] The *Times* was correct — the title reached their bestseller lists within a month of release.

The Sinclairs and Rosslyn Chapel have passing mentions in *Holy Blood, Holy Grail,* but not Jarl Henry's voyage west. That voyage is pivotal in the research of Canadian author Michael Bradley. Bradley transformed the Sinclair expedition into a desperate search for a religious sanctuary creating a successful colony of Grail guardians that settled in Canada for four centuries before being wiped out by Indians circa 1750. Over the course of his three books, Bradley connects the Sinclairs to the Book of Mormon, the Money Pit on Oak Island and the alleged Norumbega colony of Eben Norton Horsford along the Charles River near Boston.[19] Bradley's initial premise is a hybrid of previous work by Nova Scotian writers; William Crooker had first offered Henry Sinclair and his Templars as constructors of the Oak Island "Money Pit"[20] and ruins first discovered by Joan Harris grew into the Sinclair castle stronghold in New Ross, Nova Scotia.

Joan Harris believed stone ruins in her back yard were those of a 17th-century Manor House that had been dismantled by Cromwellian sympathizers. She self-published several books on the topic but Mark Finnan's book on the Sinclairs is more succinct about how her stone ruins evolved into the fantasy medieval Sinclair castle of Michael Bradley.[21]

The Temple and the Lodge, a sequel by Baigent and Leigh, cites Bradley as a possible source that indicated Sinclair may have reached North America, a somewhat cautious statement considering they follow it immediately with the suggestion that Henry Sinclair could have sailed all the way into Mexico.[22]

The theory is based on their reading of Major's translation of the Zeno Narrative which mentions a land to the south where they sacrifice men and have gold.[23] Major never suggested Zichmni traveled to the tropics; he considered the section an anecdote picked up by the fisherman from other traders who traveled further south along the coast. Beauvois' theory that there was an Irish element to the Aztec culture[24] returns as Baigent and Leigh speculate that Sinclair was actually Quetzalcoatl, the blond god whose prophesied return allowed Cortés to conquer the Aztecs in 1530. Interestingly, they do not associate this alleged voyage south to the subtropical aloe carving they claim is in Rosslyn Chapel. They acknowledge Pohl's 1974 book[25] as a source but do not appear to recognize that Pohl's research in Nova Scotia and Westford invalidates the theory they are proposing.

Research on the Westford Knight, which had slowed down after the death of Frank Glynn in 1968, was beginning to revive with Frederick Pohl's 1974 book and Westford historian Allister MacDougall's 1976 commemorative marker.[26] Up until this point, the Westford carving had not been drawn into the rapid evolution of Henry Sinclair and his expedition. That changed in 1992 with Andrew Sinclair's *The Sword and the Grail*.

Sinclair took the various Templar myths that had evolved and placed them squarely in Henry Sinclair's lap. Andrew Sinclair's theory was that the Knights Templar fled to Scotland and sent Henry Sinclair to North America to establish New Jerusalem as a safe haven for the Templars. His evidence is the secret rituals of contemporary Masonic societies, North American evidence such as the Westford Knight and Newport Tower and a grave slab he found in Rosslyn Chapel.

By the time Andrew Sinclair began researching his book on Sinclair family associations with the Knights Templar, the small grave slab had been moved into Rosslyn Chapel. The stone is carved with a sword and a stepped floriate cross, both common medieval grave stone motifs. Andrew Sinclair mentions architect Andrew Kerr's 1877 report on Rosslyn Chapel[27] but overlooked Kerr's

A sword and a stepped floriate cross mark the grave slab of Willam de Saincler, now housed in Rosslyn Chapel. Based on the sword typology, it is a marker for William de St. Clair, a crusader who was killed in 1330 Spain. The eight-spoke wheel and a sword are symbols of the martyrdom of St. Catherine, a Sinclair patron saint (detail from Plate XXIV of Andrew Kerr's 1876 article on Rosslyn Castle).

report on Rosslyn Castle in 1876, a report that might have altered his theory on the grave slab. Kerr notes the original St. Matthew's Church was located in the current Rosslyn burial ground and the local gravediggers kept finding the foundations when preparing new graves. And, Kerr notes, "several ancient slabs with incised crosses and swords have been found, one of which, inscribed 'William de Saincler,' is preserved above the entrance to the chapel grounds, another in the adjoining garden, and a third was dug up about two years ago."[28]

As a result of Sinclair's book, the slab has been put in a more prominent position along the north wall near the tomb of the 4th Earl of Caithness and placed on a new plinth to make the slab more visible. This plinth has engraved upon it "William De St. Clair- Knight Templar." Besides questions about the Templar association with the Sinclairs,[29] there remain questions as to which William Sinclair was interred beneath this grave slab. Turnbull believes it is a memorial tombstone to Jarl Henry's grandfather, William de St. Clair, a crusader who was killed in battle in Spain in 1330 while carrying the heart of Robert the Bruce to the Holy Lands.[30]

The type of sword carved on the marker seems to confirm that it is William the crusader that is commemorated by the stone. Under the typology developed by sword expert R. Ewart Oakeshott,[31] the sword portrayed is a Type XIV weapon, a short tapering blade with a long, slender and curved cross-guard and wheel-form pommel dating from the time of the Crusader Sinclair's death in 1330. Oakeshott notes that there are few surviving examples from the period but that there are more sculptured and pictorial examples than of any other type.[32]

Andrew Sinclair had attempted to explain the size discrepancy of the stone by recalling a tradition that claimed Knights Templar were often buried sitting up and as such didn't need as large a slab to cover the grave.[33] Sinclair is misinterpreting a tradition that claimed it was customary to bury Templars and other veterans of the Crusades cross-legged. This reference to recumbent slabs with one leg crossed as a symbol of military service was a persistent irritation with 19th-century antiquarians such as the Rev. Weston S. Walford and Dr. J. Charles Cox, both of whom complained about the proliferation of the myth.[34]

Cox notes that many effigies of known Crusaders are not cross-legged; there are also effigies of women in the cross-legged position and the style appears to be exclusive to the British Isles.[35] Walford goes further, stating he can find no effigy marking a Templar burial in England and only one Templar in mainland Europe.[36] Walford is referring to the grave marker of Jean de Dreux in the church of St. Yved de Braine, near Soissons, France. Although now presumed lost, Abbé Bernard de Montfaucon documented the grave and rendered it into line art in the second volume of his *Les Monumens de la Monarchie Françoise*.[37]

Dr. Helen Nicholson's book on the Templar Trials in the British Isles shows three additional Templar grave markers — two slabs of Sicilian Templars, both now stored in the civic museum in Barletta, Italy, and a third in Belgium at Villers-le-Temple.[38] The two grave stones in Italy and the Montfaucon image show the deceased Templar in his monastic robes, with a mantle over the shoulders bearing a cross over the left breast and a felt cap; they are dressed as men in a religious order. As Nicholson notes, the Templars were a religious order who were not permitted to carry weapons except in defense of Christianity. They would only be garbed in armor and carrying a sword when on a crusade.[39] The Belgian Templar is carrying a sword at his side and has a shield on the other arm. He too wears the robes and mantle, perhaps indicating a Templar fallen in battle. In all cases, the grave shows a full figure with the robes and mantle of the order.

This immediately invalidates Andrew Sinclair's claim that the William De St. Clair gravestone shows him to be a Templar. The William De St. Clair gravestone does not contain any design elements that are not found repeatedly across Scotland. His book title and underlying theme of the entire book is based on his identification of the St. Clair gravestone's floriated cross as a symbol representing the grail, and by proxy, evidence the deceased was a member of the surviving secret order of Knights Templar. Sinclair consistently identifies the floriated cross and sword stones at other Scottish locations as Templar icons, including several lost recumbent grave slabs in nearby Pentland.[40] Old Pentland is connected to the Sinclairs — the village was part of the family estates and the parish church. St. Catherine of the Hopes, flooded when Glencorse Reservoir was created in 1820, was traditionally founded by Sir William in gratitude for the Saint's response to his plea for intercession during a deer hunt in 1317.[41]

Kerr noted that the submerged ruins were still occasionally visible from the surface in his time when water levels were low. Robert Chambers also noted that during a particularly dry summer in 1842 the foundations of the chapel and at least one gravestone were uncovered.[42]

The similarity between the Pentland and Rosslyn stones should not be a revelation or a surprise to Andrew Sinclair or any other member of the Sinclair clan. As Oxbrow and Robertson point out,[43] the cross on the gravestones is not merely floriated, it has eight spokes, making it a perfectly logical choice for a Sinclair memorial. An eight-spoked wheel and a sword are symbols of the martyrdom of St. Catherine, a powerful intercessor for those who invoke her when they are dying or in great need. The location of the Pentland church is said to have been raised where Sinclair's plea was answered, in veneration of the saint.

As debatable points go, the sword's iconography is more open to interpretation than the decorated cross. Medieval studies note that almost all cruciforms on grave art were decorated in some way.[44] Swords, alternately, could be interpreted as a literal symbol, such as the emblem of a knight's grave or a figurative icon, such as guarding the soul en route to heaven.[45]

Kerr's study of Rosslyn Chapel includes an image of a second grave slab found in the old Rosslyn churchyard. It too has the sword and an eight-segment floriate cross.[46] The Sinclair slab is the only one identified with text, a possible indication that the slab was part of the floor of the original St. Matthew's church under the Canon law concept of *honor sepulturae,* which antiquarian John Di Folco notes as the privilege of burial inside a church, limited to the building's deceased founder and his family as they had a personal stake in the structure.[47] This may also explain how it survived Reformation iconoclasts — the mob couldn't destroy icons of the saints (such as St. Catherine's wheel on the cross) if the gravestone was safely hidden under vegetation and soil in the old church ruins.

If the Sinclairs were, as *The Sword and the Grail* suggests, hiding Templar treasures, it would seem very counterproductive to have so many grail symbols in plain view across burial grounds on Sinclair land. Additionally, the St. Clair family testified against the Knights Templar when the order was brought to trial at Holyrood in Edinburgh in 1309. The primary printed source for the English, Scottish and Irish interrogation transcripts is David Wilkins's

Concilia Magnae Brittaniae et Hiberniae, reprinted in *Spottiswoode Miscellany*, which notes that among those who testified against the Templars in Scotland were Henricus de Sancto Claro and Willielmus de Sancto Claro.[48] Helen Nicholson reviewed the original manuscripts of the Templar trials in the British Islands and found additional details Wilkins had not included. Henricus de Sancto Claro, or Lord Henry Sinclair, testified that he had seen the commander of Templars in neighboring Balantrodoch receive the Eucharist devoutly. Lord Hugh of Ryedale noted the same commander used to give gifts in lieu of attending General Chapters. William, Lord Henry's son, gave evidence more along the lines of other testimonies, repeating hearsay, secondhand accounts and rumors.[49]

William would be appointed the Bishop of Dunkeld in 1312, becoming ecclesiastical head of one of the larger and more important of Scotland's medieval bishoprics. His appointment was hotly contested by Dunkeld Canon John de Leche, who had the support of King Edward II of England. Any possible hint of affiliation with the Templars would mean he perjured himself during the trials, a sin that would have been exploited by de Leche, who was eventually promoted to the Archbishopric of Dublin, resolving the issue.

Nicholson's book and Aitken's study of the Templars in Scotland both paint the trials in the British Isles as hearsay and minor accusations and the general tone of the trial was less about Templar heresies and more about neighbors who disliked their Templar neighbors.[50] Evelyn Lord suggests the Templars were not particularly respected or well-liked by their neighbors out of jealousy, fueled by the previous success of the Templars in developing the lands donated to the Order.[51]

All of this leads to serious questions about Andrew Sinclair's version of events. Andrew Sinclair has the surviving Knights escaping to Scotland, where they found a safe haven at the Temple preceptory at Balantradoch near Rosslyn Castle. Sinclair hypothesizes that the regrouping Knights could have provided the impetus for Earl Henry Sinclair's expedition to the New World, with an eye toward establishing a new Temple of Jerusalem and rebuilding the Templar base of power. This is unlikely, considering Balantradoch, now the Midlothian village of Temple, was granted to the Hospitallers in 1312 by Clement after the dissolution of the Templars.

Knight and Lomas published *The Hiram Key* in 1996, deciding that half the Templars that escaped the French repression did so by sailing to Scotland while the other half landed at Cape Cod.[52] One of the proofs of this Templar voyage is the Westford Knight. *The Hiram Key* reinterprets the Gunn heraldic emblems on the shield as a medieval ship sailing west toward a star.[53]

The "Templars fled to Scotland" theory is based on the excommunication of Robert the Bruce. The logic is fallacious since although the king was persona non grata, the country was still filled with devout Catholic clergy and laity who would report such an arrival to religious authorities outside of Robert's jurisdiction. This also metamorphosed in the legend that these Templars came to the rescue of Robert the Bruce at the battle of Bannockburn in 1314.[54]

By 1837, this story was firmly entrenched in Scottish lore, with the grateful Scot monarch creating the" Order of St. Andrew" or "Knights of the Thistle" essentially to allow the Templars to function under a new name,[55] a detail that is easily dismissed by the simple fact that the Order of Knights of St. Andrew of the Thistle was not created in 1314, but in 1440 by James II. The Templars being at Bannockburn is also easily debunked. In 1355, Englishman Sir Thomas Gray was captured by Scottish forces. While being ransomed, he began writing the *Scalacronica*,[56] a history of England. Part of the book includes some reminisces of his father, also named Thomas, including his father's participation at the battle of Bannockburn. This witness's recollection does not mention the Templars who, if they had indeed caused a rout, would certainly be remembered.

Nicholson also notes that of all the Templars in the British Isles at the time of the suppression, only five were unaccounted for, a far cry from a number capable of causing the British to panic.[57] Additionally, German military historian Hans Delbrück notes that mounted Templars could not have ridden to the rescue because the battlefield was such that the fight could only be won by infantry, not calvary.[58] Nicholson also reminds readers that Templars in Western Europe were not permitted to carry weapons; they were a monastic order who had taken religious vows. They could only carry weapons when defending Christians against the enemies of Christendom. Nicholson further documents the lack of weapons in the inventories of the seized Templar properties.[59] Neither England nor Scotland qualified as an enemy of Christendom, although the argument might be made that the Templar and Papal issues in France might qualify that country as a foe.

Lord further notes that in 1291, Brian de Jay, preceptor of Balantrodoch, the most important preceptory in Scotland, swore fealty to Edward I at Edinburgh Castle. Whether this he did on behalf of the Templars or on his own behalf, de Jay was killed in 1298 at the Battle of Falkirk, fighting with the English against Scotland.[60] Lord also observes that the Knights Templars in the British Island were essentially manorial landlords with little, if any, experience in battle and that considering that Edward II had been comparatively lenient to the Order, it seemed unlikely they would side against the English even if they could.[61]

The legend of Templars at Bannockburn appears to have started with Sir

Walter Scott's "The Lord of the Isles," a poem first published in 1815.[62] In this work, Knight Giles de Argentine, a bodyguard for Edward, escorts the English king to safety as the battle of Bannockburn turns into a rout, then charges back into battle and to certain death. Some sources claim de Argentine was a Knight Hospitaller,[63] but Scott specifically refers to his "red-cross shield," a Templar emblem. Scott would continue to use the Templars in his work, and the Templar legend grew with the popularity of the battle.

About the same time that the metal framework was installed to begin drying out Rosslyn Chapel, some of the plant carvings in the building had been "identified" as aloe plants and maize. Indigenous to North America, these plants make the connection between Henry Sinclair's voyage to North America and the Knight Templar at Rosslyn Chapel. According to Sinclair, aloe is carved in patterns across a lintel on the south wall and maize decorates the stonework over a window in the south wall, evidence carved in stone that Sir William's grandfather did indeed voyage to North America in hopes of establishing a new Eden for the Templars.[64]

The claim was popularized when Barnes & Noble released a more readily available 1998 reissue of *The Hiram Key*, by Christopher Knight and Robert Lomas.[65] Lomas and Knight, although not citing a source, appear to have noted the claim[66] by Sinclair and attempted to validate the aloe and maize discovery by documenting a chance meeting with the Reverend Janet Dyer, Rosslyn's vicar (1993–97). According to their account, the Rev. Dyer had a background in botany, was married to a botanist, and was able to confirm the identity of the maize and the aloe.[67]

This story has some minor difficulties, not the least of which is that the Rev. Dyer's husband is Dr. Adrian Dyer, formerly of the University of Edinburgh and a trustee of the Royal Botanic Garden in Edinburgh. Dr. Dyer did indeed examine the carvings of plants in Rosslyn Chapel.[68] However, his findings were the exact opposite of those *The Hiram Key* authors attributed to him. Dyer found that some of the plants probably had religious symbolism, but generally, the botanical art was stylized to such a degree that there was no intent for the plants to be identifiable plants. This included the alleged pre–Columbian evidence of maize and aloe that validated the voyages of Earl Henry.

His conclusion was that the carvings were architectural designs and that any resemblance to real plant life was coincidence. This opinion was echoed by Dr. Brian Moffat,[69] a leading researcher in medieval archaeoethnopharmacology. Moffat, director of the long-term archaeological project at the House of the Holy Trinity medieval hospital site at Soutra Aisle, which has uncovered medical practices in medieval Scotland and rediscovered several forgotten medicinal plant uses, also denies the carvings are accurate or derived from nature.[70]

Oxbrow and Robertson offer the opinion that the maize carving represents sheaves of wheat, noting that the sheaves lean as they follow the arch of the window, making them appear to bow to the sheath at the top, a carved stone interpretation of the biblical story of Joseph and his first dream prophecy.[71] Considering the carvings are located on the south wall, which is known to have had modifications to the carvings, the discussion is academic; there is no documentation as to which carvings were modified, so all carvings on the east and south walls are suspect. This is particularly true with the "Freemason symbols" that have been identified in the building by authors seeking proof of connections between the Sinclairs and Freemasonry. In light of the fact that the 1861 repairs were done by Bryce, a member of the Freemasons for James Alexander St. Clair-Erskine, 3rd Earl of Rosslyn, whose family was immersed in the Freemasons, it is perfectly reasonable to assume that any Masonic influences would have crept into the chapel as replacement statuary, not that they were original decorations.[72]

An early omen of things to come, the year 2000 found the publication of *Following the Ark of the Covenant*.[73] Author Michael Boren creates a Gunn mythology to match the burgeoning Sinclair lore. Boren claims, among other things, that the Gunns were the ancestral kings of the Orkney, the Hebrides and Mann and forged an alliance by having a Gunn daughter named Guinevere marry King Arthur.[74] James Gunn, memorialized in the Westford effigy, was actually killed in battle in Fall River, Massachusetts, and was buried there, giving rise to the "Skeleton in Armor."[75] Additionally, according to Boren, the crest of the Gunns appears not only on the Westford carving but on the Boat Stone, on a ledge near Oak Island and in the crypt of Rosslyn Chapel.[76]

Boren also takes the Sinclair mythology to new depths with the claim that the Westford Knight rock rests on a granite pedestal, remaining unnoticed by locals for three centuries until Frank Glynn cleared the brush and found the pedestal.[77] He also believed the Reformation mob that damaged Rosslyn was actually looking for treasure that Oliver St. Clair had hidden at Oak Island in 1545[78] with assistance from John Dee and Francis Bacon. This treasure included the Ark of the Covenant, or The Holy Grail, which after being in Nova Scotia, was moved as needed. Westford was apparently one stop, based on the fact that John Dee acquired 10,000 acres of land that included Westford.[79] The ark/grail, according to Boren, is now in a Utah cave where Mormons hid it.

Boren's fanciful version was a precursor to a wave of materials associating the Sinclairs and Rosslyn Chapel with the Templars that culminated with

Rosslyn Chapel's pivotal role in the 2003 best-selling novel *The Da Vinci Code*.[80] The book sold over 40 million copies in hardcover alone and reinvigorated sales of *Holy Blood, Holy Grail*, especially in the wake of authors Richard Leigh and Michael Baigent suing *The Da Vinci Code* publisher Random House in 2006 for breach of intellectual copyright in British courts,[81] inciting a media frenzy on the eve of the release of the film version of *The Da Vinci Code*. The media were fairly optimistic that Dan Brown and Random House would triumph, noting that copyright infringement was difficult to prove in British courts, particularly in light of the realization that over 300 books were in print in at least 25 languages, each proposing various versions of the theory that Jesus survived the crucifixion and ended up living with Mary Magdalene.[82]

Henry Lincoln did not participate in the suit, which the media soon found was due to Lincoln, Baigent and Leigh, mirroring de Chérisey, Plantard and de Sède, and a falling out over royalties and copyrights.[83] Baigent and Leigh lost the Da Vinci copyright case and a subsequent appeal, resulting in nearly £3 million in court costs, prompting one reporter in London to slyly note that Lincoln was the only one making money from the book's return to the best-seller lists. Richard Leigh died nine months after the appeal was lost and Baigent continues to write speculative history for other publishers.

The success of *The Da Vinci Code* novel and film spawned dozens of (allegedly) non-fiction books on the topic. These books relied on previous, non-mainstream titles, hybridized with more recent material off the Internet.[84] Even the Scottish sites are not exempt. The film version of *The Da Vinci Code* was released in 2006, and within a year, Seton Collegiate College suddenly had a "murdered apprentice head" of their own, in spite of the fact that the grotesque on the sculpted corbel is illustrated in such titles as the 1897 *Ecclesiastical Architecture of Scotland*.[85] *Ecclesiastical Architecture of Scotland* demonstrated the head was extant, but neither the sculpture nor the legend is mentioned. Nor is either mentioned in the studies of Seton during the 1950s by Stewart Cruden, Inspector of Ancient Monuments for Scotland.[86] Thirty years later, Cruden's *Scottish Medieval Churches* revisited Seton, and although he mentions Rosslyn's Apprentice Pillar as so distinctive as to make the association of the apprentice story inevitable, there is no mention of Seton having a similar legend.[87]

The Sinclair-Templar connection continues to appear in print, but it has entered the mainstream of the speculative histories; instead of rehashing the story, it receives only a passing mention since the improbable hybrid is so commonplace that it no longer needs elaboration. This is not to say that there have not been a few new twists to the story. Robert Baird[88] hypothesized that

Henry Sinclair was actually the heir to Druidic tradition, sworn to protecting the Merovingians. A 2003 travel guide to mystical and spiritual sites doesn't mention Westford, but it does mention Henry Sinclair in conjunction with the Newport Tower, noting that Sinclair never claimed discovery of America because he knew his Viking ancestors had been there before him.[89]

Steven Sora, who had previously written that the Sinclairs, based on Henry's previous explorations, had hidden the Templar treasures at Oak Island in 1436, returned to the subject in 2004 with *Lost Colony of the Templars* as the French king sends Giovanni da Verrazano to the new world, not to explore but to reestablish contact with Henry Sinclair's lost Templar colony at the Newport Tower only to find it abandoned.[90] Two years later, William Mann[91] explained the treasure the Templars had found in Jerusalem was how to determine longitude and latitude, giving them the ability to reach the New World and found secret colonies to mine precious metals and that the ulterior motive of Lewis and Clark was to search for the final resting place of Prince Henry Sinclair's grave, where the lost Templar treasures were hidden.

Umberto Eco in an essay on the resurgence in interest in the Middle Ages suggests "we are at present witnessing, both in Europe and America, a period of renewed interest in the Middle Ages, with a curious oscillation between fantastic neomedievalism and responsible philological examination."[92] In this light, his novel *Foucault's Pendulum*[93] is a cautionary tale of what happens when one is confused for the other.

Duke University Professor of Religion David Morgan, in a book on the relationship between images and religious belief,[94] notes that images are forms of communication. Whether communication is designed to be informative, persuasive or emotional, it is only useful if the sender and recipient can both discern the message as interpreted. He warns that "images can also be interpreted in ways their makers or original users did not intend, serving to corroborate beliefs or desires important to a viewer or a group of viewers. In either case, an image is a visual medium that can act as an instrument of influence."[95]

From this perspective, the question is raised as to whether the Westford Knight effigy has accomplished the dissemination of its message. If it is a memorial to a fallen chieftain of the Clan Gunn, the recent spate of claims that the carving is a Templar marker, a clue to lost treasures or proof of a secret colony means that the transmittal of the original message may be lost to the ages.

Epilogue

In February 2000, yachtswoman Laura Zolo departed from Venice, beginning an epic voyage that captivated the international news media. "Progetto Zeno" was Zolo's attempt to trace the route of the Zeno Narrative from Venice to Guysborough Harbor by way of the Orkneys, Iceland and Greenland.

Zolo and colleague Captain Jack Lammiman sailed aboard *S/V Setteroses (Seven Roses)*, a 37-foot steel-hulled sloop that Zolo had rebuilt from an abandoned hulk she found in Cape Verde. *Seven Roses* arrived in Nova Scotia in early September, sailing into the harbor among tributes from the Clans Gunn and Sinclair, Guysborough officials and Mi'kmaq elders. It was a culmination of the Sinclair and Gunn clan joint celebration of the 600th anniversary of Sinclair's voyage, proving that if a sloop with a 2-man crew could make the journey, certainly a fleet of seasoned Scottish, Orcadian and Venetian sailors could also have made the trip.

Whether or not Henry Sinclair traveled to Massachusetts may never be resolved to anyone's satisfaction. If the Sinclair expedition did reach North America, it offers reinterpretation of other sites found in New England. Before he turned his attention to the Sinclair expedition, Pohl had researched Norse voyages to North America and returned to the subject repeatedly.[1] Building on Harvard botanist M. L. Fernald's research indicating the flora and fauna mentioned in the sagas pointed to the south coast of Cape Cod as Vinland,[2] Pohl traced Ericsson's route into Nantucket Sound, to the mouth of the Bass River and finally up the river to Follins Pond where they built *Leifsbudir* or "Leif's Booths," winter quarters before returning to Greenland.[3] Pohl was not the first to suggest the Bass River was a place of interest. The Reverend Abner Morse found stone hearths near South Dennis along the Bass River and he felt these were atypical of aboriginal construction.[4]

In the spring of 1952, Pohl and the Massachusetts Archaeology Society excavated a gully at Follins Pond that Pohl believed to be where the Norse brought their ship ashore for the winter.[5] Although overshadowed by the

Norse ship excavation, other members of the Massachusetts Archaeology Society also located both a burial pit and a large hearth in the vicinity.

The trees were cleared out of the gully and the first test pit uncovered a wooden post, 2 inches in diameter and 2 feet in length. It stood on a stone base with stones on each side holding it vertical, exactly what would be needed for a keel bearing. It was the first of a number of vertical posts. Soon nine vertical posts running in a line down the gully were exposed. Also found were eight slightly angled stakes, four on each side of the central keel-bearing line, which were positioned to support a ship on an even keel.[6] Using the stakes as benchmarks, the dimensions of the ship were calculated at 18 feet wide and 65 to 69 feet long, the dimensions of an oceangoing Norse knorr such as Leif would have used. Pohl was unable to radiocarbon date the wood due to groundwater contamination but the initial findings made international news with such staid media as the *New York Times* proclaiming Vikings had been located.[7]

The media support barely lasted 24 hours. The second day of excavations started with a celebrity visit by Roland Wells Robbins. Robbins looked at the excavation for three minutes and pronounced that since the stakes were above the water table, the site could not be more than 200 years old. He decided it was a hiding place for a ship during the American Revolution, neglecting to mention to the media that the trees removed the previous day had held so much water that the wooden stakes were water-soaked when found or that ditches needed to be dug earlier that day to drain the water from the trenches.

Robbins, a house painter and amateur archaeologist, had found the remains of Thoreau's cabin at Walden Pond in 1945, marking the start of a controversial but high-profile career in archaeology. Most archaeologists at the time had moved past Robbins's "pick and shovel" methods, regarding "his methods as deplorable and Robbins himself as a poseur and showman."[8] Robbins's acumen in dealing with the media outweighed his lack of science credentials and the same journalists quickly reported on the demise of Pohl's Viking theory.[9] The Follins Pond site immediately lost favor and has long since been bulldozed into oblivion in the name of development.[10]

Although he does not make such a suggestion himself, Pohl's calculations for the length and the weight-bearing capacity[11] of the stakes also matched that of a cog, the ship used into the 14th century and a likely candidate for Sinclair's voyage. The Zeno Narrative has Zichmni ordering Antonio Zeno back to Europe with most of the ships and men to avoid winter in the new land, while Zichmni remained behind with a handful of men to establish a base of operation for further explorations. If Pohl's data work for Leif's winter camp, they worked equally well as Henry's winter camp. Had not Pohl already decided that the Sinclair winter camp was in Nova Scotia, Pohl could easily have made the case that if the Sinclair expedition departed from the Merrimack River en route toward the Newport Tower in Narragansett Bay, the ships would sail around Cape Cod, a perennial favorite location for Vinland by authors dating back to the progenitor of the "Norse ruins in America" theory, C. C. Rafn.

Beyond Narragansett Bay and the Newport Tower, the Gungywamp Complex in Groton, Connecticut, consists of a series of small sites scattered over 300 acres with carbon dating from 2000 B.C. to the 18th century.[12] There are various stone remains in the area, identified as being both Native American and colonial in origin. Among the unidentified lithic structural remains is a stone chamber featuring an astronomical alignment during the equinoxes. Archaeoastronomer and educator Vance Tiede first watched the vernal equinox alignment at the Gungywamp chamber in 1988 and suspected it had European connotations. In a 1998 magazine interview,[13] Tiede explained that if the vernal equinox chamber in Gungywamp was built by Irish monks, structures in Celtic areas should exhibit similar solar alignments. Tiede went to Ireland, the Hebrides, the Orkneys, and the Shetland Islands. He found that a small eastern window in oratories, previously though to be a design feature, invariably "framed the rising solar disk on the Feast Days of selected saints."[14] Tiede was looking specifically for Celtic influences, but St. Matthew, to whom Rosslyn Chapel was dedicated, has his feast day on September 21—close enough to the autumnal equinox for the stone structure to have been built by a devoutly Catholic Scottish nobleman in need of a church. Book II, Section VII of the Apostolic Constitutions,[15] dating from the late 4th century prescribed that a church should be built with its head to the East, meaning any Catholic structure up to the Reformation would be built in such a manner.

Obviously, this doesn't support the proposal that the Sinclair expedition reached New England, but it demonstrates how malleable theories remain without conclusive evidence. And without physical evidence, The Zeno Narrative remains both the pivot point and the weak link in the chain of what is primarily circumstantial evidence.

Regardless of the accuracy of The Zeno Narrative, modern authors have taken Henry Sinclair on a voyage far beyond his imaginings. He has been credited as an heir of a Druidic tradition that built the pyramids and conspired with the Catholic Church to hide the Jesus bloodline.[16] He has been identified as a part of a metaphysical alchemist conspiracy (the author also confuses him with the Portuguese explorer Prince Henry the Navigator).[17] It is doubtful that Earl Henry would recognize himself or his exploits at this point. And the evolution of Henry Sinclair and the Westford Knight continues: one recent publication, *Gaia Matrix*,[18] identifies the Knight carving as the schematic of a time gate in a global earth energy-consciousness grid used by both the Celts and the Templars.

In 2001, Laurence Gardner's *Bloodline of the Holy Grail*[19] was re-released in an expanded edition. Originally published in 1996, it was one of the innumerable books released in the wake of the success of *Holy Blood, Holy Grail* proposing Jesus survived the crucifixion, escaped to the west and fathered children, creating a bloodline that included numerous heroes through history. Garner's book makes an interesting comparison between the Westford Knight's broken sword and the broken sword motif in Percival's quest for the Grail in Arthurian legend.[20] Glynn's images excluded the broken sword, chalking the lines of the blade as if intact. Pohl's drawing, shows one half-hearted slash across the blade as if unsure whether it was broken or not. In fact, to find a sword with a broken blade, one must travel back to Cheney's original interpretation and Lethbridge's drawings. So, Gardner's reference to a hilt and blade fragment, in one sense, completes the circle, returning the Knight to where he started. And as is often the case with traveling in circles, very little is resolved.

In 2009, the evolution of the Westford Knight again came full circle, with the release of *Cabal of the Westford Knight*[21] by Westford novelist David Brody. The book, like so many before it, associates the Westford Knight with other enigmas such as Newport Tower, Rosslyn Chapel and Oak Island. However, this book is notable because it is a well-written, fictional adventure based on the unsolved sites of New England and Europe that is clearly marketed as fiction, compared to other books of varying degree of quality previously mentioned, which are, arguably, fiction titles being marketed as non-fiction.

Whether or not (hopefully not) the Westford Knight's association with post–*Da Vinci Code* conspiracies and theories is a long-term relationship, there does seem to be an almost supernatural air to the series of events that has kept the carving intact. Minimally, it is serendipitous, to use Bob Stone's term from the foreword: only the oft-vilified William B. Goodwin had the proper combination of timing, antiquarian contacts and pre–Columbian research correspondents to learn of the Westford site and document it. Had he not wavered at the end in his opinion that the lines were an Irish "face-cross," he may not have included the Norse Sword drawing by Vincent Fagan in *Ruins of Great Ireland in New England*.[22] If the Fagan drawing had not been published, Lethbridge would not have spotted it in the book and sent Frank Glynn in search of the sword. If Cindy Glynn had not demanded her father visit the Old Indian carving, the location of the Knight may never have been recovered. Westford's carving would have been destroyed decades ago as roads were laid, underground pipes placed or driveways widened.

In 2003, a stone marker was placed on Westford's Graniteville Road at the former site of the Heywood family home. The marker commemorates three visits to Westford by Edgar Allen Poe in 1848–49, only the second marker dedicated to Poe in Massachusetts.[23]

As a result of these visits, he composed the poem "For Annie"[24] for his friend Mrs. Nancy "Annie" Lockwood Heywood Richmond. The poem of a dying man rejoicing that his lingering illness (life) was finally over was prophetic; it was written in March of 1849, and Poe died within seven months.[25]

During his visits to Westford, Poe visited the top of Prospect Hill and remarked on the scenic vista.[26] If Poe had lived longer, there might be additional visits and/or a reference in letters or print as to whether or not he was introduced to a local landmark on the hill, the crude carving of an Indian along Depot Road near the Kittredge Farm.

In 1976, a marker was placed near that "Indian carving," now known as the Westford Knight.[27] The Westford Minutemen led the bicentennial year procession as the town fathers unveiled the new marker to a small crowd on a crisp December morning. Erected by Westford historian Allister Mac-Dougall, the marker proudly reads: "*Prince Henry First Sinclair of Orkney born in Scotland made a voyage of discovery to North America in 1398. After wintering in Nova Scotia he sailed to Massachusetts and on an inland expedition in 1399 to Prospect Hill to view the surrounding countryside, one of the party died. The punch-hole armorial effigy that adorns this ledge is a Memorial to this Knight.*"

Considering that the Knight is an effigy memorializing a fallen explorer in the 14th-century expedition of Henry Sinclair, the new marker was, in effect, giving a monument its own monument.

It is not the only memorial to the Sinclair expedition. In 1998, the Scottish clans of Sinclair and Gunn gathered in Nova Scotia's Boylston Provincial Park, a wooded hilltop offering a spectacular view of Guysborough Harbor. The clans gathered to jointly celebrate the 600th anniversary of their ancestors' exploratory journey in North America. The focus of this sexcentenary gathering was the erection of an interpretative memorial overlooking Chedabucto Bay, the theoretical 1398 New World landfall of Henry Sinclair. The monument is shaped like the wooden prow of a ship and relates the story of Henry Sinclair in English, French and Mi'kmaq. Just down the road along Route 16 at Halfway Cove is another monument to Henry Sinclair. This one was erected in 1996 by the Prince Henry Sinclair Society of North America, Inc. The fifteen-ton boulder with a black granite plaque also commemorates the landing of the Sinclair expedition.

A winter snow encroaches on the ledge where the Westford Knight continues to disappear under the onslaught of frost, water and road salt (photograph courtesy of Allie Brody).

However, as fitting and impressive these testaments are, the Westford Knight itself may be the oldest memorial to the expedition, dating back to the original journey.

Unfortunately, serendipity works both ways. Had Poe lived beyond 1849 to mention the carving, it would be a literary Mecca instead of an eroded and disappearing record of history. Whether that history is of Scottish exploration or ever-evolving American pre–Columbian perceptions is an entirely different issue.

Serendipity may no longer be enough. Whether or not Henry Sinclair traveled to Massachusetts may soon be a moot issue. The Westford Knight remains exposed along an increasingly busy street, assailed by salt and ice.

The Town of Westford continues to debate how best to protect the Westford Knight effigy and perhaps make arrangements for a permanent structure to protect the remaining proof of Henry Sinclair's voyage to the New World.

At the current rate that erosion and vandalism continue to take their toll, the decision may not be in their hands much longer.

Regardless of whether you believe it to be a military effigy from a pre–Columbian expedition, a fortuitous collection of erosion and glacier damage, a Templar artifact or even a time gate, one thing is certain, the Westford Knight is a local landmark that has brought Westford and her history on a journey that Henry Sinclair never envisioned. It would be a tragedy if the Westford Knight were simply allowed to disappear into the ages without an attempt to preserve it for future generations of historians to debate, ponder and perhaps resolve.

Appendix 1: Pohl's Similarities between Glooscap and Henry Sinclair

Atlantic Crossings Before Columbus includes the statement that Pohl had found seventeen parallels between the Mi'kmaq folk hero Glooscap and Henry Sinclair's arrival in Nova Scotia. But Pohl never clearly delineates all seventeen points consecutively in this book or in his subsequent *Prince Henry Sinclair— His Voyage to the New World in 1398*. Compounding the difficulty in assessing Pohl's interpretation, *Atlantic Crossings Before Columbus* doesn't cite the specific Glooscap myth passages that Pohl uses for comparison. In *Prince Henry Sinclair— His Voyage to the New World in 1398*, Pohl does cite the specific passages, but the pagination does not always match up to the volume cited. Additionally, Pohl includes material from tales that do not feature Glooscap, and in several cases, he includes passages that even his source (Rand) feels are later European additions to the body of lore. As one example, Pohl notes passages referring to "a sword of sharpness" and "a prince" being points of the comparisons. But the tale is not a Glooscap story, and even Rand observes that the story has European fairy tale elements.

By eliminating the overtly non–Glooscap tales, Pohl's list drops to twelve comparative elements. The author has taken the liberty of adding additional points for consideration.

1. Glooscap is not a deity. "He looked and lived like other men; he ate, drank, smoked, slept, and danced along with them" (Rand, p. xliv).[1]

2. Glooscap came to this country from the east, far across the great sea (Rand, p. 232).

3. Glooscap first met the Mi'kmaq at Pictou Harbor, arriving from Newfoundland (Leland & Prince, p. 123).[2]

4. Glooscap lives in a large wigwam on an island far away (Rand, p. 23).

5. Glooscap had three daughters. Henry Sinclair had three unmarried daughters before the voyage (Rand, p. 14).

6. Glooscap explored the Nova Scotia coast by canoe (Rand, pp. 291–2).

7. He summoned a large whale. Pohl interprets a whale as a decked ship (Rand, pp. 228–9, 287).

8. Glooscap's ship is a floating island with tall trees and people. Pohl interprets this as a ship with masts and crew (Rand, p. 186, Leland & Prince, p. 77).

9. Glooscap departed to the west on a long journey (Rand, pp. 228–9, 287).

10. Glooscap goes to Newfoundland on a whale to rescue allies captured and discovers another tribe of friendly Indians. Sinclair crosses Cabot Strait by ship and explores the region (Rand, pp. 287–9).

11. Glooscap taught the Mi'kmaq how to make nets. This echoes the shipwrecked fisherman in the Zeno Narrative (Leland and Prince, p. 63).

12. Glooscap visits a mountain with smoke coming from the top (Alger, p. 51).[3]

13. Glooscap pitched his tent near Cape d'Or, and remained there all winter (Rand, p. 292).

14. Glooscap is deliberately left behind when his comrades depart (Rand, p. 270).

15. Glooscap uses a little bark dish, which gives him an advantage while pursuing enemies (early mariners' compasses were magnetized needles floating in wooden bowls of water) (Rand, p. 287).

Appendix 2: The Zeno Narrative, R.H. Major Translation (1873)

The Discovery of the Islands of Frislanda, Eslanda, Engronelanda, Estotilanda, and Icaria: made by two Brothers of the Zeno Family, namely, Messire Nicolò, the Chevalier, and Messire Antonio.

TRANSLATED BY RICHARD HENRY MAJOR, F.S.A. &C*

In the year of our Lord 1200, there was in the city of Venice a very famous gentleman named Messire Marino Zeno, who, for his great virtue and wisdom, was elected president over some of the republics of Italy; in the government of which he bore himself so discreetly, that his name was beloved and held in great respect, even by those who had never known him personally. Among other honourable actions of his, it is specially recorded that he set at rest some very serious civil disturbances which had arisen among the citizens of Verona, and from which were to be apprehended great provocations to war, had it not been for the interposition of his extreme activity and good advice. This gentleman had a son named Messire Pietro, who was the father of the Doge Rinieri, who, dying without issue, left his property to Messire Andrea, the son of his brother Messire Marco. This Messire Andrea was Captain-General and Procurator, and held in the highest reputation for his many rare qualities. His son, Messire Rinieri, was an illustrious Senator, and several times Member of the Council. His son was Messire Pietro, Captain-General of the Christian Confederation against the Turks, and bore the name of Dragone because, on his shield, he bore a Dragon in lieu of a Manfrone, which he had borne previously. He was father of the great Messire Carlo, the famous Procurator and Captain-General against the Genoese in those perilous wars which were organised amongst nearly all the leading princes of Europe against our liberty and

---

Two footnotes that specifically refer back to references in Major's introductory notes have been deleted.

167

empire, and in which, by his great prowess, as Furius Camillus delivered Rome, so he delivered his country from an imminent risk which it ran of falling into the hands of the enemy. On this account he obtained the name of the Lion, which he bore painted on his shield as an enduring memorial of his deeds of prowess. Messire Carlo had two brothers, Messire Nicolò the Chevalier and Messire Antonio, the father of Messire Dragone. This latter was the father of Messire Caterino, father of Messire Pietro, whose son was another Messire Caterino, who died last year, being the father of Nicolò, now living.[1]

Now M. Nicolò, the Chevalier, being a man of great courage, after the aforesaid Genoese war of Chioggia, which gave our ancestors so much to do, conceived a very great desire to see the world and to travel and make himself acquainted with the different customs and languages of mankind, so that when occasion offered, he might be the better able to do service to his country and gain for himself reputation and honour. Wherefore having made and equipped a vessel from his own resources, of which he possessed an abundance, he set forth out of our seas, and passing the Strait of Gibraltar, sailed some days on the ocean, steering always to the north, with the object of seeing England and Flanders.[2] Being, however, attacked in those seas by a terrible storm, he was so tossed about for the space of many days with the sea and wind that he knew not where he was; and at length when he discovered land, being quite unable to bear up against the violence of the storm, he was cast on the Island of Frislanda.[3] The crew, however, were saved, and most of the goods that were in the ship. This was in the year 1380.[4] The inhabitants of the island came running in great numbers with weapons to set upon Messire Nicolò and his men, who being sorely fatigued with their struggles against the storm, and not knowing in what part of the world they were, were not able to make any resistance at all, much less to defend themselves with the vigour necessary under such dangerous circumstances; and they would doubtless have been very badly dealt with, had it not fortunately happened that a certain chieftain was near the spot with an armed retinue. When he heard that a large vessel had just been wrecked upon the island, he hastened his steps in the direction of the noise and outcries that were being made against our poor sailors, and driving away the natives, addressed our people in Latin, and asked them who they were and whence they came; and when he learned that they came from Italy, and that they were men of the same country,[5] he was exceedingly rejoiced. Wherefore promising them all that they should receive no discourtesy, and assuring them that they were come into a place where they should be well used and very welcome, he took them under his protection, and pledged his honour for their safety. He was a great lord, and possessed certain islands called Porlanda, lying not far from Frislanda to the south, being the richest and most populous of all those parts. His name was Zichmni,[6] and besides the said small islands, he was Duke of Sorano, lying over against Scotland.

Of these north parts I have thought good to draw a copy of the sailing chart which I find that I have still amongst our family antiquities, and, although it is rotten with age, I have succeeded with it tolerably well; and to those who take pleasure in such things, it will serve to throw light on the comprehension of that which, without it, could not be so easily understood. Zichmni then, being such as I have described him, was a warlike, valiant man, and specially famous in naval exploits. Having the year before gained a victory over the King of Norway, who was lord of the island, he, being anxious to win renown by deeds of arms, had come with his men to attempt the conquest of Frislanda, which is an island somewhat larger than Ireland.[7] Whereupon, seeing that Messire Nicolò was a man of judgment, and very experienced in matters both naval and military, he gave him permission to go on board his fleet with all his men, and charged the captain to pay him all respect, and in all things to take advantage of his advice and experience.

This fleet of Zichmni consisted of thirteen vessels, whereof two only were rowed with oars; the rest were small barks and one ship. With these they sailed to the westwards, and with little trouble gained possession of Ledovo[8] and Ilofe[9] and other small islands in a gulf called Sudero, where in the harbour of the country called Sanestol[10] they captured some small barks laden with salt fish. Here they found Zichmni, who came by land with his army, conquering all the country as he went. They stayed here but a little while, and making their course still westwards, they came to the other cape of the gulf, and then turning again they fell in with certain islands and lands which they brought into possession of Zichmni. This sea through which they sailed, was in a manner full of shoals and rocks; so that had Messire Nicolò and the Venetian mariners not been their pilots, the whole fleet, in the opinion of all that were in it, would have been lost, so inexperienced were Zichmni's men in comparison with ours, who had been, one might say, born, trained up, and grown old in the art of navigation. Now the fleet having done as described, the captain, by the advice of Messire Nicolò, determined to go ashore at a place called Bondendon,[11] to learn what success Zichmni had had in his wars, and there to their great satisfaction they heard that he had fought a great battle and put to flight the army of the enemy; in consequence of which victory, ambassadors were sent from all parts of the island to yield the country up into his hands, taking down their ensigns in every town and village. They decided therefore to stay in that place to await his coming, taking it for granted that he would be there very shortly. On his arrival there were great demonstrations of joy, as well for the victory by land as for that by sea; on account of which the Venetians received from all such great honour and praise that there was no talk but of them, and of the great valour of Messire Nicolò. Whereupon the chieftain, who was a great lover of valiant men, and especially of those that were skilled in nautical matters, caused Messire Nicolò to be brought before him, and after having honoured him with many words of commendation, and complimented his great zeal and skill, by which two things he acknowledged himself to have received a very great and inestimable benefit, viz. the preservation of his fleet and the winning of so many places without any trouble to himself, he conferred on him the honour of knighthood, and rewarded his men with very handsome presents. Departing thence they went in triumphant manner towards Frislanda,[12] the chief city of that island, on the south-east of it, lying inside a bay in which there is such great abundance of fish that many ships are laden therewith to supply Flanders, Brittany, England, Scotland, Norway and Denmark, and by this trade they gather great wealth.

The description thus far is taken from a letter sent by Messire Nicolò to Messire Antonio, his brother, requesting that he would find some vessel to bring him out to him. Whereupon, he, having as great a desire as his brother to see the world and make acquaintance with various nations, and thereby make himself a great name, bought a ship, and, directing his course that way, after a long voyage in which he encountered many dangers, at length joined Messire Nicolò in safety, and was received by him with great gladness, not only as being his brother by blood, but also in courage.

Messire Antonio remained in Frislanda and dwelt there fourteen years, four years with Messire Nicolò, and ten years alone. Here they won such grace and favour with the prince that, to gratify M. Nicolò, and still more because he knew full well his value, he made him captain of his navy, and with much warlike preparation they went out to attack Estlanda [Shetland], which lies off the coast between Frislanda and Norway; here they did much damage, but hearing that the king of Norway was coming against them with a great fleet to draw them off from this attack, they departed under such a terrible gale of wind, that they were driven upon certain shoals and a good many of their ships were wrecked. The remainder took shelter in Grislanda,[13] a large island but uninhabited. The king of Norway's fleet being caught in the same storm, was utterly wrecked and lost in those seas. When Zichmni received tidings of this from one of the enemy's ships that was driven by chance upon Grislanda, he repaired his fleet, and perceiving that the Shetlands lay not far off to the northward, determined to make an attack upon Islanda[14] [or Shetland], which together with the rest was subject to the king of Norway. Here, however, he found the country so well fortified and defended, that his fleet being but small and very ill-appointed both with weapons and men, he was fain to give up that enterprise without effecting anything, but removed his attack to the other islands in those channels which are called Islande [or the Shetlands], which are seven in number, viz., Talas, Broas, Iscant, Trans, Mimant, Dambere, and Bres;[15] and having taken them all he built a fort in Bres, where he left Messire Nicolò, with some small vessels and men and stores. For his own part, thinking that he had done enough for the present, he returned with those few ships that remained to him, in all safety to Frislanda. Messire Nicolò being left behind in Bres, determined the next season to make an excursion with the view of discovering land. Accordingly he fitted out three small barks in the month of July, and sailing towards the North arrived in Engroneland.[16] Here he found a monastery of the order of Friars Preachers, and a church dedicated to St. Thomas, hard by a hill which vomited fire like Vesuvius and Etna. There is a spring of hot water there with which they heat both the church of the monastery and the chambers of the Friars, and the water comes up into the kitchen so boiling hot, that they use no other fire to dress their victuals. They also put their bread into brass pots without any water, and it is baked the same as if it were in a hot oven. They have also small gardens covered over in the winter time, which being watered with this water, are protected against the effect of the snow and cold, which in those parts, being situated far under the pole, are very severe, and by this means they produce flowers and fruits and herbs of different kinds, just as in other temperate countries in their seasons, so that the rude and savage people of those parts, seeing these supernatural effects, take those friars for Gods, and bring them many presents, such as chickens, meat, and other things, holding them as Lords in the greatest reverence and respect. When the frost and snow are very great, these friars heat their houses in the manner described, and by letting in the water or opening the windows, they can in an instant temper the heat and cold of an apartment at their pleasure. In the buildings of the monastery they use no other material than that which is supplied to them by the fire; for they take the burning stones that are cast out like cinders from the fiery mouth of the hill, and when they are at their hottest they throw water on them and dissolve them, so that they become an excellent white lime which is extremely tenacious, and when used in building never decays. These clinkers when cold are very serviceable in place of stones for making walls and arches; for when once chilled they will never yield or break unless they be cut with some iron tool, and the arches built of them are so light that they need no strong support, and are everlasting in their beauty and consistency. By means of these great advantages these good friars have constructed so many buildings and walls that it is a curiosity to witness. The roofs of their houses are for the most part made in the following manner: first, they raise up the wall to its full height; they then make it incline inwards, by little and little, in form of an arch, so that in the middle it forms an excellent passage for the rain. But in those parts they are not much threatened with rain, because the pole, as I have said, is extremely cold, and when the first snow is fallen, it does not thaw again for nine months, which is the duration of their winter. They live on wild fowl and fish; for, where the warm water falls into the sea, there is a large and wide harbour, which, from the heat of the boiling water, never freezes all the winter, and the consequence is, that there is such an attraction for sea-fowl and fish that they are caught in unlimited quantity, and prove the support of a large population in the neighbourhood, which thus finds abundant occupation in building and in catching birds and fish, and in a thousand other necessary occupations about the monastery.

Their houses are built about the hill on every side, round in form, and twenty-five feet broad, and narrower and narrower towards the top, having at the summit a little hole, through which the air and light come into the house; and the ground below is so warm, that those within feel no cold at all. Hither, in summer time, come many vessels from the islands thereabout, and from the Cape above Norway, and from Trondheim, and bring the Friars all sorts of comforts, taking in exchange fish, which they dry in the sun or by freezing, and skins of different kinds of animals. By this means they obtain wood for burning, and admirably carved timber, and corn, and cloth for clothes. For all the countries round about them are only too glad to traffic with them for the two articles just mentioned; and thus, without any trouble or expense, they have all that they want. To this monastery resort friars from Norway, Sweden, and other countries, but the greater part come from the Shetland Islands. There are continually in the harbor a number of vessels detained by the sea being frozen, and waiting for the next season to melt the ice. The fishermen's boats are made like a weaver's shuttle. They take the skins of fish, and fashion them with the bones of the self-same fish, and, sewing them together and doubling them over, they make them so sound and substantial that it is wonderful to see how, in bad weather, they will shut themselves close inside and expose themselves to the sea and the wind without the slightest fear of coming to mischief. If they happen to be driven on any rocks, they can stand a good many bumps without receiving any injury. In the bottom of the boats they have a kind of sleeve, which is tied fast in the middle, and when any water comes into the boat, they put it into one half of the sleeve, then closing it above with two pieces of wood and opening the band underneath, they drive the water out; and this they do as often as they have occasion, without any trouble or danger whatever.

Moreover, the water of the monastery being sulphureous, is conveyed into the apartments of the principal friars in vessels of brass, or tin, or stone, so hot that it heats the place like a stove, and without carrying with it any stench or offensive odour whatever.

Besides this they have another means of conveying hot water by a conduit under the ground, so that it should not freeze. It is thus conducted into the middle of the court, where it falls into a large vessel of brass that stands in the middle of a boiling fountain. This is to heat their water for drinking and for watering their gardens. In this manner they derive from the hill every comfort that can be desired. These good friars devote the greatest attention to the cultivation of their gardens, and to the erection of handsome, but, above all, commodious buildings, nor are they wanting in ingenious and painstaking workmen for this purpose; for they are very liberal in their payments, and in their gifts to those who bring them fruits and seeds they are unlimited in their generosity. The consequence is that workmen and masters in different handicrafts resort there in plenty, attracted by the handsome pay and good living.

Most of them speak the Latin language, and specially the superiors and principals of the monastery. This is all that is known of Greenland as described by Messire Nicolò, who gives also a special description of a river that he discovered, as may be seen in the map that I have drawn. At length Messire Nicolò, not being accustomed to such severe cold, fell ill, and a little while after returned to Frislanda, where he died.

Messire Antonio succeeded him in his wealth and honours; but although he strove hard in various ways, and begged and prayed most earnestly, he could never obtain permission to return to his own country. For Zichmni, being a man of great enterprise and daring, had determined to make himself master of the sea. Accordingly, he proposed to avail himself of the services of Messire Antonio by sending him out with a few small vessels to the westwards, because in that direction some of his fishermen had discovered certain very rich and populous islands. This discovery Messire Antonio, in a letter to his brother Messire Carlo, relates in detail in the following manner, saving that we have changed some old words and the antiquated style, but have left the substance entire as it was.

Six and twenty years ago four fishing boats put out to sea, and, encountering a heavy storm, were driven over the sea in utter helplessness for many days; when at length, the tempest abating, they discovered an island called Estotiland,[17] lying to the westwards above one thousand miles from Frislanda. One of the boats was wrecked, and six men that were in it were taken by the inhabitants, and brought into a fair and populous city, where the king[18] of the place sent for many interpreters, but there were none could be found that understood the language of the fishermen, except one that spoke Latin, and who had also been cast by chance upon the same island. On behalf of the king he asked them who they were and where they came from; and when he reported their answer, the king desired that they should remain in the country. Accordingly, as they could do no otherwise, they obeyed his commandment, and remained five years on the island, and learned the language. One of them in particular visited different parts of the island, and reports that it is a very rich country, abounding in all good things. It is a little smaller than Iceland, but more fertile; in the middle of it is a very high mountain, in which rise four rivers which water the whole country.

The inhabitants are very intelligent people, and possess all the arts like ourselves; and it is believed that in time past they have had intercourse with our people, for he said that he saw Latin books in the king's library, which they at this present time do not understand. They have their own language and letters. They have all kinds of metals, but especially they abound with gold. Their foreign intercourse is with Greenland, whence they import furs, brimstone and pitch. He says that towards the south there is a great and populous country, very rich in gold. They sow corn and make beer, which is a kind of drink that northern people take as we do wine. They have woods of immense extent. They make their buildings with walls, and there are many towns and villages. They make small boats and sail them, but they have not the lodestone, nor do they know the north by the compass. For this reason these fishermen were held in great estimation, insomuch that the king sent them with twelve boats to the southwards to a country which they call Drogio; but in their voyage they had such contrary weather that they were in fear for their lives. Although, however, they escaped the one cruel death, they fell into another of the cruellest; for they were taken into the country and the greater number of them were eaten by the savages, who are cannibals and consider human flesh very savoury meat.

But as that fisherman and his remaining companions were able to shew them the way of taking fish with nets, their lives were saved. Every day he would go fishing in the sea and in the fresh waters, and take great abundance of fish, which he gave to the chiefs, and thereby grew into such favour that he was very much liked and held in great consideration by everybody.

As this man's fame spread through the surrounding tribes, there was a neighbouring chief who was very anxious to have him with him, and to see how he practised his wonderful art of catching fish. With this object in view, he made war on the other chief with whom the fisherman then was, and being more powerful and a better warrior, he at length overcame him, and so the fisherman was sent over to him with the rest of his company. During the space of thirteen years that he dwelt in those parts, he says that he was sent in this manner to more than five-and-twenty chiefs, for they were continually fighting amongst themselves, this chief with that, and solely with the purpose of having the fisherman to dwell with them; so that wandering up and down the country without any fixed abode in one place, he became acquainted with almost all those parts. He says that it is a very great country, and, as it, were, a new world; the people are very rude and uncultivated, for they all go naked, and suffer cruelly from the cold, nor have they the sense to clothe themselves with the skins of the animals which they take in hunting. They have no kind of metal. They live by hunting, and carry lances of wood, sharpened at the point. They have bows, the strings of which are made of beasts' skins. They are very fierce, and have deadly fights amongst each other, and eat one another's flesh. They have chieftains and certain laws among themselves, but differing in the different tribes. The farther you go south-westwards, however, the more refinement you meet with, because the climate is more temperate, and accordingly there they have cities and temples dedicated to their idols, in which they sacrifice men and afterwards eat them. In those parts they have some knowledge and use of gold and silver.

Now this fisherman, after having dwelt so many years in these parts, made up his mind, if possible, to return home to his own country; but his companions despairing of ever seeing it again, gave him God's speed, and remained themselves where they were. Accordingly he bade them farewell, and made his escape through the woods in the direction of Drogio, where he was welcomed and very kindly received by the chief of the place, who knew him and was a great enemy of the neighbouring chieftain; and so passing from one chief to another, being the same with whom he had been before, after a long time and with much toil he at length reached Drogio, where he spent three years. Here by good luck he heard from the natives that some boats had arrived off the coast; and full of hope of being able to carry out his intention, he went down to the seaside, and to his great delight found that they had come from Estotiland. He forthwith requested that they would take him with them, which they did very willingly, and as he knew the language of the country, which none of them could speak, they employed him as their interpreter.

He afterwards traded in their company to such good purpose, that he became very rich, and fitting out a vessel of his own, returned to Frislanda, and gave an account of that most wealthy country to this nobleman [Zichmni]. The sailors, from having had much experience in strange novelties, give full credence to his statements. This nobleman is therefore resolved to send me forth with a fleet towards those parts, and there are so many that desire to join in the expedition on account of the novelty and strangeness of the thing, that I think we shall be very strongly appointed, without any public expense at all. Such is the tenor of the letter I referred to, which I [i.e., Nicolò Zeno, Junior] have here detailed in order to throw light upon another voyage which was made by Messire Antonio. He set sail with a considerable number of vessels and men, but had not the chief command, as he had expected to have, for Zichmni went in his own person; and I have a letter describing that enterprise, which is to the following effect:—

Our great preparations for the voyage to Estotiland were begun in an unlucky hour, for exactly three days before our departure the fisherman died who was to have been our guide; nevertheless Zichmni would not give up the enterprise, but in lieu of the deceased fisherman, took some sailors that had come out with him from the island. Steering westwards, we discovered some islands subject to Frislanda, and passing certain shoals, came to Ledovo,[19] where we stayed seven days to refresh ourselves and to furnish the fleet with necessaries. Departing thence we arrived on the first of July at the Island of Ilofe;[20] and as the wind was full in our favour, we pushed on; but not long after, when we were on the open sea, there arose so great a storm that for eight days we were continuously kept in toil, and driven we knew not where, and a considerable number of the boats were lost. At length, when the storm abated, we gathered together the scattered boats, and sailing with a prosperous wind, we discovered land on the west.[21] Steering straight for it, we reached a quiet and safe harbour, in which we saw an infinite number of armed people, who came running furiously down to the water side, prepared to defend the island. Zichmni now caused his men to make signs of peace to them, and they sent ten men to us who could speak ten languages, but we could understand none of them, except one that was from Shetland. He, being brought before our prince, and asked what was the name of the island, and what people inhabited it, and who was the governor, answered that the island was called Icaria,[22] and that all the kings that reigned there were called Icari, after the first king, who as they said, was the son of Dædalus, King of Scotland, who conquered that island, left his son there for king, and gave them those laws that they retain to the present time; that after this, when going to sail further, he was drowned in a great tempest; and in memory, of his death that sea was called to this day the Icarian Sea, and the kings of the island were called Icari; that they were contented with the state which God hath given them, and would neither alter their laws nor admit any stranger. They therefore requested our prince not to attempt to interfere with their laws, which they had received from that king of worthy memory, and observed up to the present time: that the attempt would lead to his own destruction, for they were all prepared to die rather than relax in any way the use of those laws. Nevertheless, that we might not think that they altogether refused intercourse with other men, they ended by saying that they would willingly receive one of our people, and give him an honourable position amongst them, if only for the sake of learning my language and gaining information as to our customs, in the same way as they had already received those other ten persons from ten different countries, who had come into their island. To all this our prince made no reply, beyond enquiring where there was a good harbour, and making signs that he intended to depart. Accordingly, sailing round about the island, he put in with all his fleet in full sail, into a harbour which he found on the eastern side. The sailors went on shore to take in wood and water, which they did as quickly as they could, for fear they might be attacked by the islanders; and not without reason, for the inhabitants made signals to their neighbours with fire and smoke, and taking to their arms, the others coming to their aid, they all came running down to the seaside upon our men with bows and arrows, so that many were slain and several wounded. Although we made signs of peace to them, it was of no use, for their rage increased more and more, as though they were fighting for their own very existence. Being thus compelled to depart, we sailed along in a great circuit about the island, being always followed on the hill tops and along the sea coasts by an infinite number of armed men. At length, doubling the northern cape of the island, we came upon many shoals, amongst which we were for ten days in continual danger of losing our whole fleet; but fortunately all that while the weather was very fine. All the way till we came to the east cape, we saw the inhabitants still on the hill tops and by the sea coast, keeping with us, howling and shooting at us from a distance to show their animosity towards us. We therefore resolved to put into some safe harbour, and see if we might once again speak with the Shetlander, but we failed in our object; for the people, more like beasts than men, stood constantly prepared to beat us back if we should attempt to come on land. Wherefore Zichmni, seeing that he could do nothing, and that if he were to persevere in his attempt, the fleet would fall short of provisions, took his departure with a fair wind and sailed six days to the westwards: but the wind afterwards shifting to the south-west, and the sea becoming rough, we sailed four days with the wind aft, and at length discovering land, as the sea ran high and we did not know what country it was, were afraid at first to approach it but by God's blessing, the wind lulled, and then there came on a great calm. Some of the crew then pulled ashore, and soon returned to our great joy with news that they had found an excellent country and a still better harbour. Upon this we brought our barks and our boats to land, and on entering an excellent harbour, we saw in the distance a great mountain that poured forth smoke, which gave us good hope that we should find some inhabitants in the island; neither would Zichmni rest, although it was a great way off, without sending a hundred soldiers to explore the country, and bring an account of what sort of people the inhabitants were. Meanwhile, they took in a store of wood and water, and caught a considerable quantity of fish and sea fowl. They also found such an abundance of birds' eggs, that our men, who were half famished, ate of them to repletion. Whilst we were at anchor here, the month of June came in, and the air in the island was mild and pleasant beyond description; but, as we saw nobody, we began to suspect that this pleasant place was uninhabited. To the harbour we gave the name of Trin, and the headland which stretched out into the sea we called Capo de Trin. After eight days the hundred soldiers returned, and brought word that they had been through the island and up to the mountain, and that the smoke was a natural thing proceeding from a great fire in the bottom of the hill, and that there was a spring from which issued a certain matter like pitch, which ran into the sea, and that thereabouts dwelt great multitudes of people half wild, and living in caves. They were of small stature, and very timid; for as soon as they saw our people they fled into their holes. They reported also that there was a large river, and a very good and safe harbour. When Zichmni heard this, and noticed that the place had a wholesome and pure atmosphere, a fertile soil, good rivers, and so many other conveniences he conceived the idea of fixing his abode there, and founding a city. But his people, having passed through a voyage so full of fatigues, began to murmur, and to say that they wished to return to their own homes, for that the winter was not far off, and if they allowed it once to set in, they would not be able to get away before the following summer. He therefore retained only the row boats and such of the people as were willing to stay with him, and sent all the rest away in the ships, appointing me, against my will, to be their captain. Having no choice, therefore, I departed, and sailed twenty days to the eastwards without sight of any land; then, turning my course towards the south-east, in five days I lighted on land, and found myself on the island of Neome, and, knowing the country, I perceived I was past Iceland; and as the inhabitants were subject to Zichnmi, I took in fresh stores, and sailed with a fair wind in three days to Frislanda, where the people, who thought they had lost their prince, in consequence of his long absence on the voyage we had made, received us with a hearty welcome.

What happened subsequently to the contents of this letter I[23] know not beyond what I gather from conjecture from a piece of another letter, which is to the effect: That Zichmni settled down in the harbour of his newly-discovered island, and explored the whole of the country with great diligence, as well as the coasts on both sides of Greenland, because I find this particularly described in the sea charts; but the description is lost. The beginning of the letter runs thus:—

> Concerning those things that you desire to know of me, as to the people and their habits, the animals, and the countries adjoining, I have written about it all in a separate book, which, please God, I shall bring with me. In it I have described the country, the monstrous fishes, the customs and laws of Frislanda, of Iceland, of Shetland, the kingdom of Norway, Estotiland, and Drogio; and, lastly, I have written the life of my brother, the Chevalier, Messire Nicolò, with the discovery which he made, and all about Greenland. I have also written the life and exploits of Zichmni, a prince as worthy of immortal memory as any that ever lived for his great bravery and remarkable goodness. In it I have described the discovery of Greenland on both sides, and the city that he founded. But of this I will say no more in this letter, and hope to be with you very shortly, and to satisfy your curiosity on other subjects by word of mouth.

All these letters were written by Messire Antonio to Messire Carlo his brother; and I[24] am grieved that the book and many other writings on these subjects have, I don't know how, come sadly to ruin; for, being but a child when they fell into my hands, I, not knowing what they were, tore them in pieces, as children will do, and sent them all to ruin: a circumstance which I cannot now recall without the greatest sorrow. Nevertheless, in order that such an important memorial should not be lost, I have put the whole in order, as well as I could, in the above narrative; so that the present age may, more than its predecessors have done, in some measure derive pleasure from the great discoveries made in those parts where they were least expected; for it is an age that takes a great interest in new narratives and in the discoveries which have been made in countries hitherto unknown, by the high courage and great energy of our ancestors.

FINIS

Appendix 3: The Zeno Narrative, Fred W. Lucas Translation (1898)

"Concerning the Discovery of the Islands Frislanda, Eslanda, Engroueland, Estotilanda, and Icaria made by the two brothers Zeni Messire Nicolò, the Knight, and, Messire Antonio. One book, with a map of the said Islands."

Family History of the Zeni by Nicolò Zeno the Younger, the Compiler of the Work

"In the year of our Salvation 1200, Messire Marin Zeno, a man very famous in Venice was elected, on account of his great abilities and the force of his Character, Governor in some of the Republics of Italy, in the administration of which he always bore himself so well that he was beloved, and his name greatly reverenced, even by those who had never known him personally. Among other good works of his, it is particularly recorded that he quelled certain grave civil discords that arose among the Veronese, which might have been expected to give rise to war, if his extreme activity and good counsel had not been interposed. To this man was born a son, Messire Pietro, who was the father of the Doge Rinieri, which Doge, dying without leaving any children of his own, made Messire Andrea, the son of his brother Messire Marco, his heir. This Messire Andrea was Captain-General and Procurator, and had a very high reputation on account of the many rare qualities which he possessed. His son, Messire Rinieri, was an illustrious Senator, and many times a Councillor. From him descended Messire Pietro, Captain-General of the League of Christians against the Turks, who was called *Dragone*, because he bore upon his shield a Dragon, instead of a Manfrone, which he had first. He was the father of the great Messire Carlo, the most illustrious Procurator and Captain-General against the Genoese, in those perilous wars which were carried on whilst almost all the greater Princes of Europe were fighting against our liberty and Empire, in which, by his own valour, as Furious Camillus did for Rome, he delivered his country from the imminent risk which it ran of becoming the prey of its enemies; for which reason he acquired the cognomen *The Lion*, bearing the figure of a lion, in perpetual memory of his prowess, depicted upon his shield. The brothers of Messire Carlo were Messire Nicolò, the Knight, and Messire Antonio, the father of Messire Dragone, to whom was born a son, Messire Caterino, who begat Messire Pietro, from whome descended another Messire Caterino, who died last year, the father of Messire Nicolò, who is still living."

The Voyage of Nicoló Zeno. From His Letter to His Brother Antonio

"Now Messire Nicolò, the Knight, being a man of high spirit, after the termination of the aforesaid Genoese war in Chioggia, which gave our ancestors so much to do, conceived a very great desire to see the world, and to travel, and to make himself acquainted with the various customs and languages of men, in order that, when occasion arose, he might be better able to do service to his country, and to acquire for himself fame and honour. Therefore, having built and fitted out a ship from his own private means, of which he possessed an abundance, he left our seas, and, having passed the Straits of Gibraltar, sailed for some days across the Ocean always holding his course towards the North, with the intention of seeing England and Flanders.

While in these seas, he was assailed by a great tempest. For many days he was carried by the waves and the winds without knowing where he might be, until, at last, discovering land, and not being able to steer against such an exceedingly fierce storm, he was wrecked upon the Island Frislanda. The crew and a great part of the goods which were in the ship were saved; and this was in the year one thousand three hundred and eighty. The Islanders, running together in great numbers, all ready-armed, attacked Messire Nicolò and his men, who, all wearied by the storm they had passed through, and not knowing in what country they might be, were not able to make the least counter attack, or even to defend themselves against the enemy so vigorously as the danger demanded. Under these circumstances, they would probably have been badly treated if good fortune had not so ordered that, by chance, a Prince with an armed following happened to be in the neighbourhood. He, understanding that a large ship had just been wrecked on the Island, hastened up, on hearing the uproar and cries which were made against our poor sailors; and, after chasing away the people of the country, he spoke in Latin, and demanded of what nation they were, and whence they came; and, when he discovered that they came from Italy, and were men of the same country, he was filled with the greatest joy. Then, assuring them all that they should receive no injury, and that they were come into a place in which they should be most kindly treated, and well looked after, he took them under his protection on his good faith.

This man was a great Lord, and possessed some Islands called Porlanda, near to Frislanda on the south side, the richest and most populous in all those parts. He was named Zichmni, and, besides the aforesaid little Islands, he ruled of the dominion of the Duchy of Sorant,[1] situated on the side towards Scotland."

By the Compiler

"Of these parts of the North it occurred to me to draw out a copy of a navigating chart which I once found that I possessed among the ancient things in our house, which although it is all rotten and many years old, I have succeeded in doing tolerably well, and which, placed before the eyes of those who delight themselves with such things, will serve as a light to make intelligible that which, without it, they would not be so well able to understand."

From Nicoló Zeno's Letter to Brother Antonio

"Besides being a man of such position I have stated, Zichmni was warlike and valiant, and, above all, most famous in maritime affairs. Having gained a victory the year before over the King of Norway, who ruled over the Island, Zichmni, being a man who desired by deeds of arms to make himself yet more illustrious than he was already, had come down with his people to attack and acquire for himself the country of Frislanda, which is an Island much larger than Ireland. Therefore, perceiving that Messire Nicolò was a prudent person, and greatly skilled in maritime and military matters, he commissioned him to go on board the fleet with all his men, directing the Captain to pay him respect, and to avail himself of his counsel in all things, as that of one who knew and understood much from his long experience in navigation and arms. This fleet of Zichmni's consisted of thirteen ships (two only propelled by oars, the rest small vessels, and one ship), with which they sailed towards the West, and with little trouble made themselves masters of Ledovo and Ilofe, and of some other small Islands. Turning into a bay called Sudero, they took, in a port of the country called Sanestol, some boats laden with salt fish. At this place finding Zichmni, who, with his army, had come by land, having taken possession of all the country behind him, they stayed there a little.

Then making sail towards the west, they came at last to the other headland of the Bay; then turning round again, they found some Islands and lands which were all reduced into the possession of Zichmni. The sea in which they were sailing was, so to speak, full of Shoals and Rocks, so that, if Messire Nicolò had not been their Pilot, with his Venetian mariners, all that fleet, in the judgment of all that were in it, would have been lost, because of the little experience which Zichmni's men had in comparison with that of ours, who were, so to say, born, bred and grown old in the art [of navigation]. The fleet having thus done those things which have been mentioned, the Captain, by the advice of Messire Nicolò, decided to put into port at a place called Bondendon, to enquire as to the success of Zichmni's campaign. There they learnt, to their great pleasure, that he had fought a great battle and routed the enemy's army. In consequence of that victory, the whole island sent Ambassadors to make submission to him, raising his standards throughout the whole country and in the villages. Therefore, they decided to wait in that place for his coming, assuring themselves confidently that he must soon be there.

Upon his arrival they made great demonstrations of joy, as well on account of the victory by land as of that by the sea; for which latter all the Venetians were so much honoured and extolled that no one could speak of anything else than of them, and of the valour of Messire Nicolò. Then the Prince, who was very fond of valiant men, and especially of those who bore themselves well in naval affairs, sent for Messire Nicolò, and, after having commended him with many honouring words, and having praised his great activity and genius in the two matters (namely, the preservation of his fleet and the acquisition of so many places without any trouble to himself), in which, as he said, he acknowledged a very great and important benefit, he made Messire Nicolò a Knight, and honoured, and made very rich presents to, all his people. Departing from that place, in the manner of a triumph for the victory achieved, he went in the direction of Frislanda, the principal city of the Island. This place is situated on its South-eastern side, at the entrance to a bay, of which there are many in that Island, in which they take fish in such abundance that they lade many ships with them, and supply Flanders, Brittany, England, Scotland, Norway and Denmark, deriving very great riches from this traffic."

Nicolò Is Joined by Antonio. Nicoló's Voyage to Greenland, from His Own Written Account

"All of the above information, Messire Nicolò wrote in one of his letters to Messire Antonio, his brother, praying him to come to find him, with some ships. And, as he was no less desirous than his brother had been to see the world and to have converse with various nations, and so to make himself illustrious and a great man, he bought a ship, and, steering in that direction, after a long voyage, and many perils passed, finally joined Messire Nicolò, safe and sound, who received him with the greatest delight, both because he was his natural brother and because he was his brother in valour also.

Messire Antonio stayed in Frislanda and lived there fourteen years, four with Messire Nicolò and ten alone. There they grew into such grace and favour with the Prince that, partly to gratify Nicolò, but even more because he was excessively useful to him, he made him Captain of his fleet, and sent him with a great armament to attack Estlanda, which is on the side between Frislanda and Norway. There they inflicted many injuries, but, understanding that the King of Norway was coming against them, with a large fleet of ships, to divert them from that war, they set sail in a Tempest so terrible that, being driven upon certain rocks, a great number of their ships were lost, and the remainder sought safety in Grislanda, a large Island, but uninhabited. The fleet of the King of Norway, likewise assailed by the same storm, was wrecked and totally lost in those seas. Zichmni, being informed of this by a small ship of the enemy which ran by good fortune into Grislanda, having first repaired the fleet, and perceiving himself to be near Islande on the North, determined to attack Islanda, which, exactly in the same manner as the others, belonged to the King of Norway; but he found the country so well fortified and furnished for defence that he could not but have been repulsed, as he had such a small fleet, and that, small as it was, likewise very badly provided both with arms and men. On this account, he abandoned that enterprise without having done anything, and attacked, in the same channels, the other Islands called Islande, which are seven in number, that is to say, Talas, Broas, Iscant, Trans, Mimant, Damberc, and Bres. Taking possession of them all, he built a fort in Bres, in which he left Messire Nicolò, with some small ships, some men and provisions; and as it appeared to him that he had done enough for the time with so small a fleet, he returned safely to Frislanda with the remainder. Messire Nicolò, remaining in Bres, determined to set forth in the spring on a voyage of discovery. So, fitting out his not very large ships, in the month of July, he made sail towards the North, and arrived in Engroueland. There he found a Monastery of the order of Preaching Friars, and a Church dedicated to St. Thomas, near to a mountain which cast out fire like Vesuvius and Etna. There is a spring of hot water with which they warm the buildings in the Church of the Monastery, and the chambers of the Friars, the water in the kitchen being so boiling that, without any other fire, it serves all their needs; and bread, being put into copper cooking-pots without the water, is cooked as in a well-heated oven. And there are little gardens covered in the winter, which being watered with this water, are protected from the snow and the cold, which in these parts, on account of their situation being so very close under the Pole, are exceedingly severe. From these are produced flowers and fruits and herbs of various kinds, just as they are in temperate climates in their seasons, so that the rough and wild people of these countries, seeing these supernatural effects, consider the Friars as Gods, and bring them fowls, flesh, and other things, and hold them all as Lords in the greatest reverence and respect. In the manner, then, which has been described, these Friars warm their habitations when the ice and snow are severe, and they can, in a moment, warm or cool a room by increasing the water to certain limits, or by opening the windows and letting in the fresh air.

In the fabric of the Monastery no other materials are used than those which are furnished by the fire, for the hot stones, which issue like sparks from the fiery mouth of the mountain, are taken at the time when they are at their hottest, and water is thrown upon them, which causes them to split open and to become pitch, or very white and very tenacious lime, which, when once set, never deteriorates. And the scoriæ, likewise, when they have become cool, serve in place of stone to make walls and arches, as, when once they have grown cold, it is no longer possible to dissolve them or to break them, unless indeed they are cut with iron; and arches made of these are so light that they need no buttresses, but always last well and remain in good order. In consequence of their possessing such conveniences, these good fathers have erected such dwellings and walls that it is a wonder to see them. Most of the roofs are made in the following manner: the wall being carried to its proper height, they then incline it inwards little by little as they go on, so that in the middle it forms a rain-proof arch; but they have not much apprehension of rain in those parts, because the Pole being, as has been said, very cold, the first-fallen snow melts no more until nine months of the year have passed, for so long does their winter last.

They live on wild fowl and fish, since, in the place where the warm water enters the sea, there is a tolerably large and capacious harbor, which, by reason of the boiling water, never freezes even in the winter. Here, therefore, there is such a concourse of sea-fowl and fish that they catch an almost infinite number, which provides support for a great many people of the vicinity, who are kept in continual employment, as well in working on the buildings as in catching birds and fish, and in a thousand other matters which are required in the Monastery.

The houses of these people surround the mountain, and are all circular in shape and twenty-five feet in diameter. They make them narrow in towards the top, in such a way as to leave above a little aperture, by which the air enters, and which gives light to the place; and the earth is so warm below that they do not feel any cold within. Hither, in the summer, come many boats from the neighbouring islands, and from the cape upon Norway, and from Treadon, and bring to the Friars all the things which they can desire, and they trade with these for fish, which they dry in the open air and in the cold, and for skins of different sorts of animals. Thus they acquire wood for burning, and timber, excellently worked, for building, and grain, and cloth for clothing; for, in exchange for the two things mentioned, nearly all the neighbouring people are desirous of selling their merchandise; and so, without trouble or expense, they have whatever they wish.

There come together in this Monastery Friars for Norway, Sweden, and other countries, but the greater part are from Islande; and there are always in this port many ships, which cannot get away because the sea is frozen, awaiting the spring thaw.

The boats of the fishermen they make like the shuttles which the weavers use to make cloth. Taking the skins of fishes, they fit them over the bones of the same fish, of which they make a frame, and sew them together, and lay them over many times double. They turn these boats out so strong and sound, that it is certainly a miraculous thing to observe how, during tempests, they fasten themselves inside, and allow them to be carried over the sea by the waves and the winds without any fear of being wrecked or drowned; and, if they do strike on the land, they stand safely many blows. They have a sleeve at the bottom which they keep tied in the middle, and, when water enters the boat, they take it in one half and close it above with two wooden shutters, then taking the ligature from below, they drive out the water. However many times they do this, they do it without any trouble or danger.

Since the water of the Monastery is sulphurous, it is conducted into the rooms of the Superiors by means of certain vessels of copper, tin, or stone, so hot that, like a stove, it warms the habitation very well, without introducing any stench or other noxious odour. Besides this, they lead other spring water through a culvert underground, so that it may not freeze, as far as the middle of the courtyard, where it falls into a large copper vessel which stands in the middle of a boiling spring, and so they warm the water for drinking and for watering their gardens.

They have in the mountains all the commodities which they can most desire. Nor do these good fathers put themselves to any other trouble than that of cultivating their gardens, and making beautiful, charming, and, above all, commodious buildings; nor for this do they want for good, clever, and industrious workmen, although pagans, and they pay them largely. To those who bring them fruits and seeds they are liberal without limit, and lavish in their expenditure. On these accounts, there is a very great concourse of people there seeking employment and instruction, in order to earn in that place such good places and better living. They use, for the most part, the Latin language, especially the Superiors and the principal men of the Monastery."

By the Compiler

"So much is known of Engroueland, concerning which Messire Nicolò described all the foregoing particulars, and more especially the river discovered by him, as may be seen in the map made by me. At last, not being used to such severe cold, he sickened, and, soon after returning to Frisland, he died there.

Messire Antonio succeeded to his riches and honours, but, although he tried many ways, and begged and prayed much, he could never succeed in getting back to his own home, because Zichmni, being a man of spirit and valour, had resolved from the bottom of his heart to make himself master of the sea. Wherefore, availing himself of the services of Messire Antonio, he desired that he should sail with several small ships towards the West, to obtain information as to the existence of some very rich and populous Islands on that side, discovered by some of his fishermen; which discovery Messire Antonio narrates in one of his letters, written to his brother Messire Carlo, with so much detail that, except that we have changed the old language and style, but we have let the matter stand as it was."

The Frisland Fisherman's Story. From Antonio Zeno's Letter to His Brother Carlo

"Twenty-six years ago, four fishing boats sailed, which driven by a great tempest, wandered many days, lost, as it were, upon the sea, until, when at last the weather moderated, they found an Island, called Estotilanda, lying to the Westward, and distant from Frislanda more than a thousand *miglia*, on which one of the boats was wrecked. Six men who were in it were seized by the islanders, and conducted to a most beautiful and largely populated city. The King who ruled there summoned many interpreters, but found none who had any knowledge of the language of these fishermen, except one who spoke Latin, and who had been cast upon the same Island by a similar tempest. This man, demanding of the castaways, on behalf of the King, who they were and whence they came, gathered all their statements, and reported their effect to the King, who, when he fully understood their case, willed that they should stay in that country. Wherefore, obeying this command, because they could not do otherwise, they remained five years in the Island and learnt the language. One of them in particular, having been in different parts of the Island, reports that it is very rich, and abundant in all the good things of this world; that it is rather smaller than Iceland, but more fertile, having in the middle a very high mountain from which spring four rivers, which water it. The inhabitants are quick-witted, and possess all the arts which we have. It is believed that in earlier times they have had commerce with our countrymen, because this man said that he saw Latin books in the King's library, which none of them at the present time understand. They have a distinct language, and letters. They get, by mining, metals of all sorts, and above all, they have abundance of gold. Their trade is with Engroueland, whence they receive furs, and sulphur, and pitch. And, towards the South, he says, there is a great country very rich in gold, and populous. They sow grain and make beer, which is a kind of beverage which the Northern people use as we do wine. They have woods of immense extent. They construct their buildings with walls, and there are many cities and villages. They make small ships and navigate them, but they have not the lodestone, nor can they indicate the North by the compass. On this account, these fishermen were held in great esteem, so much that the king dispatched them, with twelve small ships, towards the South, to the country which they call Drogio, but during the voyage they met with so great a tempest that they gave themselves up for lost. Nevertheless, in trying to escape from one cruel death, they delivered themselves into the clutches of another much more terrible, for, being taken into the country, most of them were eaten by the ferocious inhabitants, who feed upon human flesh, which they consider a most savoury viand.

But this fisherman, with his companions, by showing the natives the method of taking fish with nets, saved their lives; and, fishing every day in the sea, and in the fresh waters, they caught many fish, and gave them to the Chiefs; by which means the fisherman acquired so much favour that he was held dear, and was beloved and much honoured by everyone. His fame spread among the adjacent nations, and a neighbouring Chief conceived so great a desire to have him in his service, and to see how he exercised his wonderful art of taking fish, that he made war upon the other Chief, by whom the fisherman was protected; and prevailing at last, because he was the more powerful and warlike, the fisherman was handed over to him, with his companions. During the thirteen years which he spent continuously in the parts aforesaid, he says that he was transmitted in this manner to more than twenty-five Chiefs, they being constantly stirred up to make war one against another, solely for the sake of having him in their service; and so, as he kept wandering, without ever having a fixed abode in one place for any length of time, he came to know from actual experience almost all those parts.

He says that it is a very large country and like a new world; but the people are ignorant, and destitute of all good qualities, for they all go naked, and suffer cruelly from the cold; nor have they learnt to cover themselves with the skins of the beasts which they take in hunting. They have no metal of any sort. They live by hunting, and carry lances of wood sharpened at the point, and bows, the strings of which are made of the skins of animals. They are a people of great ferocity, and fight together to the death, and eat one another. They have Chiefs, and certain laws, which differ much amongst them.

But, the further one goes towards the South-west, the greater civilization one finds, because there the climate is more temperate, so that there are cities, and temples of idols wherein they sacrifice men, whom they afterwards eat. In these parts they have some knowledge of gold and silver, and use them.

Now this fisherman, having dwelt in these countries so many years, purposed, if he could, to return to his fatherland; but his companions, despairing of the possibility of ever seeing it again, let him depart, wishing him a successful journey, and they themselves remained where they were, Then he, commanding them to God, fled through the woods toward Drogio, and was made most welcome, and kindly treated by a neighbouring Chief who knew him, and who had great enmity against the other Chief [from whom he ran away]; and so, going from the hand of one to that of another of the same Chiefs with whom he had been before, after much time and considerable hardships and fatigues, he arrived finally in Drogio, where he dwelt the three following years. Then, by good fortune, he learnt from the Countryfolk that some ships had arrived upon the coast, and he conceived good hopes of accomplishing his desire. He went to the coast, and enquiring from what country the ships came, learnt to his great pleasure that they were from Estotilanda. Then, having begged to be taken away, he was willingly received, because he knew the language of the country; and, there being no one among the sailors who understood it, they used him as their interpreter. Afterwards, he frequently made that voyage with them, until he grew very rich, and having built and equipped a ship of his own, returned to Frislanda, bearing to the Lord of it [Zichmni] news of the discovery of that very rich country. In all this he was credited, because the sailors confirmed as true many other new things which he reported. It is on account of this affair that the Lord Zichmni has resolved to send me with a fleet towards those parts; and there are so many who wish to go over there, on account of the novelty of the thing, that I think we shall be a very strong force, without any public expense."

By the Compiler

"This is what is contained in the letter which I have cited above. I have stated its tenor here in order that another voyage which Messire Antonio made may be better understood. On this voyage he sailed with many people and ships, not, however, being appointed Captain, as he thought at first he would have been, because Zichmni decided to make the exploration in person; and I have a letter about this expedition, which states as follows:"

The Letter from Antonio Zeno to His Brother Carlo Zeno Describing His Western Voyage in Vain Search of Estotilanda and Drogio, and the Finding of Icaria and Greenland

"Our great preparations to go into Estotilanda were commenced under an evil open; for, three days exactly before our departure, the fisherman, who was to have been our guide, died. Notwithstanding this, our Chief would not abandon the intended voyage, and took with him as guides, instead of the dead fisherman, some of the sailor who had returned from the Island with the latter. And so we steered our course towards the West, and discovered some island subject to Frislanda; and, passing certain rocks, we stopped at Ledovo, where we remained seven days for the sake of the repose, and to furnish the fleet with some necessary things. Departing from thence, we arrived, on the 1st of July, at the Island of Ilofe; and, because the wind made for us, we passed onward, without the least thing to hinder us, and went far out into the deepest ocean. Not long after, a storm assailed us, so fierce that, for eight days at a stretch, it kept us at work, and cast us about so that we knew not where we might be, and we lost a large proportion of the ships. At last, the weather having become calm, we got together the ships which had been separated from the others, and, sailing with a good wind, we discovered land in the West.[2] Keeping our course directly for it, we arrived in a quiet and secure port, and we saw people, almost infinite in number, armed and ready to strike, running towards the shore to defend the Island. Thereupon, Zichmni ordered his people to make signs of peace, and the Islanders sent to us ten men, who could speak ten languages, but we could not understand any of them, except one who was from Islanda[3] [Iceland]. This man, being conducted into the presence of our Prince, and asked by him how they called the Island, and what people inhabited it, and who ruled over it, replied that the Island was called Icaria, and that all the Kings who had ruled over it were called Icarus, after its first King, who, as they said, was the son of Daedalus, King of Scotland, who, having made himself master of the Island, left his son there as King, and left also those laws which the Islanders still used; and that, after these things were done, purposing to sail further on, he was drowned in a great storm; that, on account of his death in this manner, they still called that sea Icarian, and the King of the Island Icarus. Also that, because they were satisfied with that state which God had given them, they did not wish to change their customs in any particular, nor would they receive any foreigner; that they therefore prayed our Prince that he would not seek to violate those laws which they had preserved in happy memory of their King, and had observed down to that time; adding that he would not be able to do it without his own certain destruction, they being all prepared to abandon life, rather than to give up, on any account, the use of those laws. Nevertheless, in order that it might not appear that they altogether refused intercourse with other men, they said, in conclusion, that they were willing to receive one of us, and to give him a high position amongst them, and to do so solely in order to learn my language and to have an account of our customs, just as they had already received those other ten men who had come to the Island from ten other different countries. To these things our Prince made no other reply than to make enquiry as to whether there was a good harbor. Then he feigned to depart, and, making a circuit of the Island, in full sail, put into a port pointed out to him on the Eastern side. There the sailors disembarked, to obtain wood and water, with as much dispatch as possible, as they doubted whether they might not be attacked by the Islanders; nor was their fear vain, for those who dwelt near by, making signs to the others with fire and smoke, quickly armed themselves, and, the others joining them, they came down to the shore, armed with weapons and arrows, in such numbers against our people that many were left killed and wounded; nor did it avail us that we made signs of peace to them, for, as if they were fighting for their all, they grew more and more exasperated. Therefore, we were forced to set sail, and to go along in a great circle round the Island, being always accompanied, along the mountains and shores, by an infinite number of armed men. Then, doubling the Cape at the North of the Island, we found very great shoals, amongst which, for ten days continuously, we were in much danger of losing the fleet, but, luckily for us, the weather was very fine all the while. Passing thence as far as the Cape on the East of the island, we saw the Islanders, always keeping pace with us on the summits of the mountains and along the shore, with cries and arrow-shots from afar, showing towards us more and more the same inimical mind. We therefore determined to stop in some safe port, and to see if we could not speak once more to the Icelander; but we did not succeed in this design, for the people, little better than beasts in this respect, remained continually in arms, with the deliberate intention of resisting us if we should attempt to land. Wherefore Zichmni, seeing that he could not do anything, and that, if he should remain obstinate in his purpose, victuals would soon be wanting in the fleet, set sail with a fair wind and sailed six days to the Westward; but, the wind changing to the South-west, and the sea therefore becoming rough, the fleet ran before the wind for four days. At last land was discovered, but we greatly feared to approach it, on account of the swelling seas, and because the land observed was unknown to us. Nevertheless, by God's aid, the wind dropped and it became calm. Then some men from the fleet went to the land in rowing boats, and not long after returned and reported, to their very great delight, that they had found a very good country and a still better harbor. At which news, having hauled up our ships and small vessels, we went on shore, and, having entered a good harbor, we saw afar off a great mountain which cast forth smoke; this gave us hope that inhabitants would be found in the Island, nor, for all that it was so far off, did Zichmni delay sending a hundred good soldiers to reconnoiter the country and to report what kind of people inhabited it. In the meanwhile, the fleet was supplied with water and wood, and many fishes and sea-fowl were caught; they also found there so many birds; eggs that the half-famished men were able to eat their fill.

While we remained there, the month of June[4] came in, during which season the air in the island was more temperate and mild than can be expressed. In spite of this, not seeing anyone there, we began to suspect that so beautiful a place was, nevertheless, uninhabited, and we gave to the port and to the point of land which ran out into the sea the names of Trin and Capo di Trin. The hundred soldiers who had gone away returned, after eight days, and reported that they had been over the island and to the mountain; that the smoke proceeded from it because, as they had proved, at the bottom of it was a great fire; that there was a spring from which was produced a certain matter, like pitch, which ran into the sea; that many people inhabited the neighbour-ing parts, half savage, and sheltering themselves in caves; that these were of small stature and very timid, for, directly they saw the soldiers, they fled into their caves; and that there was a large river there, and a good safe harbor. Zichmni, being informed of these things, and seeing that the place had a healthy and pure climate, and very good soil, and rivers, and so many peculiar advantages, began to think of making his dwelling there, and of building a city. But his people, who had already endured a voyage so full of hardships, began to rebel, and to say that they wished to return home, because, as the winter was near, if they let it come in, they would not be able afterwards to get away until the following summer; so he retained only the rowing boats, with those men who were willing to remain there, sending back all the others in the remaining ships; and he desired, against my will, that I should be the Captain. I departed therefore, because I could not do otherwise, and sailed towards the East for twenty days continuously without ever seeing land; then, turning towards the South-east, after five days I sighted land, and found that I had reached the island of Neome. Knowing this country, I perceived that I had passed Islanda. Wherefore, having procured fresh provisions from the Islanders, who were under the dominion of Zichmni, I sailed in three days, with a fair wind, to Frislanda, where the people there thought they had lost their Prince, because of the long time that we had spent upon the voyage, received us with signs of the greatest joy."

By the Compiler

"After this letter I find nothing further, except what I judge from conjecture. I gather, from a clause in another letter, which I give below, that Zichmni built a town in the port of the island newly discovered by him; also, that he did his best to explore the whole country, together with the rivers in various parts of Engroueland [Greenland], because I see these described in detail in the map, but the description is lost. The clause in the letter is as follows:—"

Extract From Another Letter from Antonio Zeno to Carlo Zeno

"As to those things which you seek to know from me concerning the customs of the men, the animals, and the neighbouring countries, I have written about all these in a separate book, which, please God, I shall bring home with me. In it I have described the countries, the monstrous fishes, the customs and laws of Frislanda, of Islanda [Iceland], of Estlanda [Shetland], of the Kingdom of Norway, of Estotilanda, of Drogio, and, lastly, the life of Nicoló the Knight, our brother, with the discoveries made by him, and matters relating to Grolanda[5] [Greenland]. I have also written the life and exploits of Zichmni, a Prince certainly as worthy of immortal remembrance as any other who has ever lived in this world, on account of his great valour and many good qualities. In this life may be read of his discoveries in Engrouiland [*sic*] [Greenland] on both sides, and of the city built by him. Wherefore, I will say no more to you in this letter, hoping soon to be with you, and to satisfy you concerning many other things *vivâ voce*."

By the Compiler

"All these letters were written by Messire Antonio to Messire Carlo, his brother, and I grieve that the book and many other writings, in which perhaps these very same projects may have been carried out, have come, I know not how, unhappily to harm; because, being still a boy when they came into my hands, and not understanding what they were, I tore them in pieces and destroyed them, as boys will do, which I cannot, except with keenest regret, now call to mind. Nevertheless, in order that so fair a memorial of such things may not be lost, I have placed in order in the above narrative what I have been able to recover of the aforesaid materials, to the end that I may, to some extent, make reparation to this present age, which, more than any other yet gone by, is interested in the many discoveries of new lands where, it might have been thought, they would be least expected, and which is very much given to the study both of recent accounts, and of the discoveries of unknown countries made by the great spirit and enterprise of our ancestors."

"The End."

Appendix 4: James P. Whittall's Twenty Tenets on the Newport Tower

James Whittall studied the Newport Tower extensively, drawing on his background in archaeology, his training as an architect and from a wealth of experience gained during his extensive travels in search of European counterparts. One of Whittall's final appearances before his death in 1998 was at the Sinclair Symposium, part of the annual Orkney International Science Festival in September 1997. There, he made a presentation on why he believed the Newport Tower was built by the Sinclair expedition.

Whittall's health was failing and his presentation was not published. Niven Sinclair, a fellow participant at the symposium, transcribed Whittall's data and made sure the data did not lapse into obscurity.

Whittall came to the following conclusions:

1. The architecture of the tower was pre-planned. The concept was not conceived on site or built in haste.

2. The architecture is completely based on sacred geometry.

3. The stone masons were fully conversant with the materials at hand with which to construct the tower.

4. The tower was aligned to the east and each of the eight pillars was similarly aligned on the cardinal points in the manner of the Knights Templar.

5. The tool marks created in dressing the stone can be directly identified with the tools which were used before and during the 14th century. These marks are quite distinct from those found in colonial stonework and are of an entirely different character.

6. After extensive comparisons with ancient units of measurement, it has been found that the Scottish ell is the nearest unit of measurement which coincides most accurately with the structure of Newport Tower or the Norwegian short alen (three Norse feet = one Scottish

ell). A photogrammetric survey made in 1991 showed that the unit of measurement of the tower was 23.35cm which supports the belief that the Scottish ell or the Norwegian alen may have been used as the measure when building the tower. This does not necessarily mean the tower was built using either measure but it rules out the possibility that any other measure was used. The English foot was definitely NOT used.

7. The single and double splay windows of the tower have their prototypes in medieval Europe and, more especially, in the Northern Isles of Scotland in the 1300s. The Bishop's Palace in Kirkwall, Orkney, is a typical example of this type of splayed construction of windows.

8. The arch and lintel design used in constructing Newport Tower is to be found in Orkney, Shetland and Scandinavian round church architecture before the 14th century.

9. The built-in triangular keystone feature of the arches of Newport Tower is a perfect replica of the keystones found in arches in Orkney and Shetland. Other examples have been found in Greenland (one example remaining) Ireland (two examples found) and the Western Isles of Scotland (three examples identified).

10. The built-in niches of the tower have parallels in the medieval buildings of Orkney and Shetland. These features are unknown in New England except in some stone changers.

11. The plinth, pillar, capital and arch of the tower have no parallels in New England Colonial architecture but can readily be seen in Kirkwall Cathedral, Orkney.

12. The design of the fireplace with its double flues dates to the 1300s and was out of date in Europe by the 1400s. There are prototypes of this design in Scotland. Research has indicated that the fireplace, which is situated immediately opposite the west-facing window, was probably used as a beacon or signal station. The same can be said of the windows of the third level of the tower. Of the 27 round churches in Scandinavia, 18 of them had fireplaces on the first floor.

13. The interior and exterior walls of Newport Tower were covered with plaster stucco. This type of stucco finishing began in the 1200s and is common in Orkney and Shetland.

14. The probable design of the floor joists and corbels have their parallels in the buildings in Scotland of the medieval period.

15. The entry to the 1st floor was probably by a ladder through the window/entry #3. This method of access is to be found in the round churches of Scandinavia and was a common method of entry to castles in Scotland, e.g., Braal in Caithness (the earliest Sinclair Castle in Caithness).

16. Some architectural features in Newport Tower have been aligned astronomically. Some of the alignments fall on days which have significance to the Norse and to the Knights Templar.

17. There was probably an ambulatory surrounding the tower. This is apparent from the slight overlap which circles the tower immediately above the top level of the arches. It is not known whether this was ever built at Newport but it was a common feature with other round churches, e.g., Round Church of Lanleff in Brittany.

18. Newport Tower is situated at approximately the same latitude as Rome. This would make it an ideal reference point for exploration and mapping.

19. There are no architectural parallels in Colonial New England for Newport Tower. Its specific architectural features (taken singly or collectively) are not to be found anywhere in the New World.

20. It is my considered opinion that Newport Tower was built as (and served as) a church, observatory, lighthouse and datum zero point for future exploration of the New World.

Chapter Notes

Chapter 1

1. John C. Huden, *Indian Place Names of New England* (New York: Museum of the American Indian, Heye Foundation, 1962); Samuel A. Green and Elizabeth Sewell Hill, *Facts Relating to the History of Groton, Massachusetts* (Groton, MA: J. Wilson and Son, 1912).

2. Arthur J. Krim, in *New England Prospect: Maps, Place Names, and the Historical Landscape*, edited by Peter Benes (Boston: Boston University, 1980), p. 81; Krim notes that 17th-century toponymy for renaming most swamps ranged from metaphoric descriptions (Tophet Swamp) to commercial utility (Cedar Swamp);Edwin R. Hodgman, *History of the Town of Westford in the County of Middlesex, Massachusetts — 1659–1883*, 2003 ed. (Lowell, MA: Morning Mail Co., 1883), p. 2.

3. Caleb Butler, *History of the Town of Groton* (Boston: T. R. Marvin, 1848), p. 39. The section of Groton was annexed to Westford in 1730.

4. Elias Nason, *A Gazetteer of the State of Massachusetts* (Boston: B. B. Russell, 1874), p. 542.

5. Frank Glynn, "A Unique Punched Portrait in Massachusetts," *Eastern States Archaeological Federation Bulletin* 16 (1957), 11.

6. Hodgman, p. 237.

7. Book 230, p. 590 (1892). Middlesex County Registry of Deeds, Northern District, Lowell, MA.

8. William Henry Babcock, *Early Norse Visits to North America* (Washington, DC: Smithsonian Institution, 1913).

9. William B. Goodwin, *The Truth about Leif Ericsson and the Greenland Voyages* (Boston: Meador Publishing Company, 1941), p. 197; Carl Christian Rafn, *Antiqvitates Americanæ; sive, Scriptores Septentrionales Rerum Ante-Columbianarum in America* (Copenhagen, Denmark: Typis Officinæ Schultzianæ, 1837); see Slafter et al., *Voyages of the Northmen to America* (Boston:

The Prince Society, 1877), for a summary of Rafn's geographic identifications, culled by Slafter from the 1838 English translation of Rafn (1837).

10. Now referred to as the "Pearson Chamber," a later and overdue change in the structure's identification. During Goodwin's era of research, it was simply known as the Upton Chamber or Great Beehive.

11. Pratt Pond, Jr., "Upton Traditions: A Deserted Haunt of Unknown Origin," *Milford Journal* (Milford, MA), April 26, 1893.

12. Malcolm Pearson, "Was It a Cave?" in *Upton, Massachusetts*, edited by William George Poor (Milford, MA: Charlescraft Press, 1935), pp. 149–50.

13. Babcock (1913), p. 49. "A more positive claim has been put forward by a New Hampshire judge in the latter case in the *Boston Journal* quoted by the *Philadelphia Times* of July 27, 1902, as follows — A certain field on the narrow marsh and beach on the main road up town Hampton contains the rock on which are cut the three crosses designating the grave where was buried Thorvald Ericsson in the year A.D. 1004. The rock is a large granite stone lying in the earth, its face near the top of the ground with the crosses cut thereon and other marks cut by the hand of man with a stone chisel and not by any owner. That field came into possession of the author's ancestors 250 years ago."

14. Olaf Strandwold, *Norse Runic Inscriptions along the Atlantic Seaboard* (Prosser, WA: published by author, 1939).

15. Ibid., pp. 12, 48. Both Strandwold and Cheney apparently miss the significance of Cheney finding the "Magunco Stone" in the same layer of silt as a colonial shoe buckle.

16. See David Goudsward, *Ancient Stone Sites of New England and the Debate over Early European Exploration* (Jefferson, NC: McFarland, 2006), for more of the Hampton Rune Stone, aka "Thorwald's Grave."

17. Olaf Strandwold and Thomas Sigurd-sen, *The Yarmouth Stone, Mystic Characters on Yarmouth Stone Yield Startling Evidence of Norse Discoveries* (Prosser, WA: Prosser Printing Company, 1934).

18. William B. Goodwin, *The Ruins of Great Ireland in New England* (Boston: Meador Publishing Company, 1946), p. 31. "Many persons have asked me how I became interested in the strange stone houses. The fact is that on a visit to Seattle, Washington, some fifteen years ago I was asked by Professor Olaf Strandwold of Prosser, Washington, if I knew of an unmortared stone beehive house in Upton, Massachusetts, thought to have been built by the Greenland Settlers in Vineland. To make a long story short, on my return East I went to interview Mr. Henry A. Cheney of Hopkinton, Massachusetts, who took me to Upton and introduced me to Malcolm D. Pearson on whose home place stood the great beehive to which we devote a chapter in his book, along with the little sweathouse in Hopkinton."

19. "Old Caves at Salem, N.H., Laid to Robbers, Indians," *Boston Globe*, October 24, 1935; known locally as "Pattee's Caves," the name would eventually be known as Mystery Hill. Currently, it is open to the public as "America's Stonehenge."

20. In a letter to Harral Ayres dated July 27, 1936, Goodwin wrote, "From that day when we [first] ... gazed in perplexity at the jumble of rocks on the Site at North Salem, we could not help but realize that there were no ordinary or haphazard remains of man's handiwork but the living, if silent, proof of a long forgotten past. Well do we remember our astonishment. Instinctively we had to stop and sit down on the stone by the tall pine in the plaza, covering our face with our hands to shut in the picture of desolation around us, trying to think out what this utterly un-American set-up might mean."

21. A December 1936 letter from Cheney to Goodwin asks him directly what would happen to him and Pearson if Goodwin did buy the property, reminding Goodwin that he "was the originator of the Norse story in connection with the caves."

22. Rafn (1837), p. 448.

23. Clay Perry, *Underground New England* (Brattleboro, VT: Stephen Daye Press, 1939).

24. "Local Engineer Given Credit for Solving a Mystery of the Vikings," *Daily Hampshire Gazette*, July 9, 1940.

25. Goodwin (1941), pp. 41–78. Other authors have placed the location up and down the Eastern seaboard with similar lack of confirma-tion by scholarly or archaeological sources. Currently, the only confirmed Norse colony site in North America is L'Anse aux Meadows in Newfoundland, Canada, discovered in 1960.

26. Perry (1939), pp. 154, 174.

Chapter 2

1. Goodwin was convinced the sites had been built by 9th-century Irish Catholic colonists of an order of monks known as Ceilie De or the Culdees.

2. Clay Perry, *Underground New England* (Brattleboro, VT: Stephen Daye Press, 1939).

3. After 10 years in Texas, Ayres had returned to the northeast and resumed work on a book on Indian trails. The book's original inspiration in 1915 itself appears to have been motivated by the work of Levi Badger Chase. Ayres had been exploring the origins of the Indian name of Lake Chaubunagungamaug near his home in Webster, Massachusetts, when Chase began publishing his own work on the Bay Path of the Indians. The Bay Path and the Great Trail diverge near Webster, and Chase asserted that Thomas Hooker traveled from Cambridge along the Bay Path to central Connecticut where he would found Hartford, as opposed to traveling along the Great Trail, which Ayres advocated.

4. Perry (1939), p. 167. Perry also incorrectly identifies Harry Cheney as "William Cheney."

5. Harral Ayres, *The Great Trail of New England* (Boston: Meador Publishing Company, 1940); Ayres, "Connecticut River Explorations" by William B. Goodwin, Hartford, Connecticut, pp. 111–23. Ayres also dedicated the book to Goodwin. The point where Hooker crossed the Connecticut River remained a debated point, at least locally. Ayres was still being interviewed as late as 1946 about the controversy.

6. There is no record of how far Ayres proceeded with the Mohawk Trail project, but it was not completed or published. Ayres, who was in his 70s when the first book came out in 1940, may have simply decided that between his age, distance from the research material (he was living in New Jersey) and Goodwin's fluctuating health, the project was not feasible. Ayres died in 1961 in Montclair, New Jersey.

7. Ayres, pp. 232–38.

8. Claire Augusta Wilcox Noall, in her biography of Willard Richards, an early leader in the Latter Day Saint movement and Hopkinton native, acknowledges Cheney's help in understanding the locality, specifically mentioning the 5000-volume personal library at his farm.

9. William B. Goodwin correspondence with William Sumner Appleton Jr. (July 22, 1937).

10. Goodwin and Appleton corresponded regularly on historical matters as peers; Goodwin was considered an expert on colonial cabinet makers and collected decorative art materials for the Wadsworth Athenaeum in Hartford, Connecticut, and Appleton was founder of the Society for the Preservation of New England Antiquities (SPNEA), a group that purchased and restored historic buildings as museums.

11. Unveiled in 1887, the statue by Anne Whitney still stands on Commonwealth Avenue in Boston.

12. The committee's distinguished members included Longfellow, James Russell Lowell, Oliver Wendell Holmes, Eben Norton Horsford, Harvard President Charles Eliot, publisher James Fields, Massachusetts Governor Alexander H. Rice and the mayors of Boston and Cambridge. Soon after purchasing the North Salem site, Goodwin was amazed to discover that Appleton had visited the site previously with historian George Francis Dow and archaeologist Warren K. Moorehead of the Peabody Museum of Archaeology at Phillips Academy, Andover, Massachusetts. The three had toured the site after an article in a Haverhill, Massachusetts, newspaper in 1934, a year before the Boston newspaper article that caught the attention of Cheney and Pearson

13. L. V. Grinsell, "The Breaking of Objects as a Funerary Rite," *Folklore* 72 (3) (1961), 475–91.

14. Walter Pennington, "An Irish Parallel to the Broken Sword of the Grail Castle," *Modern Language Notes* 43 (8) (1928), 534–36.

15. Carl Christian Rafn, *Antiqvitates Americanæ; sive, Scriptores Septentrionales Rerum Ante-Columbianarum in America* (Copenhagen, Denmark: Typis Officinæ Schultzianæ, 1837).

16. Carl Christian Rafn, *Supplement to the Antiquitates Americæ* (Copenhagen, Denmark: Typis Officinæ Schultzianæ, 1841).

17. Among the various Nordic-themed works are Longfellow's "Skeleton in Armor," a tale of a Viking ghost mourning his lost love at the Newport Tower in Rhode Island and Whittier's "The Norsemen," with Viking longboats sailing up the Merrimack River.

18. Charles Wingate Chase, *History of Haverhill, Massachusetts* (Haverhill, MA: published by author, 1861).

19. At least three copies of this letter exist in the Goodwin archives in the Connecticut State Library with notes indicating the letter was sent to at least ten museums and historical societies in Scandinavia. My thanks to researcher Terry Deveau for pointing these out.

20. William B. Goodwin, *The Ruins of Great Ireland in New England* (Boston: Meador Publishing Company, 1946), pp. 187, 252. Although Goodwin did visit England on at least one occasion (1906), there is no indication he actually visited Skellig Michael.

21. William B. Goodwin, *The Truth about Leif Ericsson and the Greenland Voyages* (Boston: Meador Publishing Company, 1941).

22. William B. Goodwin correspondence with David Robert Smith (December 16, 1941).

23. "Sometimes I have thought it to be a Christian cross but the face at the top and not at the cross arms of the sword inclines me to believe that it may not be a cross but as is usually said about it that it is a sword."

24. Vincent F. Fagan correspondence with William B. Goodwin (November 18, 1942).

25. Malcolm Pearson correspondence with Vincent F. Fagan (June 26, 1945).

26. Goodwin and Morison had been verbally sparring for years. Goodwin believed Morison sent Hugh Hencken to North Salem specifically to write a discrediting article on his work in 1939. Goodwin published a 1940 book that questioned Morison's location of Columbus's lost colony of La Navidad, prompting Morison to arrange to have the Hencken article republished in a larger magazine. See Goudsward and Stone, *America's Stonehenge: The Mystery Hill Story* (Wellesley, MA: Branden Books, 2002), pp. 81–86, for more on the feud.

27. Goodwin (1946), pp. 362–63.

28. Ibid., p. 54.

29. Vincent F. Fagan correspondence with William B. Goodwin (February 1, 1944); William B. Goodwin correspondence with Vincent F. Fagan (February 5, 1944).

30. William B. Goodwin correspondence with Vincent F. Fagan (September 3, 1943).

31. Goodwin (1946), p. 19.

32. Weston is the location of Norumbega Park, home to a fieldstone tower commemorating the location of Norumbega, at least in the theories of Eben Norton Horsford. Considering Goodwin's opinion of Horsford's theory, it is not a location he would include in his book under normal circumstances.

33. For additional biographic material on Goodwin, see Goudsward and Stone (2003).

34. Clay Perry, *New England's Buried Treasure* (New York: Stephen Daye Press, 1946). Perry would subsequently write a book on New York caves. The series progressed no further than the first two volumes.

35. Perry (1939), pp. 154, 174; Perry (1946), p. 245.

36. Ayres had been looking for a feeder trail leading from Lowell to the Mohawk Trail, making Westford a component along a trail.

37. The face-cross on Skellig Michael is an unusual style of standing cross. The upper arm of the cross, normally just a continuation of the vertical bar bisecting the horizontal bar, has been rounded into a stylized head, making the cross a hybrid of the crucifix and Christ. Charles Thomas notes that the style seems to appear in the 7th century and is almost certainly influenced by the "crux ansata" of the Coptic Church in Egypt, so-called because of its resemblance to the hieroglyphic ankh. The horizontal bar and the lower terminus of the vertical bar end in flares and the upper terminus of the vertical has become a double circle. See Charles Thomas, *The Early Christian Archaeology of North Britain* (Oxford: Oxford University Press, 1971), pp. 129–30, for a small comparative sketch of five face-crosses from Ireland. Thomas notes the Skellig Michael face-cross shows signs of the style "de-evolving" with the stone shaped like a face-cross with a separate cross incised on the stone instead of the stone itself being part of the cross design (p. 130). Helen Roe appears to be of the opinion this was evolution, not de-evolution, and that the style was evolving onto a "breast plate" form with the cross becoming a component of the body of Christ. See Roe, "A Stone Cross at Clogher, County Tyrone," *Journal of the Royal Society of Antiquaries of Ireland* 90 (1960), p. 193.

38. Robert Stone recollects that in the mid-1950s while starting up operations at Mystery Hill, Goodwin's publisher contacted him and offered to ship him the remaining stock that still sat in the warehouse. Stone agreed and sold the remaining books at the site for a dollar a piece.

39. Malcolm Pearson correspondence with Shaemas O'Sheel (April 2, 1948).

40. Johannes Brøndsted, *Problemet om Nordboer i Nordamerika før Columbus — en Bedømmelse af det Amerikanske Materiale* (Copenhagen, Denmark: Nordisk Oldkyndighed og Historie, 1951).

41. Ibid., pp. 145–46. Brøndsted quotes an August 15, 1949, letter from Moltke.

42. Brøndsted's overall opinion of the Norse sites in America was similarly negative — the only finds he considered remotely viable were a sword, axe and metal fragments found in Beardmore, Ontario, in 1931, but the provenance was so suspect as to render the evidence unusable.

43. Johannes Brøndsted, *Norsemen in North America before Columbus* (Washington, DC: Smithsonian Institution, 1954).

44. John Frohlin correspondence with Vincent F. Fagan (June 9, 1949); Olaf Strandwold, *Norse Inscriptions on American Stones* (Weehawken, NJ: Magnus Björndal, 1948). The second publication was dated 1948 and internal references suggest it had taken over a year to finally go to press. Pearson and Fagan did not contribute new material but are represented by scattered images not specifically supplied for the book.

45. Frank Glynn correspondence with Clay Perry (June 6, 1958).

Chapter 3

1. T. C. Lethbridge, *Merlin's Island — Essays on Britain in the Dark Ages* (London: Methuen & Co. Ltd, 1948).

2. Lethbridge (1948), Chapter 4.

3. T. C. Lethbridge, *Umiak — The European Ancestry of the 'Women's Boat.'* (Cambridge, England: privately published, 1937). The design of the currach or curragh is unique to the west coasts of Ireland and Scotland (with regional variations). See Richard Mac Cullagh, *The Irish Currach Folk* (Dublin: Wolfhound Press, 1992). St. Brendan was traditionally supposed to reach America in a currach, the possibility of which was proven feasible by Tim Severin by sailing one from Ireland to Newfoundland. See Timothy Severin, *The Brendan Voyage* (New York: McGraw-Hill, 1978).

4. T. C. Lethbridge, *Herdsmen and Hermits — Celtic Seafarers in the Northern Seas* (Cambridge, England: Bowes & Bowes, 1950), pp. 129–30. The Kensington Rune Stone is a 200-lb. stone with medieval runic writing on its face and one edge. The stone was discovered in 1898 on the property of a Minnesota farmer named Olof Öhman. The inscription tells of a Norwegian expedition in 1362 and the apparent massacre of ten men. Since it was found, the stone has continually been debated, denounced and defended. The stone currently resides in the Rune Stone Museum in Alexandria, Minnesota.

5. Glyn Daniel, "Editorial," *Antiquity* XLII (166) (June 1968), pp. 81–87.

6. Eric Forbes-Boyd, "The Dark Ages Reseen," *Christian Science Monitor* (July 28, 1948), p. 16.

7. Frank Glynn and T.C. Lethbridge, *T. C. Lethbridge — Frank Glynn Correspondence: 1950–1966* (Rowley, MA: Early Sites Research Society, 1980) [hereafter cited as Lethbridge-Glynn Correspondence].

8. Lethbridge-Glynn Correpondence (1980), p. 5.

9. Excerpt on file with Fletcher Library Westford Knight Collection. Published by permission of the Trustees of the J. V. Fletcher Library, Westford, Massachusetts.

10. Goodwin (1946), p. 19.

11. Glynn had met Goodwin in April 1949 to discuss a series of small carved stones Glynn had discovered in Guilford, Connecticut. Yale believed them to be the work of bored laborers at a nearby quarry and Goodwin agreed with Yale.

12. The photographs that appeared in Strandwold (1948) were taken by the property owner, Lawrence Rogers.

13. Iona was such a popular travel destination that, at the turn of the 20th century, art nouveau silversmiths created jewelry and flatware based on Iona funerary art motifs. See Henry Davenport Graham, *Antiquities of Iona* (London: Day & Son, 1850); James Drummond, *Archaeologia Scotica. Sculptured Monuments in Iona & the West Highlands* (Edinburgh: Society of Antiquaries of Scotland, 1881).

14. R. A. S. Macalister, "An Inventory of the Ancient Monuments Remaining in the Island of Iona," *Proceedings of the Society of Antiquaries of Scotland* 48 (1913), pp. 421–30.

15. Lethbridge (1950), pp. 128–29; Sir William died on August 25, 1330. He was killed, along with his brother John, in Spain at the Battle of Teba. They were on their way to the East with the heart of Robert the Bruce to bury in the Holy Land.

16. Andrew Sinclair, *The Sword and the Grail* (New York: Crown, 1992); Andrew Kerr, "Rosslyn Castle, Its Buildings Past and Present," *Proceedings of the Society of Antiquaries of Scotland* 12 (1876), pp. 412–24.

17. Cindy Glynn correspondence with Terry J. Deveau (2009).

18. Lethbridge (1967), pp. 147–53. Lethbridge suggests that Cindy's atypical interest in the topic was evidence of a psychic ability, using the anecdote and the story of the Westford carving to lead into a discussion of happenstance and clairvoyance.

19. Lawrence F. Willard, "Westford's Mysterious Knight," *Yankee* 22 (April 1958), pp. 60–61, 84–89.

20. Lethbridge-Glynn Correspondence (1980), pp. 31–32; Lethbridge (1967), pp. 148–49.

21. The stone is that of Roderick, 7th Chief of the MacLeods (d. c. 1498). St Columba's Church was the traditional burial place of the clan chiefs. The stone was relocated into the ruins of the church to partially protect the piece. National Monuments Record of Scotland Identification Number: NB43SE 5.

22. Inexplicably, this early, visually unimpressive Glynn image is the one included in the recent editions of the official guide book to Rosslyn Chapel.

23. Edward Hitchcock, *Final Report on the Geology of Massachusetts* (Northampton, MA: Butler, 1841); William Phillips, Henry James Brooke and William Hallows Miller, *An Elementary Introduction to Mineralogy* (London: Longman Brown Green and Longmans, 1852).

24. Andalusite also occurs in Aberdeenshire and on Unst in the Shetland Islands, two locations that Henry Sinclair may have been familiar with. So there may also been a degree of recognition when the expedition came across the ledge in Westford.

25. Fisher Buckshorn's mother, Addie Buckshorn (Adeline Maria Fisher Kittredge Buckshorn, 1860–1950) was Lila's (Eliza Capen Fisher, 1870–1957) older sister.

26. Lethbridge-Glynn Correspondence (1998), p. 31. The 1998 edition was revised to include Glynn's field notes from his first visit to the carving.

27. Ibid., p. 30.

28. Lethbridge-Glynn Correspondence (1989), pp. 70–71.

29. Joseph Killean, "Man About Town (column)," *Lowell Sun*, June 18, 1957.

30. Lethbridge-Glynn Correspondence (1980), pp. 74–75. In 1994, James Whittall used silicon rubber to create a mold of the ledge and finally succeeded in casting the Knight. Copies from the mold exist in such diverse locations as the Clan Gunn Heritage Centre in Latheron, Scotland; Rosslyn Chapel, Roslin, Scotland; Westford Museum, Massachusetts; and in the lodge at Mystery Hill in North Salem, New Hampshire.

31. Emilie Tavel, "Rock Sketch Hints Scottish Invasion of America in 14th Century," *Christian Science Monitor*, October 2, 1957.

32. Frederick J. Pohl, *The Sinclair Expedition to Nova Scotia in 1398* (Pictou, Nova Scotia: Pictou Advocate Press, 1950).

33. Lethbridge-Glynn Correspondence, p. 77. The curators also offered thoughts on an area that was perpetually perplexing Glynn — the Knight's chest, where Glynn and Lethbridge believed a falcon was drawn, either perched on the sword or attached to the shield's coronet as a heraldic symbol. Neither interpretation would last in the ongoing reexamination of the carving.

34. William S. Fowler, "The Westford Indian Rock," *Massachusetts Archaeological Society Bulletin* 21 (2) (January 1960), pp. 21–22.

35. The tomahawk, or "belt axe," is in the collections of the Rhode Island Historical Society (Call # 1858.1.1). The RIHS catalog notes the blade of the ax is inscribed "Ens Wm. Denison 1760" on blade. The dimensions of the artifact (height 17.875 inches x width 6.125 at the blade) indicate that the Westford carving would not be a life-size rendering of the object.

36. Hodgman, p. 258. According to the town history, the only house nearby was the town parsonage, built in 1727.

37. William S. Fowler, "Tomahawks of Central New England," *Massachusetts Archaeological Society Bulletin* 12 (3) (April 1951), 29–37; William S. Fowler, "Trade Tomahawks," *Massachusetts Archaeological Society Bulletin* 13 (3) (April 1952), 23–27.

38. Frederick J. Pohl, *Atlantic Crossings Before Columbus* (New York: Norton, 1961); Charles Michael Boland, *They All Discovered America* (Garden City, NY: Doubleday, 1961).

39. In a 1960 letter to Frank Glynn, Pohl unequivocally declared that Fowler had distorted the cross-guard, tapering one end and widening the other, to make it look like a tomahawk head. Pohl suggested that Glynn simply ignore the Fowler article, advice Pohl himself followed as well; Boland, pp. 335–37.

40. T. C. Lethbridge, *A Step in the Dark* (London: Routledge & Kegan Paul, 1967).

41. Frederick J. Pohl, *Prince Henry Sinclair — His Voyage to the New World in 1398* (New York: Clarkson N. Potter, 1974).

42. Sinclair (1992), p. 143.

Chapter 4

1. Frank Glynn, "A Unique Punched Portrait in Massachusetts," *Eastern States Archaeological Federation Bulletin* 16 (1957).

2. Frederick J. Pohl, *The Sinclair Expedition to Nova Scotia in 1398* (Pictou, Nova Scotia: Pictou Advocate Press, 1950).

3. Frederick J. Pohl, *Atlantic Crossings Before Columbus* (New York: Norton, 1961); Frederick J. Pohl, *Prince Henry Sinclair — His Voyage to the New World in 1398* (New York: Clarkson N. Potter, 1974).

4. Pohl (1974), p. 161.

5. Lis Rubin Jacobsen and Erik Moltke, *Danmarks Runeindskrifter* (Copenhagen, Denmark: Einar Munksgaard, 1941).

6. K. A. Steer and J. W. M. Bannerman, *Late Medieval Monumental Sculpture in the West Highlands* (Edinburgh: Royal Commission on the Ancient and Historical Monuments of Scotland, 1977), p. 22.

7. National Archives of Scotland, Liber Niger, PA5/4, f. 71v and 71r1. "que tout homme, François et Escot, ait un signe devant et derrere c'est assavoir une croiz blanche Saint Andrieu et se son jacque soit blanc ou sa côte blanche il portera la dicte croiz blanche en une piece de drap noir ronde ou quarree."

8. Pohl (1961), pp. 282–83.

9. The word "aketon" derives from Arabic and suggests the use of cotton as the quilting agent. The article is also called a gambeson but the two terms appear to be interchangeable. The name in Ireland, cotún, also implies cotton padding.

10. R. Ewart Oakeshott, *The Archaeology of Weapons; Arms and Armor from Prehistory to the Age of Chivalry* (New York: Praeger, 1960), p. 269.

11. Pohl (1974), pp. 161–63.

12. Derek Brewer and Jonathan Gibson, *A Companion to the Gawain-poet* (Woodbridge, England: Boydell & Brewer Ltd, 1997).

13. Ibid., p. 167 n4.

14. The pommel, at the end of the hilt, acted as a counterbalance against the weight of the sword's blade. Pommels came in various forms as swords evolved; the wheel pommel was popular among knights and was a simple, unadorned, round disc. It was more than decorative — in certain feinting moves, the sword reversed direction and struck the opponent in the face with the hard metal pommel. Oakeshott (1994) points out that during the late Middle Ages there was almost limitless variety in the form of sword pommels. Because of the age and simplicity of the Westford rendering, it is not possible to specifically identify which type of pommel is portrayed.

15. In the 11th and early 12th centuries, shields were long, narrow and kite-shaped, protecting most of the body. As the 12th century ended, the tops of shields became flatter, and decoration became more personalized. By the 13th century, shields were shorter and shaped like the base of a flat-iron, resulting in the name "heater shield." This type of shield, still used in heraldry, remained in use for most of the 14th century.

16. Lethbridge quotes Moncrieffe's letter at length in Lethbridge-Glynn Correspondence (1980), pp. 52–53.

17. Sir Iain Moncreiffe correspondence with unknown correspondent (March 12, 1973).

18. Sir Iain Moncreiffe, *The Highland Clans* (New York: Clarkson N. Potter, 1967), p. 161.

19. Ibid. Sir Iain also notes that based on other Caithness shields, the oars could alternatively be mast-ropes linking to a mast that had eroded away.

20. Sally Badham, " 'A New Feire Peynted Stone' — Medieval English Incised Slabs?" *Church Monuments — The Journal of The Church Monuments Society* 17 (2004), pp. 20–52.

21. James Dwight Dana, *A System of Mineralogy*, 4th ed. (New York: G. P. Putnam, 1854), p. 258; George Frederick Kunz, *Gems and Precious Stones of North America* (New York: Scientific Publishing Company, 1892), p. 171.

22. Hodgman, p. 4.

23. Pohl (1974), p. 156. Pohl also returned Indian attack to his list of possible causes of death.

24. Lethbridge-Glynn Correspondence (1980), p. 46.

25. Tim Wallace-Murphy and Marilyn Hopkins, *Templars in America: From the Crusades to the New World* (York Beach, ME: Weiser Books, 2004).

26. Ibid., p. 126. Adding insult to injury, the image is reproduced as a mirror image, with the falcon facing the wrong way and the fleurette on the wrong breast.

27. See Mark Finnan, *The Sinclair Saga* (Halifax, Nova Scotia: Formac Publishing, 1999), p. 88, and Robert Ellis Cahill, *New England's Ancient Mysteries* (Salem, MA: Old Saltbox Publishing House, 1993), p. 72, for the most readily available copies of the Whittall illustrations.

28. Robert Brydall, "The Monumental Effigies of Scotland, from the Thirteenth to the Fifteenth Century," *Proceedings of the Society of Antiquaries of Scotland* 29 (May 13, 1895), p. 329.

29. Ibid., p. 330.

30. John Hunt and Peter Harbison, *Irish Medieval Figure Sculpture, 1200–1600: A Study of Irish Tombs with Notes on Costume and Armour* (Dublin: Irish University Press, 1974).

The time period of 1200–1350 is designated as a major motif grouping, starting with the latter part of the Norman invasion of Ireland through the advent of the Black Death in 1348. In the subsequent century, little Irish funeral art exists.

31. The town acquired its name from the Knights Hospitaller who built a church in that location. Ironically, the Westford Knight carving would become associated with the rival Knights Templar order.

32. Hunt and Harbison, vol. 2, plate 15. Descriptive text is in vol. 1, p. 201.

33. There is little, if anything, remaining of the monastery founded on Iona by St. Columba in 563 A.D. A modern restoration of a Benedictine Abbey founded in 1203 A.D. is what visitors see today.

34. Royal Commission on the Ancient and Historical Monuments and Constructions of Scotland, *Argyll: An Inventory of the Ancient Monuments* (Edinburgh: Royal Commission on the Ancient and Historical Monuments and Constructions of Scotland, 1982).

35. Steer and Bannerman, pp. 23–27. Steer and Bannerman date the carving to the second half of the 14th century based on the armor and sword styles.

36. Ibid., p. 26.

37. Royal Commission on the Ancient and Historical Monuments and Constructions of Scotland, pp. 233–34. An inscription is carved in the MacKinnon pillow, which, restored and translated, reads "Here lies Gilbride MacKinnon with his sons Ewan and Cornebellus." A second inscription on the edge of the slab also notes "Here lies Finguine, son of Cormac, and Finlay, son of Finguine, and Ewan."

38. Steer and Bannerman, pp. 22–23. Creation of the effigies all but stopped as a result of the Black Death and the various wars with England. The effigies resume again in the late 14th century.

Chapter 5

1. James Graham-Campbell and Colleen E. Batey, *Vikings in Scotland: An Archaeological Survey* (Edinburgh: Edinburgh University Press, 1998).

2. *The Orkneyinga Saga: The History of the Earls of Orkney*, translated by Hermann Pálsson and Paul Geoffrey Edwards (London: Hogarth Press, 1978).

3. John Burke, *A General and Heraldic Dictionary of the Peerage and Baronetage of the British Empire*, 106th ed. (London: Burke's Peerage, Ltd, 1999).

4. B. E. Crawford, "Sinclair Family (per. 1280–c.1500)," in *Oxford Dictionary of National Biography* (Oxford: Oxford University Press, 2004).

5. *Burke's Peerage, Baronetage & Knightage*, edited by Charles Mosely, 107th ed. (Wilmington, DE: Burke's Peerage, Ltd, 2003).

6. The son of Weyland of Arde and Matilda, another daughter of Malise. De l'Arde was Governor and Commissioner of Orkney for a brief period but was not awarded the title. Henry's aunt Eupheme married Guttorm Sperra. Malise Sperra, lord of Skaldale, was Henry's first cousin.

7. Eldbjørg Haug, *Provincia Nidrosiensis i Dronning Margretes Unions- og Maktpolitikk* (Trondheim, Norway: Historisk Institutt NTNU, 1996), p. 219. Norway's Margaret drew militia from all the Scandinavian territories to defeat the usurper king of Sweden, Albrekt of Mecklenburg. This was the final battle that culminated in the Union of Kalmar in June 1397, which brought the kingdoms of Norway, Sweden, and Denmark together under a single monarch until 1523.

8. Roland William Saint-Clair, *The Saint-Clairs of the Isles* (Auckland, New Zealand: H. Brett, 1898).

9. O. S. Rydberg, *Sverges Traktater med Främmande Magter — Jemte Aandra Ditt Hörande Handlingar*, vol. 5 (Stockholm, Sweden: P.A. Norstedt & Söner, 1883), pp. 650–51. The letter does not state whether or not Sinclair was in Scandinavia for the coronation.

10. Stephen I. Boardman, *The Early Stewart Kings: Robert II and Robert III, 1371–1406* (East Linton, Scotland: Tuckwell Press, 1996).

11. Ibid., pp. 142, 280. The Battle of Otterburn pitted Scotland's James Douglas, 2nd Earl of Douglas, against Sir Henry Percy in Northumberland. Douglas defeated Percy, but was killed in the battle. Saint-Clair (p. 98) does place several cousins at the battle.

12. B. E. Crawford, "The Pledging of the Islands in 1469: The Historical Background," in *Shetland and the Outside World 1469–1969*, edited by Donald J. Withrington (Oxford: Oxford University Press, 1983), pp. 18–19 and 32–48.

13. B. E. Crawford, Lyn Blackmore and John W. Allen, *The Biggings, Papa Stour, Shetland: The History and Eexcavation of a Royal Norwegian Farm* (Edinburgh: Society of Antiquaries of Scotland, 1999).

14. B. E. Crawford, "The Historical and Archaeological Background to the Papa Stour Project," in *Papa Stour and 1299: Commemorating the 700th Anniversary of Shetland's First Document*, edited by B. E. Crawford and Jon Gunnar Jørgensen (Lerwick, Shetland: Shetland Times Ltd., 2002), pp. 13–35.

15. See John R. Tudor, *The Orkneys and Shetland; Their Past and Present State* (London: Edward Stanford, 1883), pp. 58, 467, for a fairly typical version of the story.

16. Crawford (1983), p. 38.

17. *Registrum Magni Sigilli Regum Scotorum (The Register of the Great Seal of Scotland)*, edited by John Maitland Thomson (Edinburgh: Scottish Record Society, 1984); *Diplomatarium Norvegicum*, edited by Christian C. A. Lange

and Carl R. Unger (Oslo, Norway: P.T. Mallings Forlagshandel, 1852).

18. *Registrum Magni Sigilli Regum Scotorum* (1912), vol. 1, p. 320; *Diplomatarium Norvegicum* (1852), vol. II, pp. 401–2.

19. J. Storer Clouston, *Records of the Earldom of Orkney, 1299–1614* (Edinburgh: Scottish Historical Society, 1914).

20. Thomas Sinclair, "Prince Henry Sinclair II — The Pre-Columbian Discoverer of America, One of the Ancestors of the Caithness Family," in *Caithness Events: a discussion of Captain Kennedy's historical narrative, and an account of the Broynach earls, to which is added a supplement of emendations of 1899* (Wick, Scotland: W. Rae, 1899).

21. Crawford (1999), p. 19; Clouston (p. 28) also notes the gathering of knights as "tangible evidence" of the stories of "princely magnificence" of the Sinclair Earls.

22. Boardman, pp. 205, 219.

23. "Diploma of Thomas, Bishop of Orkney and Zetland, and the Chapter of Kirkwall, addressed to Eric King of Norway, Respecting the Genealogy of William Saint Clair, Earl of Orkney," in *The Bannatyne Miscellany; containing original papers and tracts, chiefly relating to the history and literature of Scotland*, edited by Walter Scott, David Laing and Thomas Thomson (New York: AMS Press, 1973), vol. 3.

24. Clouston, pp. 35–36.

25. Ibid., pp. 36–45.

26. Menzies' misdeeds, while inexcusable, were a pale foreshadowing of the privations and oppression that Orkney would suffer when the Earldom was subsequently acquired by the Stewarts.

27. "Diploma," p. 81. "Cum quo Rege certas iniit pactiones conditiones et appunctuamenta, per quasque reversus est usque ad extremum vite sue Comesque Orcadie obitt, et pro defensione patrie inibi crudeliter ab inimicis peremtus est."

28. Pohl (1974), pp. 170–71; John Trussel, *A Continuation of the Collection of the History of England* (London: Printed by M.D. for Ephraim Dawson, 1636), pp. 68–69. Because the Orkneys were in Norwegian territory, not Scottish, this theory only works if it is a retaliatory strike aimed specifically at the Sinclairs.

29. There is evidence of the earlier structure, used as the sacristy in Rosslyn Chapel, as accessed by stairs near the Apprentice Column.

30. John Slezer, *Theatrum Scotiæ* (London: Printed by John Leake for Abell Swalle, 1693).

31. Ibid., p. 63. The entire inventory of burials includes George, Earl of Caithness;

Alexander Sutherland (William Sinclair's father-in-law); three Earls of Orkney; and nine Barons of Rosslyn.

32. Father Hay's widowed mother had married Sir James St. Clair.

33. Richard Augustine Hay, *Genealogie of the Sainteclaires of Rosslyn* (Edinburgh: T. G. Stevenson, 1835).

34. Because of the surge in interest in Rosslyn Chapel in the wake of *The Da Vinci Code*, it was reprinted in 2002 by the Grand Lodge of Scotland.

35. Hay (1835), pp. i–ii, 173. Continuing his notes, Maidment also notes obvious errors in Father Hay's transcriptions.

36. Thomas Innes, *A Critical Essay on the Ancient Inhabitants of the Northern Parts of Britain or Scotland* (Edinburgh: W. Paterson, 1879); p. 131; E. L. G. Stones, *Anglo-Scottish Relations 1174–1328* (Oxford: Clarendon Press, 1970), pp. xxxi–xxxii, 75–76, 116, 150–51, 168.

37. See Charles Purton Cooper, *An Account of the Most Important Public Records of Great Britain and the Publications of the Record Commissioners* (London: Baldwin and Cradock, 1832), pp. 179–89, for more details of the record losses.

38. Queen Margaret was a pivotal figure in Scottish history, beginning the transition of Scotland toward English influence and away from the Norse, building churches, rebuilding the monastery on Iona, and bringing the Celtic church back under control of the Roman leadership. She was canonized in 1251 by Pope Innocent IV on account of her great benefactions to the Church and is considered a patron saint of Scotland.

39. Thomas Sinclair, *The Sinclairs of England* (London: Trübner, 1887), p. 3. Sinclair later explains that William actually appears on the Dives Roll, but unlike his brother who appears as Richard de Saint-Clair. William appears as Guillaume le Blond because, even then, he was "seemly" (p. 22).

40. H. J. Lawlor, "Notes on the Library of the Sinclairs of Rosslyn," *Proceedings of the Society of Antiquaries of Scotland* 32 (1897–98), pp. 90–120.

41. Ibid., p. 93.

42. Hay (1835), p. 34.

43. Edmund Lodge, *The Genealogy of the Existing British Peerage* (London: Saunders and Otley, 1832), p. 59.

44. Colin Pilkington, *Devolution in Britain Today* (Manchester, England: Manchester University Press, 2002).

45. Ibid., p. 26.

46. Current indications are that this William is the son of Britel de St. Clair, although an unrelated line of Sinclairs appears in Scotland nearly a century earlier, as documented by an 1162 charter of the lands of Herdmanston from Richard de Moreville, Constable of Scotland.

47. Hay (1835), p. 33.

48. David Hume, *The History of the Houses of Douglas and Angus* (Edinburgh: Evan Tyler, 1643).

49. Ibid., p. 242. He lists Henry II as "Knight of the Cockle, of the Garter and Prince of Orkney."

50. James Wallace, *An Account of the Islands of Orkney by James Wallace* (London: Jacob Tonson, 1700).

51. Ibid., p. 118.

52. John Mooney, *The Cathedral and Royal Burgh of Kirkwall*, 2nd ed. (Kirkwall, Orkney: W. R. Mackintosh, 1947).

53. Håkon, showing remarkable foresight in 1379 when Henry Sinclair was granted the jarldom, stipulated one of the conditions of the grant was that Sinclair would build no permanent structures on the islands. Sinclair ignored that condition and built Kirkwall Castle.

54. *Charter: Ratification to the Earl of Caithness (16 May 1471)* [cited July 15, 2008]. Available from http://www.rps.ac.uk.

55. Bernard Sir Burke, *Vicissitudes of Families: And Other Essays*, 4th ed. (London: Longman, Green, Longman and Roberts, 1860).

Chapter 6

1. Kathleen Hughes, "Where Are the Writings of Early Scotland?" in *Celtic Britain in the Early Middle Ages: Studies in Scottish and Welsh Sources*, edited by David Dumville (Woodbridge, England: Boydell Press, 1980), pp. 1–21.

2. Ibid., p. 9. Hughes also notes that most records say little of the successes in the north, inferring that the missionary work was slow to gain momentum.

3. Ibid., pp. 14–16.

4. James Graham-Campbell and Colleen E. Batey, *Vikings in Scotland: An Archaeological Survey* (Edinburgh: Edinburgh University Press, 1998), p. 37. Graham-Campbell notes that the Norse dialects of Shetland, Orkney and Caithness were known collectively as "Norn," a term first recorded in 1485, although there were identifiable differences among the three locations. Norn remained a living language in Orkney and Shetland into the 18th century.

5. B. E. Crawford, *Scandinavian Scotland*

(Leicester, England: Leicester University Press, 1987), p. 3.

6. The Battle of St. Tears is named for the small chapel where it took place. The Gunns and Keiths decided to settle their long feud in one meeting where each clan was to come with no more than twelve men. The Gunns arrived first and entered the chapel to pray. The Keiths then arrived on twelve horses, but with two men to a horse. The Keiths caught the outnumbered Gunns unaware and George Gunn was slain along with four of his sons. His death was later avenged by Henry, one of the surviving Gunn sons, who gathered a small number of survivors to follow the Keiths back to Dirlot Castle, where they ambushed. Henry killed George Keith through an open window with an arrow while shouting "A Gunn's compliments to a Keith!"

7. Mark Rugg Gunn, *History of the Clan Gunn* (Glasgow, Scotland: Alex. McLaren & Sons, 1969), p. 44. Sir Robert Gordon's 15th-century research never mentions his name and D. Murray Rose, a 19th-century researcher, refers to him as Thomas. Gunn's final conclusion is that the name George is traditional rather than based on a definitive source.

8. John Jamieson, *Jamieson's Dictionary of the Scottish language, in which the words are explained in their different senses, authorized by the names of the writers by whom they are used, or the titles of the works in which they occur, and derived from their originals* (Edinburgh: W. P. Nimmo, 1867); Richard Henslowe Wellington, *The King's Coroner* (London: W. Clowes, 1905), p. 6.

9. Hugh Cowan, "Sheriffs and Coroners," *The Scottish Review* 30 (1897), pp. 235–36.

10. Charles Gross, "The Early History and Influence of the Office of Coroner," *Political Science Quarterly* 7 (4) (1892), pp. 659–60.

11. Ibid., p. 660. Gross supports his statements with extensive citations from English law history, more so than his contemporaries.

12. Ibid., pp. 660–61.

13. Cosmo Innes, *Lectures on Scotch Legal Antiquities* (Edinburgh: Edmonston and Douglas, 1872); Frederic William Maitland, *English Law and the Renaissance* (Cambridge, England: Cambridge University Press, 1901), pp. 19–20, 69–70.

14. Innes, p. 85.

15. John Rastell and William Rastell, *An Exposition of Certaine Difficult and Obscure Words, and termes of the lawes of this realme newly set foorth and augmented, both in French and English, for the helpe of such younge students as are desirous to attaine the knowledge of ye same: whereunto are also added the olde tenures* (London: Richardi Tottelli, 1579), pp. 51–52. This text seems to suggest that by Rastell's time, the sheriff appointed the coroner instead of the title being inherited.

16. Wellington uses a 14th-century coroner's seal as his frontispiece. The insignia uses the abbreviation Coronat.

17. Sir Iain Moncreiffe, *The Highland Clans* (New York: Clarkson N. Potter, 1967); Thomas Sinclair, *The Gunns* (Wick, Scotland: W. Rae, 1890).

18. Donald Beaton, *Some Noted Ministers of the Northern Highlands* (Inverness, Scotland: Northern Counties Newspaper and Printing and Publishing Company, 1929).

19. Moncreiffe, pp. 160–61.

20. James Traill Calder, *Sketch of the Civil and Traditional History of Caithness from the Tenth Century* (Glasgow, Scotland: Thomas Murray and Son, 1861; Jens Jakob Asmussen Worsaae, *An Account of the Danes and Norwegians in England, Scotland, and Ireland* (London: J. Murray, 1852).

21. Sinclair (1890), pp. 138–39.

22. Moncreiffe, p. 161.

23. Royal Commission on the Ancient and Historical Monuments of Scotland (RAHMS Canmore database, Edinburgh, Scotland, 2006), vol. 2006, pp. NMRS Number: ND15SE 11.

24. Sir Iain Moncreiffe correspondence with unknown correspondent (March 12 1973).

25. Michael J. Gunn, "The Scottish Expedition to America in 1398," *The Gunn Herald* 1 (1) (Winter 1987), pp. 12–25.

26. Ibid., p. 21.

27. In *LDS Family History Library — British Film 231904* (Edinburgh: Public Records Office, 1960).

28. Mawnis is interchangeable with Magnus.

29. Wellington, p. 5.

30. The Clan Gunn Society of North America website lists Croner, Crownar, Crowner, Cruiner and Cruner as sept names. The UK Clan Gunn Society does not.

31. Robert Bain, *The Clans and Tartans of Scotland* (London: Collins, 1939); George Way and Romilly Squire, *Scottish Clan & Family Encyclopedia* (New York: Barnes & Noble Books, 1999); Mark Rugg Gunn, *History of the Clan Gunn* (Glasgow, Scotland: Alex. McLaren & Sons, 1969); Robert R. Gunn, *The Gunns* (Crawfordville, GA: C.G. Moore's Print Shop, 1925).

32. Melville Henry Massue, *The Moodie Book* (Chertsey, England: privately printed, 1906), pp. 5, 7–8. His somewhat convoluted

logic is that the Moodies buried in the Sinclair Mausoleum of Ulbster's St. Martin's Burial Ground are there because the Crownars were Gunns and Ulbster belonged to the Gunns before the Sinclairs.

33. Gunn (1987), p. 13, n.9.

34. *Registrum Magni Sigilli Regum Scotorum (The Register of the Great Seal of Scotland)*, edited by John Maitland Thomson (Edinburgh: Scottish Record Society, 1984).

35. Gunn specifically cites documents 775 and 776. Document 775 is a royal charter for the church of the Holy Cross in Peebles and 776 is the charter establishing the borough of Lynlithgow. Neither mentions Sinclairs, Gunns, the Orkneys or harbors.

36. Sinclair (1890), p. 18. Sinclair doesn't specify which Gunn would have been appointed Crowner, carefully wording his text to return to the subject of Crowner George's death.

37. Alexander MacGregor, *The History of the Feuds and Conflicts among the Clans in the Northern Parts of Scotland and in the Western Isles; from the year MXXXI unto MDCXIX* (Glasgow, Scotland: Robert and Andrew Foulis, 1764). Blar-Tannie was considered the first battle in the bloody feud between the Gunns and the Keiths, precipitated by the Keith kidnapping of a Gunn bride on her wedding day. She would commit suicide rather than submit, triggering the beginning of a feud that would last for decades.

38. Sinclair (1890), pp. 1, 5, 82.

39. Ibid., p. 7.

Chapter 7

1. Carlo Zeno (1334–1418) was a Venetian admiral who commanded a fleet that lay siege to the Genoese-occupied city of Chioggia in 1380. The victory was the first time shipboard cannons were employed in battle.

2. B. E. Crawford, "[Review of Prince Henry Sinclair]," *Scottish Historical Review* 56 (161) (1977), pp. 86–87.

3. Nicolò Zeno, *De I Commentarii del Viaggio in Persia di M. Caterino Zeno il K. & delle guerre fatte nell' Imperio Persiano, dal tempo di Vssuncassano in quà. Libri due. Et dello Scoprimento dell' Isole Frislanda, Eslanda, Engrouelanda, Estotilanda & Icaria, fatto sotto il Polo Artico, da due fratelli Zeni, M. Nicolò il K. et M. Antonio* (Venice, Italy: Francesco Marcolini, 1558). [Annals of the Journey in Persia of Messire Caterino Zeno, the Knight, and of the wars carried on in the Persian Empire in the time of Ussun Cassano. Two books. And of the Discovery of the Islands Frislanda, Eslanda, Engroue-

landa, Estotilanda, and Icaria, made under the North Pole, by the two brothers Zeni, Messire Nicoló, the Knight, and Messire Antonio. One book. With a detailed map of all the said parts of the North discovered by them].

4. See Fred W. Lucas, *The Annals of the Voyages of the Brothers Nicolò and Antonio Zeno, in the North Atlantic About the End of the Fourteenth Century, and the Claim Founded Thereon to a Venetian Discovery of America; a criticism and an indictment* (London: H. Stevens Sons and Stiles, 1898), for the genealogical charts.

5. Richard Hakluyt, *The Principal Navigations, Voyages, Traffiques and Discoveries of the English nation, made by sea or overland, to the remote and farthest distant quarters of the earth, at any time within the compasse of these 1600 yeres.*, 2nd ed. (London: George Bishop and Ralph Newberie, 1589).

6. Ibid., p. 290. "For the more credite and confirmation of the former Historie of Messer Nicolas and Messer Antonio Zeni (which for some fewe respects may perhaps bee called in question) I haue heere annexed the iudgement of that famous Cosmographer Abraham Ortelius, or rather the yealding and submitting of his iudgement thereunto: who in his Theatrum Orbis, fol. 6. next before the map of Mar del Zur, boroweth proofe and authoritie out of this relation, to shew that the Northeast parte of America called Estotiland, and in the original always affirmed to bee an Islande, was about the yeere 1390 discouered by the aforesayd Venetian Gentleman Messer Antonio Zeno, aboue 100 yeeres before euer Christopher Columbus set saile for those Westerne Regions; and that the Northren Seas were euen then sayled by our Europaean Pilots through the helpe of the loadstone…"; Abraham Ortelius, *Theatrum Orbis Terrarum* (Antwerp, Belgium: Coppenium Diesth, 1590).

7. Gerhard Mercator, *Gerard Mercator's Map of the World* (Rotterdam, Netherlands: Maritiem Museum Prins Hendrik, 1961).

8. Corneille Wytfliet, *Descriptionis Ptolemaicae Augmentum, siue Occidentis Notitia: Breui Commentario Illustrata* (Louvain, Belgium: Iohannis Bogardi, 1597).

9. Hugo Grotius, "On the Origin of the Native Races of America," in *Bibliotheca Curiosa* (Edinburgh: s.n., 1884), pp. 10–11.

10. Johannes de Laet, *Notae ad Dissertationem Hugonis Grotii De Origine Gentium Americanarum: Et Observationes aliquot ad meliorem indaginem difficillimae illius Quaestionis* (Amsterdam, Netherlands: Elzevirius, 1643).

11. Ezra Stiles, *The United States Elevated to*

Glory and Honor: a sermon preached before His Excellency Jonathan Trumbull, Esq. L.L.D., governor and commander in chief, and the Honorable the General Assembly of the state of Connecticut, convened at Hartford, at the anniversary election, May 8th, 1783 (New Haven, CT: Thomas & Samuel Green, 1783).

12. Unless otherwise noted, quotes are from the 1898 translation by Fred W. Lucas.

13. Rasmus Björn Anderson, *America Not Discovered by Columbus: An Historical Sketch of the Discovery of America by the Norsemen, in the Tenth Century* (Chicago: S. C. Griggs & Co., 1877).

14. Richard Hakluyt, *Divers Voyages Touching the Discoverie of America, and the Ilands Adjacent unto the Same made first of all by our Englishmen, and afterward by the Frenchmen and Britons: and certaine notes of advertisements for observations, necessarie for such as shall heereafter make the like attempt, with two mappes annexed heereunto for the plainer understanding of the whole matter* (London: Thomas Woodcocke, 1582).

15. Johann Reinhold Forster, *Geschichte der Entdeckungen und Schiffahrten im Norden: Mit neuen Originalkarten versehen* (Frankfurt, Germany: C. G. Strauss, 1784).

16. Johann Reinhold Forster, *History of the Voyages and Discoveries Made in the North* (London: G. G. J. and J. Robinson, 1786).

17. Forster (1784); Forster (1786), p. 181 (fn).

18. Buss was first sighted by Frobisher, meaning the location is suspect from the start. Buss quickly became a "site of sunken island" notation on charts into the 19th century when Arctic explorer John Ross determined there were no shallows in the area, the ocean depths exceeding 180 fathoms. See Ross, *A Voyage of Discovery, Made under the Orders of the Admiralty in His Majesty's ships Isabella and Alexander, for the purpose of exploring Baffin's Bay, and inquiring into the probability of a North-West Passage* (London: Murray, 1819).

19. Fernando Colón and Alfonso de Ulloa, *La Vita e i Viaggi di Cristoforo Colombo* (Milan, Italy: Fasani, 1945), p. 7. Fernando quotes his father as having sailed 100 leagues beyond Thule in February 1477, to a large island now called Frisland, a land that traded with England, particularly Bristol.

20. Placido Zurla, *Dissertazione Intorno ai Viaggi e Scoperte Settentrionali di Nicolò ed Antonio Fratelli Zeni* (Venice, Italy: Dalle stampe Zerletti, 1808).

21. Ibid., pp. 85–86.

22. Ibid., pp. 29–30. "Di questo si nota, che scrisse con il fratello Nicolò K. li viaggi dell' Isole sotto il polo artico, e di quei scoprimenti del 1390, e che per ordine di Zicno Rè de Frislanda si porto nel continente d'Estotiland nell' America Settentrionale, e che se fermò 14 anni in Frislanda, cioè 4 con suo fratello Nicolò, e 10 solo."

23. Phillipe Buarche, "Mémoire sur l'Ile de Frislande," *Histoire de l'Académie Royale des Sciences* (1784 annual), pp. 430–453.

24. Ibid., p. 434.

25. Henrich Peter von Eggers, "Priisskrift om Grønlands Østerbygds sande Beliggenhed," *Kongelige Danske Landhuusholdningsselskab Skrifter* 4 (1794), pp. 239–321.

26. Christian Christopher Zahrtmann, "Bemærkninger over de Zenetianerne Zeni Tilskrevne Reiser i Norden," *Aarbøger for Nordisk Oldkyndighed og Historie* 3 (1833), pp. 1–35.

27. Christian Christopher Zahrtmann, "Remarks on the Voyages to the Northern Hemisphere, Ascribed to the Zeni of Venice," *Journal of the Royal Geographic Society of London* 5 (1835), pp. 102–28.

28. Ibid., p. 109.

29. Oscar J. Falnes, "New England Interest in Scandinavian Culture and the Norsemen," *New England Quarterly* 10 (2) (1937), pp. 211–42.

30. Carl Christian Rafn, *Antiquitates Americanæ sive scriptores septentrionales rerum antecolumbianarum in America* (Copenhagen, Denmark: Typis Officinæ Schultzianæ, 1837).

31. Andrew R. Hilen and Henry Wadsworth Longfellow, *Longfellow and Scandinavia; A Study of the Poet's Relationship with the Northern Languages and Literature* (New Haven, CT: Yale University Press, 1947).

32. The statue was created in 1886, unveiled in 1887 and rededicated in 1989. Created by noted sculptor Anne Whitney, today it is surrounded by a basin of flowers. Originally, this basin was a fountain with a longship bow on the pedestal. The statue stands at the far western end of Boston's Commonwealth Avenue mall. The Norse motif is most notable on the Longfellow Bridge that connects Boston and Cambridge. Built by the Boston Transit Commission and opened to the public in 1906, the bridge's four main piers support the center section as Viking prows extending out into the Charles River.

33. J. M. Mancini, "Discovering Viking America," *Critical Inquiry* 28 (7) (Summer 2002), pp. 868–907.

34. Janet A. Headley, "Anne Whitney's Leif Eriksson — A Brahmin Response to Christopher

Columbus," *American Art* 17 (2) (2003), pp. 40–59; Robin Fleming, "Picturesque History and the Medieval in Nineteenth-Century America," *American Historical Review* 100 (4) (1995), p. 1082.

35. Marie A. Shipley, *The Norse Colonization in America by the Light of the Vatican Finds* (Lucerne: H. Keller's Foreign Print Office, 1899).

36. Zahrtmann (1835), p. 127.

37. George Folsom, "[Review of Zahrtmann's 'Remarks on the Voyages to the Northern Hemisphere'†]," *The North American Review* 47 (100) (1838), pp. 177–206.

38. B. F. DeCosta, *The Pre-Columbian Discovery of America by the Northmen* (Albany, NY: J. Munsell, 1868); DeCosta, "Columbus and the Geographers of the North," *The American Church Review* 24 (3) (July 1872), pp. 418–38; DeCosta, "The Letter of Verrazano," *Magazine of American History* 2 (2) (February 1878), pp. 65–81.

39. Benedetto Bordone, *Isolario* (Turin, Italy: Les Belles Lettres, 2000); Zahrtmann (1833), pp. 114–15.

40. DeCosta (1872), p. 434, fn 3; DeCosta (1878), p. 469, fn 3. DeCosta (1872) further notes he had the U.S. Ambassador to Denmark request to look at the map but that the librarians were unable to find such a map in their holdings.

41. Henry Vignaud, *Toscanelli and Columbus. The Letter and Chart of Toscanelli on the Route to the Indies by Way of the West, Sent in 1474 to the Portuguese Fernam Martins, and later on to Christopher Columbus* (London: Sands & Co., 1902).

42. DeCosta (1872), pp. 431–34.

43. Richard Henry Major, "The Site of the Lost Colony of Greenland Determined, and Pre-Columbian Discoveries of America Confirmed, from 14th Century Documents," *Journal of the Royal Geographical Society of London* 43 (May 1874), pp. 156–206.

44. Richard Henry Major, *The Voyages of the Venetian brothers, Nicolò & Antonio Zeno to the Northern Seas, in the XIVth century* (London: Hakluyt Society, 1873).

45. Sinclair (1992), p. 195, fn 5.

46. See Rydberg, vol. 5, pp. 650–51 for one such occurrence.

47. Taking the Zicno question further into unexplored waters, Beauvois, a later advocate of Great Ireland being in Canada, thinks that the name Zicno was a misreading for the Scandinavian title "Thegn" or Lord. Beauvois, *Les Colonies Européennes du Markland et de l'Escociland au XIV siècle, et les Vestiges qui en Subsistèrent Jusqu'aux XVI et XVII siècles* (Nancy, France: G. Crépin-Leblond, 1877a), vol. I, p. 200.

48. When the Hakluyt Society reprinted Major's article later that year as the foreword to his new translation of *The Zeno Narrative*, it included his translation of Ivar Bardssen's *Descriptio Grœnlandiæ* (1364) as an appendix.

49. Richard Henry Major, "On the Voyages of the Venetian Brothers Zeno, to the Northern Seas, in the Fourteenth Century," *Proceedings of the Massachusetts Historical Society* 13 (October 1874), pp. 345–66; Thomas J. Schlereth, "Columbia, Columbus, and Columbianism," *Journal of American History* 79 (3) (1992), pp. 937–68; Charles Deane, "Remarks by Charles Deane on the Same," *Proceedings of the Massachusetts Historical Society* 18 (May 1880), pp. 80–81; William Everett, "Remarks by William Everett on Proposed Statue of Leif," *Proceedings of the Massachusetts Historical Society* 18 (May 1880), pp. 79–80.

50. Admiral Carl Ludvig Christian Irminger, "Zeno's Frislanda Is Iceland and Not the Færoes," *Journal of the Royal Geographical Society of London* 49 (1879), pp. 398–412.

51. Ibid., p. 405.

52. Ibid., p. 410.

53. Japetus Steenstrup, "Zeni'ernes Reiser i Norden," *Aarbøger for Nordisk Oldkyndighed og Historie* 52 (1883), pp. 55–214.

54. Adolf Erik Nordenskiöld, "Om Bröderna Zenos Resor Och de Äldsta Kartor Öfver Norden," in *Studier Och Forskningar: Föranledda af Mina Resor i Höga Norden* (Stockholm, Sweden: F&G Beijers, 1883), pp. 1–62; Nordenskiöld, *Vegas Färd Kring Asien och Europa* (Stockholm, Sweden: F&G Beijers, 1880).

55. Nordenskjöld (1883), pp. 30–32.

56. John Fiske, *The Discovery of America*, Vol. 1 (Cambridge, MA: Riverside Press, 1892), pp. 236–37.

57. Ibid., p. 255.

58. The Gogstad ship is a 9th-century Viking ship found in Sandefjord, Norway, beneath a burial mound in 1880. Clinker-built of oak, the ship was built to carry 32 oarsmen and now is displayed at the Viking Ship Museum in Oslo.

59. Thomas Sinclair, *The Gunns* (Wick, Scotland: W. Rae, 1890); Sinclair, *The Sinclairs of England* (London: Trübner, 1887); Sinclair, "Prince Henry Sinclair II — The Pre-Columbian Discoverer of America, One of the Ancestors of the Caithness Family," in *Caithness Events: a discussion of Captain Kennedy's historical narrative,*

and an account of the Broynach earls, to which is added a supplement of emendations of 1899 (Wick, Scotland: W. Rae, 1899). Henry, the first Jarl of Orkney, is cited in some genealogies as "Henry Sinclair II" to differentiate him from his great-grandfather, Henry Sinclair of Roslin or "Henry Sinclair I." In the Thomas Sinclair case, he is inexcusably merging "Henry Sinclair II" and "Henry Sinclair III."

60. Sinclair (1899), pp. 141–42.

Chapter 8

1. Rowlands Williams Sinclair was so enamored of his family history that he legally changed his name in 1886 to Roland William Saint-Clair to reflect his proud heritage. See Roland William Saint-Clair, *The Saint-Clairs of the Isles* (Auckland, New Zealand: H. Brett, 1898), pp. 161–62.

2. Ibid., pp. 445–53.

3. Fred W. Lucas, *The Annals of the Voyages of the Brothers Nicolò and Antonio Zeno, in the North Atlantic About the End of the Fourteenth Century, and the Claim Founded Thereon to a Venetian Discovery of America; a criticism and an indictment* (London: H. Stevens Sons and Stiles, 1898).

4. Fred W. Lucas, *Appendiculae Historicae or Shreds of History Hung on a Horn* (London: H. Stevens & Son, 1891).

5. C. H. Coote, "Volume VIII — Burton-Cantwell," in *Dictionary of National Biography*, edited by Leslie Stephen (London: Smith, Elder & Co., 1886); vol. 8, pp. 166–71.

6. Royal Geographic Society, "Obituary — Mr. C. H. Coote," *The Geographic Journal* 14 (1) (July 1899), pp. 99–100.

7. Lucas, who signed his name "Henry Stevens of Vermont," also mocked his peers' predilection to include degrees and memberships after their name in publications. On the title pages of his books, Stevens placed a plethora of initials after his name, ranging from FSA (Fellow of the Society of Antiquaries) to GMB (Green Mountain Boy) and BBAC (Black Balled, Athenaeum Club).

8. Henry Harrisse, *John Cabot, the Discoverer of North-America, and Sebastian, His Son; a Chapter of the Maritime History of England under the Tudors, 1496–1557* (London: B. F. Stevens, 1896).

9. Miller Christy, "Appendix B — Note on the Zeno Narrative and Chart of 1558," in *The Silver Map of the World — A Contemporary Medallion Commemorative of Drake's Great Voyage (1577–80)* (London: H. Stevens, Son & Stiles, 1900), pp. 49–67.

10. Oscar Brenner, "Die ächte Karte des Olaus Magnus vom Jahre 1539 nach dem Exemplar der Munchener Staatsbibliothek," *Forhandlinger i Videnskabs-selskabet i Christiania* 15 (1886).

11. "[Review of *The Annals of the Voyages of the Brothers Nicolò and Antonio Zeno*]," *Journal of the American Geographical Society of New York* 30 (5) (1898), pp. 459–61.

12. B. F. DeCosta, "[Review of *The Annals of the Voyages of the Brothers Nicolo and Antonio Zeno*]," *The American Historical Review* 4 (4) (1899), pp. 726–29.

13. Christy, pp. 61–66.

14. C. Raymond Beazley, "[Review — Voyages of the Zeni]," *The Geographic Journal* XIII (2) (1899), pp. 166–70.

15. Brian Smith, "Earl Henry Sinclair's Fictitious Trip to America," *New Orkney Antiquarian Journal* 2 (2002), p. 92.

16. Ibid., p. 11, fn 36. Smith makes the observation that he had unsuccessfully attempted to convince Sinclair family icon Niven Sinclair to reprint the book in a centennial edition.

17. Henry Stevens printed 400 copies, predominantly for private collectors, making the book scarce and increasingly rare in the public sector. In 2009, Online Computer Library Center's WorldCat catalog listed barely 60 libraries worldwide with holdings of the book. OCLS also lists fewer than 25 libraries with the title in the comparatively less expensive and more easily obtained microfiche format, suggesting part of the continued rarity has been lack of interest.

18. Ib Rønne Kejlbo, "Zenokortet — Dets Kilder of Dets Betydning for den Kartografiske Udforming af Det Nordlige Atlanterhav," *Fund og Forskning* 3 (1956), pp. 91–102.

19. Axel Anthon Björnbo and Carl S. Petersen, *Fyenboen Claudius Claussøn Swart (Claudius Clavus), Nordens Ældste Kartograf* (Copenhagen, Denmark: A. F. Høst & Søn, 1904).

20. Recombined, the verse reads: Der bor en mand i en -grønlands å,/og Spjeldebod monne han hedde,/mer haver han af hvide sild,/end han haver flæsk hint fede./Nordenom driver sandet på ny.

21. See Fridtjof Nansen, *In Northern Mists; Arctic Exploration in Early Times* (New York: Frederick A. Stokes Co., 1911), vol. 2, pp. 253–55, for comparative translations. The translation reads: There lives a man by a river in Greenland,/and his name is Spjeldebod/He owns more white herring/than he owns fat of pork./The sand drifts northward once more. Karl Aubert, "Grönlandsverset," *Danske Studier* 4 (1904), pp. 228–29.

22. Kejlbo, p. 94. Clavus, who was not born until 1388, was the first cartographer to represent Greenland by name, as evidenced by the Nancy Codex. This is one of several indications that Kejlbo believed were proof that the Danish Clavus had access to early Norse navigation charts. Kejlbo also notes his placement of Greenland is consistent with the text in the Sagas.

23. Major (1873), p. 6, and Lucas (1898), p. 8.

24. Placido Zurla, *Dissertazione Intorno ai Viaggi e Scoperte Settentrionali di Nicolò ed Antonio Fratelli Zeni* (Venice, Italy: Dalle stampe Zerletti, 1808); Major (1873), pp. 157–58.

25. Frederick J. Pohl, *The Sinclair Expedition to Nova Scotia in 1398* (Pictou, Nova Scotia: Pictou Advocate Press, 1950).

26. Frederick J. Pohl, *Atlantic Crossings Before Columbus* (New York: Norton, 1961), pp. 239–40.

27. Frederick J. Pohl, "Prince 'Zichmni' of the Zeno Narrative," *Terrae Incognitae—The Journal for the History of Discoveries* 2 (1970), pp. 75–86.

28. Adriano Cappelli, *Lexicon Abbreviaturarum* (Milan, Italy: Ulrico Hoepli, 1949).

29. Frederick J. Pohl, *Prince Henry Sinclair—His Voyage to the New World in 1398* (New York: Clarkson N. Potter, 1974), pp. 85–87.

30. B. E. Crawford, "[Review of Prince Henry Sinclair]," *Scottish Historical Review* 56 (161) (April 1977), pp. 86–87.

31. Andrea da Mosto, "I Navigatori Nicolò e Antonio Zeno," in *Ad Alessandro Luzio, gli Archivi di Stato Italiani*, edited by Alessandro Luzio (Florence, Italy: Le Monnier, 1933), vol. I, pp. 293–308.

32. Pohl (1974), pp. 128–30.

33. Stephen I. Boardman, *The Early Stewart Kings: Robert II and Robert III, 1371–1406* (East Linton, Scotland: Tuckwell Press, 1996).

34. Da Mosto, p. 298. Da Mosto admits he can't be certain which Nicolò Zeno is the prisoner among the several who may have been contemporaneous, but he lists reasons as to why he believes it is the Nicolò Zeno who is otherwise claimed to have been with Zichmni.

35. Ibid., pp. 299–300. In 1390, Nicolò was a military governor of Venetian bases at Corone and Modone in southern Greece. He returned to Venice in 1392 and in 1394 was accused of financial chicanery while governor. Da Mosto also notes his will was written in 1400 and he is gone from all records by 1403. Published only in Italian, the article raised some debate among Italian scholars but was not well known until Brian Smith referred to it in his 2002 article debunking the Sinclair expedition.

36. B. E. Crawford, Lyn Blackmore and John W. Allen, *The Biggings, Papa Stour, Shetland: The History and Excavation of a Royal Norwegian Farm* (Edinburgh: Society of Antiquaries of Scotland, 1999), p. 19; Richard Henry Major, *The Voyages of the Venetian brothers, Nicolò & Antonio Zeno, to the Northern Seas in the XIVth century: comprising the latest known accounts of the lost colony of Greenland and of the Northmen in America before Columbus* (London: Hakluyt Society, 1873), p. XXXIV.

Chapter 9

1. William Herbert Hobbs, "Zeno and the Cartography of Greenland," *Imago Mundi—The International Journal for the History of Cartography* 6 (1949), pp. 15–19.

2. Arlington Humphrey Mallery, *Lost America; the Story of Iron-Age Civilization prior to Columbus* (Washington, DC: Overlook Company, 1951); Arlington Humphrey Mallery and Mary Roberts Harrison, *The Rediscovery of Lost America*, 1st ed. (New York: Dutton, 1979).

3. Mallery (1979), pp. 196–97. Mallery's 1951 book was posthumously revised and released in 1979. Material on the Zeno map in the 1951 edition is also in the 1979 edition under different pagination. His material on the Piri Re'is map was among the posthumous additions and only in the 1979 edition.

4. Arlington Humphrey Mallery, M. I. Walters, Matthew Warren and Daniel Linehan, *Georgetown University Radio Forum: New and Old Discoveries in Antarctica, August 26, 1956 (transcription)* (Washington, DC: Georgetown University, 1956).

5. Charles H. Hapgood, *Earth's Shifting Crust; A Key to Some Basic Problems of Earth Science* (New York: Pantheon Books, 1958).

6. Charles H. Hapgood, *Maps of the Ancient Sea Kings; Evidence of Advanced Civilization in the Ice Age*, [1st] ed. (Philadelphia: Chilton Books, 1966).

7. Hapgood, (1966), pp. 149–58.

8. Erich von Däniken, *Chariots of the Gods?* (New York: Putnam, 1970).

9. William Herbert Hobbs, "The Fourteenth-Century Discovery of America by Antonio Zeno," *Scientific Monthly* 72 (January 1951), pp. 24–31.

10. Pohl (1952), pp. 210–13.

11. Hobbs quotes the pertinent passage in his *Scientific Monthly* article (p. 30); H. S. Poole, "The Pictou Coalfield: A Geological Revision," *Proceedings and Transactions—Nova Scotia Institute of Science* 1 (1895), pp. 228–343. Poole (p.

293) notes that methane bubbled up into Coal Brook so frequently that it could maintain a fire, and it had been utilized by women for washing purposes as late as the 1850s.

12. Samuel Eliot Morison, *Admiral of the Ocean Sea, a Life of Christopher Columbus* (Boston: Little, Brown, 1942); Samuel Eliot Morison, *The European Discovery of America* (Oxford: Oxford University Press, 1971).

13. Morison (1971), pp. 88–89, 107–8.

14. Frederick J. Pohl, *The Sinclair Expedition to Nova Scotia in 1398* (Pictou, Nova Scotia: Pictou Advocate Press, 1950).

15. Nicolas Denys, *The Description and Natural History of the Coasts of North America (Acadia)* (Toronto, Ontario: The Champlain Society, 1908).

16. Andrew Sinclair, *The Sword and the Grail* (New York: Crown, 1992).

17. Ibid., p. 136.

18. Provenience Record Number 1B6A13–1, Louisbourg Institute Archaeology Artifact Database (Fortress of Louisbourg National Historic Site).

19. George Patterson, "The Portuguese on the North East Coast of America," *Proceedings and Transactions of the Royal Society of Canada for the Year 1890* (1891), p. 164; Jean Boudriot, "La Petite Artillerie des Hunes, des Bastingages et des Embarcations," *Neptunia* 100 (September–December 1970).

20. Forster (1786), p. 179.

21. Mark Heddon, "Contact Period Petroglyphs in Machias Bay, Maine," *Archaeology of Eastern North America* 30 (2002), pp. 1–20.

22. Garrick Mallery, *Picture-writing of the American Indians* (New York: Dover Publications, 1972).

23. Heddon, p. 7.

24. Ibid., p. 8. Heddon also notes a possible visit by Pierre Dugua, the Sieur de Mons mentioned in a 1904 history of Machias but he has not located a primary source for the assertion.

25. Ibid., p. 10; Garrick Mallery, "Dangers of Symbolic Interpretation [abstract]," *Transactions of the Anthropological Society of Washington* 1 (1882), pp. 70–79.

26. James P Whittall II, "A Petroglyph of a European Ship on the Coast of Maine circa 1350–1450 A.D.," *Early Sites Research Society Bulletin* 11 (1) (1984), pp. 48–52.

27. In 1945, a suspected rune stone had been found on farmland near the ruins of an uncompleted Civil War fort. William Goodwin, Malcolm Pearson, and Olaf Strandwold traveled to Maine and documented the stone. Strandwold's translation would appear in his 1948 book

as the "Popham Beach Stone." Strandwold was the only runologist who considered the marks on the stone as man-made and the Popham Beach Stone faded into obscurity. The Spirit Pond stones, now in the Maine State Museum's custody, consist of three small stones found together along with a later additional stone found in the same area. The authenticity of the runes has been questioned by leading scholars of Norwegian and Scandinavian culture such as Einar Haugen, Professor of Scandinavian and Linguistics at Harvard University. In an article in the anthropology journal *Man in the Northeast*, Haugen declared them unquestionably to be frauds. Haugen concluded that the stones had been created by someone with minimal knowledge of runes, using a book on the Kensington Stone by Hjalmar Holand. Debate continues on the source and linguistics of the stones.

28. Erik Wahlgren, "American Runes: from Kensington to Spirit Pond," *Journal of English and Germanic Philology* 81 (1982), p. 164.

29. Hugh Marwick, *The Orkney Norn* (Oxford: Oxford University Press, 1929).

30. Ida Sedgwick Proper, *Monhegan, the Cradle of New England* (Portland, ME: Southworth Press, 1930).

31. George H. Stone, "The Inscription Rocks on the Island of Monhegan," *Science* 6 (132) (August 14, 1885).

32. Proper, pp. 5–6.

33. David B. Quinn, *North America from Earliest Discovery to First Settlements: The Norse Voyages to 1612* (New York: Harper & Row, 1978).

34. Samuel Eliot Morison, *The Maritime History of Massachusetts, 1783–1860* (Boston: Houghton Mifflin, 1961).

35. J. W. Meader, *The Merrimack River; Its Source and Its Tributaries* (Boston: B. B. Russell, 1869), pp. 24–25. Du Gua actually found the river in 1605 with Champlain. His attempt to rename the river "Gua's River" did not last long.

36. Charles Cowley, *Illustrated History of Lowell* (Boston: Lee & Shepard, 1868), pp. 16–17.

37. Donald R. Hopkins, *The Greatest Killer: Smallpox in History* (Chicago: University of Chicago Press, 2002), p. 234.

38. Paula Underwood, *The Walking People: A Native American Oral History* (San Anselmo, CA: A Tribe of Two Press & Institute of Noetic Sciences, 1993), pp. 681–94. The Walking People try to get the Stone Hill People to join with the agrarian-based Sun People, who live at a bend in a river that almost forms a circle, a reasonable description of the bend in the Merri-

mack River near Chelmsford/Tyngsboro (p. 604). Underwood later visited the America's Stonehenge at Mystery Hill location and was convinced it was the site of the Stone Hill People settlement (p. 831).

39. John J. Currier, *Historical Sketch of Ship Building on the Merrimac River* (Newburyport, MA: W. H. Huse & Co. Printers, 1877).

40. Charles Wingate Chase, *History of Haverhill, Massachusetts* (Haverhill, MA: published by author, 1861).

41. N. A. M. Rodger, *The Safeguard of the Sea: A Naval History of Britain, 660–1649*, 1st American ed. (New York: Norton, 1998); Lincoln P. Paine, *Ships of the World: An Historical Encyclopedia* (Boston: Houghton Mifflin, 1997).

42. Patricia Trainor O'Malley and Paul H. Tedesco, *A New England City: Haverhill, Massachusetts* (Northridge, CA: Windsor Publications, 1987).

43. Edwin R. Hodgman, *History of the Town of Westford in the County of Middlesex, Massachusetts — 1659–1883*, 2003 ed. (Lowell, MA: Morning Mail Co, 1883), p. 4.

44. Frederick J. Pohl, *Atlantic Crossings Before Columbus* (New York: Norton, 1961).

45. Ibid., p. 280. By his 1974 book, Pohl was also offering Indian attack or snakebite as the possible cause of death (p. 156).

46. Claire C. Gordon and Jane E. Buikstra, "Soil pH, Bone Preservation and Sampling Bias at Mortuary Sites," *American Antiquity* 46 (3) (1981), pp. 566–571.

47. Brian Smith, "Earl Henry Sinclair's Fictitious Trip to America," *New Orkney Antiquarian Journal* 2, 92 (2002); Frederick J. Pohl, *Prince Henry Sinclair — His Voyage to the New World in 1398* (New York: Clarkson N. Potter, 1974); Tim Wallace-Murphy and Marilyn Hopkins, *Templars in America: From the Crusades to the New World* (York Beach, ME: Weiser Books, 2004).

48. Thomas Innes, *A Critical Essay on the Ancient Inhabitants of the Northern Parts of Britain or Scotland* (Edinburgh: W. Paterson, 1879), p. 313.

49. John Spottiswood, *The History of the Church and State of Scotland* (London: R. Royston, 1655), p. 121. The locations specifically noted by Spottiswood are Perth, Crail, Anstruther, St. Andrews, Scone, Sterling, Cambuskenmeth, Linlithgow, Edinburgh and Glasgow.

50. See Crawford and Ballin Smith (1999), pp. 18–19, for discussion of Sinclair's acquisition of the Sperre lands in Shetland.

51. James H. Barrett, Rebecca A. Nicholson and Ruby Cerón-Carrasco, "Archaeo-icthyological Evidence for Long-term Socioeconomic Trends in Northern Scotland: 3500 BC to A.D. 1500," *Journal of Archaeological Science* 26 (1999), pp. 353–88.

52. James H. Barrett, "Fish Trade in Norse Orkney and Caithness: A Zooarchaeological Approach," *Antiquity* 71 (273) (1997), pp. 616–38; James H. Barrett, Roelf P. Beukens and Rebecca A. Nicholson, "Diet and Ethnicity during Viking Colonization of Northern Scotland: Evidence from Fish Bones and Stable Carbon Isotopes," *Antiquity* 75 (278) (2001), pp. 145–54.

53. Przemyslaw Urbanczyk, *Medieval Arctic Norway* (Warsaw, Poland: Institute of the History of Material Culture, Polish Academy of Sciences, 1992).

54. In 1474, the Portuguese navigator João Vaz Corte-Real was granted lands on the Azores as a reward for his discovery of "Terra do Bacalhau," which evidence indicates was actually the eastern end of the island of Newfoundland in Canada.

Chapter 10

1. Frederick J. Pohl, *The Sinclair Expedition to Nova Scotia in 1398* (Pictou, Nova Scotia: Pictou Advocate Press, 1950); Frederick J. Pohl, *Atlantic Crossings Before Columbus* (New York: Norton, 1961).

2. Frederick J. Pohl, *Prince Henry Sinclair — His Voyage to the New World in 1398* (New York: Clarkson N. Potter, 1974).

3. Pohl (1974), p. 133.

4. Ibid., pp. 144–51. Pohl eventually decided that Cape D'Or was the location of Sinclair's winter camp and that he built his ship in Advocate Harbor.

5. Although the modern accepted orthographic form of the hero's name is Kluscap, Pohl and his preferred source, Silas T. Rand, chose Glooscap over such other variations as Gluskab, Gluskabe, Glooskap, Gluskabi, Kluscap, Kloskomba, Kuloskap or Klose-kur-beh. For consistency with the material being discussed, this text will use Glooscap.

6. Virginia P. Miller, "Silas T. Rand, Nineteenth Century Anthropologist among the Micmacs," *Anthropologica* 22 (1) (1980), pp. 235–49; Silas Tertius Rand, *Legends of the Micmacs* (New York: Longmans Green and Co., 1893).

7. Pohl (1974), p. 135.

8. Rand (1893), p. xliv.

9. Silas Tertius Rand, *Dictionary of the Language of the Micmac Indians* (Halifax, Nova Scotia: Nova Scotia Printing Company, 1888), p. 287.

10. Barbara M. Kreutz, "Mediterranean Contributions to the Medieval Mariner's Compass," *Technology and Culture* 14 (3) (1973), pp. 367–83.

11. Pohl (1974), p. 139; Rand (1888).

12. Rand (1888), p. 149.

13. Jeremiah S. Clark, *Rand and the Micmacs* (Charlottetown, Prince Edward Island: Charlottetown Examiner, 1899), p. 42.

14. Rand (1893), p. 287 fn. "Here is evidently a clear tradition of God as the friend, companion, guide, instructor, and helper of the human race; it would suit the idea that the Indians are the Lost Tribes of Israel. This Divine Friend leaving them on account of their disobedience, and their longing expectation of his return, looks marvellously like the Jewish expectation of a Messiah, and of the reason given by the prophets why God forsook them in former days."

15. Eben Norton Horsford, *Discovery of America by Northmen: Address at the Unveiling of the Statue of Leif Eriksen, Delivered in Faneuil Hall, Oct. 29, 1887* (Boston: Houghton Mifflin, 1888); Eben Norton Horsford, *The Indian Names of Boston, and Their Meaning* (Cambridge, MA: J. Wilson and Son, 1886).

16. Clark, p. 42. Specifically "The Adventures of Kaktoogwasees"(Chapter XIII) and "The Beautiful Bride" (Chapter XXIV); Charles Godfrey Leland, *The Algonquin Legends of New England* (Boston: Houghton Mifflin, 1884).

17. Leland, p. 15.

18. Ibid., pp. 18–20.

19. Chrestien le Clercq, *Nouvelle Relation de la Gaspesie* (Paris: A. Auroy, 1691).

20. Ironically, Chatham is quite near Lake St. Clair. The name is completely unrelated to Henry Sinclair or his family, although it's probably just a matter of time before someone makes the suggestion. French explorers discovered the lake in August 1679, calling it Lac Sainte Claire in honor of Sainte Claire of Assisi because of the proximity to the date of her feast day. Government officials and map makers later changed the spelling to the present form of Saint Clair, or St. Clair.

21. Le Clercq, Chapter X (de l'origine du Culte de la Croix, Chex les Gaspesien dits Porte-Croix), pp. 266–77.

22. Chrestien le Clercq, *New Relation of Gaspesia, with the Customs and Religion of the Gaspesian Indians* (Toronto, Ontario: Champlain Society, 1910), pp. 36–40.

23. Eugène Beauvois, *Les Derniers Vestiges du Christianisme Prêché du 10 au 14 siècle dans le Markland et la Grande Irlande: Les Porte-Croix de la Gaspésie et de l'Acadie* (Paris, France, 1877b), pp. 19–20.

24. Eugène Beauvois, *La Découverte du Nouveau Monde par les Irlandais et les Premières Traces du Christianisme en Amérique avant l'an 1000* (Nancy, France: G. Crépin-Leblond, 1875), p. 86.

25. Eugène Beauvois, *Les Colonies Européennes du Markland et de l'Escociland au XIV siècle, et les Vestiges qui en Subsistèrent Jusqu'aux XVI et XVII siècles* (Nancy, France: G. Crépin-Leblond, 1877a).

26. Beavois (1875), p. 33.

27. Eugène Beauvois, *Pratiques et Institutions Religieuses d'origine Chrétienne chez les Mexicains du Moyen âge* (Louvain, Belgium: Polleunis & Ceuterick, 1896).

28. Pohl (1961), p. 39.

29. Frederick J. Pohl, *The Viking Explorers* (New York: T.Y. Crowell, 1966), p. 225.

30. Pohl (1974), p. 111.

31. Rand (1893), p. 287. If Sinclair had continued down the coast, it would be in a southwestward direction.

32. *The Orkneyinga Saga* (chapter 62) tells of a teenage Earl Rognvald sailing to Grimsby, England, a major fish market, and encountering other Orcadians.

33. Charles Godfrey Leland and John Dyneley Prince, *Kuloskap the Master, and Other Algonkin Poems* (New York: Funk & Wagnalls, 1902), p. 63.

34. Rand (1893), p. 114. Rand includes a tale where Glooscap sends his valet Marten to check the fishing-net and finds a small whale, but there's no indication that this not another reference to a weir with a case of hyperbole.

35. James P. Whittall II, "A Petroglyph of a European Ship on the Coast of Maine circa 1350–1450 A.D.," *Early Sites Research Society Bulletin* 11 (1) (1984), p. 48.

36. Anna Ritchie, "Excavation of Pictish and Viking-age Farmsteads at Buckquoy, Orkney," *Proceedings of the Society of Antiquaries of Scotland* 108 (1976–77), pp. 174–227.

37. J. M. Steane and M. F. Foreman, "The Archaeology of Medieval Fishing Tackle," in *Waterfront Archaeology*, edited by G. L. Good, R. H. Jones and M. W. Ponsford (London: Council for British Archaeology, 1991), vol. 74, pp. 88–101.

38. Molly Schauffler and George L. Jacobson, Jr., "Persistence of Coastal Spruce Refugia During the Holocene in Northern New England, USA, Detected by Stand-scale Pollen Stratigraphies," *Journal of Ecology* 90 (2) (2002).

39. Thomas Parkhill, "'Of Glooskap's Birth,

and of His Brother Malsum, the Wolf' — The Story of Charles Godfrey Leland's 'purely American creation,'" *American Indian Culture and Research Journal* 16 (1) (1992), pp. 45–69; Thomas Parkhill, *Weaving Ourselves into the Land: Charles Godfrey Leland, "Indians," and the Study of Native American Religions* (Albany: State University of New York Press, 1997).

40. Parkhill (1997), pp. 91–94.

41. Leland (1884), pp. ix–x. Leland thanks Rand for allowing him access to Rand's nine-hundred-page manuscript. Rand's work would be posthumously published in 1893; Ruth Holmes Whitehead, *Stories from the Six Worlds: Micmac Legends* (Halifax, Nova Scotia: Nimbus Publishing, 1988), p. 218.

42. Kenneth M. Morrison, *The Solidarity of Kin: Ethnohistory, Religious Studies, and the Algonkian-French Religious Encounter* (Albany: State University of New York Press, 2002).

43. In particular, see Morrison's Chapter 4, "The Mythological Sources of Wabanaki Catholicism: A Case Study of the Social History of Power."

44. Mark Finnan, *The Sinclair Saga* (Halifax, Nova Scotia: Formac Publishing, 1999), pp. 81–82.

Chapter 11

1. Governor Arnold (c. 1615–78) should not be confused with the infamous Revolutionary War figure of the same name. Governor Benedict Arnold was the 2nd great-grandfather of Major General Benedict Arnold.

2. Henry Wadsworth Longfellow, "Skeleton in Armor," in *Knickerbocker Magazine* (January 1841); James Fenimore Cooper, *The Red Rover, a Tale* (Philadelphia: Carey Lea & Carey, 1828). In the autumn of 2006, the Newport City Council approved another limited excavation, based on results of ground-penetrating radar and electrical resistivity tests. These excavations uncovered no new information.

3. Means was a former director of the National Museum of Archaeology at Lima, Peru; an associate in anthropology at the Peabody Museum, Harvard; and a widely published expert on the Spanish Conquest of the Incas and the cultures of the Andes. The article that piqued Means' interest was by F. J. Allen, "The Ruined Mill, or Round Church of the Norsemen, at Rhode Island, U.S.A., Compared with the Round Church at Cambridge and Others in Europe," *Proceedings of the Cambridge Antiquarian Society, with communications made to the society,* vol. XXII (1921), pp. 90–107.

4. Philip Ainsworth Means, *Newport Tower* (New York: Holt, 1942).

5. Charles Timothy Brooks, *The controversy touching the old stone mill, in the town of Newport, Rhode-Island. With remarks, introductory and conclusive* (Newport: C. E. Hammett Jr., 1851).

6. Hjalmar Rued Holand, *Westward from Vinland; an Account of Norse Discoveries and Explorations in America, 982–1362* (New York: Duell Sloan & Pearce, 1940); Philip Ainsworth Means, "The Mysterious Runic Stone," *New York Times,* May 26, 1940.

7. Hjalmar Rued Holand, *America, 1355–1364; a New Chapter in Pre-Columbian History* (New York: Duell Sloan and Pearce, 1946).

8. Royal Commission on the Ancient and Historical Monuments of Scotland (RAHMS Canmore database, Edinburgh, Scotland, 2006), vol. 2006, pp. NMRS Number: HY30SW 31.00.

9. *The Orkneyinga Saga: The History of the Earls of Orkney,* edited by Hermann Pálsson and Paul Geoffrey Edwards (London: Hogarth Press, 1978). "There was a great drinking-hall at Orphir, with a door in the south wall near the eastern gable, and in front of the hall, just a few paces down from it, stood a fine church" (Chapter 66).

10. Means (1942), pp. 265–67, 283.

11. A double-splayed window is a type of window where the opening is positioned in the center of the wall thickness with the surrounding wall cut away. Small splayed windows are found in buildings expecting use as a defensive stronghold such as castles, towers and signal towers.

12. Edward Adams Richardson, "The Builder of the Newport Tower," *American Society of Civil Engineers Transactions.* Paper no. 3091, Vol. 126, Part IV (1961), pp. 1–26.

13. Ibid., pp. 12–13.

14. Ibid., pp. 9–12.

15. Ibid., p. 13.

16. Ibid., p. 22.

17. William S. Penhallow, "Astronomical Alignments in the Newport Tower," in *Across Before Columbus? — Evidence for Transoceanic Contact with the Americas Prior to 1492,* edited by Donald Y. Gilmore and Linda S. McElroy (Edgecomb, ME: New England Antiquities Research Association, 1998).

18. Andrew Sinclair, *The Sword and the Grail* (New York: Crown, 1992), p. 145.

19. Samuel Lewis, *A Topographical Dictionary of Scotland Comprising the Several Counties, Islands, Cities, Burgh and Market Towns, Parishes, and Principal Villages* (London: S. Lewis, 1846);

J. Calder Ross, "The Lamp Acre," *Scottish Notes and Queries* VI (4) (September 1892), 52–53.

20. John Hale, Jan Heinemeier, Lynne Lancaster, Alf Lindroos and Asa Ringbom, "Dating Ancient Mortar," *American Scientist* 91 (2) (2003), pp. 130–38.

21. David P. Barron, "Danes Announce Carbon Dating on Newport Tower," *Stonewatch — Newsletter of the Gungywamp Society* 12 (1) (1993), pp. 1, 8.

22. "Stone Tower Theory Raises Questions," *Newport Daily News*, February 19, 1996.

23. Johannes Hertz, "Round Church or Windmill? New Light on the Newport Tower," *Newport History: Journal of the Newport Historical Society* 68 part 2 (235) (1997), p. 78.

24. Ibid.

25. Means (1942), pp. 265–67, 283.

26. *Newport History: Journal of the Newport Historical Society*, edited by Ronald M. Potvin, 68 part 2 (235) (1997). The Sinclair Symposium was held September 5–7, 1997, in conjunction with the annual Orkney International Science Festival.

27. See Appendix 4 for Whittall's conclusions on the Newport Tower.

28. Herbert C. Pell, "The Old Stone Mill, Newport," *Rhode Island History* 7 (4), (1948), pp. 105–19.

29. Manuel Luciano da Silva, "Review of the History of the Portuguese Templars," *Stonewatch — Newsletter of the Gungywamp Society* 12 (2) (Winter 1993), p. 4.

30. Dighton Rock, on the eastern bank of the Taunton River in Berkley, Massachusetts, was first identified as Portuguese in 1918 by Brown University professor Edmund Burke Delabarre. He detected the date 1511 and the name of Portuguese explorer Miguel Corte Real, who had disappeared in 1502, while searching for his brother Gaspar, who had previously disappeared while exploring the Atlantic Maritimes. The carvings on the rock had previously been attributed to, among others, Natives, Phoenicians, Norse and Celts. The 11-foot-long, 5-foot-high, 40-ton glacial erratic boulder has been removed from the river and is now protected in a small, climate-controlled museum in Dighton Rock State Park.

31. Unfortunately for Miguel, it appears that Vasco Añes Corte Real was refused a charter by Portuguese King Manuel I for undisclosed reasons. Various sources confirm the refusal without elaboration as to why. The current thought is that Manuel was attempting to keep the last male heir of the Corte Real bloodline safe and sound.

32. Pell, p. 115.

33. Manuel Luciano da Silva, *Portuguese Pilgrims and Dighton Rock: The First Chapter in American History* (Bristol, RI: published by author, 1971).

34. Ibid., p. 78.

35. Sir Howard Montagu Colvin, *Architecture and the After-life* (New Haven, CT: Yale University Press, 1991), pp. 134–35. Colvin further notes that scaled-down circular churches, evocative of the Jerusalem church but with no architectural similarities other than the shape, were popular as cemetery chapels. This actually could lend support to the Arnold theory; the first reference to the structure is a 1677 mention as a landmark noting where Arnold's granddaughter Damaris Golding was buried.

Chapter 12

1. Frank Glynn, "A Second Mediaeval Marker at Westford Massachusetts," *Eastern States Archaeological Federation Bulletin* 26 (1967).

2. Lethbridge-Glynn Correspondence (1980), p. 81.

3. Frank Glynn, "Another Possible Medieval Marker in Westford, Mass.," *NEARA Journal* 2 (2) (June 1967), pp. 21–22.

4. Sacrobosco's texts are justifiably rare to track down for comparative purposes. Jean-Étienne Montucla's *Histoire des Mathématiques* from 1758 (Tome 1, Planche XI) includes a comparative chart of early European variants of the numbers, including Sacrobosco. This chart has been widely reproduced both in print and on the Internet.

5. Joannes de Sacrobosco, *Tractatus de Sphæra* (Ferrara, Italy: Andreas Belfortis, 1472).

6. Rutger ten Broeke, "A Voyage into the Past — A New Medieval Ship Exactly Follows Evidence Uncovered by Archaeologists," *WoodenBoat* (November/December 1998), pp. 66–74.

7. Ibid., p. 73. The author includes images from a number of Hanseatic seals with cog depictions to illustrate the castles.

8. N. A. M. Rodger, *The Safeguard of the Sea: A Naval History of Britain, 660–1649*, 1st American ed. (New York: Norton, 1998), p. 63.

9. Ten Broeke, p. 73.

10. Lincoln P. Paine, *Ships of the World: An Historical Encyclopedia* (Boston: Houghton Mifflin, 1997).

11. Mark Heddon, "Contact Period Petroglyphs in Machias Bay, Maine," *Archaeology of Eastern North America* 30 (2002), pp. 1–20.

12. Lethbridge-Glynn Correspondence

(1980), pp. 63–64. Lethbridge believes this was the origin of the custom of local inns hanging signs outside their doors, which was made mandatory in England in 1393 by Richard II.

13. Ibid., p. 84. Glynn reported to Lethbridge that the property had a new owner with second-hand information from the previous owner about partially dismantling the structure and the original use of the structure as an animal pen, which Glynn considered apocryphal. The site was later mapped and measured by James Whittall of the Early Sites Research Society. File copies of Whittall's diagrams are on file in the Knight Collection at Westford's J. V. Fletcher Library.

14. Julia Fletcher and Gertrude Fletcher, *Old Houses of Westford* (Westford, MA: Daughters of the American Revolution, Colonel John Robinson Chapter, 1940).

15. Edwin R. Hodgman, *History of the Town of Westford in the County of Middlesex, Massachusetts — 1659–1883*, 2003 ed. (Lowell, MA: Morning Mail Co., 1883), p. 43.

16. The key operating word is "roughly" because attempts to standardize measurement units in the British Isles occurred regularly through 1845. A chain was 4 rods long, with the rod being the equivalent of the modern 16.5 feet (5 meters).

17. Lord Archibald Campbell, *Argyllshire Galleys: Some Typical Examples from Tomb Slabs and Crosses* (London: Charles J. Clark, 1906), p. 65.

18. W. Cecil Wade, *The Symbolisms of Heraldry, or a Treatise on the Meanings and Derivations of Armorial Bearings* (London: George Redway, 1898).

19. K. A. Steer and J. W. M. Bannerman, *Late Medieval Monumental Sculpture in the West Highlands* (Edinburgh: Royal Commission on the Ancient and Historical Monuments of Scotland, 1977).

20. Tim Wallace-Murphy and Marilyn Hopkins, *Templars in America: From the Crusades to the New World* (York Beach, ME: Weiser Books, 2004), pp. 123–24.

21. Denis Rixson, *The West Highland Galley* (Edinburgh: Birlinn, 1998).

22. Steer (p. 180, n5) cites the Register of the Privy Council of Scotland (1st series. C (1613–16), p. 347, as specifying a birlinn as having 12–18 oars and a galley 18–24 oars.

23. Scott F. Wolter and Blake Lemcke, "Petrographic Analysis of Rock" (St. Paul, MN: American Petrographic Services, 2007).

24. Richard Nielsen and Scott F. Wolter, *The Kensington Rune Stone: Compelling New Evidence* (Eden Prairie, MN: Outernet Publishing, 2005).

25. Alice Beck Kehoe, *The Kensington Runestone: Approaching a Research Question Holistically* (Long Grove, IL: Waveland Press, 2005).

26. Larry J. Zimmerman, "Unusual or "Extreme" Beliefs about the Past, Community Identity, and Dealing with the Fringe," in *Collaboration in Archaeological Practice*, edited by Chip Colwell-Chanthaphonh and T. J. Ferguson (Lanham, MD: AltaMira Press, 2008).

27. Ibid., pp. 70–72. Zimmerman also questions how Wolter, who disparages conclusions and reactions of "opinion-driven" disciplines such as archaeology and history when faced with "hard science" results such as geology, can then use science as irrefutable proof when one of the tenets of "hard science" is results that are replicable by peers, which is not possible when the process itself is not peer-reviewed.

28. Scott F. Wolter, *The Hooked X: Key to the Secret History of North America* (St. Cloud, MN: North Star Press, 2009), p. 178. Wolter's primary theory is that descendants of the Knights Templar, affiliated with Cistercian monks, were, as medieval visitors from Europe, responsible for North American rune stones, most notably the Kensington and Spirit Pond rune stones.

29. Ibid., p. 278.

30. J. A. Bennett, *The Divided Circle: A History of Instruments for Astronomy, Navigation, and Surveying* (Oxford: Phaidon, 1987).

31. James E. Morrison, *The Astrolabe* (Rehoboth Beach, DE: Janus, 2007), p. 37; Bennett, p. 33.

32. Manana Island is home of the Monhegan Island Inscription, named after the adjacent island, which appears on more maps. On top of the ledge where the alleged inscription is located are a series of drilled holes that appear to have been carved to fit the ends of poles or timbers. This could indicate a fish drying rack, a distress signal or support for an astrolabe. See Proper (1930), pp. 5–6. The introduction of the "mariner's astrolabe" in the late 15th century allowed navigators to determine the latitude at sea by measuring the sun's altitude at high noon or the altitude of the north celestial pole.

33. Wilbur Henry Siebert, *The Underground Railroad from Slavery to Freedom* (New York: Macmillan Co., 1898), pp. 36, 133; Wilbur Henry Siebert, "The Underground Railroad in Massachusetts," *Proceedings of the American Antiquarian Society* NS 45 (April 1935), pp. 25–100.

34. According to Siebert, after arriving in Concord, New Hampshire, the fugitives would

have utilized the same route north as those coming from Salem, New Hampshire, where one of the hiding places was the North Salem (Mystery Hill) site subsequently owned by William Goodwin. See Siebert (1935), p. 52.

35. The Canadian border is 199 miles due north, following nearby Route 3 on a contemporary map. This allows for the alteration of Route 3's original path when I-93 was constructed paralleling Route 3 from Manchester, New Hampshire, leading to Franconia Notch State Park, where the roads merge, veering away from each other north of the Notch.

36. John Pendergast, *The Bend in the River: A Prehistory and Contact Period History of Lowell, Dracut, Chelmsford, Tyngsborough, and Dunstable (Nashua, N.H.), Massachusetts, 17,000 BP to AD 1700* (Tyngsborough, MA: Merrimac River Press, 1991).

37. "The Wannalancet Map Rock on the Old Tyng Road in Tyngsborough, Mass.," *NEARA Journal* 5 (3) (September 1970). The unnamed author of the *NEARA* article is almost certainly the journal's esteemed editor Andrew Rothovius. Rothovius's association of the Tyngsboro map with the Westford Ship Stone has nothing to do with the Knight. Rothovius was convinced that many of the unexplained non-Indian carvings and stone ruins in New England were relics of a secret fur trading operation in the Merrimack Valley that operated outside the British tariffs.

38. James B. Kelley, "Song, Story, or History: Resisting Claims of a Coded Message in the African American Spiritual 'Follow the Drinking Gourd,'" *Journal of Popular Culture* 41 (2) (2008), p. 275.

Chapter 13

1. As early as 1984, Whittall had suggested that the Sinclair expedition was a possible inspiration for a European ship petroglyph carved by Native Americans in Machias Bay, Maine.

2. Michael Baigent, Richard Leigh and Henry Lincoln, *Holy Blood, Holy Grail* (New York: Delacorte Press, 1982); Michael Baigent and Richard Leigh, *The Temple and the Lodge*, 1st U.S. ed. (New York: Arcade, 1989); Andrew Sinclair, *The Sword and the Grail* (New York: Crown, 1992).

3. Peter Partner, *The Knights Templar & Their Myth*, 2nd ed. (Rochester, VT: Destiny Books, 1990), pp. 64–65.

4. Baphomet was the medieval French form of Mahomet or Mohammed, a detail lost on later authors.

5. Malcolm Barber, *The Trial of the Templars*, 2nd ed. (Cambridge, England: Cambridge University Press, 2006); Malcolm Barber, *The New Knighthood: A History of the Order of the Temple* (Cambridge, England: Cambridge University Press, 1994).

6. Edward McMurdo, *The History of Portugal* (London: Sampson Low, Marston, Searle, & Rivington, 1888), pp. 397–98.

7. Stanley G. Payne, *A History of Spain and Portugal* (Madison: University of Wisconsin Press, 1973).

8. Barber (2006), p. 276.

9. A. J. Forey, "Ex-Templars in England," *The Journal of Ecclesiastical History* 53 (January 2002), p. 19.

10. See Barber (2006), Chapter 8, for more on the trials in other countries.

11. Helen J. Nicholson, *The Knights Templar on Trial: The Trial of the Templars in the British Isles, 1308–1311* (Stroud, England: History Press, 2009).

12. Nicholson includes an appendix of the names and documentary sources (ibid., pp. 205–17).

13. Forey, p. 18.

14. François Raynouard, *Monumens Historiques, rélatifs à la condamnation des Chevaliers du Temple, et à l'abolition de leur ordre* (Paris: Impr. d'A. Égron, 1813).

15. Ibid., p. 258.

16. Robert Aitken, "The Knights Templars in Scotland," *The Scottish Review* 32 (1897), pp. 1–36.

17. Ibid., p. 29.

18. Ibid., pp. 33–34. Nicholson (pp. 51–52) confirms John of Usflete as one of five knights in the British Isles that was never located for interrogation, but she does not specify a presumed destination.

19. Barber (2006), p. 89.

20. Barbara Frale, *The Templars: The Secret History Revealed* (New York: Arcade, 2009).

21. Ibid., pp. 190–94.

22. Clement's death was not unexpected; he had been plagued by recurring bouts of hemorrhages, and his condition was considered terminal well before the "curse." Philip's death was caused by a cerebral ictus.

23. H. R. Trevor-Roper, "The European Witch-Craze of the Sixteenth and Seventeenth Centuries," in *The Crisis of the Seventeenth Century; Religion, the Reformation, and Social Change* (New York: Harper & Row, 1968), pp. xvi, 124.

24. Partner, p. 40.

25. Ibid., pp. 54–58. Partner considers this trend in supernatural charges to be a trigger of

the witchcraft hysteria to follow, adding two centuries of bloodshed to the religious schism that was already the legacy of Philip the Fair.

26. Peter Gay, *The Enlightenment: An Interpretation; The Rise of Modern Paganism* (New York: Knopf, 1966). See Chapter 5, "The Era of Pagan Christianity."

27. Ibid., p. 248.

28. Heinrich Cornelius Agrippa von Nettesheim, *De Occulta Philosophia Libri Tres* (New York: E. J. Brill, 1992).

29. Guillaume Paradin, *Cronique de Savoye* (Geneva, Switzerland: Gustave Revilliod et Edouard Fick, 1874); Jean Bodin, *The Six Bookes of a Common-weale* (London: Adam Islip, 1606).

30. Margaret C. Jacob, *Living the Enlightenment : Freemasonry and Politics in Eighteenth-century Europe* (Oxford: Oxford University Press, 1991).

31. Robert L. D. Cooper, *The Rosslyn Hoax?* (Hersham, England: Lewis, 2006), pp. 16–17.

32. Mary Ann Clawson, *Constructing Brotherhood: Class, Gender, and Fraternalism* (Princeton, NJ: Princeton University Press, 1989), pp. 4–5.

33. Jacob, pp. 46–51.

34. Alexander Horne, *King Solomon's Temple in the Masonic Tradition* (London: Aquarian Press, 1972); Douglas Knoop, G. P. Jones and Douglas Hamer, *The Two Earliest Masonic Mss: The Regius ms. (B.M. Bibl. reg. 17 AI) the Cooke ms. (B.M. Add. ms. 23198)* (Manchester, England: Manchester University Press, 1938).

35. Horne, p. 58.

36. Douglas Knoop and G. P. Jones, *The Genesis of Freemasonry* (Manchester, England: Manchester University Press, 1947).

37. Richard Waddington refers to it as "one of the most popular books in the sixteenth century," partly explaining the inclusion of the two pillars into mason lore within the next century. In "Rewriting the World, Rewriting the Body," in *The Cambridge Companion to English Literature, 1500–1600*, edited by Arthur F. Kinney (Cambridge, England: Cambridge University Press, 2000), pp. 287–309.

38. David Stevenson, *The Origins of Freemasonry: Scotland's Century, 1590–1710* (Cambridge, England: Cambridge University Press, 1990), p. 146. He notes that the Mason Word was already in use by the early 17th century, suggesting the Temple Pillar theme was also in place.

39. Knoop and Jones, pp. 215–16, Chapter V.

40. Robert Kirk, "London in 1689–90. By Rev. Robert Kirk, MA (Part I)," *Transactions of the London and Middlesex Archaeological Society* 6 (NS) (1933), pp. 322–42.

41. Moreau Jean Michel Voltaire, "Mélanges IV (1763–1766)," in *Œuvres Complètes de Voltaire*, edited by Louis Moland (Paris: Garnier Frères, 1877), vol. 25.

42. It is interesting to note that this statement has been widely quoted but completely out of context. "We look to Scotland for all our ideas of civilization" appears in print and on Scottish collegiate and governmental websites as if Voltaire meant it as a genuine tribute to Scottish progress. Voltaire, pp. 161–62. "It is an admirable effect of progress of the human spirit that today we must look to Scotland for the rules of taste in all arts, from the epic poem to gardening. The human spirit expands each day, and we should not despair, for soon we shall even receive the poetry and rhetoric of the Orkney Islands."

43. James Macpherson, *The Poems of Ossian and Related Works* (Edinburgh: Edinburgh University Press, 1996).

44. Goethe incorporated his translation of a part of the work into his 1774 novel *Die Leiden des jungen Werthers* (*The Sorrows of Young Werther*). A climactic scene features Goethe's own German translation of a section of Macpherson's Ossian cycle.

45. Edward Gibbon, *The Decline and Fall of the Roman Empire* (New York: Modern Library, 2005), pp. 1295–96. "The principle of the crusades was a savage fanaticism; and the most important effects were analogous to the cause. Each pilgrim was ambitious to return with his sacred spoils, the relics of Greece and Palestine; and each relic was preceded and followed by a train of miracles and visions. The belief of the Catholics was corrupted by new legends, their practice by new superstitions; and the establishment of the inquisition, the mendicant orders of monks and friars, the last abuse of indulgences, and the final progress of idolatry, flowed from the baleful fountain of the holy war. The active spirit of the Latins preyed on the vitals of their reason and religion; and if the ninth and tenth centuries were the times of darkness, the thirteenth and fourteenth were the age of absurdity and fable."

46. Cooper, (2006), p. 66; Walter Scott, *The Complete Works of Sir Walter Scott* (New York: Conner & Cooke, 1833).

47. See Nicholson's *Literary History of the Arabs* (London: T.F. Unwin, 1907) for one such example.

48. Cooper (2007) reprints the entire text of Ramsay's speech in Appendix VIII. There is some debate as to whether Ramsay actually de-

livered the speech to the Grand Lodge in 1737 France or merely wrote it with the intention of delivering it.

49. The 1913 Catholic Encyclopedia charitably notes "his knowledge of Oriental languages was extensive but not thorough."

50. Joseph von Hammer-Purgstall, "Mysterium Baphometis Revelatum," *Fundgruben des Orients* VI (1818), pp. 1–120, 445–99; Partner, p. 157. Partner dryly notes that Hammer's discourse, written in Latin and published in an Austrian periodical on Oriental philology, has been "more frequently cited than read."

51. François Raynouard, "Étude sur 'Mysterium Baphometi Revelatum,'" *Journal des Savants* (1819), pp. 151–61, 221–29.

52. Joseph-François Michaud, *Histoire des Croisades* (Paris: Furne et cie, 1841).

53. René Le Forestier, *La Franc-Maçonnerie Templière et Occultiste aux XVIII et XIX Siècles* (Paris: Aubier-Montaigne, 1970).

54. Partner, p. 110.

55. Partner's explanation is that as joining the Masons became fashionable, charlatans could create these higher grades and "assist" ambitious Masons in obtaining these secret but expensive ranks. See the second half of Partner's Chapter 5.

56. Abbé Augustin Barruel, *Memoirs Illustrating the History of Jacobinism* (New York: Hudson & Goodwin, 1799); Partner, pp. 126–31.

57. Cooper (2007), pp. 57–58. Cooper believes this exclusion to extend to Scottish, Welsh and Irish Freemasonry. See also Alexander Lawrie, *The History of Free Masonry, drawn from authentic sources of information; with an account of the Grand Lodge of Scotland, from its institution in 1736 to 1804, compiled from the records and an appendix of original papers* (Lodgeton, KY: Morris, 1856).

Chapter 14

1. Lawrie actually is not the author of the book. His signature is on the dedication so the book is referred to as "Lawrie's History," but an author is not credited. The author was David Brewster, a poorly kept secret. Maidment's notes in Father Hay's manuscript refers to it as "Brewster's Encyclopedia." Richard Augustine Hay, *Genealogie of the Sainteclaires of Rosslyn* (Edinburgh: T. G. Stevenson, 1835), p. V.

2. Hay (1835).

3. Robert L. D. Cooper, *The Rosslyn Hoax?* (Hersham, England: Lewis, 2006), pp. 93–96; Robert L. D. Cooper, *Cracking the Freemason's*

Code: the Truth about Solomon's Key and the Brotherhood (New York: Simon & Schuster, 2007). The documents are also reproduced as appendices. Cooper (2007) returns to the topic on pp. 27–34.

4. David Stevenson, *The Origins of Freemasonry: Scotland's Century, 1590–1710* (Cambridge, England: Cambridge University Press, 1990).

5. Ibid., p. 54.

6. See Cooper (2006), Chapter 2, for a more thorough dissection of the documents.

7. David Stevenson, *The First Freemasons: Scotland's Early Lodges and Their Members* (Aberdeen, Scotland: Aberdeen University Press, 1988), p. 187.

8. Hay (1835), p. 154.

9. Stevenson (1990), p. 54.

10. Mark Oxbrow and Ian Robertson, *Rosslyn and the Grail* (Edinburgh: Mainstream, 2005), p. 85.

11. Cooper (2006), pp. 96–98.

12. Hay (1835), pp. 26–27. "...his adge creeping on him, to the end that he might not seem altogither unthankfull to God for the benefices he receaved from Him, it came in his mind to build a house for God's service, of most curious worke: the which that it might be done with greater glory and splendor, he caused artificers to be brought from other regions and forraigne kingdomes, and caused dayly to be abundance of all kinde of workmen present: as masons, carpenters, smiths, barrowmen, and quarriers, with others."

13. Cooper (2006, p. 91) notes that two Collegiate Churches, Restalrig in Leith, Edinburgh, and Seton in East Lothian, began construction soon after Sinclair's death, suggesting that the tradesmen from the canceled Rosslyn church did not remain unemployed for very long.

14. George Hay, "The Architecture of Scottish Collegiate Churches," in *The Scottish Tradition; Essays in Honour of Ronald Gordon Cant*, edited by Geoffrey Wallis Steuart Barrow (Edinburgh: Scottish Academic Press, 1974), pp. 56–70.

15. Hay (1835), p. 27.

16. Ibid., p. 28.

17. Ibid. Page 136 notes a subsequent William Sinclair who rescued manuscripts from monasteries damaged by Reformation mobs.

18. H. J. Lawlor, "Notes on the Library of the Sinclairs of Rosslyn," *Proceedings of the Society of Antiquaries of Scotland* 32 (1897–98), pp. 90–120.

19. Michael Chesnutt, "The Dalhousie

Manuscript of the Historia Norvegiae," *Opuscula (Bibliotheca Arnamagnæana)* 8 (38) (1986), p. 68. There remains some questions regarding the chronology of manuscripts, which Chesnutt feels might have been carried from Orkney to Roslin when the Sinclairs surrendered the Earldom in 1470.

20. Angelo Maggi, *Rosslyn Chapel: An Icon Through the Ages* (Edinburgh: Birlinn, 2008).

21. Ibid., p. 1.

22. Colin McWilliam, *Lothian, except Edinburgh* (New Haven, CT: Yale University Press, 2000).

23. Oxbrow and Robertson, pp. 76–77.

24. Andrew Kerr, "Collegiate Church or Chapel of Rosslyn, Its Builders, Architect, and Construction," *Proceedings of the Society of Antiquaries of Scotland* 12 (May 14, 1877), p. 243.

25. Daniel Wilson, *The Archæology and Prehistoric Annals of Scotland* (Edinburgh: Sutherland and Knox, 1851), p. 630.

26. David MacGibbon and Thomas Ross, *The Ecclesiastical Architecture of Scotland from the Earliest Christian Times to the Seventeenth Century* (Edinburgh: D. Douglas, 1896), vol. 3, pp. 149–79.

27. Hay, (1835), p. 27.

28. A Green Man is a sculpture of a human foliate head — a human face intermingled with leaves. Branches or vines may sprout from the nose, mouth, or ears. It is a decorative architectural ornament, found in both secular and ecclesiastical buildings. It is believed to represent death and rebirth in medieval iconography, possibly introduced from Celtic sources.

29. Karen Ralls, *The Templars and the Grail: Knights of the Quest* (Wheaton, IL: Quest Books, 2003).

30. Michael T. R. B. Turnbull, *Rosslyn Chapel Revealed* (Stroud, England: Sutton, 2007).

31. For a discussion on whether church art served as a mimetic or mnemonic capacity, see *The Book of Memory: A Study of Memory in Medieval Culture* by Mary Carruthers (Cambridge, England: Cambridge University Press, 1993).

32. T. F. Crane, "Mediaeval Sermon-Books and Stories," *Proceedings of the American Philosophical Society* XXI (114) (1883), pp. 49–78.

33. Ibid., p. 57.

34. Thomas Kirk, "Appendix: An Account of a Tour in Scotland," in *Letters of Eminent Men, Addressed to Ralph Thoresby,* edited by Joseph Hunter (London: H. Colburn and R. Bentley, 1832), vol. 2, p. 450.

35. MacGibbon (1896), p. 179; Maggi (2008), p. 118. Maggi notes that the base was re-

placed and the dragons MacGibbon viewed were subsequently re-carved by David Bryce during 1860s restorations.

36. J. S. Richardson, *The Mediaeval Stone Carver in Scotland* (Edinburgh: Edinburgh University Press, 1964), p. 37.

37. Turnbull, p. 121.

38. John Slezer, *Theatrum Scotiæ* (London: Printed by John Leake for Abell Swalle, 1693); Daniel Defoe, *A Tour Thro' the Whole Island of Great Britain,* 1761 ed. (London: G. Strahan, 1727).

39. Richardson (1964), pp. 37–38.

40. Stewart Cruden, *Scottish Medieval Churches* (Edinburgh: John Donald, 1986), pp. 193–94.

41. Hay (1835), p. 27.

42. Nigel Saul, *English Church Monuments in the Middle Ages: History and Representation* (Oxford: Oxford University Press, 2009).

43. Ibid., pp. 69–70.

44. Among the angels carved in the chapel are two holding shields bearing the engrailed cross of the Sinclair family. One is in the chapel and a carving that is also painted is down in the crypt or sacristy.

45. Richardson (1964), pp. 37–38.

46. Kirk's 1677 version does not specifically mention the widowed mother or the master mason's execution. The weeping mother figure does not start appearing in print for another century.

47. Robert Forbes, "An Account of the Chapel of Roslin &C," *Edinburgh Magazine* (January 1761).

48. Robert Forbes, *An Account of the Chapel of Roslin,* edited by Philo-Roskelynsis (Edinburgh: William Auld, 1774), p. 28.

49. John Thompson, *The Illustrated Guide to Rosslyn Chapel and Castle, Hawthornden, &c.,* 10th ed. (Edinburgh: J. Menzies, 1892); Maria Hornor Lansdale, *Scotland, Historic and Romantic* (Philadelphia: H. T. Coates & Co., 1901), p. 186.

50. Joseph Robertson, ed., *Concilia Scotiae; Ecclesiae Scoticanae Statuta tam Provincialia quam Synodalia quae Supersunt. MCCXXV–MDLIX* (Edinburgh: The Bannatyne Club, 1866). The Gray Manuscript is a collection of manuscripts that are notes and texts believed to be written by James Gray, priest, notary public, and secretary to William Schevez, Archbishop of St. Andrews, 1478–1497.

51. B. E. Crawford, "Earl William Sinclair and the Building of Roslin Collegiate Church," in *Medieval Art and Architecture in the Diocese of St. Andrews,* edited by John Higgitt (Tring, En-

gland: British Archaeological Association, 1994), vol. 14.

52. Ibid., pp. 105–7.

53. Robertson (1866), vol. 2, p. 73. "De Reconciliacione Ecclesie"; David Patrick, *Statutes of the Scottish Church, 1225–1559, Publications of the Scottish History Society* (Edinburgh: Edinburgh University Press, 1907); see Patrick's 1907 translation of Synodal Statue #164 (pp. 76–77). Of the reconciliation of a church: "Furthermore, we decree that when a church or churchyard shall have been profaned by the shedding of blood or of sexual seed, if this church or churchyard have been profaned by the rector or the vicar or a parishioner of the said church, or by any other person whatsoever, he who profaned it, provided he be solvent, shall pay the dues in respect of the reconciliation of this church or churchyard. But if either have been profaned by some one who has nowise compeared, or has perchance compeared but has been found to be non-solvent, the rector of this parish or his vicar, if there be both in the said parish, shall provide the dues in respect of the reconciliation in this connection, at their own and the parishioners' expense in equal proportions, since it is their common interest, with reservation also to them of the right of raising an action against the desecrator. Now when there are a rector and a vicar in the same parish, the one half of the dues shall be paid by them in proportion to their respective incomes, and the other half shall be paid by the parishioners themselves, and if need be, they shall be compelled by ecclesiastical censure. Also we interdict, under pain of excommunication in force from this time forth, any one from daring in the future to have dances, or to hold wrestling matches, or to hold or engage in any other kind of unseemly sports in churches or in churchyards at any festivals or seasons whatsoever, since the occasion of profaning churches or churchyards has been wont to arise from such causes." Sartell Prentice discusses Masons at various projects, including a passing mention of a medieval mason named "Lente, who never outgrew his boyhood but 'worstyled [wrestled] and playde, and ran about in werkyng tyme.'" *The Voices of the Cathedral; Tales in Stone and Legends in Glass* (New York: W. Morrow and Company, 1938), p. 132.

54. Jean François Pommeraye, *Histoire de l'Abbaye Royale de S. Ouen de Rouen* (Rouen, France: Chez Richard Lallemant et Louys du Mesnil, 1662).

55. The story doesn't always end with the apprentice specifically as a homicide victim. The Lincoln Cathedral and Melrose Abbey versions have the master committing suicide in shame. See *History and Antiquities of Lincoln: Lincoln Cathedral* (Lincoln, England: Brookes and Vibert, 1865), pp. 103–4.

56. Mark Bambrough, "Rosslyn Chapel: A Glazing History," *The Journal of Stained Glass: The Journal of the British Society of Master Glass Painters* 30 (2006), pp. 12–28.

57. G. G. Coulton, "Artist Life in the Middle Ages," *The Burlington Magazine for Connoisseurs* 21 (114) (September 1912), 336–44.

58. Ibid., p. 344; see W. Crooke's article "'Prentice Pillars: The Architect and His Pupil," *Folklore* 29 (3) (September 1918), pp. 219–25, for a discussion on the myth, which Crooke believes dates back to the classic tale of Daedalus and Talos.

59. Stewart Cruden, "Seton Collegiate Church," *Proceedings of the Society of Antiquaries of Scotland* 89 (1955–56), p. 422.

60. John Bilson, "A French Purchase of English Alabaster in 1414," *The Archaeological Journal* LXIV (1) (March 1907), pp. 32–37.

61. Richardson (1964), p. 37.

62. Ibid., pp. 36–37.

63. Louise O. Fradenburg, "Scotland: Culture and Society," in *A Companion to Britain in the Later Middle Ages*, edited by Stephen Henry Rigby (Oxford: Blackwell, 2003), pp. 521–40.

64. Dunbar belonged to a group of influential late-medieval Scottish poets, generally referred to as the Scottish Makars. This group also includes the author of *The Kingis Quair*, the only surviving copy of which, housed in Bodleian Library at Oxford, was owned by the Sinclairs, dating back minimally to 1489, which bears a sketch of the coat of arms of Henry Sinclair, the grandson of Rosslyn's founder. The bound manuscript also includes a copy of Chaucer's *Troilus*, which has been identified as written by James Gray, the protégé of Lord Sinclair and the same Gray who was the secretary to St. Andrews Archibishop Scheves whose manuscript recorded the privilege of reconciling churches by proxy because of bloodshed at Rosslyn. See Eleanor P. Hammond, *Chaucer: A Bibliographical Manual* (New York: Macmillan, 1908), pp. 341–42, for more on MS. Arch. Selden. B. 24. Also see Joanne S. Norman, "Sources for the Grotesque in William Dunbar's 'Dance of the Sevin Deidly Synnis,'" *Scottish Studies* 29 (1989), pp. 55–75.

65. When the new St. Peter's Basilica was constructed, Gian Lorenzo Bernini's design of the baldacchino (1624–33) over the new high altar derived the design for the new columns from the twisted design of the old columns.

66. Eric Fernie, "The Spiral Piers of Durham Cathedral," in *Medieval Art and Architecture at Durham Cathedral*, edited by Nicola Coldstream and Peter Draper (London: British Archaeological Association, 1980), vol. 3. This could also explain a subsequent elaboration of the "Murdered Apprentice" story that specifies that the Master Mason went to Rome to study the original column before attempting to recreate the pillar.

67. Forbes (1774), p. 33.

68. Hays (1835), pp. 124–25.

69. *The History and Antiquities of Lincoln* (1865) specifically blames the "Puritan Soldiery" for the loss of the stained glass in the cathedral after stabling horses in the building (p. 103).

70. Betty Willsher, *Understanding Scottish Graveyards* (Edinburgh: Council for Scottish Archaeology, 2005), pp. 4–5.

71. Ibid., p. 6.

72. Royal Commission on the Ancient and Historical Monuments of Scotland, (RAHMS Canmore database, Edinburgh, Scotland, 2008), vol. 2008.

73. In spite of Monck and iconoclastic mobs, the chapel was already being visited by the curious — an Edinburgh physician mentions a visit to "that rare peece of Architecture, the old Chappell of Rosline" in 1618. See Patrick Anderson, *The Colde Spring of Kinghorne Craig, his admirable and new tryed properties, so far foorth as yet are found true by experience* (Edinburgh: Thomas Finlason, 1618).

74. J. Douglas Stewart, "Rome, Venice, Mantua, London — Form and Meaning in the 'Solomonic' Column from Veronese to George Vertue," *British Art Journal* 8 (3) (Winter 2007), pp. 15–23; Jean Calvin, *Sermons of Maister John Calvin, upon the Booke of Job* (London: George Bishop, 1584).

75. *History and Antiquities of Lincoln* (1865), pp. 103–4. "The two circular windows in the Great Transept are of great beauty and interest. The idle legend of a master and apprentice which used to be related to visitors, is scarcely worth noticing, in these days of better information; half the cathedrals and castles of this country and the continent have similar fables attached to them, but the fact of one of the Lincoln windows being nearly a century older than the other, adds somewhat to the absurdity of the story."

76. Jules Quicherat, "Documents Inédits sur la Construction de Saint-Ouen de Rouen," *Bibliothèque de l'École des Chartes* 13 (1) (1852), pp. 464–76.

77. Francis Grose, *The Antiquities of Scotland* (London: Hooper & Wigstead, 1797); *The Topographical, Statistical, and Historical Gazetteer of Scotland* (Edinburgh: A. Fullarton, 1853).

78. Thompson, p. 10.

79. The Wilsons operated the inn from 1763 to 1783, then took it over again in 1786. David Wilson died in 1801. He also grew strawberries alongside Rosslyn Castle, rented and catered events at Rosslyn Castle, lumbered boards and sold charcoal. His widow and their children kept the inn for several years. The building, now known as Collegehill House, remains adjacent to the chapel and still accepts bookings.

80. Antony Todd Thomson's "Journal of a Vacation in Parts of England and Scotland" (1823), quoted by Maggi (2008), p. 142, fn11.

81. Maggi expressed the opinion in a 2009 interview with Catriona Stuart. Even if Scott picked up the tale elsewhere, he was well aware of Annie and her tours. See Gillies (1837), pp. 105–7 for a recounting of Scott's encounter with the formidable Annie Wilson.

82. R.S., in *The Gentleman's Magazine* (September 1817), p. 209. Maggi (2008) also notes a number of paintings of the chapel interior that include her iconic pointing stick, either perched by itself or in the hands of subsequent guides.

83. One of the popular types of dramas during the time when the Wilsons were running the inn was the "domestic tragedy," where the trials and tribulations of the working class replaced those featuring persons of nobility. The genre, dating back to the late Elizabethan period with such dramas as "Arden of Feversham" (c. 1591), was revitalized in 1731 with the debut of George Lillo's "The London Merchant, or the History of George Barnwell," which featured an apprentice who robs his master and murders his uncle in 1588 London. It was performed regularly through 1789 and then revived in 1796. Lillo based the drama on a popular ballad, "The tale of George Barnwell, a young apprentice undone by a strumpet who having thrice robbed his master and murdered his uncle in Ludlow was hanged in chains in Polonia" (1610 version title).

84. Douglas Knoop and G. P. Jones, *The Genesis of Freemasonry* (Manchester, England: Manchester University Press, 1947); Knoop and Jones, *The Mediaeval Mason* (Manchester, England: Manchester University Press, 1933), pp. 160–68; Knoop and Jones, "Masons and Apprenticeship in Mediæval England," *Economic History Review* 3 (3) (1932), pp. 346–66. Knoop and Jones believe that new masons were recruited from the quarries and from family members. Although they do find records of masons training other masons, it was not within the

structure of indenture that would suggest an apprenticeship.

85. William Miller, "The Restorations at Roslin Chapel," *The Scotsman*, June 18, 1861.

86. "Roslin Chapel," *The Building News* VII (1861), p. 560.

87. McWilliam, pp. 416–17.

88. James Alexander St. Clair-Erskine Rosslyn, "Lord Rosslyn's Reply," *The Scotsman*, June 18, 1861.

89. Cuthbert Bede, *A Tour in Tartan-land* (London: Richard Bentley, 1863).

90. "May 12," in *The Book of Days*, edited by Robert Chambers (London: W & R Chambers, 1863), vol. 1, p. 624.

91. Author and chapel researcher Jeff Nisbet also believes the beard removal occurred after Bryce's work was completed. He notes that Bryce would be more inclined to replace the entire head with a beardless version rather than simply modifying the existing one. Additionally, based on the work done for Bryce, his stonemasons/carvers were highly skilled and certainly would have made the apprentice's chin look naturally unshaven, rather than the head's current state, which upon close examination, looks exactly like what it is — a face with a beard chiseled off (2009 correspondence with author). See Nisbet, "Secrets of Rosslyn Chapel Unveiled," *Atlantis Rising*, no. 38 (March/April 2003), for other alterations to the carvings he has noted.

92. Nigel Llewellyn, *The Art of Death: Visual Culture in the English Death Ritual c. 1500–c. 1800* (London: Reaktion Books, 1991), p. 144.

93. See Maggi (2008), Chapter 4, for the controversy over restorations of the chapel. The chapel was essentially a moss-covered ruin when restorations began in 1837, and there was much debate over whether reroofing the building and scouring the moss would destroy the building's appeal and whether the algae and moss were actually the only things holding the sculptures together.

94. Claire Smith, "Rosslyn Trust Seeks Millions in Funding to Save Crumbling Chapel," *The Scotsman*, May 23, 2006.

Chapter 15

1. Barbara Frale, *The Templars: The Secret History Revealed* (New York: Arcade, 2009).

2. Norman L. Jones, *The English Reformation: Religion and Cultural Adaptation* (Oxford: Blackwell, 2002), pp. 2–4.

3. Scottish Record Office, (RCAHMS) no GD 164/Box12/21.

4. Andrew Kerr, "Collegiate Church or Chapel of Rosslyn, Its Builders, Architect, and Construction," *Proceedings of the Society of Antiquaries of Scotland* 12 (May 14, 1877), pp. 232–33 and fn.

5. Andrew Kerr, "Rosslyn Castle, Its Buildings Past and Present," *Proceedings of the Society of Antiquaries of Scotland* 12 (1876), pp. 412–24.

6. Peter St. Clair-Erskine Rosslyn, *Rosslyn Chapel* (Roslin, Scotland: Rosslyn Chapel Trust, 1997).

7. "Grand Lodge of Scotland — The Festival of St. Andrew," *The Scotsman*, December 1, 1870.

8. See *Roslin Chapel* (1997), p. 49.

9. Eugene Taylor, *Shadow Culture: Psychology and Spirituality in America* (Washington, DC: Counterpoint, 1999).

10. Taylor identifies the first Great Awakening as being in the 1730s and 1740s, when mainstream religion saw a resurgence simultaneously with the rise of the Shakers and the Pietists of Ephrata Cloister. Taylor places the Second Great Awakening as being in the early to mid-19th century, with abolitionists, tent-revivals and waves of missionaries coexisting with the rise of mesmerism and transcendentalism.

11. Andrew Sinclair, *The Sword and the Grail* (New York: Crown, 1992).

12. Michael Baigent, Richard Leigh and Henry Lincoln, *Holy Blood, Holy Grail* (New York: Delacorte Press, 1982).

13. The book was retitled *Holy Blood, Holy Grail* for the United States market. For simplicity's sake, the U.S. title is cited throughout.

14. Gérard de Sède, *Les Templiers Sont Parmi Nous, ou, L'énigme de Gisors* (Paris: R. Julliard, 1962).

15. Henry Lincoln, "The Lost Treasure of Jerusalem?" in *Chronicle, Essays from Ten Years of Television Archaeology*, edited by Ray Sutcliffe (London: British Broadcasting Corporation, 1978); René Descadeillas, "Mythologie du Trésor de Rennes," *Mémoires de la Société des Arts et des Sciences de Carcassonne* VII (2) (July 1974).

16. Philippe de Chérisey, *L'Enigme de Rennes* (Paris: s.n., 1978). For more sources on the Rennes-le-Château and Priory of Scion hoaxes, visit Paul Smith's collection of smoking guns, documents and interviews at http://priory-of-sion.com.

17. Jean Luc Chaumeil, *Le Tresor du Triangle d'Or* (Nice, France: Alain Lefeuvre, 1979).

18. Edwin McDowell, "Publishing: When Book Does Its Own Promotion," *New York Times*, February 5, 1982.

19. Michael Anderson Bradley and Deanna

Theilmann-Bean, *Holy Grail across the Atlantic: The Secret History of Canadian Discovery and Exploration* (Willowdale, Ontario: Hounslow Press, 1988); Michael Anderson Bradley, *Grail Knights of North America: On the Trail of the Grail Legacy in Canada and the United States* (Toronto, Ontario: Hounslow Press, 1998); Michael Anderson Bradley and Joelle Lauriol, *Swords at Sunset: The Last Stand of North America's Grail Knights* (Ancaster, Ontario: Manor House Publishing, 2005); Eben Norton Horsford, *The Discovery of the Ancient City of Norumbega. A Communication to the President and Council of the American Geographical Society at Their Special Session in Watertown, November 21, 1889* (Boston: Houghton, 1890); Bradley and Lauriol (2005), pp. 168–69. As a side note, or a testament to Bradley's research skills, he confuses Horsford with character actor Edward Everett Horton, best remembered as the narrator of the "Fractured Fairy Tales" segment of the *Rocky & Bullwinkle* cartoon show.

20. William S. Crooker, *Oak Island Gold* (Halifax, Nova Scotia: Nimbus, 1993).

21. These books are difficult to locate but supporters have placed her materials, published and drafts, online at http://thelibraryof hope. com. Mark Finnan, *The Sinclair Saga* (Halifax, Nova Scotia: Formac Publishing, 1999). Finnan's Chapters 2 and 11 discuss the matter.

22. Michael Baigent and Richard Leigh, *The Temple and the Lodge*, 1st U.S. ed. (New York: Arcade, 1989), p. 113.

23. Richard Henry Major, *The Voyages of the Venetian brothers, Nicolò & Antonio Zeno to the Northern Seas, in the XIVth century: comprising the latest known accounts of the lost colony of Greenland and of the Northmen in America before Columbus* (London: Hakluyt Society, 1873), p. 200.

24. Eugène Beauvois, *Pratiques et Institutions Religieuses d'origine Chrétienne chez les Mexicains du Moyen âge* (Louvain, Belgium: Polleunis & Ceuterick, 1896).

25. Frederick J. Pohl, *Prince Henry Sinclair—His Voyage to the New World in 1398* (New York: Clarkson N. Potter, 1974), p. 111. Pohl briefly mentions Beauvois but only regarding his placement of Great Ireland in Canada.

26. "Many Attend Unveiling of Knight Marker," *Westford Eagle*, December 16, 1976.

27. Kerr (1877).

28. Kerr (1876), p. 415.

29. The Templars took three vows — chastity, poverty and obedience. The Sinclairs were neither chaste nor poor.

30. Michael T. R. B. Turnbull, *Rosslyn Chapel Revealed* (Stroud, England: Sutton, 2007), p. 152. This also the stance of the official guidebook.

31. R. Ewart Oakeshott, *The Archaeology of Weapons; Arms and Armor from Prehistory to the Age of Chivalry* (New York: Praeger, 1960).

32. Ibid., p. 210. Oakeshott calculates that upwards of eight out of ten English military effigies from c.1290–1330 have swords of Type XIV and nearly all of effigies of Alsace and Lorraine and the Rhineland dating between 1300 and 1330 have this kind of sword.

33. Sinclair (1992), p. 3.

34. Weston S. Walford, "On Cross-legged Effigies Commonly Appropriated to Templars," *Archaeological Journal* 1 (1844), pp. 49–52; J. Charles Cox, "On Some Popular Archaeological Errors and Fictions," *Antiquary* XXX (July–December 1894), pp. 48–54.

35. Cox, p. 49.

36. Walford, p. 50.

37. Bernard de Montfaucon, *Les Monumens de la Monarchie Françoise* (Paris: J. M. Gandouin, 1730).

38. Helen J. Nicholson, *The Knights Templar on Trial: The Trial of the Templars in the British Isles, 1308–1311* (Stroud, England: History Press, 2009), plates 2–4.

39. Ibid., pp. 75–76.

40. Thomas Arnold, "Note on Two Sculptured Sepulchral Slabs in Old Pentland Churchyard," *Proceedings of the Society of Antiquaries of Scotland* 14 (1879), pp. 49–51.

41. According to family lore, the Sinclairs acquired Pentland as a result of a wager with King Robert where Sinclair boasted his hounds could capture a white hind that had evaded the king's dogs. Robert took the bet and staked Pentland against Sinclair's head. When it appeared the dogs would fail, Sinclair beseeched St. Catherine and the fleeing deer suddenly paused in flight, allowing Sinclair's hounds to close the distance and kill the hind.

42. Andrew Kerr, "Glencorse and Its Old Buildings," *Proceedings of the Society of Antiquaries of Scotland* 13 (1879), pp. 129–36; Robert Chambers, "On the Skirts of the Pentlands," *Chamber's Journal* VI (October 17, 1903), pp. 733–36.

43. Mark Oxbrow and Ian Robertson, *Rosslyn and the Grail* (Edinburgh: Mainstream, 2005), pp. 127–28.

44. Edward Lewes Cutts, *A Manual for the Study of the Sepulchral Slabs and Crosses of the Middle Ages* (London: J. H. Parker, 1849), p. 29. "It is noticeable that the plain cross is very seldom used upon these monuments, but almost

always an ornamented cross. The symbolists considered the plain cross to be the cross of shame, and we very rarely find it used in ancient Gothic work; the floriated cross was the cross of glory, and alluded to the triumph of our blessed Lord."

45. Ibid., p. 39; John Di Folco, "Some Aspects of Funerary Monuments in Lowland Scotland," in *The Scottish Tradition; Essays in Honour of Ronald Gordon Cant*, edited by Geoffrey Wallis Steuart Barrow (Edinburgh: Scottish Academic Press, 1974), p. 150.

46. Kerr (1877), plate XXIV.

47. Di Folco, p. 149.

48. David Wilkins, *Concilia Magnae Britanniae et Hiberniae a Synodo Verolamiensi A.D. CCCCXLVI. ad Londinensem A.D. [MD]CCXVII. Accedunt Constitutiones et alia ad Historiam Ecclesiae Anglicanae spectantia* (London, 1737), book II, p. 381, reprinted in John Spottiswoode, *The History of the Church and State of Scotland* (London: R. Royston, 1655), pp. 14–15; *The Spottiswoode Miscellany: A Collection of Original Papers and Tracts, Illustrative Chiefly of the Civil and Ecclesiastical History of Scotland* (Edinburgh: Spottiswoode Society, 1845).

49. Nicholson, pp. 140–41. Her source is Folio 158V of MS 454 in Oxford's Bodleian Library.

50. Robert Aitken, "The Knights Templars in Scotland," *The Scottish Review* 32 (July and October 1898), pp. 29–32.

51. Evelyn Lord, *The Knights Templar in Britain* (Harlow, England: Longman, 2002), pp. 98–99. Lord (pp. 130–31) believes that when the Templar properties were seized in 1308, the general disrepair of many buildings indicated that the Templars, after the fall of Acre and the elimination of their Holy Land imperative, lost momentum in keeping the properties profitable, compounded by the lack of new recruits to help with maintenance.

52. Christopher Knight and Robert Lomas, *The Hiram Key: Pharaohs, Freemasons, and the Discovery of the Secret Scrolls of Jesus* (New York: Barnes & Noble, 1998), pp. 288–89.

53. The book hypothesizes that Freemasonry origins predate the Knights Templar to the Essene Church and Pharaoic Egypt. The star is a symbol, the authors state, that connects the Essenes and Egyptian theologies to Freemasonry.

54. In 1314, the famous battle of Bannockburn was fought by English troops against Scottish forces under Robert the Bruce. A decisive victory for the Scots, it would be a pivotal point on the battle for Scottish independence. The outnumbered Scottish forces were able to bottle up the English in an area where their greater numbers were a disadvantage. As the British struggled in crowded tight quarters, the mobile Scottish were able to advantage of the confusion. By the second day, the English troops were beginning to break under the Scottish onslaught. A cry of encouragement by the Scots was heard by the Scottish servants and camp followers, who gathered weapons and banners and charged forward. The English army saw the new arrivals and panicked at what they thought to be fresh reserves. They broke ranks and the battle became a rout.

55. See James Burnes, *Sketch of the History of the Knights Templars* (Edinburgh: W. Blackwood & Sons, 1837), p. 39, as one example.

56. Thomas Gray, *Scalacronica* (Edinburgh: The Maitland Club, 1836).

57. Nicholson, p. 52.

58. Hans Delbrück, *History of the Art of War Within the Framework of Political History* (Westport, CT: Greenwood Press, 1975), vol. 3, pp. 438–42.

59. Nicholson, pp. 75–76.

60. Lord, pp. 145–46. Lord also suggests that de Jay may have been the prototype for Brian de Bois Guilbert, the evil Templar villain in Sir Walter Scott's *Ivanhoe*.

61. Ibid., pp. 109, 154.

62. Walter Scott, *The Lord of The Isles: A Poem in Six Cantos* (Edinburgh: James Ballantyne and Co., 1815).

63. There was a Templar knight named Reginald di Argentine who was killed at Antioch in 1153. No relationship has been ascertained.

64. Sinclair (1992), p. 192.

65. The book had originally been released in England in 1996 with less distribution.

66. Sinclair's book is cited in a footnote regarding alleged Templar involvement in the Battle of Bannockburn in *The Hiram Key* (p. 299, fn 2), indicating their familiarity with the book.

67. Knight and Lomas, p. 302.

68. A. F. Dyer, "A Botanist Looks at the Medieval Plant Carvings at Rosslyn Chapel. Part 1: The Chapel and the Leaf Carvings," *Botanical Society of Scotland News* (76) (2001), pp. 26–33; A. F. Dyer, "A Botanist Looks at the Medieval Plant Carvings at Rosslyn Chapel. Part 3: Assessing the Evidence for a Pre-Columbian contact with the New World, or: the Indian Corn Mystery," *Botanical Society of Scotland News* (78) (2002), pp. 31–40; A. F. Dyer, "A Botanist Looks at the Medieval Plant Carvings at Rosslyn Chapel. Part 2: The Fruits and Flowers and Their Possible Symbolism," *Botanical Society of Scotland News* (77) (2001), pp. 33–41.

69. Brian Moffat, "Rosslyn Aloes in Veritas?" *Textualities* (1) (2006), pp. 9–15.

70. Moffat's article is a direct challenge to Andrew Sinclair's book, which states the Rosslyn Chapel is a medieval herbarium of medicinal plants. See Sinclair (1992), Chapter 9.

71. Oxbrow and Robertson, pp. 63–64; Genesis 37 (KJV).

72. His father, Sir James St. Clair-Erskine, 2nd Earl of Rosslyn, and his son, Robert Francis St. Clair-Erskine, 4th Earl of Rosslyn, were each elected to Grand Master Mason of Scotland. A December 1, 1870, article in *The Scotsman* reported the installment of Robert Francis St. Clair-Erskine, the 4th Earl of Rosslyn, as the Grand Master Mason of Scotland and David Bryce as the Grand Architect.

73. Kerry Ross Boren and Lisa Lee Boren, *Following the Ark of the Covenant: The Treasure of God: Solving the Mystery of Sanpete Valley, Utah* (Springville, UT: Cedar Fort, 2000).

74. Ibid., pp. 68, 185.

75. Ibid., p. 72.

76. Ibid., pp. 71–72.

77. Ibid., p. 71.

78. Ibid., pp. 84–85.

79. Ibid., p. 166.

80. Dan Brown, *The Da Vinci Code*, 1st ed. (New York: Doubleday, 2003).

81. Technically the suit was against their own publisher—a series of acquisitions and takeovers left Random House as the publisher of both the plaintiffs' and defendant's books.

82. Simon Edge, "Secrets of the Da Vinci Code," *The Express* (London), March 1, 2006.

83. Nigel Blundell, Fidelma Cook and James Tapper, "Solved: Riddle of the Da Vinci Code's Third Man," *The Mail on Sunday* (London), April 9, 2006.

84. One way to see which authors are borrowing from other authors is to trace the egregious errors and typos as they migrate from one title to another. As an example, Goodwin's 1946 book *Ruins of Great Ireland in New England* is incorrectly mentioned as *Ruins of "Greater Ireland" in New England* in one book, which then is carried forward in subsequent books, including Andrew Sinclair's.

85. Joanna Vallely, "Free Ticket on Time Machine to the Past," *Edinburgh Evening News*, April 17, 2007; David MacGibbon and Thomas Ross, *The Ecclesiastical Architecture of Scotland from the Earliest Christian Times to the Seventeenth Century* (Edinburgh: D. Douglas, 1896).

86. Stewart Cruden, "Seton Collegiate Church," *Proceedings of the Society of Antiquaries of Scotland* 89 (1955–56), pp. 417–37.

87. Stewart Cruden, *Scottish Medieval Churches* (Edinburgh: John Donald, 1986), p. 192.

88. Robert Baird, *Diverse Druids* (Arlington, VA: Invisible College Press, 2003).

89. Brad Olsen, *Sacred Places, North America: 108 Destinations* (Santa Cruz, CA: Consortium of Collective Consciousness, 2003).

90. Steven Sora, *The Lost Treasure of the Knights Templar: Solving the Oak Island Mystery* (Rochester, VT: Destiny Books, 1999); Steven Sora, *The Lost Colony of the Templars: Verrazano's Secret Mission to America* (Rochester, VT: Destiny Books, 2004).

91. William F. Mann, *The Templar Meridians: The Secret Mapping of the New World* (Rochester, VT: Destiny Books, 2006).

92. Umberto Eco, "Dreaming of the Middle Ages," in *Travels in Hyper Reality* (San Diego: Harcourt Brace Jovanovich, 1986), pp. 61–72.

93. Umberto Eco, *Foucault's Pendulum* (San Diego: Harcourt Brace Jovanovich, 1989).

94. David Morgan, *The Sacred Gaze: Religious Visual Culture in Theory and Practice* (Berkeley: University of California Press, 2005).

95. Ibid., p. 68.

Epilogue

1. Frederick J. Pohl, "Leif Ericsson's Visit to America," *American-Scandinavian Review* 36 (1948), pp. 17–29; Pohl, *The Lost Discovery; Uncovering the Track of the Vikings in America* (New York: Norton, 1952); Pohl, *The Vikings on Cape Cod: Evidence from Archaeological Discovery* (Pictou, Nova Scotia: Pictou Advocate Press, 1957); Pohl, *Atlantic Crossings Before Columbus* (New York: Norton, 1961); Pohl, *The Viking Settlements of North America* (New York: Clarkson N. Potter, 1972).

2. M.L. Fernald, "Notes on the Plants of Wineland the Good," *Rhodora* 12 (134), 17–38 (1910); Fernald, *Bulletin of the American Geographical Society* 47, 9 (1915).

3. Frederick J. Pohl, "Can the Ship's Shoring at Follins Pond Be Radiocarbon Dated?" *Massachusetts Archaeological Society Bulletin* 16 (3) (1955), pp. 56–60.

4. Abner Morse, *Traces of the Ancient Northmen in America: being a paper read before the New England Historical Genealogical Society August, 1861 : also supplement to same* (Boston: Mudge Printers, 1887); Morse, *Further Traces of the Ancient Northmen in America : with geological evidences of the location of their Vineland* (Boston: H. W. Dutton, 1861).

5. Benjamin L. Smith, "A Report on the

Follins Pond Investigation," *Massachusetts Archaeological Society Bulletin* 14 (2) (1953), pp. 82–88; Pohl (1957), pp. 47–48.

6. See Pohl (1957), p. 51, or Pohl (1972), p. 198, for a diagram of the wooden artifacts.

7. Pohl (1955); Donald Allan, "Cape Cod Diggers Find 'Norse Relics,'" *New York Times*, May 11, 1952.

8. Donald W. Linebaugh, *The Man Who Found Thoreau: Roland W. Robbins and the Rise of Historical Archaeology in America* (Hanover, NH: University Press of New England, 2005).

9. Robbins, as documented in his 1959 book *Hidden America*, also visited William Goodwin's site in North Salem and removed several roof slabs from the entrance to the Oracle Chamber. Robbins was not authorized to be on the site, let alone undertake excavations and was physically removed from the site by Malcolm Pearson. Donald Allan, "Cape Cod Timbers Are Not Viking; 'Artifacts' Are Only a Century Old," *New York Times*, May 12, 1952.

10. Pohl (1957), p. 43. Pohl dryly notes that two new housing developments on the north side of the pond were kind enough to name streets after figures in the sagas.

11. Pohl (1961), pp. 119–22.

12. David P. Barron and Sharon Mason, *The Greater Gungywamp: A Guidebook* (Noank, CT: Gungywamp Society, 1990), p. 6.

13. Jack Hitt, "How the Gungywampers Saved Civilization," *Gentlemen's Quarterly* 68 (January 1998), pp. 128–35.

14. Vance R. Tiede, "Solar Orientation of Irish Early Christian Oratories [abstract]," *HAD News — The Newsletter of the Historical Astronomy Division of the American Astronomical Society* (60) 2 (2002).

15. Alexander Roberts and James Donaldson, *Constitutions of the Holy Apostles* (Grand Rapids, MI: W. B. Eerdmans, 1950).

16. Robert Baird, *Diverse Druids* (Arlington, VA: Invisible College Press, 2003).

17. Tracy R. Twyman, *Solomon's Treasure* (Portland, OR: Dragon Key Press, 2005), p. 17. In the same sentence, "occult expert" Tracy Twyman also credits Sinclair with being "one of the hereditary lords of Rosslyn," referring to the chapel that would later be built by Henry's grandson.

18. Peter Champoux, *Gaia Matrix: Arkhom and the Geometries of Destiny in the North American Landscape*, 1st ed. (Washington, MA: Franklin Media, 1999).

19. Laurence Gardner, *Bloodline of the Holy Grail: The Hidden Lineage of Jesus Revealed* (Gloucester, MA: Fair Winds Press, 2001).

20. Ibid., p. 253.

21. David S. Brody, *Cabal of the Westford Knight* (Groton, MA: Martin & Lawrence Press, 2009).

22. William B. Goodwin, *The Ruins of Great Ireland in New England* (Boston: Meador Publishing Company, 1946).

23. The first marker was a plaque on a brick wall in an access alley that was the remnant of the street in Boston where Poe was born. The Commonwealth did not like their native son and the disaffection was mutual. He rewrote his biography to claim Richmond, Virginia, as his birthplace and railed endlessly about Boston's literary elitism. Boston in return built the Massachusetts Transportation Building over his actual birthplace on Carver Street. In 2009, Boston finally made amends and dedicated a small square to the author near the Boston Common.

24. Edgar Allan Poe, "For Annie," *Flag of Our Union* (Boston), July 7, 1849.

25. Ironically, considering the theme of this text, Poe has two monuments in Baltimore's Westminster Burying Ground. Controversy swirls unabated as to under which stone Poe is actually interred.

26. Frederick W. Coburn, "Poe as Seen by the Brother of 'Annie,'" *New England Quarterly* 16 (3) (1943), pp. 468–76.

27. "Many Attend Unveiling of Knight Marker," *Westford Eagle*, December 16, 1976.

Appendix 1

1. Silas Tertius Rand, *Legends of the Micmacs* (New York: Longmans Green and Co., 1893).

2. Charles Godfrey Leland and John Dyneley Prince, *Kuloskap the Master, and Other Algonkin Poems* (New York: Funk & Wagnalls, 1902).

3. Abby Langdon Alger, *In Indian Tents: Stories Told by Penobscot, Passamaquoddy and Mimac Indians* (Boston: Roberts Brothers, 1982).

Bibliography

Agrippa von Nettesheim, Heinrich Cornelius. *De Occulta Philosophia Libri Tres.* New York: Brill, 1992.

Aitken, Robert. "The Knights Templars in Scotland." *The Scottish Review* 32 (July and October 1898), 1–36.

Alger, Abby Langdon. *In Indian Tents: Stories Told by Penobscot, Passamaquoddy and Mimac Indians.* Boston: Roberts Brothers, 1982.

Allan, Donald. "Cape Cod Diggers Find 'Norse Relics.'" *New York Times*, May 11, 1952.

_____. "Cape Cod Timbers Are Not Viking; 'Artifacts' Are Only a Century Old." *New York Times*, May 12, 1952.

Allen, F.J. "The Ruined Mill, or Round Church of the Norseman, at Newport, Rhode Island, U.S.A., Compared with the Round Church at Cambridge and Others in Europe." *Proceedings of the Cambridge Antiquarian Society, with communications made to the society*, Vol. XXII (1921), pp. 90–107.

Anderson, Patrick. *The Colde Spring of Kinghorne Craig, his admirable and new tryed properties, so far foorth as yet are found true by experience.* Edinburgh: Thomas Finlason, 1618.

Anderson, Rasmus Björn. *America Not Discovered by Columbus: An Historical Sketch of the Discovery of America by the Norsemen, in the Tenth Century.* Chicago: S. C. Griggs & Co., 1877.

Arnold, Thomas. "Note on Two Sculptured Sepulchral Slabs in Old Pentland Churchyard." *Proceedings of the Society of Antiquaries of Scotland* 14, 49–51.

Atherton, Ian. *Norwich Cathedral: Church, City, and Diocese, 1096–1996.* London: Hambledon Press, 1996.

Aubert, Karl "Grönlandsverset." *Danske Studier* 4 (1907), 228–29.

Ayres, Harral. *The Great Trail of New England.* Boston: Meador Publishing Company, 1940.

Babcock, William Henry. *Early Norse Visits to North America.* Washington, DC: Smithsonian Institution, 1913.

Badham, Sally. " 'A New Feire Peynted Stone'—Medieval English Incised Slabs?" *Church Monuments—The Journal of The Church Monuments Society* 17 (2004), 20–52.

Baigent, Michael, and Richard Leigh. *The Temple and the Lodge.* New York: Arcade, 1989.

Baigent, Michael, Richard Leigh, and Henry Lincoln. *Holy Blood, Holy Grail.* New York: Delacorte Press, 1982.

Bain, Robert. *The Clans and Tartans of Scotland.* London: Collins, 1939.

Baird, Robert. *Diverse Druids.* Arlington, VA: Invisible College Press, 2003.

Bambrough, Mark. "Rosslyn Chapel: A Glazing History." *The Journal of Stained Glass: The Journal of the British Society of Master Glass Painters* 30 (2006), 12–28.

Barber, Malcolm. *The New Knighthood: A History of the Order of the Temple.* Cambridge, England: Cambridge University Press, 1994.

_____. *The Trial of the Templars.* 2nd ed. Cambridge, England: Cambridge University Press, 2006.

Barrett, James H. "Fish Trade in Norse Orkney and Caithness: A Zooarchaeological Approach." *Antiquity* 71, no. 273 (Sept.), 616–38.

Barrett, James H., Roelf P. Beukens, and Rebecca A. Nicholson. "Diet and Ethnicity during Viking Colonization of Northern Scotland: Evidence from Fish Bones and Stable Carbon Isotopes." *Antiquity* 75, no. 278 (2001), 145–54.

Barrett, James H., Rebecca A. Nicholson, and Ruby Cerón-Carrasco. "Archaeo-icthyological Evidence for Long-term Socioeconomic Trends in Northern Scotland: 3500 BC to AD 1500." *Journal of Archaeological Science* 26 (1999), 353–88.

Barron, David P. "Danes Announce Carbon Dating on Newport Tower." *Stonewatch — Newsletter of the Gungywamp Society*, Vol. 12, No. 1 (Fall 1993), pp. 1, 8.

Barron, David P., and Sharon Mason. *The Greater Gungywamp: A Guidebook.* Noank, CT: Gungywamp Society, 1990.

Barruel, Abbé Augustin. *Memoirs Illustrating the History of Jacobinism.* Translated by Robert Clifford. 4 vols. New York: Hudson & Goodwin, 1799.

Beaton, Donald. *Some Noted Ministers of the Northern Highlands.* Inverness, Scotland: Northern Counties Newspaper and Printing and Publishing Company, 1929.

Beauclerk-Dewar, Peter de Vere. "The Kingdom in Scotland." In *Burke's Landed Gentry of Great Britain.* Wilmington, DE: Burke's Peerage and Gentry, 2001.

Beauvois, Eugène. *La Découverte du Nouveau Monde par les Irlandais et les Premières Traces du Christianisme en Amérique avant l'an 1000.* Nancy, France: G. Crépin-Leblond, 1875.

———. *Les Colonies Européennes du Markland et de l'Escociland au XIV siècle, et les Vestiges qui en Subsistèrent Jusqu'aux XVI et XVII siècles.* Nancy, France: G. Crépin-Leblond, 1877a.

———. *Les Derniers Vestiges du Christianisme Prêché du 10 au 14 siècle dans le Markland et la Grande Irlande: Les Porte-Croix de la Gaspésie et de l'Acadie.* Paris, France, 1877b.

———. *Pratiques et Institutions Religieuses d'origine Chrétienne chez les Mexicains du Moyen âge.* Louvain, Belgium: Polleunis & Ceuterick, 1896.

Beazley, C. Raymond. "[Review — Voyages of the Zeni]." *The Geographic Journal* XIII, no. 2 (February 1899), 166–70.

Bede, Cuthbert. *A Tour in Tartan-land.* London: Richard Bentley, 1863.

Bennett, J. A. *The Divided Circle: A History of Instruments for Astronomy, Navigation, and Surveying.* Oxford: Phaidon, 1987.

Billings, Robert William. *The Baronial and Ecclesiastical Antiquities of Scotland.* 4 vols.. Edinburgh: W. Blackwood and Sons, 1845.

Bilson, John. "A French Purchase of English Alabaster in 1414." *The Archaeological Journal* LXIV, no. 1 (March 1907), 32–37.

Björnbo, Axel Anthon, and Carl S. Petersen. *Fyenboen Claudius Claussøn Swart (Claudius Clavus), Nordens Ældste Kartograf.* Copenhagen, Denmark: A. F. Høst & Søn, 1904.

Blundell, Nigel. "Holy Authors in Stand-off." *Daily Telegraph*, April 10, 2006.

Blundell, Nigel, Fidelma Cook, and James Tapper. "Solved: Riddle of the Da Vinci Code's Third Man." *The Mail on Sunday*, April 9, 2006.

Boardman, Stephen I. *The Early Stewart Kings: Robert II and Robert III, 1371–1406.* East Linton, Scotland: Tuckwell Press, 1996.

Bodin, Jean. *The Six Bookes of a Commonweale.* Translated by Richard Knolles. London: Adam Islip, 1606.

Boland, Charles Michael. *They All Discovered America.* Garden City, NY: Doubleday, 1961.

Bordone, Benedetto. *Isolario.* Turin, Italy: Les Belles Lettres, 2000.

Boren, Kerry Ross, and Lisa Lee Boren. *Following the Ark of the Covenant: The Treasure of God: Solving the Mystery of Sanpete Valley, Utah.* Springville, UT: Cedar Fort, 2000.

Boudriot, Jean. "La Petite Artillerie des Hunes, des Bastingages et des Embarcations." *Neptunia* 100, September–December 1970.

Boynton, Susan, and Eric Rice. *Young Choristers, 650–1700.* Rochester, NY: Boydell Press, 2008.

Bradley, Michael Anderson. *Grail Knights of North America: On the Trail of the Grail Legacy in Canada and the United States.* Toronto, Ontario: Hounslow Press, 1998.

Bradley, Michael Anderson, and Joelle Lauriol. *Swords at Sunset: The Last Stand of North America's Grail Knights.* Ancaster, Ontario: Manor House Publishing, 2005.

Bradley, Michael Anderson, and Deanna Theilmann-Bean. *Holy Grail across the Atlantic: The Secret History of Canadian Discovery and Exploration.* Willowdale, Ontario: Hounslow Press, 1988.

Brenner, Oscar. "Die ächte Karte des Olaus Magnus vom Jahre 1539 nach dem Exemplar der Munchener Staatsbibliothek." *Forhandlinger i Videnskabs-selskabet i Christiania* 15 (1886).

Brewer, Derek, and Jonathan Gibson. *A Companion to the Gawain-poet.* Woodbridge, England: Boydell & Brewer Ltd, 1997.

Brody, David S. *Cabal of the Westford Knight.* Groton, MA: Martin & Lawrence Press, 2009.

Brooks, Charles Timothy. *The controversy Touching the Old Stone Mill, in the town of Newport, Rhode-Island. With remarks, introductory and conclusive.* Newport, RI: C.E. Hammett Jr., 1851.

Brøndsted, Johannes. *Norsemen in North America before Columbus.* Washington, DC: Smithsonian Institution, 1954.

_____. *Problemet om Nordboer i Nordamerika før Columbus — en Bedømmelse af det Amerikanske Materiale.* Copenhagen, Denmark: Nordisk Oldkyndighed og Historie, 1951.

Brown, Dan. *The Da Vinci Code.* New York: Doubleday, 2003.

Brydall, Robert. "The Monumental Effigies of Scotland, from the Thirteenth to the Fifteenth Century." *Proceedings of the Society of Antiquaries of Scotland* 29 (May 13, 1895), 329–410.

Buarche, Phillipe. "Mémoire sur l'Ile de Frislande." *Histoire de l'Académie Royale des Sciences* 1784 annual, 430–53.

Burke, Bernard Sir. *Vicissitudes of Families: And Other Essays.* 4th ed. London: Longman, Green, Longman and Roberts, 1860.

Burke, John. *A General and Heraldic Dictionary of the Peerage and Baronetage of the British Empire.* 106th ed. London: Burke's Peerage, Ltd, 1999.

Burke's Peerage, Baronetage & Knightage. Edited by Charles Mosely. 107th ed. Wilmington, DE: Burke's Peerage, Ltd, 2003.

Burnes, James. *Sketch of the History of the Knights Templars.* Edinburgh: W. Blackwood & Sons, 1837.

Butler, Caleb. *History of the Town of Groton.* Boston: T.R. Marvin, 1848.

Cahill, Robert Ellis. *New England's Ancient Mysteries.* Salem, MA: Old Saltbox Publishing House, 1993.

Calder, James Traill. *Sketch of the Civil and Traditional History of Caithness from the Tenth Century.* Glasgow, Scotland: Thomas Murray and Son, 1861.

Calvin, Jean. *Sermons of Maister John Calvin, upon the Booke of Job.* Translated by Arthur Golding. London: George Bishop, 1584.

Campbell, Ian. "A Romanesque Revival and the Early Renaissance in Scotland, c.1380–1513." *Journal of the Society of Architectural Historians* 54, no. 3 (September 1995), 302–25.

Campbell, Lord Archibald. *Argyllshire Galleys: Some Typical Examples from Tomb Slabs and Crosses.* London: Charles J. Clark, 1906.

Cappelli, Adriano. *Lexicon Abbreviaturarum.* Milan, Italy: Ulrico Hoepli, 1949.

Carlyle, Thomas. *The Early Kings of Norway.* New York: Harper, 1875.

Carruthers, Mary J. *The Book of Memory: A Study of Memory in Medieval Culture.* Cambridge, England: Cambridge University Press, 1993.

Chambers, Robert. "On the Skirts of the Pentlands." *Chamber's Journal* VI, October 17, 1903, 733–36.

Champoux, Peter. *Gaia Matrix: Arkhom and the Geometries of Destiny in the North American Landscape.* 1st ed. Washington, MA: Franklin Media, 1999.

Charter: Ratification to the Earl of Caithness (16 May 1471) [cited July 15, 2008]. Available from http://www.rps.ac.uk.

Chase, Charles Wingate. *History of Haverhill, Massachusetts.* Haverhill, MA: published by author, 1861.

Chase, Levi B. *The Bay Path and Along the Way.* Norwood, MA: printed for the author, 1919.

Chaumeil, Jean Luc. *Le Tresor du Triangle d'Or.* Nice, France: Alain Lefeuvre, 1979.

Cheney, Harry. Correspondence with William B. Goodwin, December 20, 1936.

Chesnutt, Michael. "The Dalhousie Manuscript of the Historia Norvegiae." *Opuscula (Bibliotheca Arnamagnæana)* 8, no. 38 (1985), 54–95.

Christy, Miller. "Appendix B — Note on the Zeno Narrative and Chart of 1558." In *The Silver Map of the World — A Contemporary Medallion Commemorative of Drake's Great Voyage (1577–80)* 49–67. London: H. Stevens, Son & Stiles, 1900.

Clark, Jeremiah S. *Rand and the Micmacs.* Charlottetown, Prince Edward Island: Charlottetown Examiner, 1899.

Clawson, Mary Ann. *Constructing Brotherhood: Class, Gender, and Fraternalism.* Princeton, NJ: Princeton University Press, 1989.

Clouston, J. Storer. *Records of the Earldom of Orkney, 1299–1614.* Vol. VII. Edinburgh: Scottish Historical Society, 1914.

Coburn, Frederick W. "Poe as Seen by the Brother of 'Annie.'" *New England Quarterly* 16, no. 3 (September 1943), 468–76.

Colón, Fernando, and Alfonso de Ulloa. *La Vita e i Viaggi di Cristoforo Colombo.* Translated by Rinaldo Caddeo. Milan, Italy: Fasani, 1945.

Colvin, Sir Howard Montagu. *Architecture and the After-life.* New Haven, CT: Yale University Press, 1991.

Constitutions of the Holy Apostles. Edited by Alexander Roberts and James Donaldson. Grand Rapids, MI: W.B. Eerdmans Publishing Company, 1950.

Cooper, Charles Purton. *An Account of the Most Important Public Records of Great Britain and the Publications of the Record Commissioners.* 2 vols. London: Baldwin and Cradock, 1832.

Cooper, James Fenimore. *The Red Rover, The Works of James Fenimore Cooper.* New York: G.P. Putnam's & Sons, 1850.

_____. *The Red Rover, a Tale.* Philadelphia: Carey Lea & Carey, 1828.

Cooper, Robert L. D. *Cracking the Freemason's Code: The Truth about Solomon's Key and the Brotherhood.* New York: Simon & Schuster, 2007.

_____. *The Rosslyn Hoax?* Hersham, England: Lewis, 2006.

Coote, C. H. "Volume VIII — Burton-Cantwell." In *Dictionary of National Biography*, edited by Leslie Stephen, pp.166–71. London: Smith, Elder & Co., 1886.

Coulton, G. G. "Artist Life in the Middle Ages." *The Burlington Magazine for Connoisseurs* 21, no. 114 (September 1912), 336–44.

Cowan, Hugh. "Sheriffs and Coroners." *The Scottish Review* 30 (July 1897), 235–51.

Cowley, Charles. *Illustrated History of Lowell.* Boston: Lee & Shepard, 1868.

Cox, J. Charles. "On Some Popular Archaeological Errors and Fictions." *Antiquary* XXX (July–December 1894), 48–54.

Crane, T. F. "Mediaeval Sermon-Books and Stories." *Proceedings of the American Philosophical Society* XXI, no. 114 (1883), 49–78.

Crawford, B. E. "Earl William Sinclair and the Building of Roslin Collegiate Church." In *Medieval Art and Architecture in the Diocese of St. Andrews*, edited by John Higgitt. Tring, England: British Archaeological Association, 1994.

_____. "The Historical and Archaeological Background to the Papa Stour Project." In *Papa Stour and 1299: Commemorating the 700th Anniversary of Shetland's First Document*, edited by B. E. Crawford and Jon Gunnar Jørgensen, 13–35. Lerwick, Shetland: Shetland Times Ltd., 2002.

_____. "The Pledging of the Islands in 1469: The Historical Background." In *Shetland and the Outside World 1469–1969*, edited by Donald J. Withrington, 32–48. Oxford: Oxford University Press, 1983.

_____. "[Review of Prince Henry Sinclair]." *Scottish Historical Review* 56, no. 161 (April 1977), 86–87.

_____. *Scandinavian Scotland.* Leicester, England: Leicester University Press, 1987.

_____. "Sinclair Family (per. 1280–c.1500)." In *Oxford Dictionary of National Biography.* Oxford: Oxford University Press, 2004.

Crawford, B. E., Lyn Blackmore, and John W. Allen. *The Biggings, Papa Stour, Shetland: The History and Excavation of a Royal Norwegian Farm.* Edinburgh: Society of Antiquaries of Scotland, 1999.

Crooke, W. "'Prentice Pillars: The Architect and His Pupil." *Folklore* 29, no. 3 (September 1918), 219–25.

Crooker, William S. *Oak Island Gold.* Halifax, Nova Scotia: Nimbus, 1993.

Cruden, Stewart. *Scottish Medieval Churches.* Edinburgh: John Donald, 1986.

_____. "Seton Collegiate Church." *Proceedings of the Society of Antiquaries of Scotland* 89 (1955–56), 417–37.

Currier, John J. *Historical Sketch of Ship Building on the Merrimac River.* Newburyport, MA: W.H. Huse & Co. Printers, 1877.

Cutts, Edward Lewes. *A Manual for the Study of the Sepulchral Slabs and Crosses of the Middle Ages.* London: J.H. Parker, 1849.

da Mosto, Andrea. "I Navigatori Nicolò e Antonio Zeno." In *Ad Alessandro Luzio, gli Archivi di Stato Italiani*, edited by Alessandro Luzio, 293–308. Florence, Italy: Le Monnier, 1933.

da Silva, Manuel Luciano. *Portuguese Pilgrims and Dighton Rock: The First Chapter in American History.* Bristol, RI: published by author, 1971.

_____. "Review of the History of the Portuguese Templars." *Stonewatch — Newsletter of the Gungywamp Society* 12, no. 2 (Winter 1993), 4.

Dana, James Dwight. *A System of Mineralogy.* 4th ed. New York: G.P. Putnam, 1854.

Daniel, Glyn. "Editorial." *Antiquity* XLII, no. 166 (June 1968), 81–87.

Däniken, Erich von. *Chariots of the Gods?* New York: Putnam, 1970.

de Chérisey, Philippe. *L'Enigme de Rennes.* Paris: s.n., 1978.

de Sède, Gérard. *Les Templiers Sont Parmi Nous, ou, L'énigme de Gisors.* Paris: R. Julliard, 1962.

_____. *L'Or de Rennes ou la Vie insolite de Bérenger Saunière, curé de Rennes-le-Château.* Paris: Julliard, 1967.

Deane, Charles. "Remarks by Charles Deane on the Same." *Proceedings of the Massachusetts Historical Society* 18 (May 1880), 80–81.

DeCosta, B. F. "Columbus and the Geographers of the North." *The American Church Review* 24, no. 3 (July 1872), 418–38.

_____. "The Letter of Verrazano." *Magazine of American History* 2, no. 2 (February 1878), 65–81.

_____. *The Pre-Columbian Discovery of America by the Northmen.* Albany, NY: J. Munsell, 1868.

_____. "[Review of *The Annals of the Voyages of the Brothers Nicolo and Antonio Zeno*]." *The American Historical Review* 4, no. 4 (July 1899), 726–29.

Defoe, Daniel. *A Tour Thro' the Whole Island of Great Britain.* 1761 ed. 3 vols. London: G. Strahan, 1727.

Delabarre, Edmund Burke. *Dighton Rock. A Study of the Written Rocks of New England.* New York: Walter Neale, 1928.

Delbrück, Hans. *History of the Art of War Within the Framework of Political History.* Translated by Walter J. Renfroe. 4 vols. Westport, CT: Greenwood Press, 1975.

Denys, Nicolas. *The Description and Natural History of the Coasts of North America (Acadia).* Translated by William Francis Ganong. Toronto, Ontario: The Champlain Society, 1908.

Descadeillas, René. "Mythologie du Trésor de Rennes." *Mémoires de la Société des Arts et des Sciences de Carcassonne* VII, no. 2 (July 1974).

Di Folco, John. "Some Aspects of Funerary Monuments in Lowland Scotland." In *The Scottish Tradition; Essays in Honour of Ronald Gordon Cant,* edited by Geoffrey Wallis Steuart Barrow. Edinburgh: Scottish Academic Press, 1974.

Dillon, H. A., and W. St. J Hope. "Inventory of the Goods and Chattels Belonging to Thomas, Duke of Gloucester." *Archaeological Journal* 54, 274–308.

"Diploma of Thomas, Bishop of Orkney and Zetland, and the Chapter of Kirkwall, addressed to Eric King of Norway, Respecting the Genealogy of William Saint Clair, Earl of Orkney." In *The Bannatyne Miscellany; Containing Original Papers and Tracts, Chiefly Relating to the History and Literature of Scotland,* edited by Walter Scott, David Laing and Thomas Thomson. New York: AMS Press, 1973.

Diplomatarium Norvegicum. Edited by Christian C.A. Lange and Carl R. Unger. Vol. 2. Oslo, Norway: P.T. Mallings Forlagshandel, 1852.

The Diplomatic Correspondence of Richard II. Edited by Édouard Perroy. Vol. 48, *Royal Historical Society. Publications; Camden third series.* London: Royal Historical Society, 1933.

Drummond, James. *Archaeologia Scotica. Sculptured Monuments in Iona & the West Highlands.* Edinburgh: Society of Antiquaries of Scotland, 1881.

Dyer, A. F. "A Botanist Looks at the Medieval Plant Carvings at Rosslyn Chapel. Part 1: The Chapel and the Leaf Carvings." *Botanical Society of Scotland News* no. 76 (2001), 26–33.

_____. "A Botanist Looks at the Medieval Plant Carvings at Rosslyn Chapel. Part 2: The Fruits and Flowers and Their Possible Symbolism." *Botanical Society of Scotland News,* no. 77 (2001), 33–41.

_____. "A Botanist Looks at the Medieval Plant Carvings at Rosslyn Chapel. Part 3: Assessing the Evidence for a Pre-Columbian contact with the New World, or: the Indian Corn Mystery." *Botanical Society of Scotland News,* no. 78 (2002), 31–40.

Eco, Umberto. "Dreaming of the Middle Ages." In *Travels in Hyper Reality,* 61–72. San Diego: Harcourt Brace Jovanovich, 1986.

_____. *Foucault's Pendulum.* San Diego: Harcourt Brace Jovanovich, 1989.

Edge, Simon. "Secrets of the Da Vinci Code." *The Express,* March 1, 2006.

Eggers, Henrich Peter von. "Priisskrift om Grønlands Østerbygds sande Beliggenhed." *Kongelige Danske Landhuushold-ningsselskab Skrifter* 4, no. 1794, 239–321.

Everett, William. "Remarks by William Everett on Proposed Statue of Leif." *Proceedings of the Massachusetts Historical Society* 18 (May 1880), 79–80.

The Exchequer Rolls of Scotland (Rotuli Scaccarii Regum Scotorum). Edited by John Stuart and George Burnett. 23 vols. Edinburgh: HM General Register House, 1878.

Fagan, Vincent F. Correspondence with William B. Goodwin, November 18, 1942.

_____. Correspondence with William B. Goodwin, February 1, 1944.

Falnes, Oscar J. "New England Interest in Scandinavian Culture and the Norsemen." *New England Quarterly*, Vol. 10, No. 2 (June 1937), pp. 211–242.

Fernald, M.L. "Notes on the Plants of Wineland the Good." *Rhodora*, Vol. 12, No. 134 (February 1910), pp. 17–38.

Fernie, Eric. "The Spiral Piers of Durham Cathedral." In *Medieval Art and Architecture at Durham Cathedral*, edited by Nicola Coldstream and Peter Draper. London: British Archaeological Association, 1980.

Finnan, Mark. *The Sinclair Saga.* Halifax, Nova Scotia: Formac Publishing, 1999.

Fiske, John. *The Discovery of America.* 2 vols. Cambridge, MA: Riverside Press, 1892.

Fleming, Robin. "Picturesque History and the Medieval in Nineteenth-Century America." *The American Historical Review*, Vol. 100, No. 4 (October 1995), pp. 1061–1094.

Fletcher, Julia, and Gertrude Fletcher. *Old Houses of Westford.* Westford, MA: Daughters of the American Revolution, Colonel John Robinson Chapter, 1940.

Folsom, George. "[Review of Zahrtmann's 'Remarks on the Voyages to the Northern Hemisphere']." *The North American Review* 47, no. 100 (July 1838), 177–206.

Forbes, Robert. *An Account of the Chapel of Roslin.* Edited by Philo-Roskelynsis. Edinburgh: William Auld, 1774.

_____. "An Account of the Chapel of Roslin &C." *Edinburgh Magazine*, January 1761.

Forbes-Boyd, Eric. "The Dark Ages Reseen." *Christian Science Monitor.* (July 28, 1948): 16.

Forey, A. J. "Ex-Templars in England." *The Journal of Ecclesiastical History* 53 (January 2002), 18–37.

Forster, Johann Reinhold. *Geschichte der Entdeckungen und Schifffahrten im Norden: Mit neuen Originalkarten versehen.* Frankfurt, Germany: C. G. Strauss, 1784.

_____. *History of the Voyages and Discoveries Made in the North.* London: G. G. J. and J. Robinson, 1786.

Fowler, William S. "Tomahawks of Central New England." *Massachusetts Archaeological Society Bulletin* 12, no. 3 (April 1951), 29–37.

_____. "Trade Tomahawks." *Massachusetts Archaeological Society Bulletin* 13, no. 3 (April 1952), 23–27.

_____. "The Westford Indian Rock." *Massachusetts Archaeological Society Bulletin* 21, no. 2 (January 1960), 21–22.

Fradenburg, Louise O. "Scotland: Culture and Society." In *A Companion to Britain in the Later Middle Ages*, edited by Stephen Henry Rigby, 521–40. Oxford: Blackwell, 2003.

Frale, Barbara. *The Templars: The Secret History Revealed.* New York: Arcade, 2009.

Frohlin, John. Correspondence with Vincent Fagan, June 9, 1949.

Gardner, Laurence. *Bloodline of the Holy Grail: The Hidden Lineage of Jesus Revealed.* Gloucester, MA: Fair Winds Press, 2001.

Gay, Peter. *The Enlightenment: An Interpretation; The Rise of Modern Paganism.* 2 vols. New York: Knopf, 1966.

Gibbon, Edward. *The Decline and Fall of the Roman Empire.* New York: Modern Library, 2005.

Gillies, R.P. *Recollections of Sir Walter Scott.* London: Fraser, 1837.

Glynn, Cindy. Correspondence with Terry J. Deveau, 2009.

Glynn, Frank. "Another Possible Medieval Marker in Westford, Mass." *NEARA Journal* 2, no. 2 (June 1967), 21–22.

_____. Correspondence with Clay Perry, June 6, 1958.

_____. "A Second Mediaeval Marker at Westford Massachusetts." *Eastern States Archaeological Federation Bulletin* 26, 1967.

_____. "A Unique Punched Portrait in Massachusetts." *Eastern States Archaeological Federation Bulletin* 16 (1957), 11.

Glynn, Frank, and T. C. Lethbridge. *T. C. Lethbridge — Frank Glynn Correspondence: 1950–1966.* Edited by James P. Jr. Johnson Whittall. Rowley, MA: Early Sites Research Society, 1980.

_____. *T. C. Lethbridge — Frank Glynn Correspondence: 1950–1966.* Edited by James

P. Jr. Johnson Whittall. Rowley, MA: Early Sites Research Society, 1998.

Goodwin, William B. "An Ancient Norse Relic." *The Chronicle* 228 (November 1938), 36–39.

_____. Correspondence with David Robert Smith, December 16, 1941.

_____. Correspondence with Harral Ayres, July 27, 1936.

_____. Correspondence with Vincent Fagan, February 5, 1944.

_____. Correspondence with Vincent Fagan, September 3, 1943.

_____. Correspondence with William Sumner Appleton Jr., July 22, 1937.

_____. *The Lure of Gold.* Boston: Meador Publishing Company, 1940.

_____. *The Ruins of Great Ireland in New England.* Boston: Meador Publishing Company, 1946.

_____. *The Truth about Leif Ericsson and the Greenland Voyages.* Boston: Meador Publishing Company, 1941.

Gordon, Claire C., and Jane E. Buikstra. "Soil pH, Bone Preservation and Sampling Bias at Mortuary Sites." *American Antiquity* 46, no. 3 (July 1981), 566–71.

Goudsward, David. *Ancient Stone Sites of New England and the Debate over Early European Exploration.* Jefferson, NC: McFarland, 2006.

Goudsward, David, and Robert Stone. *America's Stonehenge: The Mystery Hill Story.* Wellesley, MA: Branden Books, 2002.

Graham, Angus. "Headstones in Post-Reformation Scotland." *Proceedings of the Society of Antiquaries of Scotland* 91 (1958), 1–9.

Graham, Henry Davenport. *Antiquities of Iona.* London: Day & Son, 1850.

Graham-Campbell, James, and Colleen E. Batey. *Vikings in Scotland: An Archaeological Survey.* Edinburgh: Edinburgh University Press, 1998.

"Grand Lodge of Scotland — The Festival of St. Andrew." *The Scotsman*, December 1, 1870.

Gray, Thomas. *Scalacronica.* Edinburgh: The Maitland Club, 1836.

Green, Samuel A., and Elizabeth Sewell Hill. *Facts Relating to the History of Groton, Massachusetts.* Groton, MA: J. Wilson and Son, 1912.

Grinsell, L. V. "The Breaking of Objects as a Funerary Rite." *Folklore* 72, no. 3 (1961), 475–91.

_____. "The Breaking of Objects as a Funerary Rite: Supplementary Notes." *Folklore* 84, no. 2, 111–14.

Grose, Francis. *The Antiquities of Scotland.* 2 vols. London: Hooper & Wigstead, 1797.

Gross, Charles. "The Early History and Influence of the Office of Coroner." *Political Science Quarterly* 7, no. 4 (December 1892), 656–72.

Grotius, Hugo. "On the Origin of the Native Races of America." In *Bibliotheca Curiosa.* Edinburgh: s.n., 1884.

Gunn, Mark Rugg. *History of the Clan Gunn.* Glasgow, Scotland: Alex. McLaren & Sons, 1969.

Gunn, Michael J. "The Scottish Expedition to America in 1398." *The Gunn Herald* 1, no. 1 (Winter 1987), 12–25.

Gunn, Robert R. *The Gunns.* Crawfordville, GA: C.G. Moore's Print Shop, 1925.

Hakluyt, Richard. *Divers Voyages Touching the Discoverie of America, and the Ilands Adjacent unto the Same made first of all by our Englishmen, and afterward by the Frenchmen and Britons: and certaine notes of advertisements for observations, necessarie for such as shall heereafter make the like attempt, with two mappes annexed heereunto for the plainer understanding of the whole matter.* London: Thomas Woodcocke, 1582.

_____. *The Principall Navigations, Voyages and Discoveries of the English nation, made by sea or overland, to the remote and farthest distant quarters of the earth, at any time within the compasse of these 1600 yeres.* 2nd ed. London: George Bishop and Ralph Newberie, 1589.

Hale, John, Jan Heinemeier, Lynne Lancaster, Alf Lindroos, and Asa Ringbom. "Dating Ancient Mortar." *American Scientist,* Vol. 91, No. 2 (March-April 2003), pp. 130–138.

Hammer-Purgstall, Joseph von. "Mysterium Baphometis Revelatum." *Fundgruben des Orients* VI, 1–120, 445–99.

Hammond, Eleanor P. *Chaucer: A Bibliographical Manual.* New York: Macmillan, 1908.

Hapgood, Charles H. *Earth's Shifting Crust; A Key to Some Basic Problems of Earth Science.* New York: Pantheon Books, 1958.

_____. *Maps of the Ancient Sea Kings; Evidence of Advanced Civilization in the Ice Age.* [1st] ed. Philadelphia: Chilton Books, 1966.

Harde, Ellen, and Marilyn Day. *The New Old*

Houses of Westford. 2nd ed. 1 vol. Westford, MA: Westford Historical Commission, 2004.

Harrisse, Henry. *John Cabot, the Discoverer of North-America, and Sebastian, His Son; a Chapter of the Maritime History of England under the Tudors, 1496–1557.* London: B. F. Stevens, 1896.

Haug, Eldbjørg. *Provincia Nidrosiensis i Dronning Margretes Unions- og Maktpolitikk, Nr. 14 i Skriftserie fra Historisk institutt.* Trondheim, Norway: Historisk Institutt NTNU, 1996.

Haugen, Einar. "The Rune Stones of Spirit Pond Maine." *Man in the Northeast* 4 (Fall 1972), 62–80.

Hay, George. "The Architecture of Scottish Collegiate Churches." In *The Scottish Tradition; Essays in Honour of Ronald Gordon Cant,* edited by Geoffrey Wallis Steuart Barrow, 56–70. Edinburgh: Scottish Academic Press, 1974.

Hay, Richard Augustine. *Genealogie of the Sainteclaires of Rosslyn.* Edited by James. Maidment. Edinburgh: T. G. Stevenson, 1835.

Hay, Richard Augustine, Robert L. D. Cooper, and the Grand Lodge of Scotland Freemasons. *Genealogie of the Sainteclaires of Rosslyn.* Edinburgh: Grand Lodge, 2002.

Headley, Janet A. "Anne Whitney's Leif Eriksson — A Brahmin Response to Christopher Columbus." *American Art,* Vol. 17, No. 2 (Summer 2003), pp. 40–59.

Heddon, Mark. "Contact Period Petroglyphs in Machias Bay, Maine." *Archaeology of Eastern North America* 30 (2002), 1–20.

Hertz, Johannes. "Round Church or Windmill? New Light on the Newport Tower." *Newport History: Journal of the Newport Historical Society* 68 part 2, no. 235 (1997), 55–91.

Hilen, Andrew R. and Henry Wadsworth Longfellow. *Longfellow and Scandinavia: A Study of the Poet's Relationship with the Northern Languages and Literature.* New Haven, CT: Yale University Press, 1947.

Hill, Rosalind M. T. "Fourpenny Retirement: the Yorkshire Templars in the Fourteenth Century." *Studies in Church History* 24, 123–28.

History and Antiquities of Lincoln: Lincoln Cathedral. Lincoln, England: Brookes and Vibert, 1865.

Hitchcock, Edward. *Final Report on the Geology of Massachusetts.* 2 vols. Northampton, MA: Butler, 1841.

Hitt, Jack. "How the Gungywampers Saved Civilization." *Gentlemen's Quarterly* 68 (January 1998), 128–35.

Hobbs, William Herbert. "The Fourteenth-Century Discovery of America by Antonio Zeno." *Scientific Monthly* 72 (January 1951), 24–31.

_____. "Zeno and the Cartography of Greenland." *Imago Mundi—The International Journal for the History of Cartography* 6 (1949), 15–19.

Hodgman, Edwin R. *History of the Town of Westford in the County of Middlesex, Massachusetts—1659–1883.* 2003 ed. Lowell, MA: Morning Mail Co, 1883.

Holand, Hjalmar Rued. *America, 1355–1364; a new chapter in pre-Columbian history.* New York: Duell Sloan & Pearce, 1946.

_____. *Westward from Vinland; an account of Norse discoveries and explorations in America, 982–1362.* New York: Duell Sloan & Pearce, 1940.

Hopkins, Donald R. *The Greatest Killer: Smallpox in History.* Chicago: University of Chicago Press, 2002.

Horne, Alexander. *King Solomon's Temple in the Masonic Tradition.* London: Aquarian Press, 1972.

Horsford, Eben Norton. *Discovery of America by Northmen: Address at the Unveiling of the Statue of Leif Eriksen, Delivered in Faneuil Hall, Oct. 29, 1887.* Boston: Houghton Mifflin & Co, 1888.

_____. *The Discovery of the Ancient City of Norumbega. A Communication to the President and Council of the American Geographical Society at Their Special Session in Watertown, November 21, 1889.* Boston: Houghton, 1890.

_____. *The Indian Names of Boston, and Their Meaning.* Cambridge, MA: J. Wilson and Son, 1886.

Huden, John C. *Indian Place Names of New England.* New York: Museum of the American Indian, Heye Foundation, 1962.

Hughes, Kathleen. "Where Are the Writings of Early Scotland?" In *Celtic Britain in the Early Middle Ages: Studies in Scottish and Welsh Sources,* edited by David Dumville, 1–21. Woodbridge, England: Boydell Press, 1980.

Hume, David. *Godscroft's The History of the House of Douglas.* Edited by David Reid.

2 vols. Edinburgh: Scottish Text Society, 1996.

_____. *The History of the Houses of Douglas and Angus.* Edinburgh: Evan Tyler, 1643.

Hunt, John, and Peter Harbison. *Irish Medieval Figure Sculpture, 1200–1600: A Study of Irish Tombs with Notes on Costume and Armour.* 2 vols. Dublin: Irish University Press, 1974.

Innes, Cosmo. *Lectures on Scotch Legal Antiquities.* Edinburgh: Edmonston and Douglas, 1872.

Innes, Thomas. *A Critical Essay on the Ancient Inhabitants of the Northern Parts of Britain or Scotland.* Vol. 8. Edinburgh: W. Paterson, 1879.

Irminger, Admiral Carl Ludvig Christian. "Zeno's Frislanda Is Iceland and Not the Færoes." *Journal of the Royal Geographical Society of London* 49 (1879), 398–412.

Jacob, Margaret C. *Living the Enlightenment: Freemasonry and Politics in Eighteenth Century Europe.* Oxford: Oxford University Press, 1991.

Jacobsen, Lis Rubin, and Erik Moltke. *Danmarks Runeindskrifter.* Copenhagen, Denmark: Einar Munksgaard, 1941.

Jamieson, John. *Jamieson's Dictionary of the Scottish language, in which the words are explained in their different senses, authorized by the names of the writers by whom they are used, or the titles of the works in which they occur, and derived from their originals.* Edinburgh: W.P. Nimmo, 1867.

Jones, Norman L. *The English Reformation: Religion and Cultural Adaptation.* Oxford: Blackwell, 2002.

Kehoe, Alice Beck. *The Kensington Runestone: Approaching a Research Question Holistically.* Long Grove, IL: Waveland Press, 2005.

Kejlbo, Ib Rønne. "Zenokortet — Dets Kilder of Dets Betydning for den Kartografiske Udforming af Det Nordlige Atlanterhav." *Fund og Forskning* 3, 91–102.

Kelley, James B. "Song, Story, or History: Resisting Claims of a Coded Message in the African American Spiritual 'Follow the Drinking Gourd.'" *Journal of Popular Culture* 41, no. 2 (April 2008), 262–80.

Kelly, Francis M. "A Knight's Armour of the Early XIV Century. Being the Inventory of Raoul de Nesle." *Burlingon Magazine for Connoisseurs* 6, no. 24 (March 1905), 457–59, 462–69.

Kerr, Andrew. "Collegiate Church or Chapel of Rosslyn, Its Builders, Architect, and Construction." *Proceedings of the Society of Antiquaries of Scotland* 12 (May 14, 1877), 218–44.

_____. "Glencorse and Its Old Buildings." *Proceedings of the Society of Antiquaries of Scotland* 13 (1879), 129–36.

_____. "Rosslyn Castle, Its Buildings Past and Present." *Proceedings of the Society of Antiquaries of Scotland* 12 (1876), 412–24.

Killean, Joseph. "Man About Town (column)." *Lowell Sun*, June 18, 1957.

Kirk, Robert. "London in 1689–90. By Rev. Robert Kirk, MA (Part I)." *Transactions of the London and Middlesex Archaeological Society* 6 (NS), 1933, 322–42.

Kirk, Thomas. "Appendix: An Account of a Tour in Scotland." In *Letters of Eminent Men, Addressed to Ralph Thoresby* edited by Joseph Hunter. London: H. Colburn and R. Bentley, 1832.

Knight, Bernard. "The Medieval Coroner." *The Medico-legal Journal* 58, no. 2.

Knight, Christopher, and Robert Lomas. *The Hiram Key: Pharaohs, Freemasons, and the Discovery of the Secret Scrolls of Jesus.* New York: Barnes & Noble, 1998.

Knoop, Douglas, and G. P. Jones. *The Genesis of Freemasonry.* Manchester, England: Manchester University Press, 1947.

_____. "Masons and Apprenticeship in Mediæval England." *The Economic History Review* 3, no. 3 (April 1932), 346–66.

_____. *The Mediaeval Mason.* Manchester, England: Manchester University Press, 1933.

Knoop, Douglas, G. P. Jones, and Douglas Hamer. *The Two Earliest Masonic Mss: The Regius ms. (B.M. Bibl. reg. 17 AI) the Cooke ms. (B.M. Add. ms. 23198).* Manchester, England: Manchester University Press, 1938.

Kreutz, Barbara M. "Mediterranean Contributions to the Medieval Mariner's Compass." *Technology and Culture* 14, no. 3, 367–83.

Krim, Arthur J. "Acculturation of the New England Landscape: Native and English Toponymy of Eastern Massachusetts." In *New England Prospect: Maps, Place Names, and the Historical Landscape,* edited by Peter Benes. Boston: Boston University, 1980.

Kunz, George Frederick. *Gems and Precious Stones of North America.* New York: Scientific Publishing Company, 1892.

Lacy, Norris J. "The Da Vinci Code: Dan Brown and the Grail That Never Was." *Arthuriana* 14, no. 3, 81–93.

Laet, Johannes de. *Notae ad Dissertationem Hugonis Grotii De Origine Gentium Americanarum: Et Observationes aliquot ad meliorem indaginem difficillimae illius Quaestionis.* Amsterdam, Netherlands: Elzevirius, 1643.

Lambert, Joanne Dondero. *America's Stonehenge—An Interpretive Guide.* Kingston, NH: Sunrise Publications, 1996.

Lansdale, Maria Hornor. *Scotland, Historic and Romantic.* 2 vols. Philadelphia: H. T. Coates & Co., 1901.

Lawlor, H. J. "Notes on the Library of the Sinclairs of Rosslyn." *Proceedings of the Society of Antiquaries of Scotland* 32 (1897–98), 90–120.

Lawrie, Alexander. *The History of Free Masonry, drawn from authentic sources of information; with an account of the Grand Lodge of Scotland, from its institution in 1736 to 1804, compiled from the records and an appendix of original papers.* Lodgeton, KY: Morris, 1856.

le Clercq, Chrestien. *New Relation of Gaspesia, with the Customs and Religion of the Gaspesian Indians.* Translated by William Francis Ganong. Toronto, Ontario: Champlain Society, 1910.

_____. *Nouvelle Relation de la Gaspesie.* Paris: A. Auroy, 1691.

Le Forestier, René. *La Franc-Maçonnerie Templière et Occultiste aux XVIII et XIX Siècles.* Paris: Aubier-Montaigne, 1970.

Leland, Charles Godfrey. *The Algonquin Legends of New England.* Boston: Houghton Mifflin and Company, 1884.

Leland, Charles Godfrey, and John Dyneley Prince. *Kuloskap the Master, and Other Algonkin Poems.* New York: Funk & Wagnalls, 1902.

Lethbridge, T. C. *Herdsmen and Hermits—Celtic Seafarers in the Northern Seas.* Cambridge, England: Bowes & Bowes, 1950.

_____. *Merlin's Island—Essays on Britain in the Dark Ages.* London: Methuen & Co. Ltd, 1948.

_____. *A Step in the Dark.* London: Routledge & Kegan Paul, 1967.

_____. *Umiak—The European Ancestry of the 'Women's Boat.'* Cambridge, England: privately published, 1937.

Lewis, Gordon T. *The Cruise of the Knorr; an account of early Norse exploration in America.* Yarmouth, Nova Scotia: s.n., 1938.

Lewis, Samuel. *A Topographical Dictionary of Scotland Comprising the Several Counties, Islands, Cities, Burgh and Market Towns, Parishes, and Principal Villages.* 2 vols. London: S. Lewis, 1846.

Lincoln, Henry. "The Lost Treasure of Jerusalem?" In *Chronicle, Essays from Ten Years of Television Archaeology,* edited by Ray Sutcliffe. London: British Broadcasting Corporation, 1978.

Llewellyn, Nigel. *The Art of Death: Visual Culture in the English Death Ritual c. 1500–c. 1800.* London: Reaktion Books, 1991.

"Local Engineer Given Credit for Solving a Mystery of the Vikings." *Daily Hampshire Gazette,* July 9, 1940.

Lockhart, Robert Hamilton Bruce. *My Scottish Youth.* London: Putnam, 1937.

Lodge, Edmund. *The Genealogy of the Existing British Peerage.* London: Saunders and Otley, 1832.

Longfellow, Henry Wadsworth. "Skeleton in Armor." *Knickerbocker Magazine,* January 1841.

Lord, Evelyn. *The Knights Templar in Britain.* Harlow, England: Longman, 2002.

Louisbourg Institute Archaeology Artifact Database. "Cannon, Petrieroe, Swivel Gun-Provenience Record Number 1B6A13–1." Fortress of Louisbourg National Historic Site.

Lucas, Fred W. *The Annals of the Voyages of the Brothers Nicolò and Antonio Zeno, in the North Atlantic About the End of the Fourteenth Century, and the Claim Founded Thereon to a Venetian Discovery of America; a criticism and an indictment.* London: H. Stevens Sons and Stiles, 1898.

_____. *Appendiculae Historicae or Shreds of History Hung on a Horn.* London: H. Stevens & son, 1891.

Lucas, Fred W., and Henry Stevens. *The New Laws of the Indies for the Good Treatment and Preservation of the Indians, Promulgated by the Emperor Charles the Fifth 1542–1543. A facsimile reprint of the original Spanish edition, together with a literal translation into the English language.* London: Chiswick Press, 1893.

Mac Cullagh, Richard. *The Irish Currach Folk.* Dublin: Wolfhound Press, 1992.

Macalister, R. A. S. "An Inventory of the Ancient Monuments Remaining in the Island of Iona." *Proceedings of the Society of Antiquaries of Scotland* 48 (1913), 421–30.

MacCormick, Iain, and Alexander Ritchie. *The Celtic Art of Iona: drawings and reproductions from the manuscripts of the late Alex Ritchie of Iona, and from the Iona Press of 1887.* Iona, Scotland: New Iona Press, 1994.

MacGibbon, David, and Thomas Ross. *The Castellated and Domestic Architecture of Scotland from the Twelfth to the Eighteenth Century.* 5 vols. Edinburgh: D. Douglas, 1887.

_____. *The Ecclesiastical Architecture of Scotland from the Earliest Christian Times to the Seventeenth Century.* 3 vols. Edinburgh: D. Douglas, 1896.

MacGregor, Alexander. *The History of the Feuds and Conflicts among the Clans in the Northern Parts of Scotland and in the Western Isles; from the year MXXXI unto MDCXIX.* Glasgow, Scotland: Robert and Andrew Foulis, 1764.

Macmillan, Archibald, and Robert Brydall. *Iona: Its History, Antiquities, Etc.* London: Houlston, 1898.

Macpherson, James. *The Poems of Ossian and Related Works.* Edited by Howard Gaskill. Edinburgh: Edinburgh University Press, 1996.

Maggi, Angelo. "Poetic Stones: Roslin Chapel in Gandy's Sketchbook and Daguerre's Diorama." *Architectural History* 42, 263–83.

_____. *Rosslyn Chapel: An Icon Through the Ages.* Edinburgh: Birlinn, 2008.

Maitland, Frederic William. *English Law and the Renaissance.* Cambridge, England: Cambridge University Press, 1901.

Major, Richard Henry. "On the Voyages of the Venetian Brothers Zeno, to the Northern Seas, in the Fourteenth Century." *Proceedings of the Massachusetts Historical Society* 13 (October 1874), 345–66.

_____. "The Site of the Lost Colony of Greenland Determined, and Pre-Columbian Discoveries of America Confirmed, from 14th Century Documents." *Journal of the Royal Geographical Society of London* 43 (May 1874), 156–206.

_____. *The Voyages of the Venetian brothers, Nicolò & Antonio Zeno to the Northern Seas, in the XIVth century: comprising the latest known accounts of the lost colony of Greenland and of the Northmen in America*

before Columbus. London: Hakluyt Society, 1873.

Major, Richard Henry, Niccolo Zeno, and Ivarr Barðarson. *The voyages of the Venetian brothers, Nicolo & Antonio Zeno, to the Northern Seas in the XIVth century: comprising the latest known accounts of the lost colony of Greenland and of the Northmen in America before Columbus.* London: Hakluyt Society, 1873.

Mallery, Arlington Humphrey. *Lost America; the Story of Iron-Age Civilization prior to Columbus.* Washington, DC: Overlook Company, 1951.

Mallery, Arlington Humphrey, and Mary Roberts Harrison. *The Rediscovery of Lost America.* 1st ed. New York: Dutton, 1979.

Mallery, Arlington Humphrey, M. I. Walters, Matthew Warren, and Daniel Linehan. *Georgetown University Radio Forum: New and Old Discoveries in Antarctica, August 26, 1956 (transcription).* Washington, DC: Georgetown University, 1956.

Mallery, Garrick. "Dangers of Symbolic Interpretation [abstract]." *Transactions of the Anthropological Society of Washington* 1 (Feb. 1879–Jan. 1882), 70–79.

_____. *Picture-writing of the American Indians.* New York: Dover Publications, 1972.

Mancini, J. M. "Discovering Viking America." *Critical Inquiry* 28, no. 4 (Summer 2002): 868–907.

Mann, William F. *The Templar Meridians: The Secret Mapping of the New World.* Rochester, VT: Destiny Books, 2006.

"Many Attend Unveiling of Knight Marker." *Westford Eagle*, December 16, 1976.

Marwick, Hugh. *The Orkney Norn.* Oxford: Oxford University Press, 1929.

Massue, Melville Henry. *The Moodie Book.* Chertsey, England: privately printed, 1906.

"May 12." In *The Book of Days*, edited by Robert Chambers. London: W & R Chambers, 1863.

McClintock, H. F. *Old Irish and Highland Dress; with notes on that of the Isle of Man.* Dundalk, Ireland: Dundalgan Press, 1943.

McDowell, Edwin. "Publishing: When Book Does Its Own Promotion." *New York Times*, February 5, 1982.

McMurdo, Edward. *The History of Portugal.* London: Sampson Low, Marston, Searle, & Rivington, 1888.

McWilliam, Colin. *Lothian, except Edinburgh.* New Haven, CT: Yale University Press, 2000.

Meader, J. W. *The Merrimack River; Its Source and Its Tributaries.* Boston: B. B. Russell, 1869.

Means, Philip Ainsworth. "The Mysterious Runic Stone." *New York Times*, May 26, 1940, p. BR5.

_____. *Newport Tower.* New York: Holt, 1942.

Mercator, Gerhard. *Gerard Mercator's Map of the World.* 1961 ed. Rotterdam, Netherlands: Maritiem Museum Prins Hendrik, 1569.

Michaud, Joseph-François. *Histoire des Croisades.* 6 vols. Paris: Furne et cie, 1841.

Miller, Crichton E. M. *The Golden Thread of Time.* Rugby, England: Pendulum Publishing, 2001.

Miller, Virginia P. "Silas T. Rand, Nineteenth Century Anthropologist among the Micmacs." *Anthropologica* 22, no. 1 (1980), 235–49.

Miller, William. "The Restorations at Roslin Chapel." *The Scotsman*, June 18, 1861.

Moffat, Brian. "Rosslyn Aloes in Veritas?" *Textualities*, no. 1 (2006), 9–15.

Moncreiffe, Sir Iain. Correspondence (unknown recipient), March 12, 1973.

_____. *The Highland Clans.* New York: Clarkson N. Potter, Inc., 1967.

Montfaucon, Bernard de. *Les Monumens de la Monarchie Françoise.* 5 vols. Paris: J. M. Gandouin, 1730.

Montucla, Jean-Etienne. *Histoire des Mathematiques dans laquelle on rend compte de leurs progres depuis leur origine jusqu'a nos jours.* Paris: Jombert, 1758.

Mooney, John. *The Cathedral and Royal Burgh of Kirkwall.* 2nd ed. Kirkwall, Orkney: W. R. Mackintosh, 1947.

Morgan, David. *The Sacred Gaze: Religious Visual Culture in Theory and Practice.* Berkeley: University of California Press, 2005.

Morison, Samuel Eliot. *Admiral of the Ocean Sea, a life of Christopher Columbus.* Boston: Little, Brown, 1942.

_____. *The European Discovery of America.* 2 vols. Oxford: Oxford University Press, 1971.

_____. *The Maritime History of Massachusetts, 1783–1860.* Boston: Houghton Mifflin, 1961.

Morrison, James E. *The Astrolabe.* Rehoboth Beach, DE: Janus, 2007.

Morrison, Kenneth M. *The Solidarity of Kin: Ethnohistory, Religious Studies, and the Algonkian-French Religious Encounter.* Albany: State University of New York Press, 2002.

Morse, Abner. *Further Traces of the Ancient Northmen in America: with geological evidences of the location of their Vineland.* Boston: H.W. Dutton, 1861.

_____. *Traces of the Ancient Northmen in America: being a paper read before the New England Historical Genealogical Society August, 1861: also supplement to same.* Boston: Mudge Printers, 1887.

Nansen, Fridtjof. *In Northern Mists; Arctic Exploration in Early Times.* Translated by Arthur G. Chater. 2 vols. New York: Frederick A. Stokes Co., 1911.

Nason, Elias. *A Gazetteer of the State of Massachusetts.* Boston: B. B. Russell, 1874.

Needham, Joseph, and Ling Wang. *Mathematics and the Sciences of the Heavens and the Earth.* Vol. III. Cambridge, England: Cambridge University Press, 1979.

Newport History: Journal of the Newport Historical Society. Edited by Ronald M. Potvin. Vol. 68, part 2. Newport, RI: Newport Historical Society, 1997.

Nicholson, Helen J. *The Knights Templar on Trial: The Trial of the Templars in the British Isles, 1308–1311.* Stroud, England: History Press, 2009.

Nicholson, Reynold Alleyne. *A Literary History of the Arabs.* London: T.F. Unwin, 1907.

Nielsen, Richard, and Scott F. Wolter. *The Kensington Rune Stone: Compelling New Evidence.* Eden Prairie, MN: Outernet Publishing, 2005.

Nisbet, Jeff. "Secrets of Rosslyn Chapel Unveiled." *Atlantis Rising*, no. 38 (March/April 2003): 42–43; 68–70.

Noall, Claire Augusta Wilcox. *Intimate Disciple; a portrait of Willard Richards, apostle to Joseph Smith, cousin of Brigham Young.* Salt Lake City: University of Utah Press, 1957.

Nordenskiöld, Adolf Erik. "Om Bröderna Zenos Resor Och de Äldsta Kartor Öfver Norden." In *Studier Och Forskningar: Föranledda af Mina Resor i Höga Norden* 1–62. Stockholm, Sweden: F&G Beijers, 1883.

_____. *Vegas Färd Kring Asien och Europa.* Stockholm, Sweden: F&G Beijers, 1880.

Norman, Joanne S. "Sources for the Grotesque in William Dunbar's 'Dance of the Sevin Deidly Synnis.'" *Scottish Studies* 29 (1989), 55–75.

Oakeshott, R. Ewart. *The Archaeology of Weapons; Arms and Armor from Prehistory to the Age of Chivalry*. New York: Praeger, 1960.

_____. *The Sword in the Age of Chivalry*. Woodbridge, England: Boydell & Brewer Ltd, 1994.

"Old Caves at Salem, N.H., Laid to Robbers, Indians." *Boston Globe*, October 24, 1935.

Olsen, Brad. *Sacred Places, North America: 108 Destinations*. Santa Cruz, CA: Consortium of Collective Consciousness, 2003.

O'Malley, Patricia Trainor, and Paul H. Tedesco. *A New England City: Haverhill, Massachusetts*. Northridge, CA: Windsor Publications, 1987.

The Orkneyinga Saga: The History of the Earls of Orkney. Translated by Hermann Pálsson and Paul Geoffrey Edwards. London: Hogarth Press, 1978.

Orme, Nicholas. *English Schools in the Middle Ages*. London: Methuen 1973.

Ortelius, Abraham. *Theatrum Orbis Terrarum*. Antwerp, Belgium: Coppenium Diesth, 1590.

Oxbrow, Mark, and Ian Robertson. *Rosslyn and the Grail*. Edinburgh: Mainstream, 2005.

Paine, Lincoln P. *Ships of the World: An Historical Encyclopedia*. Boston: Houghton Mifflin, 1997.

Paradin, Guillaume. *Cronique de Savoye*. Geneva, Switzerland: Gustave Revilliod et Edouard Fick, 1874.

Parkhill, Thomas. "'Of Glooskap's Birth, and of His Brother Malsum, the Wolf'—The Story of Charles Godfrey Leland's 'purely American creation.'" *American Indian Culture and Research Journal* 16, no. 1, 45–69.

_____. *Weaving Ourselves into the Land: Charles Godfrey Leland, "Indians," and the Study of Native American Religions*. Albany: State University of New York Press, 1997.

Partner, Peter. *The Knights Templar & Their Myth*. 2nd ed. Rochester, VT: Destiny Books, 1990.

Patrick, David. *Statutes of the Scottish Church, 1225–1559, Publications of the Scottish History Society*. Edinburgh: University Press, 1907.

Patterson, George. "The Portuguese on the North East Coast of America." *Proceedings and Transactions of the Royal Society of Canada for the Year 1890* (1891), 164.

Payne, Stanley G. *A History of Spain and Portugal*. 2 vols. Madison: University of Wisconsin Press, 1973.

Pearson, Malcolm. Correspondence with Shaemas O'Sheel, April 2, 1948.

_____. Correspondence with Vincent Fagan, June 26, 1945.

_____. "Was It a Cave?" In *Upton, Massachusetts*, edited by William George Poor, 149–50. Milford, MA: Charlescraft Press, 1935.

Pell, Herbert C. "The Old Stone Mill, Newport." *Rhode Island History* 7, no. 4 (October 1948), 105–19.

Pendergast, John. *The Bend in the River: A Prehistory and Contact Period History of Lowell, Dracut, Chelmsford, Tyngsborough, and Dunstable (Nashua, N.H.), Massachusetts, 17,000 BP to AD 1700*. Tyngsborough, MA: Merrimac River Press, 1991.

Penhallow, William S. "Astronomical Alignments in the Newport Tower." In *Across Before Columbus?—Evidence for Transoceanic Contact with the Americas Prior to 1492*, edited by Donald Y. Gilmore and Linda S. McElroy. Edgecomb, ME: New England Antiquities Research Association, 1998.

Pennington, Walter. "An Irish Parallel to the Broken Sword of the Grail Castle." *Modern Language Notes* 43, no. 8 (1928), 534–36.

Perley, Frank E. "Is Hooker Problem Settled at Last?" *Hartford Courant*, April 7, 1946.

Perry, Clay. *New England's Buried Treasure*. New York: Stephen Daye Press, 1946.

_____. *Underground Empire; Wonders and Tales of New York Caves*. New York: Stephen Daye Press, 1948.

_____. *Underground New England*. Brattleboro, VT: Stephen Daye Press, 1939.

Phillips, William, Henry James Brooke, and William Hallows Miller. *An Elementary Introduction to Mineralogy*. London: Longman Brown Green and Longmans, 1852.

Pilkington, Colin. *Devolution in Britain Today, Politics Today*. Manchester, England: Manchester University Press, 2002.

Pinkerton, John. *Pinkerton's Lives of the Scottish Saints*. Translated by William M. Metcalfe. 2 vols. Paisley, Scotland: Alexander Gardner, 1889.

Poe, Edgar Allan. "For Annie." *Flag of Our Union* (Boston), July 7, 1849.

Pohl, Frederick J. *Atlantic Crossings Before Columbus*. New York: Norton, 1961.

_____. "Can the Ship's Shoring at Follins Pond Be Radiocarbon Dated?" *Massachusetts Archaeological Society Bulletin* 17 (1955), 49–50.

_____. Correspondence with Frank Glynn, February 6, 1960.

_____. "Leif Ericsson's Visit to America." *American-Scandinavian Review* 36 (March 1948), 17–29.

_____. *The Lost Discovery; Uncovering the Track of the Vikings in America*. New York: Norton, 1952.

_____. *Prince Henry Sinclair—His Voyage to the New World in 1398*. New York: Clarkson N. Potter, 1974.

_____. "Prince 'Zichmni' of the Zeno Narrative." *Terrae Incognitae—The Journal for the History of Discoveries* 2 (1970), 75–86.

_____. "The Ship's Shoring at Follins Pond." *Massachusetts Archaeological Society Bulletin* 16, no. 3, 56–60.

_____. *The Sinclair Expedition to Nova Scotia in 1398*. Pictou, Nova Scotia: Pictou Advocate Press, 1950.

_____. *The Viking Explorers*. New York: T.Y. Crowell, 1966.

_____. *The Viking Settlements of North America*. New York: Clarkson N. Potter, Inc, 1972.

_____. *The Vikings on Cape Cod: Evidence from Archaeological Discovery*. Pictou, Nova Scotia: Pictou Advocate Press, 1957.

Pommeraye, Jean François. *Histoire de l'Abbaye Royale de S. Ouen de Rouen*. Rouen, France: Chez Richard Lallemant et Louys du Mesnil, 1662.

Pond Jr., Pratt. "Upton Traditions: A Deserted Haunt of Unknown Origin." *Milford Journal*, April 26, 1893.

Poole, H. S. "The Pictou Coalfield: a Geological Revision." *Proceedings and Transactions—Nova Scotia Institute of Science* 1 (1895), 228–343.

Portors, Frank E. "Problem for Archaeologists." *Haverhill Evening Gazette*, August 15, 1934.

Prentice, Sartell. *The Voices of the Cathedral; Tales in Stone and Legends in Glass*. New York: W. Morrow and Company, 1938.

Proper, Ida Sedgwick. *Monhegan, the Cradle of New England*. Portland, ME: Southworth Press, 1930.

Quicherat, Jules. "Documents Inédits sur la Construction de Saint-Ouen de Rouen." *Bibliothèque de l'École des Chartes* 13, no. 1 (May–June 1852), 464–76.

Quinn, David B. *North America from Earliest Discovery to First Settlements: The Norse Voyages to 1612*. New York: Harper & Row, 1978.

R.S. "[untitled letter to editor]." *The Gentleman's Magazine* (September 1817), 209.

Rafn, Carl Christian. *Antiqvitates Americanæ; sive, Scriptores Septentrionales Rerum Ante-Columbianarum in America*. Copenhagen, Denmark: Typis Officinæ Schultzianæ, 1837.

_____. *Supplement to the Antiquitates Americæ*. Copenhagen, Denmark: Typis Officinæ Schultzianæ, 1841.

Ralls, Karen. *The Templars and the Grail: Knights of the Quest*. Wheaton, IL: Quest Books, 2003.

Rand, Silas Tertius. *Dictionary of the Language of the Micmac Indians*. Halifax, Nova Scotia: Nova Scotia Printing Company, 1888.

_____. *Legends of the Micmacs*. New York: Longmans Green and Co., 1893.

Rastell, John, and William Rastell. *An Exposition of Certaine Difficult and Obscure Words, and termes of the lawes of this realme newly set foorth and augmented, both in French and English, for the helpe of such younge students as are desirous to attaine the knowledge of ye same: whereunto are also added the olde tenures*. London: Richardi Tottelli, 1579.

Raynouard, François. "Étude sur 'Mysterium Baphometi Revelatum.'" *Journal des Savants*, 151–61, 221–29.

_____. *Monumens Historiques, rélatifs à la condamnation des Chevaliers du Temple, et à l'abolition de leur ordre*. Paris: Adrien Égron, 1813.

Registrum Magni Sigilli Regum Scotorum (The Register of the Great Seal of Scotland). Edited by John Maitland Thomson. 11 vols. Edinburgh: Scottish Record Society, 1984.

Reid, Alan. "Monumental Remains in Pitlochry District, and Churchyard Memorials at Moulin, Temple, and Clerkington." *Proceedings of the Society of Antiquaries of Scotland* 46 (1911–12), 389–423.

"[Review of The Annals of the Voyages of the Brothers Nicolò and Antonio Zeno]." *Journal of the American Geographical Society of New York* 30, no. 5 (1898), 459–61.

Richardson, Edward Adams. "The Builder of the Newport Tower." *American Society of Civil Engineers Transactions* . Paper no. 3091, Vol. 126, Part IV (1961), pp. 1–26.

Richardson, J. S. *The Mediaeval Stone Carver in Scotland*. Edinburgh: Edinburgh University Press, 1964.

Ritchie, Anna. "Excavation of Pictish and Viking-age Farmsteads at Buckquoy, Orkney." *Proceedings of the Society of Antiquaries of Scotland* 108, 174–227.

Rixson, Denis. *The West Highland Galley*. Edinburgh: Birlinn, 1998.

Robbins, Roland Wells. *Hidden America*. New York: Knopf, 1966.

Robertson, Joseph, ed. *Concilia Scotiae: Ecclesiae Scoticanae Statuta tam Provincialia quam Synodalia quae supersunt MCCXXV–MDLIX*. 2 vols. Vol. 2, *Publications of the the Bannatyne Club*. Edinburgh: The Bannatyne Club, 1866.

Rodger, N. A. M. *The Safeguard of the Sea: A Naval History of Britain, 660–1649*. 1st American ed. New York: Norton, 1998.

Roe, Helen M. "A Stone Cross at Clogher, County Tyrone." *Journal of the Royal Society of Antiquaries of Ireland* 90 (1960), 191–206.

"Roslin Chapel." *The Building News* VII (July 5, 1861), 560.

Ross, J. Calder. "The Lamp Acre." *Scottish Notes and Queries* VI, no. 4 (September 1892), 52–53.

Ross, John. *A Voyage of Discovery, Made under the Orders of the Admiralty in His Majesty's ships Isabella and Alexander, for the purpose of exploring Baffin's Bay, and inquiring into the probability of a North-West Passage*. London: Murray, 1819.

Rosslyn, James Alexander St. Clair-Erskine. "Lord Rosslyn's Reply." *The Scotsman* (June 18, 1861), 2.

Rosslyn, Peter St. Clair-Erskine. *Rosslyn Chapel*. Roslin, Scotland: Rosslyn Chapel Trust, 1997.

Royal Commission on the Ancient and Historical Monuments and Constructions of Scotland. *Argyll: An Inventory of the Ancient Monuments*. 5 vols. Vol. 4 — Iona. Edinburgh: Royal Commission on the Ancient and Historical Monuments and Constructions of Scotland, 1982.

_____. "Lewia, Aignish, St. Columba's Church." NMRS Number: NB43SE 5. Edinburgh: RAHMS Canmore Database, 2006.

Royal Commission on the Ancient and Historical Monuments of Scotland. "General Monck's Battery, Roslin." Edinburgh: RAHMS Canmore database, 2008.

_____. "Orphir, St Nicholas's Church." NMRS Number: HY30SW 1.00. Edinburgh: RAHMS Canmore database, 2006.

_____. "St. Magnus Hospital And Chapel, Spittal." NMRS Number: ND15SE 1. Edinburgh: RAHMS Canmore database, 2006.

Royal Geographic Society. "Obituary — Mr. C. H. Coote." *The Geographic Journal* 14, no. 1 (July 1899), 99–100.

Rydberg, O. S. *Sverges Traktater med Främmande Magter — Jemte Aandra Ditt Hörande Handlingar*. Vol. 5. Stockholm, Sweden: P.A. Norstedt & Söner, 1883.

Sacrobosco, Joannes de. *Tractatus de Sphæra*. Ferrara, Italy: Andreas Belfortis, 1472.

Saint-Clair, Roland William. *The Saint-Clairs of the Isles*. Auckland, New Zealand: H. Brett, 1898.

Saul, Nigel. *English Church Monuments in the Middle Ages: History and Representation*. Oxford: Oxford University Press, 2009.

Schauffler, Molly, and George L. Jacobson Jr. "Persistence of Coastal Spruce Refugia during the Holocene in Northern New England, USA, Detected by Stand-scale Pollen Stratigraphies." *Journal of Ecology* 90, no. 2 (April 2002): 235–250.

Schlereth, Thomas J. "Columbia, Columbus, and Columbianism." *Journal of American History* 79, no. 3 (December 1992), 937–68.

Scott, Walter. *The Complete Works of Sir Walter Scott*. 7 vols. New York: Conner & Cooke, 1833.

_____. *The Lord of The Isles: A Poem in Six Cantos*. Edinburgh: James Ballantyne and Co, 1815.

Severin, Timothy. *The Brendan Voyage*. New York: McGraw-Hill, 1978.

Shelby, Lon R. "Mediaeval Masons' Templates." *Journal of the Society of Architectural Historians* 30, no. 2 (May 1971), 140–54.

Shipley, Marie A. *The Norse Colonization in America by the Light of the Vatican Finds*. Lucerne, Switzerland: H. Keller's Foreign Print Office, 1899.

Siebert, Wilbur Henry. *The Underground Railroad from Slavery to Freedom*. New York: Macmillan Co., 1898.

_____. "The Underground Railroad in Massachusetts." *Proceedings of the American Antiquarian Society* NS 45 (April 1935), 25–100.

_____. "The Underground Railroad in Massachusetts." *New England Quarterly* 9, no. 3 (September 1936), 447–67.

Sinclair, Andrew. *The Sword and the Grail.* New York: Crown, 1992.

Sinclair, Thomas. *The Gunns.* Wick, Scotland: W. Rae, 1890.

_____. "Prince Henry Sinclair II — The Pre-Columbian Discoverer of America, One of the Ancestors of the Caithness Family." In *Caithness Events: a discussion of Captain Kennedy's historical narrative, and an account of the Broynach earls, to which is added a supplement of emendations of 1899.* Wick, Scotland: W. Rae, 1899.

_____. *The Sinclairs of England.* London: Trübner, 1887.

Slafter, Edmund F., North Ludlow Beamish, and Carl Christian Rafn. *Voyages of the Northmen to America.* Boston: The Prince Society, 1877.

Slezer, John. *Theatrum Scotiæ.* London: Printed by John Leake for Abell Swalle, 1693.

Smith, Benjamin L. "A Report on the Follins Pond Investigation." *Massachusetts Archaeological Society Bulletin,* Vol. 14, No. 2 (January 31, 1953), pp. 82–88.

Smith, Brian. "Earl Henry Sinclair's Fictitious Trip to America." *New Orkney Antiquarian Journal* 2 (2002), 92.

Smith, Claire. "Rosslyn Trust Seeks Millions in Funding to Save Crumbling Chapel." *The Scotsman,* May 23, 2006.

Sora, Steven. *The Lost Colony of the Templars: Verrazano's Secret Mission to America.* Rochester, VT: Destiny Books, 2004.

_____. *The Lost Treasure of the Knights Templar: Solving the Oak Island Mystery.* Rochester, VT: Destiny Books, 1999.

Spofford, Jeremiah. *A Historical and Statistical Gazetteer of Massachusetts.* Haverhill, MA: E. G. Frothingham, 1860.

Spottiswood, John. *The History of the Church and State of Scotland.* London: R. Royston, 1655.

The Spottiswoode Miscellany: A Collection of Original Papers and Tracts, Illustrative Chiefly of the Civil and Ecclesiastical History of Scotland. Edited by James Maidment. Vol. 2. Edinburgh: Spottiswoode Society, 1845.

Steane, J. M. , and M. F. Foreman. "The Archaeology of Medieval Fishing Tackle." In *Waterfront Archaeology,* edited by G. L. Good, R. H. Jones and M. W. Ponsford, 88–101. London: Council for British Archaeology, 1991.

Steenstrup, Japetus. "Zeni'ernes Reiser i Norden." *Aarbøger for Nordisk Oldkyndighed og Historie* 52 (1883), 55–214.

Steer, K. A., and J. W. M. Bannerman. *Late Medieval Monumental Sculpture in the West Highlands.* Edinburgh: Royal Commission on the Ancient and Historical Monuments of Scotland, 1977.

Stefansson, Vilhjalmur. *My Life with the Eskimo.* New York: Macmillan Company, 1913.

Stephen, William. *History of the Scottish Church* Edinburgh: D. Douglas, 1894.

Stevenson, David. *The First Freemasons: Scotland's Early Lodges and Their Members.* Aberdeen, Scotland: Aberdeen University Press, 1988.

_____. *The Origins of Freemasonry: Scotland's Century, 1590–1710.* Cambridge, England: Cambridge University Press, 1990.

Stewart, J. Douglas. "Rome, Venice, Mantua, London — Form and Meaning in the 'Solomonic' Column from Veronese to George Vertue." *British Art Journal* 8, no. 3 (Winter 2007/8), 15–23.

Stiles, Ezra. *The United States Elevated to Glory and Honor: a sermon preached before His Excellency Jonathan Trumbull, Esq. L.L.D., governor and commander in chief, and the Honorable the General Assembly of the state of Connecticut, convened at Hartford, at the anniversary election, May 8th, 1783.* New Haven, CT: Thomas & Samuel Green, 1783.

Stokhuyzen, Frederick. *The Dutch Windmill.* New York: Universe Books, 1963.

Stone, George H. "The Inscription Rocks on the Island of Monhegan." *Science* 6, no. 132 (August 14, 1885).

"Stone Tower Theory Raises Questions." *Newport Daily News,* February 19, 1996.

Stones, E. L. G. *Anglo-Scottish Relations 1174–1328.* Vol. LVI, *Oxford medieval texts.* Oxford: Clarendon Press, 1970.

Strandwold, Olaf. *Norse Inscriptions on American Stones.* Weehawken, NJ: Magnus Björndal, 1948.

_____. *Norse Runic Inscriptions along the Atlantic Seaboard.* Prosser, WA: published by author, 1939.

Strandwold, Olaf, and Thomas Sigurdsen. *The Yarmouth Stone, Mystic Characters on Yarmouth Stone Yield Startling Evidence of Norse Discoveries.* Prosser, WA: Prosser Printing Company, 1934.

Stuart, Catriona. "Rosslyn Chapel." *Scots—Journal of the Scots Heritage Society* 43, February 2009, pp. 54–59.

Stubbs, William. *The Constitutional History of England in its Origin and Development.* 6th ed. 3 vols. Oxford: Clarendon Press, 1903.

Stylegar, Frans-Arne, and Liv Kjørsvik Schei. "'Lords of Norroway'— The Shetland Estate of Herdis Thorvaldsdatter ." In *West over Sea: Studies in Scandinavian Seaborne Expansion and Settlement before 1300: A Festschrift in Honour of Dr. Barbara E. Crawford,* edited by Beverley Ballin Smith, Simon Taylor, and Gareth Williams. Leiden, Netherlands: Brill, 2007.

Tavel, Emilie. "Rock Sketch Hints Scottish Invasion of America in 14th Century." *Christian Science Monitor,* October 2, 1957.

Taylor, Eugene. *Shadow Culture: Psychology and Spirituality in America.* Washington, DC: Counterpoint, 1999.

Telepneff, Gregory. *The Egyptian Desert in the Irish Bogs: the Byzantine character of early Celtic monasticism.* Etna, CA: Center for Traditionalist Orthodox Studies, 1998.

ten Broeke, Rutger. "A Voyage into the Past — A New Medieval Ship Exactly Follows Evidence Uncovered by Archaeologists." *WoodenBoat* (November/December 1998), 66–74.

Thomas, Charles. *The Early Christian Archaeology of North Britain.* Oxford: Oxford University Press, 1971.

Thompson, John. *The Illustrated Guide to Rosslyn Chapel and Castle, Hawthornden, &c.* 10th ed. Edinburgh: J. Menzies, 1892.

Tiede, Vance R. "Solar Orientation of Irish Early Christian Oratories [abstract]." *HAD News—The Newsletter of the Historical Astronomy Division of the American Astronomical Society,* No. 60 (May 2002), p. 2.

The Topographical, Statistical, and Historical Gazetteer of Scotland. 2 vols. Edinburgh: A. Fullarton, 1853.

Þorgilsson, Ari. *The Íslendingabók.* Translated by Halldór Hermannsson. Ithaca, NY: Cornell University Library, 1930.

"Transcripts from Retours or Returns: 1302– 1622, in Latin and English, among the papers of Alexander MacDonald." In *LDS Family History Library— British Film 231904.* Edinburgh: Public Records Office, 1960.

Trevor-Roper, H. R. "The European Witch-Craze of the Sixteenth and Seventeenth Centuries." In *The Crisis of the Seventeenth Century; Religion, the Reformation, and Social Change.* New York: Harper & Row, 1968.

Trompf, Garry W. "The Hiram Key (book review)." *Aries* 3, no. 1, 114–17.

Trussel, John. *A Continuation of the Collection of the History of England.* London: Printed by M.D. for Ephraim Dawson, 1636.

Tudor, John R. *The Orkneys and Shetland; Their Past and Present State.* London: Edward Stanford, 1883.

Turnbull, Michael T. R. B. *Rosslyn Chapel Revealed.* Stroud, England: Sutton, 2007.

Twyman, Tracy R. *Solomon's Treasure.* Portland, OR: Dragon Key Press, 2005.

Underwood, Paula. *The Walking People: A Native American Oral History.* San Anselmo, CA: A Tribe of Two Press & Institute of Noetic Sciences, 1993.

Urbańczyk, Przemyslaw. *Medieval Arctic Norway.* Warsaw, Poland: Institute of the History of Material Culture, Polish Academy of Sciences, 1992.

Vallely, Joanna. "Free Ticket on Time Machine to the Past." *Edinburgh Evening News,* April 17, 2007, 2.

Vignaud, Henry. *Toscanelli and Columbus. The Letter and Chart of Toscanelli on the Route to the Indies by Way of the West, Sent in 1474 to the Portuguese Fernam Martins, and later on to Christopher Columbus.* London: Sands & Co., 1902.

Voltaire, Moreau Jean Michel. "Mélanges IV (1763–1766)." In *Œuvres Complètes de Voltaire,* edited by Louis Moland. Paris: Garnier Frères, 1877.

Waddington, Richard. "Rewriting the World, Rewriting the Body " In *The Cambridge Companion to English Literature, 1500– 1600,* edited by Arthur F. Kinney, 287– 309. Cambridge, England: Cambridge University Press, 2000.

Wade, W. Cecil. *The Symbolisms of Heraldry, or a Treatise on the Meanings and Derivations of Armorial Bearings.* London: George Redway, 1898.

Wainwright, F. T., ed. *The Northern Isles.* Edinburgh: Nelson, 1962.

Walford, Weston S. "On Cross-legged Effigies Commonly Appropriated to Templars." *Archaeological Journal* 1, 49–52.

Wahlgren, Erik. "American Runes: from Kensington to Spirit Pond." *Journal of English and Germanic Philology*, Vol. 81, No. 2 (April 1982), pp. 157–185.

Wallace, James. *An Account of the Islands of Orkney by James Wallace. Early English Books, 1641–1700 / 1079:03*. London: Jacob Tonson, 1700.

Wallace-Murphy, Tim, and Marilyn Hopkins. *Templars in America: From the Crusades to the New World*. York Beach, ME: Weiser Books, 2004.

"The Wannalancet Map Rock on the Old Tyng Road in Tyngsborough, Mass." *NEARA Journal* 5, no. 3, September 1970.

Way, George, and Romilly Squire. *Scottish Clan & Family Encyclopedia*. New York: Barnes & Noble Books, 1999.

Wellington, Richard Henslowe. *The King's Coroner*. London: W. Clowes, 1905.

Whitehead, Ruth Holmes. *Stories from the Six Worlds: Micmac Legends*. Halifax, Nova Scotia: Nimbus Publishing, 1988.

Whittall II, James P. "A Petroglyph of a European Ship on the Coast of Maine circa 1350–1450 A.D." *Early Sites Research Society Bulletin* 11, no. 1 (December 1984), 48–52.

Whittall II, James P., and Mark Stoughton. *Ground penetrating radar survey, Newport Tower Site, Touro Park, Newport, Rhode Island, 1994, Bulletin / Early Sites Research Society; Variation: Bulletin (Early Sites Research Society)*. Rowley, MA: Early Sites Research Society, 1995.

Wilkins, David. *Concilia Magnae Britanniae et Hiberniae a Synodo Verolamiensi A.D. CCCCXLVI. ad Londinensem A.D. [MD]CCXVII. Accedunt Constitutiones et alia ad Historiam Ecclesiae Anglicanae spectantia*. 4 vols. Vol. 2 (AD 446–1718). London, 1737.

Willard, Lawrence F. "Westford's Mysterious Knight." *Yankee*, (April 1958): 60–61; 84–89.

Willoughby, Charles C. "Book review of 'The Dighton Rock.'" *American Anthropologist* 31, no. 3 (July–Sept. 1929), 518–21.

Willsher, Betty. *Understanding Scottish Graveyards*. Edinburgh: Council for Scottish Archaeology, 2005.

Wilson, Daniel. *The Archæology and Prehistoric Annals of Scotland*. Edinburgh: Sutherland and Knox, 1851.

Wolter, Scott F. *The Hooked X: Key to the Secret History of North America*. St. Cloud, MN: North Star Press of St. Cloud, 2009.

Wolter, Scott F., and Blake Lemcke. "Petrographic Analysis of Rock." St. Paul, MN: American Petrographic Services, 2007.

Wordsworth, Dorothy. *Recollections of a Tour Made in Scotland A.D. 1803*. Edited by John Campbell Shairp. New York: G. P. Putnam's Sons, 1874.

Worsaae, Jens Jakob Asmussen. *An Account of the Danes and Norwegians in England, Scotland, and Ireland*. London: J. Murray, 1852.

Wytfliet, Corneille. *Descriptionis Ptolemaicae Augmentum, siue Occidentis Notitia: Breui Commentario Illustrata*. Louvain, Belgium: Iohannis Bogardi, 1597.

Zahrtmann, Christian Christopher. "Bemærkninger over de Zenetianerne Zeni Tilskrevne Reiser i Norden." *Aarbøger for Nordisk Oldkyndighed og Historie* 3 (1833), 1–35.

_____. "Remarks on the Voyages to the Northern Hemisphere, Ascribed to the Zeni of Venice." *Journal of the Royal Geographic Society of London* 5 (1835), 102–28.

Zeno, Nicolò. *De I Commentarii del Viaggio in Persia di M. Caterino Zeno il K. & delle guerre fatte nell' Imperio Persiano, dal tempo di Vssuncassano in quà. Libri due. Et dello Scoprimento dell' Isole Frislanda, Eslanda, Engrouelanda, Estotilanda & Icaria, fatto sotto il Polo Artico, da due fratelli Zeni, M. Nicolò il K. et M. Antonio*. Venice, Italy: Francesco Marcolini, 1558.

Zimmerman, Larry J. "Unusual or "Extreme" Beliefs about the Past, Community Identity, and Dealing with the Fringe." In *Collaboration in Archaeological Practice*, edited by Chip Colwell-Chanthaphonh and T. J. Ferguson. Lanham, MD: AltaMira Press, 2008.

Zurla, Placido. *Dissertazione Intorno ai Viaggi e Scoperte Settentrionali di Nicolò ed Antonio Fratelli Zeni*. Venice, Italy: Dalle stampe Zerletti, 1808.

Index

Numbers in *bold italics* indicate pages with photographs.